The India–Pakistan Conflict: An Enduring Rivalry

The India–Pakistan rivalry remains one of the most enduring and unresolved conflicts of our times. It began with the birth of the two states in 1947, and it has continued ever since, with the periodic resumption of wars and crises. The conflict has affected every dimension of interstate and societal relations between the two countries and, despite occasional peace initiatives, shows no signs of abating. This volume brings together leading experts in international relations theory and comparative politics to explain the persistence of this rivalry. Together they examine a range of topics including regional power distribution, great power politics, territorial divisions, the nuclear weapons factor, and incompatible national identities. Based on their analyses, they offer possible conditions under which the rivalry could be terminated. The book will be of interest to scholars of politics and international relations, as well as those concerned about stability and peace in South Asia.

T. V. PAUL is James McGill Professor of International Relations in the Department of Political Science at McGill University, Montreal, Canada. His previous publications include *Power Versus Prudence: Why Nations Forgo Nuclear Weapons* (2000) and *India in the World Order: Searching for Major Power Status* (with Baldev Raj Nayar, 2002).

The India–Pakistan Conflict
An Enduring Rivalry

Edited by

T. V. Paul
McGill University

CAMBRIDGE
UNIVERSITY PRESS

Published in South Asia by

Foundation Books Pvt. Ltd.
CAMBRIDGE HOUSE
4381/4, Ansari Road
Daryaganj, New Delhi – 110002

ISBN 81-7596-364-6
This edition is for sale in South Asia only, not for export elsewhere.

This edition of *T. V. Paul / The India-Pakistan Conflict : An Enduring Rivalry*
is published by arrangement with Cambridge University Press, The Edinburgh
Building, Shaftesbury Road, Cambridge CB2 2RU, UK.

Published by Manas Saikia for Foundation Books Pvt. Ltd. and printed &
bound at Raj Press, R-3 Inderpuri, New Delhi 110 012.

In fond memory of my father, Varkey (1912–1998), my mother, Thresa (1915–1978), and my brother, Joseph (1952–1998)

Contents

Figures and tables

Figures

Tables

Notes on contributors

REETA CHOWDHARI TREMBLAY is Chair and Professor of Political Science at Concordia University, Montreal, Canada. Her research interests include comparative politics, South Asian political economy, nation-state and secessionist movements in India, and Indian popular cinema. Her publications include *Mapping the Political Landscape* (2004) and articles and reviews in *Journal of Comparative Policy Analysis: Research and Practice, Pacific Affairs, Contemporary South Asia, Canadian Journal of Political Science, Encyclopedia on World Terrorism, Peacekeeping and International Relations,* and *Political Studies.*

PAUL F. DIEHL is Professor of Political Science and University Distinguished Teacher/Scholar at the University of Illinois at Urbana-Champaign. His books include *War and Peace in International Rivalry* (2000), *A Road Map to War: Territorial Dimensions of International Conflict* (1999), *The Dynamics of Enduring Rivalries* (1998), *International Peacekeeping* (1994), and *Territorial Changes and International Conflict* (1992).

DANIEL S. GELLER is Professor and Chair of the Department of Political Science at Wayne State University and a consultant with the US Department of State, Office of Technology and Assessments. His latest books are *Nations at War: A Scientific Study of International Conflict,* coauthored with J. David Singer (1998) and *The Construction and Cumulation of Knowledge in International Relations,* coedited with John A. Vasquez (2004).

GARY GOERTZ is Professor of Political Science at the University of Arizona. His books include *Contexts of International Politics* (Cambridge University Press, 1994), *International Norms and Decision Making: A Punctuated Equilibrium Model* (2003), and with Paul Diehl, *Territorial Change and International Conflict* (1992) and *War and Peace in International Rivalry* (2000).

WILLIAM HOGG is a Ph.D. Candidate in the Department of Political Science at McGill University and Lecturer in the Political Studies Department at Bishop's University. His publications include "Controlling Weapons in Turbulent Times: Canada and the Future of the Conventional Armed Forces in Europe Treaty," *International Journal* (Spring 2004), "Plus ça Change: Continuity, Change and Culture in Foreign Policy White Papers," *International Journal* (Summer 2004), and "Canada and Arms Control" (with Michel Fortmann) in David DeWitt (ed.), *Uncertain Times: Canadian Defence and Security Policy in the 21st Century* (2005).

ASHOK KAPUR is Chair and Professor of the Department of Political Science at the University of Waterloo. His recent publications include *Pokhran and After: India's Nuclear Weapons Capability* (2000), *India: Fifty Years of Democracy and Development*, with Y. K. Malik (eds.), (1998), "China and Proliferation: Implications for India," in P. R. Kumara-Swamy (ed.), *China and the Middle East* (1999), 162–78.

SAIRA KHAN is Assistant Professor of International Relations at the American University in Cairo. Her research interests encompass South Asia and the Middle East. She is the author of *Nuclear Proliferation Dynamics in Protracted Conflict Regions: A Comparative Study of South Asia and the Middle East* (2002), *The Power of Nuclear Weapons in Protracted Conflict Transformation: The India-Pakistan Case* (forthcoming).

RUSSELL J. LENG is James Jermain Professor of Political Economy and International Law at Middlebury College, Vermont. His research interests include international politics, interstate crisis behavior, diplomacy, and the causes of war. His recent publications include *Bargaining and Learning in Recurring Crises: The Soviet–American, Egyptian–Israeli, and Indo-Pakistani Rivalries* (2000); "Cumulation in Q.I.P.: 25 Years After Ojai," *Conflict Management and Peace Science* (Fall 1999): 133–47, "Reducing Intergang Violence: Norms from the Interstate System," *Peace and Change* (October 1999): 476–504.

VALI NASR is a Professor in the Department of National Security Affairs at the Naval Postgraduate School, Monterey. He is author of *The Islamic Leviathan: Islam and the Making of State Power* (2001); *Mawdudi and the Making of Islamic Revivalism* (1996); *The Vanguard of the Islamic Revolution: The Jama'at-i Islami of Pakistan* (1994); and editor, *Muslim World*, Special Issue on South Asian Islam (July–October 1997); and an editor of *Oxford Dictionary of Islam* (2003).

T. V. PAUL is James McGill Professor of International Relations in the Department of Political Science at McGill University, Montreal, Canada, where he has been teaching since 1991. He specializes and teaches courses in international relations, especially international security, international conflict and conflict resolution, regional security and South Asia. He received his M.A. and Ph.D. from the University of California, Los Angeles. He is the author or coeditor of several books, including *India in the World Order: Searching for Major Power Status* (2003, with B. Nayar); *Power versus Prudence: Why Nations Forgo Nuclear Weapons* (2000), *Balance of Power: Theory and Practice in the 21st Century* (with J. Wirtz and M. Fortman, 2004); *The Nation-State in Question* (2003, with G. John Ikenberry and John A. Hall); *International Order and the Future of World Politics* (1999, with John A. Hall).

STEPHEN M. SAIDEMAN is Associate Professor of Political Science and Canada Research Chair in International Security and Ethnic Conflicts at McGill University. He specializes in issues related to political competition and foreign policy and the international and domestic politics of ethnic conflicts. He is the author of *The Ties that Divide: Ethnic Politics, Foreign Policy and International Conflict* (1998).

JULIAN SCHOFIELD is Assistant Professor of Political Science at Concordia University, Montreal. His research interests include South, Southeast, and East Asian security issues, the theory of strategic and naval arms control, and the political economy of military regimes. His articles have appeared in the *Journal of South Asian and Middle Eastern Studies, Journal of Conflict, Security and Development, Proceedings of the U.S. Naval Institute, Canadian Journal of Political Science, Armed Forces & Society, International Relations*, and *Journal of Strategic Studies*.

JOHN A. VASQUEZ is the Thomas Mackie Scholar in International Relations and Professor of Political Science at the University of Illinois at Urbana-Champaign. He has published over a dozen books, including *What Do We Know about War?* (editor); *Realism and the Balancing of Power: A New Debate?* (coedited with Colin Elman), *The Power of Power Politics*, and *The War Puzzle*. His articles have appeared in journals such as *International Studies Quarterly, Journal of Peace Research, American Political Science Review, World Politics*, and *Journal of Politics*. He has been president of the International Studies Association, and the Peace Science Society (International).

Acknowledgments

This volume emerges out of the need for a comprehensive analysis of the enduring conflict between India and Pakistan. A deeper understanding of the root causes of the India–Pakistan rivalry has become all the more important in the context of nuclear acquisitions by the rival states, and the emergence of South Asia as a fulcrum of international security challenges in both the domains of transnational terrorism and nuclear proliferation, especially in the post-September 11, 2001 international environment. While there exists a substantial literature on enduring inter-state rivalries and protracted conflicts, none of the international relations theorists in this vein has focused specifically on the South Asian conflict, which has remained an enduring rivalry *par excellence* for over half a century, with no endpoint in sight. Comparative politics scholars of South Asia, on the other hand, have made some strides in understanding the particular national identity and domestic variables that perpetuate the India–Pakistan conflict. Yet, previous works have made little effort to integrate the findings of both these two strands of literature by exploring the multiple causes and consequences of the India–Pakistan conflict in a broad yet rigorous theoretical and analytical manner. This volume represents a pioneering effort to bring together the theoretical and empirical frameworks developed in international relations and comparative politics in order to offer a comprehensive, yet in-depth, understanding of the conflict. The effort is to link the works of scholars who have made major advances in understanding the patterns and processes of enduring rivalries with those of regional specialists.

The volume grew out of papers presented at a conference I hosted at McGill University, Montreal, in December 2003. After the conference, paper-givers received extensive comments and criticisms. The ensuing chapters are the result of careful revisions by the contributors, and I thank them for their efforts. The conference was cosponsored and funded by the McGill-University of Montreal Research Group in International Security (REGIS), the McGill Peace Studies Program through a grant from the Arsenault Foundation, the Canadian Department of Foreign Affairs and

International Trade through its John Holmes Fund, the Canadian Department of National Defence through its Security and Defence Forum, and the McGill conference grant program. Scholars and officials who helped the project in different ways include: Michael Brecher, Theressa de Haan, Michel Fortmann, John Galaty, Nirmala George, John A. Hall, Ajit Jain, George Joseph, C. Raja Mohan, Venu Rajamony, Norrin Ripsman, K. Subrahmanyam, B. Vijayan, and Marie-Joëlle Zahar. Baldev Raj Nayar and William Hogg deserve special thanks for reading and commenting on several chapters.

The hospitality of the following individuals who organized work-in progress seminars at their institutions is gratefully acknowledged: Carlos Juarez and Michael Pavkovic at the Hawaii Pacific University, Honolulu; Shankaran Krishna at the East-West Center, University of Hawaii; Mohan Malik and Satu Limaye at the Asia-Pacific Security Center, Honolulu; Swaran Singh and Varun Sahni at the Jawaharlal Nehru University, New Delhi; Raju Thadikakran at Mahatma Gandhi University, Kottayam; G. Gopakumar and Syam Lal at Kerala University, Thiruvananthapuram; Lawrence Prabhakar and Kamala Aravind at Stella Mary's College, Chennai; N. K. Jha at the Pondicherry University; M. N. Varma at the University of Allahabad; C. P. Barathwal at the University of Lucknow; Arpit Rajain, General V. P. Malik, and Sathya Moorthy at the Observer Foundation, New Delhi and Chennai; Deepankar Banerjee and P. R. Chari at the Institute of Peace and Conflict Studies, New Delhi; C. Uday Bhaskar at the Institute for Defense Studies and Analysis, New Delhi; and in Colombo, Darshani Das at the Regional Center for Strategic Studies; the scholars at the Colombo University's Department of Political Science and the Bandaranaike Institute. I also thank the panelists and discussants at the roundtable on this subject at the American Political Science Association Convention in Chicago in September 2004, especially Scott Sagan, Devin Hagerty and James Wirtz. The comments by the two anonymous reviewers of the original manuscript were also useful. The interest in the volume by the Cambridge University Press Editor Marigold Acland has been very encouraging. Last, but not least, I thank my family members – Rachel, Kavya, and Leah – for their support and understanding.

T. V. PAUL

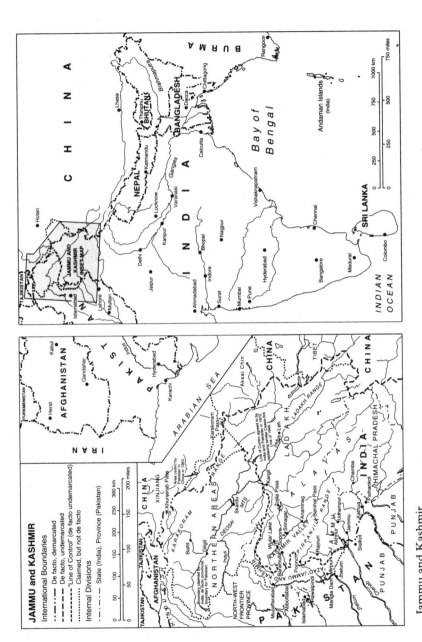

Jammu and Kashmir
Source: From Suntra Bose, Kashmir: Roots of Conflict: Paths to Peace

Part I

Introduction

1   Causes of the India–Pakistan enduring rivalry

T. V. Paul

The India–Pakistan rivalry remains one of the most enduring and unresolved conflicts of our times. Begun in the aftermath of the birth of the two states from British colonial rule in 1947, it has continued for well over half a century with periodic wars and crises erupting between the two rivals. The conflict has affected all key dimensions of inter-state and societal relations of the two antagonists. Despite occasional peace overtures and periods of détente, it shows no signs of a permanent settlement in the near future. Since the late 1980s, the open acquisition of nuclear weapons by the two states, the increasing number of crises involving them, and the introduction of terrorist tactics into the conflict have led to the heightened possibility of a cataclysmic war breaking out in South Asia with unimaginable consequences.

What explains the persistence of this rivalry even when some other long-running conflicts in different parts of the world have come to an end? Do existing theories of enduring rivalries provide compelling explanations for this ongoing conflict? Can the rivalry and its persistence be understood on the basis of factors at the international, societal, and decisionmaker levels of analysis? Is it the convergence of these factors that keeps the conflict enduring in nature? Why do the near- and medium-term prospects of negotiating an end to this enduring rivalry look bleak? Does the answer lie in the territorial nature of the rivalry, disparate national identities of the two states, and the peculiar power asymmetry between the two parties, or the fundamental incompatibility in the strategic goals they seek? Can the extensive works on enduring rivalries and the emerging literature on asymmetric conflicts shed light on this conflict?

Theories of enduring rivalries and asymmetric conflicts

Enduring rivalries are defined as conflicts between two or more states that last more than two decades with several militarized inter-state disputes punctuating the relationship in between. An enduring rivalry is characterized by a "persistent, fundamental, and long term incompatibility of

goals between two states," which "manifests itself in the basic attitudes of
the parties toward each other as well as in recurring violent or potentially
violent clashes over a long period of time."[1] Although there is difference
of opinion among analysts on the number of disputes and inter-state
crises required for calling a rivalry "enduring," I accept the categorization
by Paul Diehl and Gary Goertz, who treat an enduring rivalry as one that
involves at least six militarized disputes during a twenty-year period. This
specification, according to them, allows defining the concept along "spatial consistency, duration and militarized competition."[2] In other words,
an enduring rivalry cannot be episodic or of short duration; it should be
ongoing for a reasonably long period on a continuous basis before it can
be termed "enduring." Enduring rivalries are also called "protracted
conflicts," but the main difference between the two concepts perhaps
lies in the inter-state dimension of the former.[3] Whereas a protracted
conflict can be internal or intra-state, involving state and/or non-state
actors, an enduring rivalry specifically refers to inter-state conflicts.

An enduring rivalry is often characterized by zero-sum perspectives on
the part of the participants. The conflict can become entrenched and
societal as parties view each other as highly threatening to their security
and physical survival. Enduring rivalries tend to be typified by periodic
inter-state crises and, in some instances, war, although war is not a
necessary condition for a rivalry to be categorized as "enduring."[4] John
Vasquez argues that relative equality in power capabilities is necessary for
a rivalry to remain enduring, since in a highly unequal power situation the

[1] According to Zeev Maoz and Ben Mor, these conflicts tend to have four major characteristics: (1) an outstanding set of unresolved issues; (2) strategic interdependence between
the parties; (3) psychological manifestations of enmity; and (4) repeated militarized
conflict. See Maoz and Mor, *Bound by Struggle: The Strategic Evolution of Enduring
International Rivalries* (Ann Arbor: University of Michigan Press, 2002), 5.
[2] Paul Diehl and Gary Goertz, *War and Peace in International Rivalry* (Ann Arbor:
University of Michigan Press, 2001), 44, 48; see also their chapter in this volume; and
Paul F. Diehl (ed.), *The Dynamics of Enduring Rivalries* (Urbana and Chicago: University
of Illinois Press, 1998). Some key samples of this literature are: William R. Thompson,
"Principal Rivalries," *Journal of Conflict Resolution* 39 (June 1995), 195–223; Frank
W. Wayman, "Rivalries: Recurrent Disputes and Explaining War," in John Vasquez
(ed.), *What Do We Know about War?* (Oxford: Rowman and Littlefield, 2000), 219–34;
and Scott D. Bennett, "The Dynamics of Enduring Rivalries," *American Political Science
Review* 93 (September 1999), 749–50.
[3] On protracted conflicts, see Edward Azar, Paul Jureidini, and Ronald McLaurin,
"Protracted Social Conflict: Theory and Practice in the Middle East," *Journal of
Palestine Studies* 29 (1978), 41–60; Michael Brecher and Jonathan Wilkenfeld, *A Study
of Crisis* (Ann Arbor: University of Michigan Press, 2000), 6.
[4] On crisis, see Patrick James, *International Relations and Scientific Progress* (Columbus: Ohio
State University Press, 2002), 57–62.

stronger party will in general be able to impose its will on the weaker side and put an end to the conflict.[5]

Asymmetric conflicts involve states of unequal aggregate power capability, measured in terms of material resources, i.e., size, demography, military capability, and economic prowess. Intangible factors such as will and morale are not included in assessing national power capabilities as these are difficult to measure.[6] Further, these factors tend to change over time and are difficult to notice until a real military contest takes place. Weaker parties in asymmetric power dyads often use these intangible means to bolster their military and political positions during both war and peace. Within asymmetric conflict dyads one may notice wide disparity in power capabilities (as in the US–Cuba or China–Taiwan cases) or limited disparity (as in the North Korea–South Korea case).

The India–Pakistan conflict is both enduring and asymmetric, but the power asymmetry is truncated and mitigated by many factors. In particular, the weaker party, Pakistan, has been successful in reducing the asymmetry through strategy, tactics, alliances with outside powers, acquisition of qualitatively superior weapons and nuclear arms since the late 1980s, and, for over a decade, low-intensity warfare. The materially stronger power, India, is not overwhelmingly preponderant in the theater of conflict – Kashmir – and has been vulnerable to asymmetric challenges by the weaker state, Pakistan. Nor is Pakistan too small or incapable of mounting a sustained challenge, as it has proved over half a century. Pakistan, with a population of over 141 million, is the seventh largest country in the world. Its territorial size is larger than most Middle Eastern and Gulf states, except Saudi Arabia and Iran, and its elite has sufficient wherewithal and high level of motivation to sustain the conflict even if at a high cost to its society in terms of economic and political underdevelopment. The asymmetry is built into the structure of the conflict, the power balance, and the goals and objectives that the two parties seek. I argue

---

[5] John A. Vasquez, "Distinguishing Rivals that Go to War from Those that Do Not: A Quantitative Comparative Case Study of the Two Paths to War," *International Studies Quarterly* 40 (December 1996), 531–58. Although there is good logic in this argument, empirically this may not be the case, unless one is willing to include intangible factors in assessing the power capability of states. The overwhelming preponderance of one side as contrasted with limited overall superiority is critical here in determining the impact of asymmetry on the type of rivalry.

[6] This definition is elaborated in T. V. Paul, *Asymmetric Conflicts: War Initiation by Weaker Powers* (Cambridge: Cambridge University Press, 1994), 20. On this subject, see also Andrew Mack, "Why Big Nations Lose Small Wars: The Politics of Asymmetric Conflict," *World Politics* 27 (January 1975), 175–200; and Ivan Arreguín-Toft, "How the Weak Win Wars: A Theory of Asymmetric Conflict," *International Security* 26 (Summer 2001), 93–128.

that this peculiar asymmetry makes the conflict deadly and prolonged. This truncated asymmetry, in recent years buttressed by nuclear weapons, makes the resolution of the conflict unlikely any time soon.

Origins of the rivalry: the historical legacy

A brief historical survey of the origins of the conflict is necessary at this point. The roots of the India–Pakistan rivalry lie in the two visions of statehood that arose within the context of the nationalist movement in the Indian subcontinent. The Indian National Congress, spearheaded by Mohandas Gandhi and Jawaharlal Nehru, sought a unified country built around the principles of secularism and liberal democracy. Although the majority of the Congress Party membership came from the mainstream Hindu population, the party embodied all major ethnic groups of India and had a vision of a state not supporting any single religion. Many Muslim leaders were wary of majority rule which they viewed as tantamount to Hindu rule and demanded safeguards by way of separate electorates. In order to press for their demands with the colonial rulers, they formed the Muslim League Party in December 1906. Their claim for separate electorates was accepted by the British in the Government of India Act of 1909, which offered limited political rights to the Indian subjects. The British rulers were sympathetic to separate constituencies for Muslims which they hoped would weaken the incipient nationalist movement, spearheaded by the Congress Party. However, over time this policy helped to unify the Muslim community in a communal and political sense and sowed the seeds for the idea of Pakistan. Although the Congress Party initially accepted separate Muslim electorates in 1916, it subsequently rejected the idea in the constitutional proposals it made in 1928. Alienation from both the British and the Congress Party led to the proposal for a separate Muslim homeland by the League, which was first put forward by the poet Muhammad Iqbal in 1930.[7]

The Government of India Act of 1935 was pivotal in the rise of Muslim separatist nationalism, with the League under Mohammad Ali Jinnah deciding to contest elections for limited self-governing provincial governments in 1937. The overwhelming electoral victory of the Congress Party in six provinces and that party's decision not to form coalition governments with the Muslim League – which had not fared well even in the separate Muslim constituencies – disillusioned Jinnah, who then began to propagate the merits of the two-nation theory. The Congress Party's

[7] Stanley Wolpert, *A New History of India* (Oxford: Oxford University Press, 2000), 317.

rejection of Jinnah's demand that the League be recognized as the sole party of Indian Muslims (because the Congress itself had a substantial Muslim membership) and the misdeeds of some Congress provincial leaders embittered Jinnah and his followers even further.

In March 1940, at its meeting in Lahore, the League proclaimed as its goal the creation of Pakistan as a separate homeland for Indian Muslims and the Congress–League schism widened even further. The May 1944 Gandhi–Jinnah talks and the June 1945 Simla conference of top Congress and Muslim League leaders failed to break the deadlock between them. The League also benefited from its somewhat supportive position of the war effort by Britain. The arrival of the Labour Party government under Clement Atlee in July 1945 speeded up the Indian independence process. In 1946, the Cabinet Mission sent by Britain proposed that a union between British India and the princely states be established and a constitution drafted. However, this proposal failed to resolve the divide between the Congress and the League. During this time, Hindu–Muslim communal clashes intensified in many parts of India and the last British viceroy, Lord Louis Mountbatten, came to the conclusion that the creation of Pakistan was inevitable. Accordingly, the two independent states of India and Pakistan were born on August 15, 1947, with Pakistan gaining the Muslim majority British-administered areas in the northwest and Bengal and India obtaining the rest of British India, while the fate of the 500-odd princely states remained undecided.[8] The partition was followed by one of history's largest mass migrations – over 10 million people from both sides – and was accompanied by brutal violence.

The Indian Independence Act of 1947 contained a provision that the 562 princely states – scattered throughout the subcontinent and partially autonomous under British rule – had the option to join either India or Pakistan. Thanks largely to the efforts of Sardar Vallabhai Patel, almost all states within India joined the Indian Union while Jinnah succeeded in gaining the accession by the Muslim princes within Pakistan's territorial domain. Three princely states decided to stay independent from both India and Pakistan: Jammu and Kashmir in the north, Hyderabad in the south, and Junagadh in the west. While the rulers of the latter two were Muslim, the majority of their population was Hindu and their accession to India occurred through internal revolt or Indian police actions. New Delhi legitimized these accessions through subsequent popular referenda. Only Jammu and Kashmir emerged as the most contentious, given its geographical proximity to Pakistan and a majority Muslim population

---

[8] For historical accounts on this, see Percival Spear, *A History of India* (New Delhi: Penguin Books, 1999), vol. II, 226–29; Wolpert, *A New History of India*, 324–49.

(concentrated largely in the northern areas and Kashmir Valley) even as a substantial Hindu population inhabited the Jammu area and a Buddhist population lived in the Ladakh region. The Hindu ruler of Kashmir, Maharaja Hari Singh, first chose to remain independent from both India and Pakistan, but in reaction to an invasion in October 1947 by tribal forces from Pakistan's Northwest Frontier Province (which were aided by Pakistani regular troops), he sought India's help. Following his signing an agreement to accede to India and the approval of Kashmir's undisputed leader of the time, Sheikh Mohammad Abdullah, the Indian forces intervened and managed to partially evict the intruders. Jinnah's decision to send in Pakistani troops escalated the conflict to a short war between the two states, which lasted until the end of 1948.

A ceasefire agreement was reached between the two states under the auspices of the United Nations, which came into effect on January 1, 1949. A ceasefire line was established dividing Kashmir, with nearly two thirds of the state under Indian control and the rest under Pakistan, which the latter called "Azad" or "Free" Kashmir. The ceasefire line was monitored by a UN observer mission until 1972, when it was renamed Line of Control (LoC), and has been actively manned by the regular forces of the two countries, with sporadic shellings, occasional skirmishes, and limited incursions. Three major wars (1947–48, 1965, and 1971) and a minor war, Kargil (1999), have been fought over control of the territory, but neither country has succeeded in changing the line to its advantage.[9] This military stalemate is only part of the story of the rivalry between the two states. Understanding the structure of the conflict is critical to explaining why the India–Pakistan conflict persists as an enduring rivalry.

The structure of the conflict: asymmetry in goals

The India–Pakistan conflict is simultaneously over territory, national identity, and power position in the region. The political status of Kashmir, from Pakistan's perspective, is the unfinished business of the partition of the subcontinent on a religious basis in 1947. Successive Pakistani leaders have viewed the gaining of the entire Jammu and Kashmir state from Indian control as their core national mission for identity and strategic reasons.[10] To the Pakistanis, the Indian-controlled Muslim-majority state

[9] For a history of the conflict, see Victoria Schofield, *India, Pakistan and the Unfinished War* (London: I. B. Tauris, 2000).

[10] For an excellent assessment of Pakistan's identity and the role of Kashmir in it, see Stephen Philip Cohen, *The Idea of Pakistan* (Washington, DC: Brookings Institution Press, 2004).

of Kashmir, if given full freedom to choose in a plebiscite, would join Pakistan. However, as Bose puts it: "this state-centered, legalistic interpretation of the 'right to self-determination' is significantly different from the highly populist version articulated by proponents of an independent Kashmir."[11] Thus, despite the preference of most Kashmiri nationalist groups for independence or greater autonomy from both countries, Pakistan steadfastly holds the view that the partition of the sub-continent is still incomplete and that Pakistan's Islamic identity will not be total until the territory is unified with that country.

From India's standpoint, besides being an integral part of India legally by virtue of the instrument of accession signed by the Maharaja, Kashmir is very much a part of the nation's secular identity. To New Delhi, partition was completed in 1947 and no further territorial concessions to Pakistan are feasible. Further, India argues that the several democratic elections that it has held have legitimized the accession. The pressure of the nearly 125 million (12 percent of the total) strong Muslim population in India attests to the Indian belief that partition on the basis of religion was an unfortunate historical *fait accompli* and that ceding Jammu and Kashmir, or even portions of the Kashmir Valley or the Vale of Kashmir, where the Muslims constitute a majority, to Pakistan would result in a second partition, negating India's secular credentials. Indians in general fear that letting Kashmir go could open the floodgates of separatist movements in other parts of India and that it may be followed by inter-communal violence reminiscent of the partition days. There exists no serious constituency in India from the left to the right that believes that Kashmir should be ceded to Pakistan.[12] Extreme right-wingers in the Bharatiya Janata Party (BJP) would want to forcefully integrate Kashmir and even recover the portion held by Pakistan (Azad Kashmir), since ceding it to Pakistan or allowing independence to Kashmiris will be tantamount to placating the minority Muslims, while more moderate political groups would like to see a peaceful integration of Kashmir within the Indian Union. It seems that restoring Kashmir's pre-1953 autonomous status is the maximum concession that most Indian moderates would agree to.[13]

[11] Sumantra Bose, *Kashmir, Roots of Conflict, Paths to Peace* (Cambridge, MA: Harvard University Press, 2003), 165, 168.

[12] On various Indian perspectives on Pakistan, see Kanti Bajpai, "Indian Strategic Culture," in Michael R. Chambers (ed.), *South Asia in 2020* (Carlisle, PA: Strategic Studies Institute, US War College, 2002), 245–303; see also, Maya Chadda, *Ethnicity, Security, and Separatism in India* (New York: Columbia University Press, 1997).

[13] If implemented, the central government in Delhi will limit its jurisdiction in Kashmir to defense, foreign affairs, communications, and currency while the authority of the Indian

10   T. V. Paul

Despite the rhetoric about the indivisibility of Kashmir, it seems that the Indian elite and public could live with the status quo on the territorial division, i.e., acceptance of the Line of Control separating the Indian and Pakistani sides of Kashmir as the permanent border.[14] However, even in this instance, compromise has been constrained by the disparate positions within the Kashmiri liberation movement. This movement is a conglomerate of groups, some of which want to create an Islamic state while others are more tolerant toward the inclusion of the minority Hindu and Buddhist populations. The involvement of Islamic insurgent groups from Pakistan, Afghanistan, and other parts of the Middle East and Central Asia and the deadly terrorist tactics they employ have undermined their cause within India. In the post-September 11, 2001 context, they also have lost much international sympathy as the intimate links between some such groups and al-Queda have been exposed. Despite this, the fact remains that a peace settlement between India and Pakistan would require the fulfillment of Kashmiri aspirations in some meaningful way. The challenge remains how the three mutually exclusive claims of India, Pakistan, and the Kashmiri movements can be accommodated, satisfying the aspirations of the three contestants simultaneously.[15]

Some of India's domestic constraints arise from the tendency of democratic states not to make territorial concessions, especially to non-democratic countries. This is because the political leader and party that make territorial concessions, especially under threat of violence, are not likely to get re-elected.[16] The Indian political parties seem to be unwilling to make territorial concessions to either China or Pakistan partly because of this factor. Despite its position of no revision to the territorial status quo, India has not been successful in fully integrating the Kashmiri population and legitimizing its control. This lack of success is due partly to the sometimes highhanded tactics of the Indian security forces in dealing

Election Commission and Supreme Court will still be maintained over the state. Harish Khare, "Kashmir: New Roadmap Taking Shape," http://www.hinduonnet.com, November 18, 2004.
[14] In November 2004, Prime Minister Manmohan Singh reiterated the inviolability of India's territorial boundaries, but hinted at the possible Indian concession of loose borders between the two Kashmirs and considerable autonomy for the Kashmiri population. Singh was responding to Pakistani President Pervez Musharaff who had proposed the creation of seven demilitarized autonomous regions on both sides of Kashmir, granting some of them independence or giving the option of joint control by India and Pakistan, or placing them under UN mandate. "Indian PM Rejects Kashmir Proposal," BBC News, http://newsvote.bbc.co.uk/mpapps/pagetools/print/news.bbc.co.uk/2/hi/south_asia/40203, November 17, 2004.
[15] Bose, *Kashmir, Roots of Conflict*, 165.
[16] On the constraints that democracies face in war and peace, see Paul K. Huth and Todd L. Allee, *The Democratic Peace and Territorial Conflict in the Twentieth Century* (Cambridge: Cambridge University Press, 2002), ch. 4.

with Kashmiri opposition groups and the general population, and the questionable past electoral practices of the national political parties and their allies in the state. Although the Indian side of Kashmir is more economically prosperous and politically democratic than the Pakistani counterpart, India has not been able to attract a majority of the Kashmiris to its secular/democratic identity. The Indian strategy has been to give time (as it did in the cases of other insurgencies in the Punjab and the northeast) for the major groups to become exhausted and reconciled to integration with India, and to engage in both coercive and non-coercive measures to quell the insurgency in the meantime. This strategy seems to have worked in the Punjab in stemming the tide of a violent separatist movement in the 1980s. The major difference is the irredentist dimension and the extensive involvement of outside actors in the Kashmir conflict. Further, India has maintained the separate identity and autonomy of Kashmir through a constitutional provision, and in recent years has agreed to include the issue of Kashmir as one of the topics in the composite dialogue for rapprochement with Pakistan.

Even after more than half a century of conflict, neither India nor Pakistan is willing to compromise on the Kashmir issue, nor do they have the capacity to force a settlement on each other. None of the wars that they fought was decisive enough to settle the issue once and for all. The 1971 War resulted in a military debacle for Pakistan and the loss of the eastern wing of its territory, but the secession of Bangladesh consolidated Pakistan's military assets on the western front. India was not able to translate the victory into a lasting political settlement. The war also increased the Pakistani elite's perception that India is out to destroy Pakistan as a state, and some of its members still harbor vengeance for the humiliation of 1971. A compromise has also become difficult given that the societal dominance of the Pakistani army has been built largely around the acquisition of Kashmir from India and balancing the power of its larger neighbor. Although the army will still retain numerous internal and external security missions, reducing the significance of the Kashmir issue could diminish the value of the army in Pakistani society and the extensive corporate interests built around it.[17]

Thus the fundamental asymmetry is about national identities and the role that the territory in dispute plays in each state's conceptions about

---

[17] The Pakistani army has emerged not only as the defender of the country, but a major player in the country's agrarian economy. The officer corps holds not only considerable social-political prestige, but its members are major landowners in the country and, as a result, they have benefited from the semi-feudal politico-economic order. Owen Bennett Jones, *Pakistan: Eye of the Storm* (New Haven: Yale University Press, 2002), 277–78.

statehood, although the identity linkage may have changed since the 1980s.[18] Since the territory in dispute is crucially tied to its national identity, the challenger plays the irredentist game on a continuous basis, given that the majority of the population of the Jammu and Kashmir state is Muslim and the terrain allows low-intensity military and guerrilla operations. This, in turn, encourages the defender to remain unyielding, given that compromise would negate its own identity as a secular state. The inability of either state to impose a settlement or convince the other to make significant concessions is because of the peculiar power asymmetry that has existed between the two states.

The power asymmetry

The India–Pakistan power relationship is characterized by a distinct form of power asymmetry which I term *truncated asymmetry*. India is over seven times larger than Pakistan in population and size of national economy, and four times in territorial size. In 2002, India's population stood at 1 billion, while that of Pakistan was 141 million. The latter's population is smaller than India's largest state, Uttar Pradesh, which holds 181 million people. However, Pakistan has been able to borrow power to balance India through externally procured military capabilities and alignment with outside powers. Until the 1980s, the Pakistani economy also performed slightly better than India's (in terms of GDP growth rates and per capita income) due largely to external aid, remittances of Pakistani expatriate workers, and its embrace of limited free market economic policies. However, this situation began to change after India launched its policy of economic liberalization in 1991. As the power differential between the two countries in terms of economic and conventional military strength began to alter in India's favor after the early 1990s – with India's economic and military capabilities showing steady growth over Pakistan's – Islamabad increasingly resorted to asymmetric strategies such as supporting insurgency and proxy war to continue its struggle with India. This strategy, although launched in the aftermath of the Soviet withdrawal from Afghanistan in 1989, began to pick up momentum in the 1990s. The increasing unrest in Indian Kashmir, the rise of Islamic fundamentalism in Afghanistan and elsewhere spearheaded by the Taliban, and the availability of a steady stream of mujahidin fighters from the wider Muslim world, facilitated this strategy.

---

[18] Sumit Ganguly, *Conflict Unending: India–Pakistan Tensions since 1947* (New York: Columbia University Press, 2001), 6–7.

The military asymmetry, especially in the theater of conflict, Kashmir, has not therefore been all that favorable to the larger power, India. While India is dramatically larger in physical size, GNP, and overall military size, it is not overwhelmingly preponderant in Kashmir. Pakistan benefits from the terrain, the support of sympathetic segments among the Kashmiri population, and, during several phases of the conflict, qualitatively superior conventional weapons systems. There is a near-parity in the army divisions deployed against each other, since about half of India's land forces are stationed on the border with China. This near-parity in the theater gives Pakistan several advantages in a short war. The terrain of Kashmir permits limited incursions and guerrilla operations undetected by the defender. The possession of superior weaponry allows Pakistan to checkmate India during the initial stages of a conflict, and this option has been an asset in a short war. Only in a long war can India muster its aggregate superiority, but this has been constrained by the great powers that have often intervened to put an end to the conflict before it escalated beyond a limited war. Since the introduction of nuclear weapons, a long war has also become inconceivable without the likelihood of a nuclear escalation. In a short war, the Pakistani leaders tend to believe that their superior strategy, tactics, and resolve could enable them to compensate for their overall material weaknesses.

Until 1965, India's defense posture against Pakistan was based on "matching capabilities," but since 1965 India's policy has been to maintain "sufficient deterrence" or a "slight edge" in its force deployments *vis-à-vis* Pakistan. Thus, in 1965 India possessed seven divisions while Pakistan had six, with Pakistan holding qualitative superiority in tanks and aircraft. Since 1971, India has maintained the "slight edge" in both qualitative and quantitative defense areas.[19] This slight edge is not sufficient for the defense of Kashmir or deterrence against a determined assault from Pakistan. Islamabad holds several advantages in asymmetric warfare, especially in deploying a holding force and supporting insurgents at low cost. For India, the mountainous terrain of Kashmir makes it difficult to seal off the border or conduct counter-insurgency operations. Moreover, India has to rely on a single road to the area near the LoC, and its direct frontal offensives may not succeed in advancing beyond the territory in its control. According to some Indian military commanders, to secure some areas of the Kashmir frontline, a 30:1 superiority is needed.[20]

[19] Raju G. C. Thomas, *Indian Security Policy* (Princeton: Princeton University Press, 1986), 22–23.
[20] For this assessment, see Anthony H. Cordesman, *The India–Pakistan Military Balance*, (Washington, DC: Center for Strategic and International Studies, 2002), 3.

Kashmir thus remains vulnerable to surprise attacks by Pakistan, as is evident in the 1999 Kargil incursion. It took a considerable amount of manpower and resources for India to eject the Pakistani intruders from the Kargil Hills. Even at this high cost, the intrusion did not come to an expeditious end until the US, under President Bill Clinton, intervened and compelled the then Pakistani Prime Minister Nawaz Shariff to withdraw his troops.[21] With the acquisition of nuclear weapons, Pakistan believes that it has obtained a "great equalizer" at the strategic level, since its missiles can hit most parts of India. New Delhi's overall conventional superiority has thus been severely constrained in the event of a war. Its earlier strategic posture of deterrence by denial and deterrence by punishment (i.e., in response to an attack on Kashmir, India would escalate the conflict across Pakistan's vulnerable strategic underbelly in Punjab) may have become less plausible. The previous Indian strategy, as practiced in 1965, was to open up a second front in the Punjab if Pakistan crossed the LoC in Kashmir as this sector offers India major tactical advantages. In that war, Pakistan had to pull its forces out of Kashmir to defend its heartland, the Punjab.[22] The Indians realized this as is evident in their adoption of strategies such as military mobilization and limited war, hoping that Pakistan could be contained and that it would suffer economically and militarily in a long-term competition with India.[23]

Furthermore, the politico-military support that Pakistan enjoyed off and on from the US and continuously from China since the 1960s, has enabled it to reduce the power asymmetry with India. During some periods (especially in the 1960s and 1980s), Pakistan acquired from the US qualitatively superior weapons compared to those of India's. Pakistan's geostrategic location has been a crucial factor in its importance to the US and its allies. During the early stages of the Cold War, Pakistan offered bases and staging posts to the US spy planes to watch the Soviet nuclear and missile activities. Under the Eisenhower administration, Pakistan became "the most allied ally" of the US in the region. The conclusion of the 1954 mutual defense agreement and membership in the Southeast Asian Treaty Organization (SEATO) and the Central Treaty Organization (CENTO) were key elements of this cooperation. During the 1950s and early 1960s, massive amounts of American arms and economic aid flowed to Pakistan, and some argue that the aid was

---

[21] On this see Strobe Talbott, *Engaging India* (Washington, DC: Brookings Institution Press, 2004), ch. 8.

[22] On the 1965 War, see Paul, *Asymmetric Conflicts*, ch. 6.

[23] On the changing Indian strategy, see C. Raja Mohan, *Crossing the Rubicon: The Shaping of India's New Foreign Policy* (New York: Palgrave-Macmillan, 2003), ch. 7.

part of the reason for the strengthened position of the armed forces in Pakistani society, the creation of a vast military infrastructure, and the tendency among the Pakistani ruling elite to pursue risky military behavior.[24] In the early 1970s, Pakistan acted as a go-between for the US and China in the diplomatic opening between the two states. During the 1980s, Pakistan was the frontline state for the US and the conduit for American assistance to the Afghan mujahedin forces fighting the Soviet Union; this cooperation also resulted in substantial US economic and military transfers to Pakistan. Since September 11, 2001, it has become a pivotal state in the fight against terrorism. In all these cases, Pakistani leaders astutely negotiated diplomatic bargains with the US. While the US gave aid with the intention of using Pakistan for its larger strategic goals, Pakistan's main goal has always been to increase its capabilities *vis-à-vis* India.

In asymmetric conflict relationships, the initiator of crises and wars, if it achieves surprise, can derive certain benefits. The crisis initiator can gain an early advantage in terms of upsetting the status quo, and if that advantage can be converted into a long-lasting politico-military *fait accompli*, the materially weaker party can gain politically, if not militarily.[25] In other words, the revisionist state has temporary advantages in challenging the status quo militarily, although it may not be able to translate these advantages into a long-term permanent settlement in its favor unless outside powers come to its rescue. In its rivalry with India, Pakistan, the state seeking territorial revisions, on several occasions when it gained temporary military advantage, engaged in crisis/war activity. The examples of such activity include the Rann of Kutch skirmishes in 1965, the Kashmir War of 1965, and the Kargil conflict of 1999. While launching the military initiatives, Pakistani decisionmakers invariably expected the support or intervention of China and the US, the latter as a diplomatic rescuer. But often these initiatives strengthened the Indian determination to stand firm and not to concede, similar to a pattern of crisis learning identified by Russell Leng.[26] Such a response, however, further encouraged the weaker party to try harder, hoping to avoid the

---

[24] See Robert J. McMahon, *Cold War in the Periphery: The United States, India and Pakistan* (New York: Columbia University Press, 1994), 209–10. See also Dennis Kux, *The United States and Pakistan 1947–2000* (Washington, DC: Woodrow Wilson Center Press, 2002).

[25] On this, see Paul, *Asymmetric Conflicts*, 24–25.

[26] As Leng puts it: "Far from showing signs of improved crisis management, each successive Indo-Pakistani crisis escalated to a more violent conclusion than its predecessor." *Bargaining and Learning in Recurring Crises* (Ann Arbor: University of Michigan Press, 2000), 270.

16   *T. V. Paul*

previous lack of success or resolve. The cycle of escalating crisis behavior has thus continued.

Some argue that the period of Indian military preponderance was associated with stability or absence of war and crises in South Asia. During 1972–87, Pakistan was weakened considerably following its defeat in the Bangladesh War of 1971.[27] The notion of "preponderance deters war," developed in the power transition theory of A. F. K. Organski and others, seems to have relevance to the subcontinent. According to this notion, peace is obtained when a satisfied state has preponderance of strength, while war is more likely when a dissatisfied challenger approximates its capability with the status quo power.[28] Since the late 1980s, when Pakistan acquired nuclear weapons and delivery systems such as F-16 aircraft and medium-range missiles that can hit most parts of India, the Pakistani posture has changed. Thus, nuclear acquisition is viewed by the Pakistani military elite as a way to equalize the power relationship with India and as a cover for conducting substrategic-level operations in Kashmir with more vigor.

Sensing these constraints, India had by 2002 developed a limited war strategy (somewhat similar to the Israeli strategy) of attacking insurgent camps within the Pakistani side of Kashmir without escalating it into a war, while holding a no-first-use nuclear posture, if it were provoked through terrorist attacks similar to the attack on the Indian Parliament in December 2001. New Delhi has also revamped its intelligence and defense networks and fenced the LoC. However, Pakistan maintains a first-use nuclear posture, thereby attempting to deter India from launching a conventional attack. By threatening nuclear war, the Pakistani strategy appears to be to raise international alarm and thereby diplomatic intervention, especially by the US. In these strategic postures of the opponents lie potential risks for nuclear war, as either state during a crisis time – fearing pre-emption or due to miscalculation – could initiate an early nuclear launch in order not to be the first one to be struck.

The peculiar power asymmetry between India and Pakistan has also generated different patterns of resolve and resentment. Most often, the weaker party has shown more resolve to acquire the territory through military means, including guerrilla/terrorist operations. However,

---

[27] Raju G. C. Thomas, "The South Asian Security Balance in a Western Dominant World," in T. V. Paul, James J. Wirtz, and Michel Fortman (eds.), *Balance of Power: Theory and Practice in the 21st Century* (Stanford: Stanford University Press, 2004), 317–18.

[28] A. F. K. Organiski, *World Politics*, 2nd edn (New York: Alfred A. Knopf, 1968), 364–66; Inis L. Claude, *Power and International Relations* (New York: Random House, 1964), 56; and Jacek Kugler and Douglas Lemke (eds.), *Parity and War* (Ann Arbor: University of Michigan Press, 1996).

because the crisis decisions in Pakistan have been made secretly by a small group within the military elite, these decisionmakers have also displayed a tendency to waffle in the face of escalation by the other side and diplomatic intervention by the great powers. The sense of resentment is higher in the weaker party as the status quo seems to favor the stronger side. Further, the territorial dismemberment in 1971 solidified the existing resentment of Pakistanis about the "unfairness" of territorial divisions. The passage of time seems to favor the stronger side, given that India's economy is growing more rapidly than Pakistan's since the former began economic reforms in 1991.

This higher level of resentment among Pakistanis tends to manifest itself intensely in societal dimensions, especially in the teaching of history that perpetuates negative and stereotypical images of India and the Hindu religion. The widespread *madrassa* educational system, which handles a large portion of the elementary and middle-level schools, and the absence of authentic democratic institutions, a civil society, or a free press, have made virtually impossible a secular understanding of other religious beliefs for ordinary Pakistanis. Indians also hold stereotypical images of Pakistanis, as is evident in the often negative media coverage of that country and the burgeoning number of Bollywood movies with anti-Pakistan themes. The rise of Hindu fundamentalism since the 1980s (with the hostility toward Pakistan having played a part in it) has further strengthened the anti-Pakistan, anti-Muslim forces in India.[29] Moreover, there is a tendency among the Indian political leaders to blame Pakistan for every terrorist strike in the country, at times offering little evidence, thereby generating credibility problems for the Indian position.

The India–Pakistan power asymmetry is affected by perceptions that each side holds of the other. Much of the Pakistani elite believes that India and Pakistan ought to be coequals geopolitically and it sees relative parity in military and diplomatic terms as a goal worth striving for, even at a high cost to society. It is, indeed, an ardent believer in the Westphalian notion of *de jure* equality of states and balance of power politics. Thus, India's efforts at achieving major power status and gaining permanent membership in the UN Security Council are viewed with great alarm and all means are employed to avert this prospect.[30] Pakistan fears that Indian

---

[29] On the broader issue of Hindu–Muslim violence in India, see Ashutosh Varshney, *Ethnic Conflict and Civic Life: Hindus and Muslims in India* (New Haven: Yale University Press, 2002).

[30] A Pakistani scholar puts it succinctly: "Pakistan's abhorrence to India's commanding role in view of its historical experiences and the distrust of the latter is deeply ingrained into Pakistan's strategic culture." See Hasan-Askari Rizvi, "Pakistan's Strategic Culture," in Chambers (ed.), *South Asia in 2020*, 305–28. On India's effort to achieve great power

hegemony in the subcontinent will adversely affect its security and power position.[31] Its perception of parity also arises from its historical under-standing of the subcontinent, where Muslims ruled for over six centuries. Pakistan's founding father, Jinnah, and the Muslim League, were driven by the perception of coequality with India (or 'Hindustan' as they called it) and the territorial division they demanded included this notion. Since independence, Pakistan has consistently pursued a policy of obtaining parity with India, often through military and diplomatic means. Alignment with outside powers and the acquisition of qualitatively superior weaponry have been two key planks of this strategy. Although Pakistan's dismemberment in the Bangladesh War dampened any hopes of maintaining or obtaining real strategic parity, the logic of balancing India militarily and diplomatically still runs deeply in the Pakistani elite's calculations.

The Pakistani aim of achieving symmetry between the two states has been further augmented by outside powers, which treated these two states as strategic and political equals during the Cold War era. In the Western official and media worlds, bracketing India and Pakistan as equals has been a common practice, and the American alignment with Islamabad reinforced the equality notion. The nuclear arms race between the two states has been another basis for the parity notion. Only with the end of the Cold War, and the substantial improvement in US–India relations, has this approach become less salient, although it has not fully disappeared. At the same time, Pakistan's search for parity with India has been greatly helped by its military and strategic relationship with China, which has emerged as the main source of Islamabad's nuclear and missile capabilities and, in recent years, conventional weapons. China has maintained its "all-weather relationship" with Pakistan as a way to contain India, even when Beijing has maintained a policy of engagement with New Delhi.[32]

The conflict with a larger neighbor has also created peculiar domestic power structures and political configurations in Pakistan. The armed

status, see Baldev Raj Nayar and T. V. Paul, *India in the World Order: Searching for Major Power Status* (Cambridge: Cambridge University Press, 2003); Stephen P. Cohen, *India: Emerging Power* (Washington, DC: Brookings, 2001); and Dinshaw Mistry, "A Theoretical and Empirical Assessment of India as an Emerging Power," *India Review* 3 (January 2004), 64–87.

31 Jean-Luc Racine, "Pakistan and the 'India Syndrome': Between Kashmir and the Nuclear Predicament," in Christophe Jaffrelot (ed.), *Pakistan: Nationalism Without a Nation?* (London: Zed Books, 2002), ch. 9.

32 On this, see T. V. Paul, "The Enduring Sino-Pakistani Nuclear/Missile Relationship and the Balance of Power Logic," *Nonproliferation Review* 10 (Summer 2003), 1–9; and J. Mohan Malik, "South Asia in China's Foreign Relations," *Pacifica Review* 13 (February 2001), 73–90.

forces have emerged as the most powerful societal actor with excessive institutional and corporatist interests, largely due to Pakistan's asymmetric conflict with India. The successive military coups have led to Pakistan being ruled by military dictators for more than half of its existence as a nation-state, its failure to develop democratic institutions, and its excessive defense burden.[33] From the beginning, the Pakistani ruling elite vested unlimited power in the military and other central bureaucratic authorities, withholding devolution of power to regional and local levels. Successive governments made policies that favored central rule, bolstering the role of the military and undermining popular participation.[34] The war-making aspect of the Pakistani state is strong, but it has not resulted in a stronger nation-state, unlike the European historical experience.

In the Indian case, five decades of conflict have built considerable institutional rigidity. The armed forces seem to be reluctant to make any territorial concessions to neighbors which they fear would neutralize their strategic and tactical positions. The political parties have shown substantial opposition to any concessions, although in recent years there has been a subtle change in their positions. The Indian External Affairs Ministry is another stakeholder, with a rather conservative approach toward diplomacy and change in relations with neighboring countries. It seems there is a general perception in Indian strategic circles that small territorial concessions will have a domino effect and will lead to demands for more concessions and that no minor concessions will placate Pakistan. Under these circumstances, stasis, not conflict resolution, has become the chief characteristic of the rivalry.

Resolving the conflict

The existing literature on conflict resolution points to several avenues for an end to an enduring rivalry. For instance, using a punctuated equilibrium model,[35] Diehl and Goertz argue that the arrival of some sort of internal or external political shock is a necessary condition for the termination of a conflict of this kind. Mediation by outside powers tends to have limited value as it could delay a settlement. To Diehl and Goertz, what seems

---

[33] Babar Sattar, "Pakistan: Return to Praetorianism," in Muttiah Alagappa (ed.), *Coercion and Governance* (Stanford: Stanford University Press, 2001), 385–412.

[34] Ayesha Jalal, *The State of the Martial Law: The Origins of Pakistan's Political Economy of Defense* (Cambridge: Cambridge University Press, 1990), 295–328.

[35] They draw the theory from biology about the uneven rates of species evolution occurring in spurts followed by long periods of stasis and no change. "Species evolve rapidly, change little, and then go extinct quickly." Similarly, "states lock-in to enduring rivalries, which then change little until their rapid demise." Diehl and Goertz, *War and Peace in International Rivalry*, 132.

necessary is "a dramatic change in the international system or its subsystems that fundamentally alters the processes, relationships, and expectations that drive nation-state interactions." War and domestic regime changes are two such shocks.[36] Other theorists have argued for the role of imaginative leadership along with the arrival of favorable structural conditions for peace.[37] Yet others view major crises or imminent threats of war as preconditions for change.[38] Moreover, parties should feel exhausted with a mutually hurting stalemate affecting their thinking on the subject. One thing is certain, however, for an enduring rivalry to end, both favorable general conditions and imaginative leaders are needed. Conditions may be ripe for rapprochement but, if leaders are reluctant to translate them into concrete negotiating opportunities, peace will remain elusive. Similarly, leaders may be genuinely interested in accommodation, but the background conditions may not be there that would allow them to strike a deal that satisfies key domestic and international constituencies.

Several questions emerge as important in this context. In the India–Pakistan context, could a major nuclear crisis or a substantial change in political regimes serve as a necessary catalyst for the termination of the rivalry? If external shocks are catalysts, why did the end of the Cold War not make a big difference for South Asia as it did in many other parts of the world? Is the continuing truncated asymmetry partly the reason why the conflict does not show signs of ending?[39] Is overwhelming preponderance of the status quo power – similar to the pattern of the US–Mexico and US–Canada cases in which the US had obtained hegemony – a necessary condition for the ending of this conflict? How will this settle the aspirations of the Kashmiri people? Or, does it make any difference in a nuclearized context? Is ideological and regime compatibility crucial in conflict termination? Are domestic structural changes in Pakistan and societal-level attitudinal changes in India necessary precursors for accommodation? Or does the contiguous-territorial

---

[36] Ibid., 215–17, 221.

[37] On the role of leaders who used favorable conditions for negotiating an end to three enduring rivalries – East–West Germany, US–China and Egypt–Israel – see Tony Armstrong, *Breaking the Ice* (Washington, DC: United States Institute of Peace, 1993).

[38] For the role of crisis as a catalyst in rapprochement between long-standing enemies, see Richard Ned Lebow, *Between Peace and War* (Baltimore: Johns Hopkins University Press, 1984); and Stephen Rock, *Why Peace Breaks Out* (Chapel Hill: University of North Carolina Press, 1989).

[39] According to one study, diplomatic negotiations involving dyads of low power asymmetry tend to deadlock because neither has the power to force the other to move. Both sides tend to lock in their side of the symmetry and prolong and reinforce their hostility. See I. William Zartman and Jeffrey Z. Rubin, "Symmetry and Asymmetry in Negotiations," in Zartman and Rubin (eds.), *Power and Negotiations* (Ann Arbor: University of Michigan Press, 2000), 272.

nature of the conflict, combined with strong ideological and irredentist dimensions, not lend itself to easy resolution unless there is a major catalyst such as war or regime change? Are there sufficient domestic and international level factors that allow leaders to come to terms?[40] Are active mediation and internationalization required before a settlement can be reached?

The various chapters in this volume address these and the following additional questions:

1. To what extent is the India–Pakistan conflict an enduring rivalry? How does it vary from other enduring rivalries, past and present? Why have some similar conflicts ended but not this one?
2. What specific factors explain the persistence of this conflict? The main factors identified are:
   - Particular power asymmetry
   - Incompatible national identities
   - Differing domestic power structures (democracy versus authoritarianism)
   - Irredentism
   - Great power involvement (as supporter of one or more parties, source of weapons and also as source of conflict/crisis management). A pertinent question is: what difference has the end of the Cold War – the change from bipolarity to near unipolarity – made to the persistence of the conflict? If shifts in the distribution of power at the global level make a major difference, why has no substantial change occurred in this conflict as in the Middle East and other former rivalries such as Cambodia and Southern Africa? Did the September 11, 2001 terrorist attacks influence the contours of this rivalry? If so, how?
   - The presence of nuclear weapons
3. What changes are required in these factors that could bring this conflict to an end?

Responses of contributors

The contributors to this volume offer answers to these and related questions in their chapters. In general, most contributors seem pessimistic

---

[40] Robert Putnam conceives international negotiations as a two-level game in which, at the national level, domestic groups pressure governments to pursue favorable policies while at the international level national governments seek to maximize their ability to meet domestic demands and minimize adverse consequences. See Putnam, "Diplomacy and Domestic Politics: The Logic of Two-Level Games," *International Organization* **42** (Summer 1988), 427–60.

regarding an immediate end to the conflict, despite minor changes in the positions of the parties and their great power supporters, most visible since early 2004. The second section of the volume addresses the theoretical issues relating to enduring rivalries. The chapters by Diehl, Goertz and Saeedi, Vasquez, Geller, and Leng review the existing literature on enduring rivalries and apply its findings to the South Asian conflict. The factors that lead to such a rivalry, its different phases – including lock-in and stasis – are discussed. The crucial role that territory plays in an enduring conflict is a particular focus. John Vasquez also gives territory a key role in his analysis – built around his prominent work on steps to war – states in conflict tend to make certain foreign policy choices that have the effect of increasing hostility and threat perception, eventually leading to war.

In his chapter, Daniel Geller argues that the India–Pakistan conflict is shaped by the complex conjunction of structural factors such as the ongoing territorial dispute over Kashmir; the opportunity to exercise military force because of the contiguous border; the absence of paired democratic regimes, non-violent norms for conflict resolution, and shared institutional constraints on war decisions; and the low levels of economic development for both states, which make possible the use of force with minimal economic consequences. To Russell Leng, the elites of both states have been learning, but are predisposed by their realpolitik beliefs to draw only certain types of lessons from their behavior. Each successive crisis raises the reputational stakes for both sides, and success or failure in each crisis is attributed to the state's ability to demonstrate superior resolve. The coercive bargaining strategies of the parties have created a self-fulfilling prophecy, while the pervading realpolitik culture constricts the range of actions available to leaders of the two states, as it colors their historical memories and narrows their collective identities.

Two other chapters crossing international and domestic aspects are offered by Ashok Kapur and Saira Khan. To Kapur, the conflict became enduring because of the continued support of the US and China to the regional challenger Pakistan and the desire of the great powers to reduce the power asymmetry between the two states and to balance India's power capabilities. India remained defensive and reactive toward this great power challenge and, only with the end of Nehruvian approaches in the late 1990s, has India become more proactive in the rivalry. The great powers were also driven by motives arising out of their own conflict, especially during the Cold War era. Until recently, conflict management was the norm of behavior of the great powers that have been heavily involved in the region. Khan argues that the induction of nuclear weapons has made the dyad more crisis-prone and the parties less willing to compromise. With the understanding that full-scale war is unlikely to occur, both India and Pakistan have become less interested in making meaningful compromises to terminate the rivalry. Nuclear weapons have helped to increase the pace of low- to medium-level violence in the rivalry, reinforcing each state's view of hostility on the part of the other.

The comparative and regional dimensions of the conflict are presented in the chapters by Vali Nasr, Stephen Saideman, and Reeta Tremblay and Julian Schofield. For Nasr, national identity has played a complex role in the India–Pakistan conflict, with both countries becoming more reliant on religious ideology than was the case at independence. The lack of an adequate national identity in Pakistan has made it imperative that it create an identity that is in opposition to India's. While in India the rise of Hindu nationalism has strengthened anti-Pakistani attitudes, in Pakistan the military has successfully used Islamic identity to defend its own political position and interests that are conducive to the perpetuation of the rivalry. To Saideman, the key reasons for the persistence of the conflict have to be located in domestic politics associated with irredentism. In comparison with the Sino-Indian conflict, the India–Pakistan rivalry has remained at a higher intensity due to the irredentist aims of Pakistan and the anti-irredentist policies of India while the majority Kashmiri population desires independence from both states. The international costs of aggressive foreign polices are not necessarily sufficient to stop a country from engaging in self-destructive behavior associated with irredentism if domestic pressures are strong enough to continue such policies. Tremblay and Schofield argue that both military and hybrid regimes (democratic in name only as they are heavily controlled by the military) are dispute and war prone because they have a tendency to become involved in conflicts which carry domestic symbolic importance, while democratic regimes are constrained by institutional structures and normative factors. Despite the regime incompatibility, both states have responded cooperatively to possibly contentious issues, such as water sharing, due to the influence of different policy communities and policy networks involved in these areas.

The conditions under which the conflict could end are part of the focus of the concluding chapter. In this context, the peace efforts by India and Pakistan since 2004 assume significance. To an extent, the peace initiatives were the result of changing external and internal conditions. The political shock of the events of September 11, 2001 has been more profound in South Asia than the systemic shock resulting from the end of the Cold War. In the aftermath of the terrorist strikes in the US, the great power involvement in the region has to a certain extent changed. By early 2004, some general background conditions for deescalation had emerged. The shifting positions of the great powers (US and China more prominently) in the post-September 11 international context were a key source of change in the region. With the shifting approaches of the US and China and the rapid economic growth of India, the Pakistani elite's notion of maintaining parity with India has been somewhat battered. Both internal and external political considerations for the leaders of the two states, such as electoral victory in the Indian case and exoneration from involvement in transnational terrorism and nuclear proliferation in the Pakistani case, were significant as well. Durable peace, however, will require drastic changes in several factors well ingrained in this conflict, and the ensuing chapters address them one by one in order to understand why the India–Pakistan rivalry remains one of the world's most enduring and deadly conflicts devoid of easy resolution.

Part II

Theories of enduring rivalry and the South Asian conflict

2 Theoretical specifications of enduring rivalries: applications to the India–Pakistan case

Paul F. Diehl, Gary Goertz, and Daniel Saeedi

Introduction

Although there are various conceptual[1] and operational definitions of enduring rivalries, and these may result in different compilations of the phenomena,[2] the India–Pakistan rivalry appears on all lists. From shortly after both states gained their independence in 1947 until the present day, India and Pakistan have clashed repeatedly, with several wars and a larger number of military crises the most notable manifestations of that competition.

To say that India and Pakistan are engaged in an enduring rivalry does not necessarily mean that we understand all aspects of that competition. Nevertheless, there have been several theoretical formulations that seek to explain and predict enduring rivalry behavior. In addition, there is a growing body of research[3] that tests many of the propositions from those models, and we have accumulated some significant knowledge about enduring rivalries. Using these theoretical formulations and empirical evidence, this chapter will examine the India–Pakistan rivalry. Specifically, we will examine the origins of the India–Pakistan rivalry in light of enduring rivalry research, focusing the conditions that led to its initiation and development. We then examine the dynamics of the rivalry, and its patterns of persistence over the last six decades. Although the India–Pakistan rivalry is ongoing, we also consider theoretical and empirical specifications for rivalry termination, with special attention to the prospects of those conditions arising in the India–Pakistan context.

---

[1] See Paul F. Diehl and Gary Goertz, *War and Peace in International Rivalry* (Ann Arbor: University of Michigan Press, 2000).

[2] William R. Thompson, "Identifying Rivals and Rivalries in World Politics," *International Studies Quarterly* 45 (1995), 557–87.

[3] See Gary Goertz and Paul F. Diehl, "(Enduring) Rivalries," in Manus Midlarsky (ed.), *Handbook of War Studies*, 2nd edn (Ann Arbor: University of Michigan Press, 2000), 222–67.

Throughout this analysis, special attention is directed to how the India–Pakistan rivalry compares to other long-standing rivalries.

The India–Pakistan rivalry presents something of a puzzle for international relations theory. Conventional treatments of war, such as the power transition model,[4] regard preponderance as a pacifying condition. Yet, despite apparent Indian military advantages, the India–Pakistan rivalry has experienced multiple wars and numerous other confrontations with little sign of abatement. Some rational choice approaches regard military conflict and war as an information problem; once states recognize their opponent's preferences and likely actions, future conflict becomes costly and unlikely.[5] States that fail to obtain their goals repeatedly, often losing in war, should learn from such failure and thereby be restrained from future challenges under such formulations. Nevertheless, Pakistan has repeatedly and unsuccessfully challenged India over Kashmir; indeed, it may be as Leng has argued, any learning that did occur by Pakistan may have been largely dysfunctional.[6] Therefore, understanding the India–Pakistan rivalry is not only valuable for its own sake, but it may also provide insight into rivalries that seem to defy extant theoretical frameworks.

We begin with a specification of the most developed theoretical treatment of enduring rivalries, namely the "punctuated equilibrium" model developed by Diehl and Goertz.[7] Yet we also review some of the tenets of alternative specifications, namely what has been referred to as "evolutionary approaches" to rivalries.[8] Along with empirical findings, these models provide the road map for our understanding of the origins, dynamics, and possible termination of the India–Pakistan rivalry.

The conclusions below are largely derived from an analysis of all the militarized confrontations between India and Pakistan from 1947 to 2001, the latter being the last year for which data are available. Specifically, we analyze "militarized disputes," as defined by the Correlates of War (COW) Project. These are "a set of interactions between or among states involving threats to use military force, displays of military force, or actual uses of military force ... these acts must be explicit, overt, nonaccidental, and

[4] A. F. K. Organski and Jacek Kugler, *The War Ledger* (Chicago: University of Chicago Press, 1980).
[5] James Fearon, "Rationalist Explanations for War," *International Organization* 49 (1995), 379–414.
[6] See Leng in this volume.   [7] Diehl and Goertz, *War and Peace.*
[8] For example, see Paul R. Hensel, "An Evolutionary Approach to the Study of Interstate Rivalry," *Conflict Management and Peace Science* 17 (1999); Zeev Maoz and Ben D. Mor, *Bound by Struggle: The Strategic Evolution of Enduring International Rivalries* (Ann Arbor: University of Michigan Press, 2002).

government sanctioned."[9] Forty-three confrontations between India and Pakistan over the period of study meet this definition.[10] Our analysis focuses on the characteristics of individual disputes and their patterns over time in relation to what models of enduring rivalries can tell us about the phenomena.

Theoretical guides to enduring rivalries

Traditional realist conceptions of interstate conflict focus heavily on power considerations.[11] In such formulations, enduring rivalries might be expected to form and sustain themselves as states of relatively equal capability contend for regional or global influence. Competitions between mismatched protagonists may never develop into enduring rivalries as the stronger side can impose its will on its weaker opponent or defeat it militarily if necessary. Accordingly, initial confrontations might result in the stronger side winning the nascent rivalry, and the rivalry thereby terminating. Enduring rivalries will likely occur between states that are unable to dominate or defeat each other, such as major powers in the international system, who have both the intersecting interests and military capabilities to sustain a long-term competition. Realist conceptions of rivalry development, however, may provide limited insight into the India–Pakistan rivalry. At first glance, India appears to hold a military advantage throughout most, if not all, of the rivalry (see more on this point below), and Pakistan's repeated failure in challenging India has not ameliorated the frequency or intensity of the military confrontations.

Rational choice treatments are equally limited in helping understand enduring rivalries. Such approaches, heavily influenced by realist logic, may even regard enduring rivalries as epiphenomenal. If one conceives of rivalries as repeated games, rivalries can be understood as the repetition of the same conditions producing the same outcomes over time. The future is very much like the past until the cycle is broken. This is largely the argument made by Gartzke and Simon, who claim that the distribution of enduring rivalries across a continuum of dispute frequency is similar to that predicted by a random events model.[12] In effect, they

---

[9] Charles S. Gochman and Zeev Maoz, "Militarized Interstate Disputes, 1816–1976: Procedures, Patterns, and Insights," *Journal of Conflict Resolution* 28 (1984), 587.

[10] These data, and indeed data on all militarized disputes in the international system, are available at http://www.correlatesofwar.org

[11] Jeffrey Legro and Andrew Moravcsik, "Is Anybody Still a Realist?," *International Security* 24 (1999), 5–55.

[12] Erik Gartzke and Michael Simon, "Hot Hand: A Critical Analysis of Enduring Rivalries," *Journal of Politics* 63 (1999), 777–98.

are arguing that repeated militarized disputes, and therefore enduring rivalries, might easily occur by chance. Nevertheless, the research that has directly or indirectly examined their claim without exception (that we are aware of) finds a very strong interconnection between the same rivals over time. All of these studies find very significant correlations between rivalry history and the current dispute.[13] Furthermore, it would be ludicrous to argue that the various confrontations between India and Pakistan are unrelated to each other or that earlier crises did not influence the strategies of the two sides.

Better insights into the India–Pakistan rivalry are available from two theoretical treatments of enduring rivalries: the punctuated equilibrium and evolutionary model approaches. The punctuated equilibrium model of rivalries[14] starts with a longitudinal view of international relations, which does not atomize disputes and wars and rip them from their historical context. Roughly, there are three phases in the maturation of a rivalry. In the onset phase, the rivalry begins following a "political shock," a dramatic change endogenous to one or both of the rivals (e.g., regime change) or to the international environment as a whole (e.g., aftermath of a world war). The punctuated equilibrium model is not very specific as to the other conditions that prompt the initiation of rivalries, although it suggests that structural factors (e.g., power distributions, issues in dispute) may be important. During this initial phase, the rivals either resolve the disputes relatively quickly or patterns of hostility "lock-in," with the consequence that the rivalry becomes enduring.

Evolutionary conceptions of enduring rivalries argue that the outcomes of the first confrontations are critical for the maturation of a enduring rivalry. The severity levels and who wins (and the effect on satisfaction) determine whether a rivalry dies out or festers.[15] For example, a confrontation that ends in a stalemate is likely to increase distrust and hostility between two adversaries without resolving any of the disputed issues to either side's

---

[13] Paul R. Hensel, "One Thing Leads to Another: Recurrent Militarized Disputes in Latin America, 1816–1986," *Journal of Peace Research* 31 (1994), 281–98; Paul R. Hensel, "Hot Hands and Cold Wars: A Reassessment of the Stochastic Model of Rivalry." Presented at the Annual Meeting of the American Political Science Association, San Francisco (September) 2001; Mark Crescenzi and Andrew Enterline, "Time Remembered: A Dynamic Model of Interstate Interaction," *International Studies Quarterly* 45 (2001), 409–32; Michael Colaresi and William Thompson, "Hot Spots or Hot Hands?: Serial Crisis Behavior, Escalating Risks, and Rivalry," *Journal of Politics* 64 (2002), 1175–98.

[14] Diehl and Goertz, *War and Peace*; see also Claudio Cioffi-Revilla, "The Political Uncertainty of Interstate Rivalries: A Punctuated Equilibrium Model," in Paul F. Diehl (ed.), *The Dynamics of Enduring Rivalries* (Urbana: University of Illinois Press, 1998), 64–97.

[15] Hensel, "An Evolutionary Approach"; Maoz and Mor, *Bound by Struggle*.

satisfaction. In contrast, a dispute that ends in a negotiated compromise – *ceteris paribus* – is more likely to help resolve the issues between the adversaries, or at least to help create a more trusting environment because of the experience of negotiating a satisfactory resolution to the dispute. Similarly, a dispute that ends in a decisive victory for one side (whether through a battlefield victory or by compelling the opponent to back down) is likely to reduce conflict levels in its immediate aftermath, if only because the defeated side requires time to recover or to prepare for another challenge at a more propitious moment. Beyond the outcome of the previous confrontation, the evolutionary approach suggests that the severity level is likely to be quite important. All else remaining equal, more severe confrontations appear likely to intensify the distrust and hostility between two adversaries relative to more trivial confrontations that end quickly and with little bloodshed or destruction, thus increasing subsequent conflict levels.

Following the "lock-in" phase is one of "stasis," in which hostile interactions persist between the rivals with some regularity or consistency. It is not until another political shock (although only a necessary condition) arises that enduring rivalries end, and they do so abruptly. The punctuated equilibrium model of rivalry depends centrally on the concept of a "basic rivalry level" or BRL.[16] Azar proposed that each pair of countries has a "normal relations range," or an average level of hostile or cooperative interaction, around which their relations vary;[17] Goertz and Diehl reformulate this as a BRL around which relations fluctuate. The punctuated equilibrium model anticipates that conflict patterns within rivalries will "lock in" around this BRL at the outset of the rivalry relationship, and will remain similar throughout the rivalry. Periods of conflict and détente are seen as random variations around this basic level, with no secular trend toward more conflictual or more peaceful relations. This is not to suggest, though, that all conflict within a rivalry is exactly the same over time. This model expects some variation in severity and duration across different disputes, occasionally including large deviations (full-scale interstate wars) from the basic rivalry level. BRLs also vary across rivalries; that is, not all enduring rivalries have the same level, and enduring rivalries do not necessarily have more severe BRLs than lesser rivalries.

Hensel argues that after two adversaries have engaged in several confrontations the push of the past (the lengthening history of past conflict) and the pull of the future (the expectation of continued future conflict) begin to have

---

[16] Diehl and Goertz, *War and Peace*.

[17] Edward Azar, "Conflict Escalation and Conflict Reduction in an International Crisis: Suez 1956," *Journal of Conflict Resolution* 16 (1972), 183–201.

an important impact on conflict behavior.[18] The advanced phase of rivalry is characterized by substantial threat perception and competition between the rivals. This conception is largely consistent with that of McGinnis and Williams, who argue that belief systems and bureaucratic policies harden over time in a rivalry, making rivalry behavior (such as arms races) hard to dislodge.[19] Similarly, Leng indicates that the belief systems of leaders are critical in crisis behavior, and these systems are largely defined by prior disputes and crises.[20] Over time, the external rivalry becomes entrenched in the domestic politics of the two rival states.[21]

We use the punctuated equilibrium model and various insights from the evolutionary model as a framework to analyze patterns evident in the India–Pakistan rivalry.

Origins of enduring rivalries

The origins of enduring rivalries are perhaps the least developed area of research given that scholars have concentrated on the more policy applicable concerns of rivalry dynamics and termination. Nevertheless, there are a number of clues as to how violent conflict in rivalries begins and what leads to the development of enduring competitions from that early conflict.

The punctuated equilibrium model of rivalries posits that political shocks are necessary, but not sufficient, conditions for the onset of enduring rivalries.[22] That is, they set the environmental context for the rivalries to develop, but they by no means guarantee that such rivalries will occur. Political shocks may come in a variety of forms and at different levels of analysis. System level shocks include world wars, rapid and dramatic changes in the power distribution, and significant transfers of territory between states. Such changes reorder international relations and create opportunities for new coalitions to form. Old enemies may become friends but, equally important for our purposes, new sources of contention may arise between states that were formally allies or at least were not rivals with one another. The emergence of the US–USSR rivalry at the end of World War II is a classic example.

[18] Hensel, "An Evolutionary Approach."
[19] Michael D. McGinnis and John T. Williams, *Compound Dilemmas: Democracy, Collective Action and Superpower Rivalry* (Ann Arbor: University of Michigan Press, 2001).
[20] Russell Leng, *Bargaining and Learning in Recurrent Crises: The Soviet–American, Egyptian–Israeli, and Indo-Pakistani Rivalries* (Ann Arbor: University of Michigan Press, 2000).
[21] Hensel, "An Evolutionary Approach."
[22] Diehl and Goertz, *War and Peace*; see also Michael P. Colaresi, "Shocks to the System: Great Power Rivalry and the Leadership Long Cycle," *Journal of Conflict Resolution* 45 (2001), 569–74.

Shocks may also occur at the domestic level, affecting one or both of the potential rivals. Most notable is a newly independent state, which has been found to be especially vulnerable to armed confrontations in its first years as a member of the international community.[23] This may be the result of the unsettled borders, something especially characteristic of new states. Yet new states may also have dramatic effects on regional security, disrupting power balances or causing shifts in alignment between friends and foes. Other domestic level shocks affecting rivalry initiation include the presence of a civil war in one state; this could open opportunities for another state to exploit its rival's preoccupation with and commitment of resources to the civil war. A regime change in one or both of the rivals may also be a shock that is a precursor to the onset of militarized competition. Regime changes may signal significant changes in preferences of the state affected, and this may lead to sudden clash of interests with another state, even one that was formerly a friend.

In the case of India and Pakistan, their joint independence is obviously the event that sets the stage for their initial confrontation. Yet, a rivalry was by no means inevitable. States centered on different religions did not help matters, but differing religions were not necessarily the causal factor in the conflict. Ganguly notes that it was the differing ideologies of the two leaderships, exacerbated by the legacy of the British colonial disengagement, that set the conflict in motion, and continues to influence the relationship to this day.[24]

That the first militarized confrontation was a war was important in establishing high hostility levels, but not a necessary condition for the development of an enduring rivalry. Many enduring rivalries began without wars early in their existence; indeed, some enduring rivalries never experience a war (e.g., US–USSR after 1945). Still other proto rivalries (e.g., US–Spain in the late nineteenth century) experience a war very early on, but the fighting resolved the disputed issues between the participants and an enduring rivalry never developed. Indeed, our research suggests that wars occur at various times throughout enduring rivalries, without a pattern that can be generalized across rivalries.

The independence of Pakistan and India was a political shock to the region that set the stage for the rivalry, but it was the presence of unresolved territorial issues as a consequence of independence that encouraged its development. Stinnett and Diehl demonstrate that when

---

[23] Zeev Maoz and Nasrin Abdolali, "Regime Types and International Conflict, 1817–1976," *Journal of Conflict Resolution* 33 (1989), 3–35.

[24] Sumit Ganguly, *The Origins of War in South Asia: Indo-Pakistani Conflicts Since 1947* (Boulder, CO: Westview Press, 1986).

the first confrontation between states is over a territorial issue, the likelihood of that pair of states becoming involved in an enduring rivalry is increased.[25] The first militarized dispute between India and Pakistan is the 1947 Kashmir War, which was clearly over territorial control.

Not every enduring rivalry involves primarily or exclusively territorial issues. Nevertheless, Tir and Diehl report that 81 percent of enduring rivalries were partly or predominantly fought over territorial issues.[26] Not surprisingly, India and Pakistan have clashed forty-three times since 1947, with thirty-seven or approximately 86 percent involving territory, most commonly Kashmir. What is it about territorial disputes that seem to lend themselves to protracted competition between states? Scholars have found that territorial disputes are the most salient to decision-makers, and the ones most likely to escalate to war.[27] Specifically, standing firm in territorial disputes is often essential for political leaders to maintain or enhance support from domestic political audiences. Even when inclined to do otherwise, leaders may have their hands tied by the public, who are loath to make concessions to an enemy.[28] Accordingly, disputes over territorial control tend to repeat. Democratic states, although perhaps more pacific in general, are still strongly subject to such pressures in territorial disputes. Democratic states may be more coercive or conciliatory toward their opponents depending on election cycle timing and other domestic political factors.[29] Indian and Pakistani leaders would be committing political (and perhaps more) suicide if they abandoned their claims to Kashmir.

Beyond domestic political aspects, territory is often valued as much or more for its symbolic or intangible value as it is for its economic or strategic importance. That is, states and their peoples attach historical, religious, or related significance to a piece of territory, independent of its material value (which may in fact be limited). Jerusalem is an obvious example. Intangibly

---

[25] Douglas M. Stinnett and Paul F. Diehl, "The Path(s) to Rivalry: Behavioral and Structural Explanations of Rivalry Development," *Journal of Politics* 63 (2001), 717–40.

[26] Jaroslav Tir and Paul F. Diehl, "Geographic Dimensions of Enduring Rivalries," *Political Geography* 21 (2002), 263–86.

[27] Paul K. Huth, "Territory: Why Are Territorial Disputes Between States a Central Cause of International Conflict?" in John A. Vasquez (ed.), *What Do We Know about War?* (Lanham, MD: Rowman & Littlefield, 2000), 85–110; John A. Vasquez and Marie T. Henehan, "Territorial Disputes and the Probability of War, 1816–1992," *Journal of Peace Research* 38 (2001), 123–38.

[28] Paul Senese and John A. Vasquez, "A Unified Explanation of Territorial Conflict: Testing the Impact of Sampling Bias, 1919–1992," *International Studies Quarterly* 47 (2003), 275–98.

[29] Paul Huth and Todd Allee, *The Democratic Peace and Territorial Conflict in the Twentieth Century* (New York: Cambridge University Press, 2003).

or symbolically valued territory inhibits the construction of solutions or compromises acceptable to both parties. Economically valued territory can be divided between states, or access can be guaranteed to both parties. The same can be done for some strategic territory, or at least other security guarantees can be substituted for territorial control. Yet intangibly valued territory is not divisible in the eyes of disputants, who view territorial control as a zero-sum game. Division of territory as a solution to competing claims failed in Palestine (both as a whole and with respect to Jerusalem). The absence of a solution that falls within the "win set" of both parties is a recipe for long-term, militarized competition.

Competing claims over Kashmir illustrate the significance of territory in the origins of enduring rivalries. Kashmir clearly has value for Pakistan for religious reasons, given the majority Muslim population in that territory and the origins of the Pakistani state as a Muslim entity. More importantly, Kashmir is perceived as part of Pakistani identity, and therefore a powerful force in Pakistani domestic politics.[30] For India, Kashmir represents a beachhead against autonomy or independence claims from groups in other parts of India. Territorial concessions in India may be viewed as a sign of weakness, and precipitate further problems for the Indian state. In addition, Kashmir possesses significant water resources, vital to agriculture, especially for Pakistan. Hagerty refers to Kashmir as a "zero-sum test for each state's legitimizing ideology."[31] Another element of territorial disputes, irredentism, is a critical factor in this rivalry. Indeed, Ganguly refers to Pakistani irredentism (and Indian anti-irredentism) as a precipitating factor in the First Kashmir War.[32] Even with the passage of more than fifty years, irrendentist motivations are still manifest in the rivalry.[33] As a result of these aspects of territorial importance, dividing Kashmir, as was done at the time of independence for Pakistan and India, has proven no more successful in heading off conflict than has partition in other parts of the world.

Rivalry development, maintenance, and dynamics

Although rivalries share many common origins, the overwhelming majority of them die out quickly. That is, the first one or two militarized confrontations between two states take place in a confined time period (less than ten

---

[30] For more, see Nasr in this volume.
[31] Devin T. Hagerty, *The Consequences of Nuclear Proliferation: Lessons from South Asia* (Cambridge, MA: MIT Press, 1998), 67.
[32] Ganguly, *The Origins of War in South Asia*.
[33] See Saideman in this volume for more on irredentism and the domestic political concerns underlying it.

years) and are not followed by another crisis or dispute for many years, if ever. Indeed, our research suggests that of states that have an initial dispute, approximately 76 percent end their "rivalry" quickly, about 19 percent develop in proto-rivalries (something akin to adolescence in a lifecycle), and only 5.4 percent ever become enduring rivalries. The India–Pakistan rivalry belongs among those in the tiny, last category.

Enduring rivalry development and maintenance

What distinguishes nascent rivalries that develop into enduring ones from those that die out quickly? Several scholars note that enduring rivalries are more typical of pairs of states that are roughly equal in power or capability.[34] Such parity is said to be a prerequisite for competition between the states; significantly weaker states are thought not to be able to challenge stronger ones. Asymmetry may also lead to the stronger side deterring a weaker opponent or prevailing in a decisive way in early confrontations such that future challenges are precluded. Indeed, realist approaches suggest that asymmetric competitions will be short lived, and therefore unlikely to develop into enduring rivalries. Nevertheless, Diehl and Goertz identify a number of cases of enduring rivalries (e.g., US–Cuba after 1959) in which there are great disparities in power between the rivals, but the competition persists for decades nonetheless.[35] From the punctuated equilibrium model and other perspectives, what matters more is the source of the disputes, the orientations of the rivals toward the status quo, and whether the initial disputes resolve the conflict or not.

Preponderance by one rival may make a rivalry more likely to end quickly if the stronger side can impose its will, but this is by no means assured. There is no guarantee that military or other capability superiority can lead to an alteration of the status quo favorable to the stronger side. Furthermore, it may take overwhelming preponderance, rather than simple superiority, in any case, to achieve this. The aforementioned US–Cuba rivalry is illustrative of this. In addition, it may be that the stronger side is the status quo power, and military challenges come from the weaker rival. We know that weaker states may initiate war, and by implication lower order military conflict as well.[36] Thus, the driving force behind the rivalry may be the repeated challenges of the weaker side, and mere capability superiority may not

---

[34] William R. Thompson, "Principal Rivalries," *Journal of Conflict Resolution* 39 (1995), 195–224; John A. Vasquez, *The War Puzzle* (New York: Cambridge University Press, 1993).

[35] Diehl and Goertz, *War and Peace*.

[36] T. V. Paul, *Asymmetric Conflicts: War Initiation by Weaker Powers* (Cambridge: Cambridge University Press, 1994).

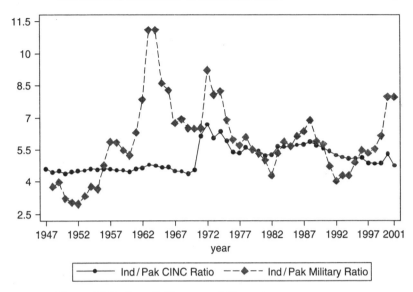

Figure 2.1 India to Pakistan capability ratios

deter such challenges.[37] The other dimension of rivalry maintenance is that the disputed issues in the rivalry are not resolved, best indicated by repeated stalemate or indecisive outcomes to the militarized confrontations. Thus, the status quo, which is unacceptable to one or both of the participants, remains, and this generates future attempts to change it. In the absence of changed preferences or the ability of one side in the conflict to disable the challenger, the rivalry may persist for many years, until the conditions for termination occur (more on this below).[38]

The pattern of interactions in the India–Pakistan rivalry is consistent with the above formulation. According to standard measures, India is clearly preponderant in aggregate conventional capabilities over Pakistan over the full life of their rivalry. Figure 2.1 charts the relative capabilities of the two sides since 1947.[39] Whether looking at military capabilities

[37] Joseph Grieco, "Repetitive Military Challenges and Recurrent International Conflict, 1918–1994," *International Studies Quarterly* 45 (2001), 295–316.

[38] Maoz and Mor, *Bound by Struggle.*

[39] Capabilities are measured according to yearly military expenditures and the number of military personnel in each state. A broader measure of capabilities includes two additional indicators each on demographic (total population and urban population) and economic (steel production and energy consumption) dimensions. See J. David Singer, Stuart Bremer, and John Stuckey, "Capability Distribution, Uncertainty, and Major Power War, 1820–1965," in Bruce Russett (ed.), *Peace, War, and Numbers* (Beverly Hills: Sage, 1972), 19–48. Data are taken from http://www.correlatesofwar.org

only or at a broader, multidimensional measure of power, India has enjoyed *at least* a 2.5:1 military advantage and a 4:1 overall capability advantage; such advantages have been relatively consistent over time. Nevertheless, there is considerable evidence that Pakistan overestimated its capabilities, leading to a false optimism about its ability to challenge India successfully.[40]

Although data suggest Indian preponderance, the distribution of power between the two rivals is better understood, as argued by Paul, as "truncated asymmetry."[41] First, India's military forces and planning are concentrated on two fronts, directed at China as well as Pakistan. India is forced to defend a much larger border (including against China). Second, it has always had to commit a sizeable portion of its troops to international security (in Punjab and elsewhere). Meanwhile, until recent operations near the Afghan border, Pakistan had a simpler defense task, to deal with the threat from India.

In addition, military capabilities in the likely theatre of conflict (Kashmir) reflect a distribution nearer to parity than aggregate, national data indicate. Furthermore, Pakistan has maintained some qualitative superiority in certain weapons systems (e.g., fighter aircraft). It might also be argued that something approaching parity has been achieved following nuclear weapons acquisition by both states.[42] Whether India is preponderant or not, several things are clear. First, whatever capability advantages it possesses are not sufficient to facilitate a decisive victory that will pre-empt future Pakistani challenges. Second, even if Pakistan approaches parity, this is probably not enough to compel India to give up or even make concessions on Kashmir. This is critical, because in this rivalry Pakistan is the clear revisionist state and this is reflected in the pattern of militarized dispute initiation over the history of the rivalry.[43]

India's preferences are such that if Kashmir were to remain in its hands and be peaceful, it would be satisfied. In contrast, Pakistan is the revisionist state, seeking to acquire the territory for its own. Thus, to achieve its goal, Pakistan must compel India to change its policy on negotiations over Kashmir and ultimately allow a change in sovereignty for that area. Not surprisingly, it is Pakistan that has been the initiator (the state that

---

[40] Sumit Ganguly, *Conflict Unending: India–Pakistan Tensions since 1947* (New York: Columbia University Press, 2001).

[41] See Paul in this volume.

[42] Although nuclear tests did not occur until 1998, both states had some nuclear capability as early as the mid-1980s and this was reflected in each state's policymaking toward the other. I thank Stephen Cohen and an anonymous reviewer for this point.

[43] Nevertheless, Pakistanis believe that India has revisionist ambitions, seeking to reverse the partition of the Indian subcontinent. Thus, it is admittedly simplistic to say that Pakistan is exclusively the revisionist power and therefore somehow responsible for starting all the conflict.

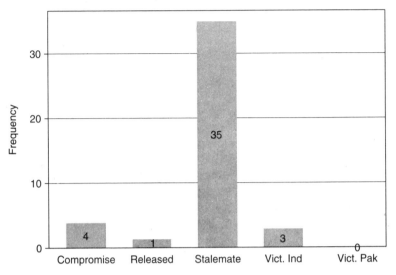

Figure 2.2 Frequency of dispute outcomes

threatened, displayed, or used military force first) of the clear majority of disputes in the rivalry. Over 65 percent (28/43) of the disputes have been initiated by Pakistan. All twelve cases of Indian initiation, however, have Pakistan as the revisionist power in the dispute; typically, India might threaten military force, accusing the Pakistanis of covertly supporting rebels in Kashmir. Thus, this is a rivalry in which the nominally weaker side is repeatedly challenging the stronger side, with some exceptions.

For a rivalry to maintain itself under these conditions, the weaker side must leave the confrontations unsuccessful and unsatisfied, but still capable of mounting future challenges. Overwhelming defeats are rare and often confined to world wars. In the case of India–Pakistan, most of the disputes end in stalemate or indeterminate outcomes. Figure 2.2 provides an overview of the outcomes of the forty-three disputes between these two rivals.[44] As predicted by the punctuated equilibrium model, most of the military confrontations have ended in stalemates; 35 (or 81.4 percent) of the disputes ended with such indecisive results. Even though it enjoys conventional superiority, India has scored a clear victory only three times (the first confrontations over Kashmir in the late 1940s and the 1971 war), although one could argue that stalemates that preserve the status quo also serve Indian interests to a large degree. In forty-three confrontations, Pakistan was *never* successful in achieving its goals. Compromise outcomes

[44] Outcomes are taken directly from the COW militarized data set referenced earlier.

are also relatively rare – only four instances, which suggests that negotiated settlements to crises are not the norm in this rivalry.

Rivalry stability

Once a rivalry is established or "locked-in," it exhibits an extended period of stability until termination. Rivalry scholars may disagree about the timing of the lock-in, but there is consensus about the element of stability. The punctuated equilibrium model posits that hostile policies by rival governments become established and are hard to dislodge.[45] Furthermore, many responses to the threats posed by a rival involve fundamental alterations in security strategy and actions of a long-term character. For example, alliance formation and strategic planning are not transitory. In addition, weapons acquisition and deployment are multiyear processes, and their effects may linger many years after, sometimes even after a rivalry ends. Note that US and Soviet defense planning and nuclear targeting remained unchanged for many years following the end of the Cold War. McGinnis and Williams argue also that domestic political attitudes harden over time in a rivalry, such that they become a brake on leaders' efforts to ameliorate rivalry hostilities.[46]

The net effect of rivalry stability is that there should be consistent patterns of rivalry interaction over the course of the rivalry. Diehl and Goertz noted that this does not resemble a "volcano" pattern of rising hostility ending in war. Rather, over two-thirds of enduring rivalries exhibit a "flat" pattern of rivalry interaction.[47] This signifies that repeated confrontations between rivals are similar to one another in terms of their severity, length, and other characteristics. Wars represent deviations from this pattern, but they are very much anomalies and may occur at various junctures over the life of the rivalry.

Not surprisingly, the India–Pakistan rivalry exhibits significant stability over time, albeit at a higher level of hostility and with greater frequency of war than other enduring rivalries. Figure 2.3 plots the severity scores of the forty-three disputes in the rivalry over time.[48] The apparent pattern is one of a series of relatively high hostility confrontations, often followed by a

---

[45] For a more detailed analysis of the strategic interaction between India and Pakistan, see Russell Leng, *Bargaining and Learning in Recurrent Crises* (Ann Arbor: University of Michigan Press, 2000).

[46] McGinnis and Williams, *Compound Dilemmas.*   [47] Diehl and Goertz, *War and Peace.*

[48] The severity measure is based on COW "level of hostility" scores (reflecting the threat, display, and uses of military force) for both rivals in the dispute and the number of fatalities for both sides. Scores of less than 100 are those disputes without fatalities, and scores greater than 100 are those with fatalities including those that escalated to full-scale war. See Diehl and Goertz, *War and Peace.*

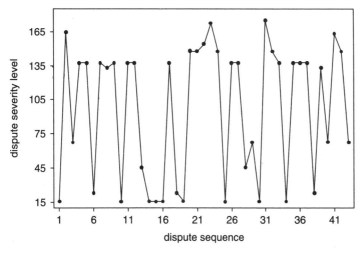

Figure 2.3 Dispute severity levels over time

single lower-level dispute. Although this is not a perfectly "flat" distribution, it does reveal a consistent guide for tracking hostile interactions in the rivalry.

Every enduring rivalry is posited to have its unique basic rivalry level (BRL), or baseline around which rivalry interactions fluctuate. Some BRLs are relatively low, such as the one between the Soviet Union and Norway during the Cold War; typically, violations of territorial waters by submarines with no active military hostilities characterized this rivalry. In contrast, Israel and Jordan's confrontations have involved war or near-war situations on a regular basis. India and Pakistan's BRL (the mean severity is 97.3, the median is 137.2) is closer to the latter example than the former. The average severity level for an enduring rivalry is approximately 80, with only a handful above 100. Notably, the presence of nuclear capabilities makes little difference to the severity of confrontations, with the average severity being quite high (mean = 111.2 and median = 155.1) after 1990 and approximately the same number of months in disputes as the previous period. Nevertheless, nuclear weapons may have contributed to limiting the escalation potential of conflicts (immediate deterrence), even if they were unable to deter the initiation of those confrontations (general deterrence). The Kargil "war" in 1999 was fought more as an indirect battle between Indian, unofficial Pakistani, and local Kashmiri forces. Both sides took pains to avoid a declaration of war or even admit that their forces were directly engaged with one another. India was careful to launch its attacks only on Indian-controlled territory. Furthermore, India and Pakistan went to the brink of war again in 2002, but backed off, perhaps in part because of nuclear concerns. Another indicator of rivalry stability is the average duration of militarized confrontations. Once again, with the exception of one dispute (the long-standing dispute that eventually becomes the Kargil confrontation), there is not much variation; the duration is very similar from dispute to dispute. The average dispute lasts slightly less than six months. This tends to be longer than the standard rivalry disputes, many of which last only a single day and may be composed of only a single incident. India–Pakistan confrontations tend to be more drawn out affairs and involve more give and take than other disputes between rivals; for example, some rivalries (e.g., China–Vietnam) revolve around competing claims to the Spratley Islands and the typical dispute involves a fishing boat seizure with the "crisis" usually resolved within a few days.

Although the India–Pakistan rivalry shows similar patterns of stability to other enduring rivalries, it is considerably more conflict and war prone. Its forty-three disputes are greater than almost all enduring rivalries, except the US–USSR (beginning in 1946) and Russia/USSR–China (beginning in 1862) rivalries, the latter of which extended over a much longer historical period. Not only have India–Pakistan disputes been relatively severe, their frequency rate of roughly four disputes every five years also puts them on the high end of the scale. India and Pakistan have also fought four wars:[49] First Kashmir (1947), Second Kashmir (1965), Bangladesh (1971), and Kargil (1999).[50] These rivals have also gone to the brink of war several other times, most recently in 2002, when India and Pakistan put their military forces on alert and massed thousands of troops near their borders. This frequency of high-level conflict is greater than almost all other enduring rivalries; only the Israel–Egypt and China–Japan rivalries have had more.

Beyond wars, India and Pakistan have also engaged in significant arms acquisition competitions, most notably after wars. This is typical of many enduring rivalries, as military buildups become the vehicles for states to

---

[49] War is defined as a military confrontation resulting in 1,000 or more battle-related fatalities. See Meredith R. Sarkees, "The Correlates of War Data on War: An Update to 1997," *Conflict Management and Peace Science* 18 (2000), 123–44. See also Kristian Gleditsch, "A Revised List of Wars Between and Within Independent States, 1816–2002," *International Interactions* 30 (2004), 231–62.

[50] Kargil represents something of a special case. In the COW collection, it barely meets the 1,000 death threshold. Some dispute the accuracy of this estimate, arguing for a lower number. It is clear that precise figures may be difficult to obtain given that Pakistani forces were never officially committed to the conflict. Still, Kargil also appears as a war with over 1,000 fatalities on Gleditsch's list, and he uses data independent of the COW Project. For our purposes, we accept Kargil as a war, but recognize that it represents a military conflict of a very different type and scale from the other three wars.

strengthen themselves in the hope of changing the pattern of unsuccessful outcomes in military confrontations.[51] Looking at military spending patterns,[52] both sides increase their military expenditures substantially just after the 1947 war. More notable, however, is the arms race that occurs after the 1971 Bangladesh War. In the period 1974–82, Pakistan averages more than a 19 percent yearly increase in military spending. Ganguly argues that the crushing military defeat in the 1971 war ended the myth of Pakistani military superiority pervasive in the decisionmaking circles of that country.[53] It is perhaps not surprising that a result of this defeat was an attempt to build up military forces to challenge India sometime in the future. The origins of the Pakistani nuclear program can also be traced to this time period and as a consequence of the 1971 war.[54] Pakistan desperately sought parity with India, "an echo of the pre-independence era when the Muslim League claimed equality with Congress."[55] India did not stand idly by during the Pakistani buildup as it had double-digit (over 10 percent) yearly increases in its military spending as well during this period; of course, some of this was directed at China and internal security threats. Although this arms race period was less dispute prone that earlier or later periods, it was clear that this was merely an interlude in the rivalry as Pakistan sought to position itself better for future challenges.

Influences on rivalry dynamics

Among the other factors thought to influence the dynamics of enduring rivalries are their linkages to other competitions. There are a variety of ways that enduring rivalries can be linked: common foes, alliances, geography, and participation on opposite sides in multilateral disputes. Generally, rivalries that had linkages to other competitions experienced higher levels of hostility, more volatility, and a greater chance of war. Indeed, contagion is one of the two paths to war for rivalries cited by Vasquez.[56] There are twenty-seven of these different linkages between twenty-two different enduring rivalries and the India–Pakistan one.

---

[51] Paul F. Diehl and Mark Crescenzi, "Reconfiguring the Arms Race–War Debate," *Journal of Peace Research* 35 (1998), 111–18.

[52] Military spending data are taken from the COW Project at http://www.correlatesofwar.org

[53] Ganguly, *Conflict Unending.*   [54] *Ibid.*

[55] Anand K. Verma, *Reassessing Pakistan: Role of Two-Nation Theory* (New Delhi: Lancer Publishers, 2001), 152.

[56] John A. Vasquez, "Distinguishing Rivals that Go to War from Those that Do Not: A Quantitative Comparative Case Study of the Two Paths to War," *International Studies Quarterly* 40 (1996), 531–58.

Indeed, Ganguly and Bajpai note that South Asia and surrounding areas are characterized by mutually entangling rivalries.[57]

Consistently, the most dangerous kind of rivalry linkage has been when two or more rivalries coalesce in one or more militarized confrontations.[58] Most notable about the India–Pakistan rivalry, however, is the exclusively dyadic military confrontations between the two states. This makes the number of militarized disputes, forty-three, even more significant. India and Pakistan are not involved in proxy conflicts with one another and do not oppose each other in conflicts primarily involving opposing allies of the two states. Thus, whatever hostility is manifest in the rivalry is concentrated on the other rival and not secondarily to other states. The bilateral character of the rivalry also suggests that resolving the conflict will need to be a more direct process. In contrast, resolving Israel's rivalry with Syria clearly involves some bilateral issues (e.g., Golan Heights), but probably cannot be divorced from an Israeli–Palestinian or an Israeli–Lebanese resolution. Therefore, the most dangerous form of rivalry linkage is not responsible for exacerbating the India–Pakistan rivalry. We must note, however, one caveat to this conclusion. Although no other *states* were involved in these disputes, local Kashmiri forces, not wholly under the control of Pakistan, were part of several of the confrontations, especially in recent years. Accordingly, such forces have the ability to create crises between India and Pakistan, and could also play the role of "spoiler" in any agreement (whether it be a limited ceasefire or a comprehensive peace agreement) reached between the two rivals.

Other forms of rivalry linkage are less associated with the dynamics of a given rivalry. India and Pakistan share borders with China, which has historically been involved in a number of enduring rivalries. Yet, these rivalries have not diffused to affect India and Pakistan. Similarly, most of the rivalries linked by alliances to India–Pakistan are irrelevant to the latter's dynamics. The exceptions, however, are critical in some cases. Pakistan's ties to China are an important factor in exacerbating tensions with India. This is true, because China has also been engaged in an enduring rivalry with India (linkage by common foe). China has provided military and other support to Pakistan, largely to offset the growth of Indian power on the subcontinent. Similarly, India and Pakistan have been on opposite sides of the Cold War rivalry between the United States and the Soviet Union. Each superpower provided arms, intelligence, and

---

[57] Sumit Ganguly and Kanti Bajpai, "India and the Crisis in Kashmir," *Asian Survey* 43 (1994), 401–16.
[58] Diehl and Goertz, *War and Peace.*

political support to their client states. Despite this, however, we note that the India–Pakistan rivalry was more than a simple proxy conflict between the superpowers. Indeed, the end of the Cold War precipitated no significant change in the dynamics of the rivalry, at least from our examination of conflict behavior.

Just as rivalry linkages can exacerbate rivalry conflict, conflict management attempts have the potential to mitigate, and perhaps even resolve, enduring rivalries. Yet our research suggests that most conflict management attempts in enduring rivalries are ineffective in altering the basic rivalry level, much less in producing rivalry termination.[59] This does not suggest, however, that third parties avoid enduring rivalries. Rather, not surprising given their dangers, enduring rivalries are more likely than other conflicts to attract the diplomatic attentions of other states and international organizations, even though those mediation efforts most frequently fail.

The India–Pakistan rivalry has attracted significant international attention over the last fifty years. Various third-party mediation attempts have sometimes produced short-term successes in the form of ceasefires, but as yet have not produced a negotiated agreement to end hostilities, much less a successful implementation of such an agreement. The United Nations has been involved in diplomatic efforts since the beginning of the rivalry. The UN established a five-member United Nations Commission on India and Pakistan (UNCIP) in 1948, and shortly thereafter deployed a peace observer force (UNMOGIP or United Nations Military Observer Group in India and Pakistan), which technically is still in existence today, although largely ineffective. Many UN efforts were predicated on holding a plebiscite in Kashmir to resolve the conflict, but this has never occurred. The UN has appointed a number of special representatives or mediators over the years. Similarly, the UN Security Council (and periodically the UN General Assembly and European Union) has passed resolutions calling for ceasefires and negotiations between India and Pakistan. At best, all these efforts have produced some short-term abatement in the conflict, but no long-term impact on the rivalry. The failure of international organizations is largely because such entities cannot impose solutions on disputants, but depend in large part on the cooperation of the conflicting parties. Divisions within the membership of those organizations have also limited the scope of initiatives to those in which there is consensus; this has largely been confined to

---

[59] *Ibid.*; Jacob Bercovitch and Paul F. Diehl, "Conflict Management of Enduring Rivalries: Frequency, Timing, and Short-Term Impact of Mediation," *International Interactions* 22 (1997), 299–320.

limiting conflict escalation and not to the configuration of any political settlement.

Conflict management efforts have not been confined to international organizations. Various states, such as the United States, United Kingdom, Yugoslavia, Egypt, and the Soviet Union, to name a few, have intervened in the rivalry diplomatically. Such efforts have been primarily appeals for negotiation or offers of mediation. Not coincidentally, such initiatives have been concentrated around the times of major wars and crises. Some of these efforts produced limited, short-term successes. For example, USSR Prime Minister Kosygin mediated negotiations in 1965–66 that produced the Tashkent Declaration, in 1965, in which India and Pakistan agreed to withdraw troops from the border region. Yet the conditions for short-term mediation success (conflict management) in enduring rivalries are quite different than for long-term success (conflict resolution).[60] Thus, none of the conflict management efforts so far have produced an agreement that resolved all or part of the disputed issues between India and Pakistan.

Rivalry termination

Although the India–Pakistan rivalry is ongoing and shows no signs of abating, it is instructive to consider the conditions for rivalry termination, if only to assess the likelihood they might arise in the India–Pakistan context. We are first drawn to the "democratic peace," or the proposition that two democratic states will not fight each other in a war. There is now broad consensus on this phenomenon.[61] The democratic peace effect is confined to two states that each have stable democracies: that is, states must have consolidated democratic institutions and norms, and thereby have been democracies for a period of years. Nevertheless, the transition to the point at which both states are stable democracies may be especially dangerous. Snyder reports that during the democratizing period, the state involved is actually *more* prone to militarized conflict.[62]

For our purposes, the question arises as to how the democratic peace applies to enduring rivalries. Most notably, the presence of a pair (dyad) of democratic states serves as a pacifying influence in rivalry development. Hensel, Goertz, and Diehl report only 66 (out of 1,166, or less than

---

[60] J. Michael Greig, "Moments of Opportunity: Recognizing Conditions of Ripeness for International Mediation," *Journal of Conflict Resolution* 45 (2001), 691–718.

[61] See, for example, Bruce Russett and John Oneal, *Triangulating Peace: Democracy, Interdependence, and International Organizations* (New York: W. W. Norton, 2001).

[62] Jack Snyder, *From Voting to Violence: Democratization and Nationalist Conflict* (New York: Norton Books, 2000).

6 percent) rivalry relationships begin when both states are democratic, much less than might be predicted by chance.[63] Additionally, almost all those rivalries remained confined to low levels of conflict, with only eleven becoming proto or adolescent rivalries, and only two developing into full-fledged enduring rivalries. Thus, the democratic peace has a significant impact on rivalries, not merely on the outbreak of war. Initial conflicts between democracies are less likely to occur, and even when they do, they rarely mature into more advanced rivalries.

India and Pakistan begin their rivalry without the requisite democratic dyad, but have had some periods of joint democracy since 1947. Most instructive then is an analysis of what changes, if any, occur in a rivalry when both rivals become democratic. Hensel, Goertz, and Diehl examined twenty-three rivalries that change regime type during the duration of the rivalry, meaning that they experienced both joint democratic and non-democratic periods.[64] Consistent with Maoz's findings, they report that militarized conflict in "regime change" rivalries is less likely in periods when both rivals are democratic than in periods in which at least one rival is non-democratic.[65] Note that disputes are not completely avoided, suggesting that the dynamics of the rivalry are strong enough to resist, at least in part, the pacifying effects of democracy. There are some important qualifications to this finding. Despite the decrease in conflict frequency under democracy, the transition year (the year in which rivalry first qualifies as a joint democratic dyad) is an especially dangerous time. The likelihood of a dispute is greater in that year than in any other time during the rivalry; this is consistent with Snyder's warning about the dangers of democratization. Nevertheless, there is a substantial drop off in conflict propensity after the transition year, with the mean number of disputes per year quickly declining by almost half within five years and then approaching zero. This suggests that joint democracy may be associated with rivalry termination after a period of time.

In the period 1947–2001, India and Pakistan oscillate back and forth between joint democracy and non-democracy.[66] Except perhaps during the period of emergency rule in India (under Indira Gandhi), India was a

---

[63] Paul R. Hensel, Gary Goertz, and Paul F. Diehl, "The Democratic Peace and Rivalries," *Journal of Politics* 62 (2000), 1173–88.

[64] *Ibid.*

[65] Zeev Maoz, "The Debate over the Democratic Peace: Rearguard Action or Cracks in the Wall?", *International Security* 32 (1997), 162–98.

[66] In order to qualify as a democracy, a state must have a score of 7 or greater on the Polity regime type scale (10 is the maximum democracy score), which considers several democracy dimensions. Data are take from the most recent Polity IV collection and available at http://www.cidcm.umd.edu/inscr/polity/. We lag the democracy

stable democracy throughout the period. In contrast, Pakistan has an elected, democratic government less than a third of the time. Yet, as Tremblay and Schofield argue, Pakistan is best understood as a hybrid democracy/autocracy during this time.[67] The influence of the military in the Pakistani government was strong even in so-called democratic periods, and because of several military coups, at no time does Pakistan probably qualify as a stable democracy in which democratic institutions and norms are well ingrained in society. For example, Hagerty notes that even though Pakistan was a democracy at the time of a serious crisis with India in 1990, "the country's most sensitive national security decisions were not made by Prime Minister Bhutto, but by the army and by a civilian president with close ties to the army."[68] According to democratic peace theorists then, the full effect of democracy was unlikely to be felt in this rivalry.[69] Still, we look to see if Pakistani conflict behavior was different during periods of democratic rule as opposed to those periods in which the military was in full control of government.

Consistent with the broad results above, however, the India–Pakistan rivalry was less dispute-prone under joint democracy than during other periods. The probability of a new dispute arising in any given year during the joint democracy period was approximately 40 percent (seven disputes in seventeen years) as opposed to almost 100 percent (thirty-six disputes in thirty-eight years) when there was no joint democracy. This should not imply that the democratically elected leaders of Pakistan (e.g., Bhutto, Sharif) were less supportive of claims toward Kashmir than their military counterparts. Rather, they resorted to military force less frequently to pursue those claims, and may have concentrated more on domestic concerns (as they were more accountable to domestic audiences) than the military leaders.

There is mixed evidence for the dangers of democratic transition in this rivalry. The years 1957–58, the first time joint democracy occurs, experience three new disputes between India and Pakistan. This democracy period is short lived and therefore no long-term impact on the rivalry can be seen. In contrast, however, the next period of democratization, beginning in 1974, is dispute free. Yet, that period of no militarized confrontation begins before democracy is established in Pakistan and continues a few years after military

score one year to be sure that the state is really a democracy at the beginning of a year in which a dispute might have or has occurred rather than at the end of the year, the reporting method of Polity.

[67] Tremblay and Schofield in this volume.

[68] Devin T. Hagerty, "Nuclear Deterrence in South Asia: The 1990 Indo-Pakistani Crisis," *International Security* 20 (1995), 11.

[69] E.g., Bruce Russett, *Grasping the Democratic Peace: Principles for a Post-Cold War World* (Princeton: Princeton University Press, 1993).

rule is restored. One might give greater weight to the impact of the Bangladesh War than democracy in explaining the absence of Pakistani challenges to India during this period. The terrible territorial, military, and political losses suffered by Pakistan may have inhibited it from launching any more challenges to India, at least until it had recovered from the war. Finally, the next restoration of joint democracy in the late 1980s finds several disputes occurring in the early transition period, but gradually tapering off. Although there is almost a decade of joint democracy in this rivalry during the 1990s, the rivalry does not end.

The major puzzle for democratic peace theorists is the Kargil War. That conflict has its origins in a militarized dispute beginning in 1993. Although there were a number of incidents between India and Pakistan over the next several years, the conflict doesn't escalate until March 1999 when Pakistani troops occupied peaks in Kargil. After a few months of fighting, the war ended with the withdrawal of Pakistani forces. During this whole period, both states were democratic. The military coup that ousted Prime Minister Sharif does not come until the following October.

Is this the first war between democratic states in the modern era?[70] At first glance, it would appear that the India–Pakistan rivalry breaks the democratic peace mold. Yet there are several significant caveats to this conclusion. First, Pakistan was clearly not a stable democracy, a prerequisite according to democratic peace theorists for the pacifying effect to be manifest. That the military overthrew the democratic government shortly thereafter, and did so with substantial public support, is itself evidence that Pakistan was not a stable democracy with democratic norms and institutions deeply embedded in society. Second, one might question whether Pakistan was truly a liberal democracy in the first place, even though it technically meets certain coding criteria for democracies. Such classifications generally do include civilian control over the military among those criteria, but such a factor is critical for democratic political processes to have a pacifying effect. This was clearly lacking in Pakistan. The military assisted Prime Minister Nawaz Sharif in the early stages of his political movement and retained significant autonomy and influence on military decisions during his regime. Third, the existence of a war during the democratic transition is validation of those who point out the dangers of the democratization period, an important qualification to the democratic peace. Finally, one might argue that Pakistan did not overtly launch a war against India. The Pakistani troops participating in the conflict were not in uniform, did not carry army badges, and had no

---

[70] Once again, the Kargil War meets the COW criteria for an interstate war. Regardless, it is still a serious confrontation between two democratic states that deserves scrutiny.

identity cards. Indeed, the Pakistani action might better be considered a covert action, something that theorists have also discovered is not subject to the democratic peace effect.[71]

At best, joint democracy has had a modest, mitigating effect on the India–Pakistan rivalry. Yet Pakistan has never fully qualified as a stable democracy during this period, and thus the full effects of the democratic peace are not evident. In addition, past patterns of democratic transition in the rivalry suggest that the establishment of joint democracy in this rivalry could not end it. Taking the most optimistic perspective, even if Pakistan restored democracy immediately (an unlikely prospect), it may be years before Pakistan is a stable democracy, and therefore any pacifying effects may be apparent only in the distant future.

A second factor in rivalry termination is the appearance of other security threats for the rivals. Specifically, Bennett argues that common external threats make rivals less likely to continue their competition.[72] One might assume that common external enemies engender greater feelings of amity ("the enemy of my enemy is my friend"). The rapprochement between the United States and China in the 1970s and 1980s was, in part, related to concerns with their common rival, the Soviet Union. Other rivalries also reduce the resources and attention that can be directed to extant rivalries; states must make choices on which enemies to focus on and this may mean ending one rivalry in order to pursue others.

Over the course of their rivalry, India and Pakistan also engaged in rivalries with other states. Most notably, India clashed with China over the northern border between the states. Pakistan has had an ongoing disagreement with Afghanistan over the Pashtun region that straddles the border. Neither of these other rivalries has been so significant as to distract India or Pakistan from their primary rivalry with each other. Indeed, as noted above, the India–China rivalry may have strengthened the India–Pakistan competition because of China's support of Pakistan. It is difficult to imagine at this point from where a common security threat to both India and Pakistan might arise. None of the neighboring countries, save perhaps China, is powerful enough to present a challenge to both countries and to require some kind of cooperative response to meet such a threat. Chinese and Indian relations have improved somewhat in recent years and few credible scenarios exist such that China would become an

[71] David P. Forsythe, "Democracy, War, and Covert Action," *Journal of Peace Research* 29 (1992), 385–95.
[72] D. Scott Bennett, "Security, Bargaining, and the End of Interstate Rivalry," *International Studies Quarterly* 40 (1996), 157–83; D. Scott Bennett, "Integrating and Testing Models of Rivalry Duration," *American Journal of Political Science* 42 (1998), 1200–32.

enemy of both rivals (or even that such an occurrence would be sufficient for India and Pakistan to end their rivalry). Our judgment is that the India–Pakistan rivalry is unlikely to end because of new common security threats.

As with the origins of rivalries, Diehl and Goertz argue that political shocks are associated with rivalry termination.[73] Yet, such shocks are only necessary conditions for termination, indicating that other pacifying conditions must be present for long-standing military competitions to end. We don't focus on shocks such as world wars or massive territorial changes, largely because neither is likely in the foreseeable future. Instead, we consider other political shocks that are potentially relevant to the India–Pakistan rivalry.

Major alterations in the international system may reconfigure alliance patterns, offer new opportunities for cooperation, or just make rivalry competition more costly than in earlier periods. As evident from the end of the Cold War, such systemic changes are hard to foresee. We should also note, however, that the end of the Cold War did not lead to the end of the India–Pakistan rivalry, even as it contributed to the termination of some superpower proxy conflicts in Africa. Closer ties between the United States and Pakistan after the terrorist attacks of 11 September may have moderated the latter's policies toward India, but they do not appear to be able to prompt an end to the rivalry.[74] All this reminds us of the stability of rivalries, and of the India–Pakistan rivalry in particular. Even systemic shocks, at best necessary conditions, may have little effect on a well-established, regional rivalry.

Perhaps more significant are endogenous shocks, those occurring within each of the states. We have already discussed the impact that a democratic transition in Pakistan might have on the rivalry. We turn now to other internal changes. Diehl and Goertz hypothesized that a civil war in one or both of the rivals might lead to the end of a rivalry, as the state affected might direct its attention and resources inward to deal with that threat.[75] Yet they did not find much impact empirically. This may be because a rival may actually exploit internal unrest in its neighbor, either supplying arms to the rebel forces or taking advantage of the rival's distraction to press claims on the issues underlying the rivalry. Although internal unrest exists in several parts of India (outside of Kashmir), none of it is serious enough to threaten the Indian regime or end the rivalry. Indeed, Pakistan's sponsorship of internal conflict in Kashmir has

---

[73] Diehl and Goertz, *War and Peace.*
[74] For more on major power effects, see Kapur in this volume.
[75] Diehl and Goertz, *War and Peace.*

intensified the rivalry and precipitated several crises just short of war. Pakistan would seem to be a better bet for internal unrest, especially as the Musharraf regime faces challenges near the Afghan–Pakistani border from fundamentalist groups. Perhaps a civil war in Pakistan would lead to a temporary respite in the India–Pakistan rivalry as the military and various groups competed for power. Yet such an abeyance would probably not be synonymous with rivalry termination. Whichever faction gained control of the Pakistani government would likely renew claims to Kashmir, and domestic opinion in Pakistan is strongly supportive of such a policy.

A second element hypothesized by Goertz and Diehl, although not fully investigated, is that a change in leadership in one or both countries might produce a breakthrough in diplomacy that produces a peace agreement. Specific, *new* policies, which involve the end of hostility with an enemy, need to be formulated and implemented in order for conflict resolution to occur. Major policy changes require new ideas, and these usually come in the form of new people. New leadership is frequently divorced from past policies, often comes into power because past policies have failed, and is not inhibited by the sunk costs of old leadership. US President Nixon's trip to China is often cited as an example of how a leader can have a significant impact on rivalry termination. Similarly, Egyptian President Anwar Sadat's dramatic peace initiative toward Israel is another common example. Yet although the subsequent Camp David Accords significantly ameliorated the Israel–Egypt rivalry (less frequent and much less severe disputes), that rivalry did not end immediately, and still persists today. Perhaps a better example is the transition away from an apartheid government in South Africa to one led by Nelson Mandela and his African National Congress Party. This was quickly followed by the end of rivalries between South Africa and several of its neighbors.

As with some other political shocks, leadership changes that lead to a reorientation of foreign policy are often unexpected. Although foreign policy differences exist between the Bharatiya Janata Party (BJP) and Congress Party in India, neither supports significant concessions on Kashmir. Even if the present prime minister of India wanted to make concessions on Kashmir, it is unlikely that they would be significant enough to placate Pakistani society. Similarly, no major political figure in Pakistan has supported abandoning or significantly revising Pakistani positions on that disputed territory. Recent assassination attempts against the Pakistani president point to the instability in that country; had those attempts been successful, it is far more likely that chaos rather than a reformulation of Kashmir policy would have been the result. At least in the short term, any leader in either country doing otherwise would likely achieve little political benefit and would do so at some personal risk.

Lebow has attempted to use the Cold War case to develop a set of conditions he believes accounts for the thawing of US–Soviet relations under Gorbachev and the winding down of rivalries in general.[76] For accommodation to occur, he argues that the presence of the following three conditions for one of the rivals is critical: (1) a leader committed to domestic reforms where foreign cooperation is necessary for those reforms; (2) that rivalry and confrontation has failed in the past to achieve a rival's goals and will likely fail in the future; and (3) the belief that conciliatory gestures will be reciprocated. Thus, Lebow sees the end of rivalries beginning from domestic political considerations. Might these conditions arise in the India–Pakistan rivalry? This is very difficult to say, and indeed Lebow's conditions are more evident in retrospect. It is clear that Pakistan's attempts at securing Kashmir have failed, but the policy still remains popular on the domestic front. Pakistan is suffering some of the economic problems that plagued the Soviet Union before its demise. Resolving the Kashmir problem might increase international economic aid and lessen the crushing defense burden. Yet, the emergence of a conciliatory leader who wants to resolve the conflict, as opposed to one who merely wants to prevent escalation, is largely dismissed above. That leaves the third condition as largely speculative and therefore uncertain.

Overall, we do not paint an optimistic picture for the end of the India–Pakistan rivalry any time soon. The competition is deeply ingrained in each society, both in the public psyche and in military and government planning. A political shock alone, even if one were to occur, is insufficient to lead to the end of the rivalry. The other conditions associated with enduring rivalry termination are not present and probably unlikely for the foreseeable future.

---

[76] Richard Ned Lebow, "The Search for Accommodation: Gorbachev in Comparative Perspective," in Richard Ned Lebow and Thomas Risse-Kappen (eds.), *International Relations Theory and the End of the Cold War* (New York: Columbia University Press, 1995), 167–86.

3   The India–Pakistan conflict in light of general theories of war, rivalry, and deterrence

John A. Vasquez

Introduction

This chapter examines the India–Pakistan conflict in light of international relations theory. What can some of these theories tell us about the causes of the conflict, why the conflict goes to war, why it persists, and whether nuclear weapons will increase or decrease the probability of war? Two major theories will be the focus of the analysis: the steps to war explanation and classical deterrence theory, with an emphasis on the former. The chapter will begin with an overview of the steps to war explanation. It will then review some of the research on that explanation. Next, this explanation will be utilized to see how it can explain the India–Pakistan conflict and what new insights it might offer. Then, deterrence theory will be reviewed and criticized in light of the steps to war explanation. Lastly, the possibility of deterrence failure in the India–Pakistan conflict will be discussed.

The steps to war explanation: an overview

The steps to war explanation attempts to make sense of a welter of empirical findings on war by thinking about what these findings tell us about the foreign policy behavior between two or more states that makes them go to war. Since I have presented this explanation both in detailed and summary form, I will give only a brief overview here.[1] Out of this foreign policy perspective comes the idea that as states adopt certain goals and objectives and then take action to support those objectives, they engage in behavior that has the effect of increasing hostility and threat

My thanks to T. V. Paul, Daniel Geller, Marie Henehan, David Stuligross, and the anonymous reviewers of the book for valuable comments. The responsibility for the analysis remains mine alone however.
[1] See John A. Vasquez, *The War Puzzle* (Cambridge: Cambridge University Press, 1993); John A. Vasquez, "Reexamining the Steps to War: New Evidence and Theoretical Insights," in Manus Midlarsky (ed.), *Handbook of War Studies II* (Ann Arbor: University of Michigan Press, 2000), 371–406.

perception. This has both external effects (in terms of a state's relations with an opponent) and internal effects (in terms of the number of foreign policy hardliners and accommodationists). The end result is that certain foreign policy actions can be seen as a series of steps to war in that each step increases the probability of war.

The explanation posits that territorial issues are an underlying cause of war. Of all the issues over which states contend, territorial issues can be regarded as the most likely to become life and death issues worthy of going to war. They are highly salient and tend to fester unless both sides can resolve the issues to their mutual satisfaction or one side can achieve an overwhelming victory over the other. In the absence of these outcomes protracted conflict and even recurrent wars are not surprising, even if not the modal pattern.

For obvious reasons, territorial disagreements are most likely to occur between neighbors, and empirical evidence supports the claim that most wars and rivalries involve neighbors.[2] Whether a territorial disagreement goes to war, however, depends on how it is handled. The same is true for whether territorial conflicts persist – how they are handled, given the domestic and external context, will have a major impact on whether the contending states become enduring rivalries, as we will see when we examine the India–Pakistan case.

The foreign policy practices of a state, how it handles issues between itself and those that contend with it, are posited as the proximate cause of war. These practices, including the institution of war, should not be seen as given. It is assumed that war is a social invention that is learned in history and changes in history. It is also argued that leaders, diplomats, and others create folklores or diplomatic cultures that guide states and inform their leaders when it is appropriate to handle a situation with the use of force.

In the West, one of the most important roles of realist thinking, beginning with Thucydides and going down to Morgenthau and beyond, is that it has provided a folklore that tells leaders how they should act when faced with security issues. Realist folklore or culture informs leaders that, in the face of security issues, they should increase their power. The two main ways of doing that for realism are to either make alliances and/or build up one's military. The problem, however, as realists recognize, is that this gives rise to a security dilemma in that taking these actions makes one's opponent insecure and encourages them to do the same thing. The end result can often be that alliance making leads to counter-alliances and

---

[2] Stuart A. Bremer, "Dangerous Dyads: Conditions Affecting the Likelihood of Interstate War, 1816–1965," *Journal of Conflict Resolution* 36 (1992), 309–41; John A. Vasquez and Marie T. Henehan, "Territorial Disputes and the Probability of War, 1816–1992," *Journal of Peace Research* 38 (2001), Tables I–IV.

military buildups lead to arms racing. One of the ironies of realism is that, among relative equals,[3] each of these steps increases insecurity, threat perception, and hostility. In this sense, they can be seen as steps that bring each party closer to war.

States adopt these practices not only to increase their security, but also to press their claims or defend their positions. Alliance making and military buildups not only signal resolve, but also provide a means of attaining foreign policy objectives. To attain an objective, however, a state must do more than make alliances or build up its military; it must take action, and in the face of action, a target must defend itself. Realism sees the threat and use of force (and a host of realpolitik tactics) as one of the main ways (and of course it is the only unilateral way) of bringing about changes (or redistributions) in the existing allocation of valued things in the international system. Since territory is so salient, resorting to the threat or use of force is not apt to result in many concessions, especially among equals. It is more likely to lead to a stalemate or simply to no resolution at all. Nevertheless, because the issue is salient to leaders (and to hardliners within the polity) territorial disputes tend to recur. The theory posits that crises and militarized interstate disputes that recur promote escalatory behavior and increase the number and influence of hardliners domestically, even though this may not occur in a straight uninterrupted linear fashion. Eventually, a crisis emerges that escalates to war.

Power politics can be seen as a set of proximate causes of war in that it tells leaders how to handle security issues, including territorial issues. It is a *proximate* cause in that it is closer to the outbreak of war. It is a *cause* in that if issues could be handled in other ways, then war could be avoided, or at least have a higher probability of being avoided. Power politics, because it involves a way of handling issues that increases the probability of war, will increase the probability of any issue going to war and not just territorial issues.

---

[3] Equals is defined here in terms of status, which is assumed to have some relationship, but not a perfect one, to material capability in terms of demographic, economic, and military resources. All major states (e.g., Britain, Germany, Russia, Japan, etc. in the late nineteenth century) are treated as equal to each other, and all minor states are treated as equal to each other, even though they have different capabilities. At their birth India and Pakistan are equal in status, both being minor states, even though India has greater capability on a number of standard measures. See Russell J. Leng, *Bargaining and Learning in Recurring Crises* (Ann Arbor: University of Michigan, 2002), 197–99; Sumit Ganguly, *Conflict Unending: India–Pakistan Tension since 1947* (New York: Columbia University Press 2001), 19; Baldev Raj Nayar and T. V. Paul, *India in the World Order: Searching for Major Power Status* (Cambridge: Cambridge University Press, 2003). Later, especially after the Bangladesh War, India seems to be emerging as a dominant state in South Asia, and in the long run India can be seen as a potential major state. Pakistan tries to counter this by acquiring nuclear weapons – the quick technological fix.

The point here is not to deny that the structure of the situation also promotes power politics, but to maintain that the institutionalization of realist ideas in the diplomatic culture makes leaders more aware of and more likely to follow realist strategies, as well as more likely to see them as legitimate ways of handling certain situations. Realist theory becomes a way of predicting what kinds of policies leaders will adopt to handle highly salient security issues. Realist theory, however, underestimates the extent to which these policies actually encourage a decision for war.[4]

The language of "steps" is meant to convey that the pursuing of certain objectives by adopting realist practices, such as the making of alliances, buildups of the military, and resorting to the threat and use of force, increases the probability of war each time one of these is adopted. These steps, however, should not be seen as necessarily following a particular sequence. Alliances may precede or follow military buildups, and militarized disputes are likely to punctuate the entire relationship, thereby occurring before and after certain practices are adopted. While there might be a sequential pattern to the steps that can be theoretically derived and/or inductively established, such precision is not necessary at this stage of research. What is important is that the presence of more than one step, regardless of its order, results in an increase in the probability of war.

One of the problems in applying general international relations theories to a specific case is that sometimes these theories may not have had many tests to see if the general patterns they posit actually hold across history. While such applications of theory to current situations can be enlightening, they also can lead to misleading conclusions if the theory upon which they are based turns out to be empirically inaccurate. Since the initial publication of the steps to war explanation a number of empirical studies have been conducted that have tested aspects of the explanation. A review of this research will help us see the extent to which various aspects of the explanation have empirical corroboration.

Previous research

One of the main things we now know about territorial disputes that we did not know before 1996 is that they are, in fact, highly war prone. This has been established by a number of studies employing different research designs and databases, so that the finding seems to be robust.[5] It should

---

[4] See Vasquez, *The War Puzzle*, 114–17.
[5] Paul Hensel, "Charting a Course to Conflict: Territorial Issues and Interstate Conflict, 1816–1992," *Conflict Management and Peace Science* 15 (Spring 1996), Table 2; Paul

be noted that most of these studies define a militarized interstate dispute (MID) as over territory only when official representatives make specific claims of territory in another state's jurisdiction *before* the actual threat or use of force made in relation to that claim.[6] In this way, the concept of territorial dispute is not so elastic as to make every war a war over territory simply because battles may be fought to hold and capture territory or territory may be exchanged after a war even though it was not officially claimed before.[7]

The research on territorial disputes has also found that territorial disputes are more apt to recur between the parties, which suggests that dyads that have territorial disputes are more apt to become enduring rivals, a prediction that has been subsequently substantiated by research.[8] There has been research also on whether certain types of territorial claims, like those related to ethnic conflict, are more apt to escalate to more intense levels of military confrontation.[9] One of the reasons that ethnic territorial issues are the most likely to escalate is because domestic hardliners demand that leaders take more drastic actions and oppose attempts to compromise.[10] The tendency of ethnic territorial issues to generate domestic hardline constituencies may be an important factor for explaining why territorial disputes recur,

---

Senese, "Geographic Proximity and Issue Salience: Their Effects on the Escalation of Militarized Interstate Conflict," *Conflict Management and Peace Science* 15 (1996), 151, 153–54; Vasquez and Henehan, "Territorial Disputes and the Probability of War," Tables I–IV; Hemda Ben-Yehuda, "Territoriality, Crisis and War in the Arab–Israel Conflict, 1947–94," *Journal of Conflict Studies* 21 (2001), 78–108.

[6] See Daniel Jones, Stuart Bremer, and J. David Singer, "Militarized Interstate Disputes, 1816–1992: Rationale, Coding Rules, and Empirical Patterns," *Conflict Management and Peace Science* 15 (1996), 178.

[7] Without a rigorously narrow definition of territorial disputes, the territorial explanation of war would be tautological. For an empirical examination of whether the territorial explanation is tautological, see Vasquez, "Reexamining the Steps to War," in Midlarsky (ed.), *Handbook of War Studies II*, 383–86. This study shows that the territorial explanation of war is testable and falsifiable. This analysis shows that only 28.7 percent of the 2,034 MIDs are coded as territorial and that policy disputes with 46.3 percent are the modal dispute in the data. It should also be noted that coding of territorial MIDs was done by those who had no knowledge of the territorial explanation of war, since it did not exist at that time, and therefore there was no unconscious tendency of finding territorial disputes because the coder thought it was going to go to war.

[8] See respectively, Paul Hensel, "One Thing Leads to Another: Recurrent Militarized Disputes in Latin America, 1816–1986," *Journal of Peace Research* 31 (1994), 281–98; John A. Vasquez and Christopher Leskiw, "The Origins and War Proneness of Interstate Rivalries," *Annual Review of Political Science* 4 (2001), 295–316.

[9] Paul Huth, *Standing Your Ground: Territorial Disputes and International Conflict* (Ann Arbor: University of Michigan Press, 1996).

[10] *Ibid.*; A. Bikash Roy, "Intervention Across Bisecting Borders," *Journal of Peace Research* 34 (1997), 3–14. One example of this just prior to the Second Kashmir War are the calls in Pakistan for Ayub Khan to fight a jihad to liberate Kashmir, see Leng, *Bargaining and Learning in Recurring Crises*, 224–25, 227–28.

especially when the two sides are relatively equal. Such hardline behavior can even extend to the point where non-state actors take matters into their own hands by engaging in communal strife or attacking the other side, something which has frequently happened in Kashmir.

The research on the other steps to war – alliances, rivalry, and arms races – is too extensive to review here in detail. Nevertheless, an overview of the research most relevant to the model reveals a general consistency with the claim that taking these steps is often associated with war, although little of this work examines the steps in combination with each other. Evidence on alliances shows that certain types of alliances increase the probability of war.[11]

Research on recurring crises finds that as disputes between the same two parties repeat, war is more likely.[12] Pairs of states or dyads that have recurring disputes are conceptualized as rivalries,[13] and a key conclusion of this literature is that most wars that have been fought since 1816 have rivals in them.

Early research on arms races supported the claim that militarized confrontations between major states that occur in the context of an ongoing arms race are more apt to escalate to war. This research, however, generated a heated debate as to whether there really is a relationship between arms races and the escalation of disputes to war or whether these findings are a function of the research design and measures.[14] Recent research, however, has shown that while the relationship between arms races and a given MID escalating to war is at best of only moderate strength (although statistically significant), the probability of an MID between the parties arms racing escalating to war within five years is fairly high during the pre-nuclear era.[15]

---

[11] See Douglas M. Gibler, "Alliances: Why Some Cause War and Why Others Cause Peace," in John Vasquez (ed.), *What Do We Know about War?* (Lanham, MD: Rowman and Littlefield, 2000), 145–64; Paul Senese and John Vasquez, "Alliances, Territorial Disputes, and the Probability of War: Testing for Interactions," in Paul Diehl (ed.), *The Scourge of War* (Ann Arbor: University of Michigan Press, 2004); Jack S. Levy, "Alliance Formation and War Behavior: An Analysis of the Great Powers, 1495–1975," *Journal of Conflict Resolution* 25 (December 1981), Table 7.

[12] Russell Leng, "When Will They Ever Learn? Coercive Bargaining in Recurrent Crises," *Journal of Conflict Resolution* 27 (September 1983), 379–419.

[13] Paul Diehl and Gary Goertz, *War and Peace in International Rivalry* (Ann Arbor: University of Michigan Press, 2000); see also Frank Whelon Wayman, "Rivalries: Recurrent Disputes and Explaining War," in Vasquez (ed.), *What Do We Know about War?*, 219–34.

[14] Michael D. Wallace, "Arms Races and Escalation: Some New Evidence," *Journal of Conflict Resolution* 23 (March 1979), 3–16; Paul Diehl, "Arms Races and Escalation: A Closer Look," *Journal of Peace Research* 20 (1983), 205–12.

[15] Susan G. Sample, "Arms Races and Dispute Escalation: Resolving the Debate," *Journal of Peace Research* 34 (1997), 7–22; Susan G. Sample, "The Outcomes of Military Buildups: Minor States vs. Major Powers," *Journal of Peace Research* 39 (2002), 669–92.

The steps to war in the India–Pakistan conflict

To what extent are these findings and the steps to war explanation relevant to the India–Pakistan conflict? Can such aggregate findings and theory elucidate specific historical cases? Table 3.1 lists the various steps to war. It will be interesting to see how many of these steps can be found in the India–Pakistan case. Territory as an underlying cause will be treated first and the power politics proximate causes second.

The role of territory

One of the initial things that the steps to war explanation can tell us is what is driving these wars and how typical are they in terms of their underlying causes. The steps to war explanation asserts that territorial conflict is frequently an underlying cause of war. Among neighbors, the explanation goes further and says that: "*Ceteris paribus*, two states bordering on each other will early on in their history use aggressive displays to establish a border in an area where they both have frequent contact."[16]

The India–Pakistan case provides an interesting test of this proposition on borders because two new nation-states are being created from a colonial empire through a process being structured by the former colonial power in light of those demanding independence. In general, the entire process of colonial independence and contemporary state creation provides a set of cases for seeing the extent to which borders are demarked through aggressive displays. One path-breaking study maintains that whether the borders of new states are challenged militarily depends very much on how the states come into existence.[17] If new states arise through revolution or other forms of violence, they are more apt to have their borders challenged by neighbors. If these states arise through a more evolutionary process and their borders are consistent with the norms of the time, then the probability of their being challenged goes down. Thus, among sub-Saharan African states that gained independence peacefully in the 1960s, an agreement is reached through the Organization of African Unity (OAU) that the borders made by the colonial powers will be honored and recognized. This has the effect of preventing many interstate wars,[18] but such borders are not always recognized internally

---

[16] Vasquez, *The War Puzzle*, 310; see also 140–41.

[17] Zeev Maoz, "Joining the Club of Nations," *International Studies Quarterly* 33 (June 1989), 199–231.

[18] Douglas Lemke, *Regions of War and Peace* (Cambridge: Cambridge University Press, 2002).

Table 3.1 *Steps to war*

Rise of Territorial Disputes (underlying cause)
  handled in a power politics fashion (proximate causes):
    Recurrent disputes
    Alliance making
    Arms races
  One Crisis Escalates to War

and have been associated with civil wars and ethnic conflict. Whether such an OAU consensus will continue as certain states become stronger and more able to expand remains to be seen, but the territorial explanation of war would predict that it would. Nevertheless, even if it does not, sub-Saharan Africa has been spared the kind of warfare that was attendant at the birth of India and Pakistan or the birth of modern Israel.

India and Pakistan are states that are born in disagreement about their border and specifically about the future of Jammu and Kashmir. Note that there are several disagreements here: (1) initially the disagreement is not about the demarked border around Jammu and Kashmir (although where it is not clearly demarked will later become an issue) but about whether Jammu and Kashmir will accede to India or Pakistan or be independent; (2) whether the process agreed upon for accession has been properly followed; and (3) whether the norm of nationalism and self-determination should be the principle followed for the transfer of territory that is in dispute.

The territorial concerns at the time of independence and the fundamental territorial issues underlying the rivalry should not be interpreted narrowly as the concrete stakes associated with the "land" of Kashmir. According to the territorial explanation of war, what makes territorial disputes so intractable is that concrete tangible territorial stakes, like pieces of land, that are in principle divisible, become infused with "symbolic" and even "transcendent" qualities that make them intangible, perceived in zero-sum terms, and hence difficult to divide.

Symbolic stakes involve the idea that a given stake is important not for its intrinsic value, but because it stands for a number of other stakes.[19] Reputational concerns play a key role in making symbolic stakes

---

[19] The Rann of Kutch is an example of symbolic stake. Here is a fairly worthless piece of ground that takes on importance because it stands for Kashmir. See Leng, *Bargaining and Learning in Recurring Crises*, 215–16. For further elaboration on the concepts of concrete,

intractable.[20] Leaders will fight for a symbolic stake from fear that failure to do so will encourage further attacks or probes. Transcendent stakes frame issues in terms of fundamental disagreements over values (like democracy *vs.* dictatorship). These can easily become a fight for survival and one's way of life or culture, which in turn can be seen as a battle between good and evil. Such issues become zero-sum, and because they cannot be compromised, they fester and tend to end relatively quickly primarily when one side is completely destroyed.

None of the questions involving major territorial disagreements at the time of independence are successfully negotiated even though there are a number of intermediaries, including the United Nations, trying to prevent the demarcation of the border through war. The steps to war explanation and existing research on territorial disputes suggest that this is a situation where the conflict of which norm to follow (nationalism or the process laid out for accession) is going to provide an ambiguity where both sides will be unwilling to accept the outcome of the decision game that will result in their losing potential territory. The steps to war explanation assumes, as does Clausewitz, that war occurs when the goals of policy cannot be attained by the normal means available. This is precisely what happens in the First Kashmir War. Pakistan and nationalists in Kashmir who do not want to accede to India resort to arms because they feel that they will lose if they do not. Added to this is the dual notion that the decision game that will lead to Jammu and Kashmir acceding to India is rigged and in violation of the greater principle of nationalism and self-determination.

The First Kashmir War is fundamentally a territorial war. In one way or another all the subsequent wars (even the Bangladesh War) are derivative from the set of territorial concerns at the time of independence, as are most of the MIDs between the wars.[21] From an international relations theory perspective, the India–Pakistan wars arise out of an initial typical war between neighbors over territorial boundaries. As a set of interrelated

symbolic, and transcendent stakes, see Richard Mansbach and John Vasquez, *In Search of Theory: A New Paradigm for Global Politics* (New York: Columbia University Press, 1981), 61–67.

[20] Monica Duffy Toft, *The Geography of Ethnic Conflict* (Princeton: Princeton University Press, 2003), 26–29; Barbara Walter, "Explaining the Intractability of Territorial Conflict," *International Studies Review* 5 (2003), 137–53; Mansbach and Vasquez, *In Search of Theory*, 61–62.

[21] On how the Bangladesh War is related to territorial dispute over Kashmir see Leng, *Bargaining and Learning in Recurring Crises*, 256–57, 260–61. For a more detailed discussion see Richard Sisson and Leo E. Rose, *War and Succession: Pakistan, India, and the Creation of Bangladesh* (Berkeley: University of California Press, 1990). Put simply, the Bangladesh War is triggered by the huge influx of refugees into India, but at the same time India uses this opportunity to dismember and weaken its rival, while enhancing its own strategic position *vis-à-vis* Pakistan and China.

wars, they are not unusual in their causes and are fairly straightforward in terms of their underlying fundamentals. They are also typical in terms of how they compare to other wars fought since 1816. If one classifies wars in terms of what they are fought over and who fights them, then one finds that the modal interstate war since 1816 is the dyadic war over territory.[22] Of these, the most common is between minor states fighting over territory.[23]

The steps to war explanation posits, and existing empirical findings show, that territorial disputes that fail to be resolved tend to recur. This is because the revisionist state will not permit the status quo to persist unmolested. This too is the pattern in the India–Pakistan conflict with Pakistan assuming the role of the revisionist state. Figure 3.1 plots all the MIDs between the two parties from 1947 through 1992. The Y axis portrays the level of hostility with 1 equal to non-militarized action (these are not included in the data), 2 equal to the threat to use force, 3 equal to a display of force, 4 equal to an actual use of force, and 5 equal to those uses of force that result in war (with at least 1,000 combined battle deaths). The lightly colored lines portray the MIDs that each state had with the other. As can be seen, this is a very disputatious dyad; indeed it is one of the most contentious in the post-1945 era.

The steps to war explanation posits that territorial disputes are so salient that they will continue to fester unless they are resolved either through an overwhelming victory or through a mutually accepted settlement that recognizes the border as legal.[24] The India–Pakistan conflict is so disputatious because neither side has been able to attain that overwhelming victory, and as a result they have had a sufficient number of recurring disputes that they have become an interstate rivalry (conventionally defined as six or more MIDs within twenty years).[25] Again this is not unusual, as research has shown a pair of states that has a territorial dispute has a greater probability of developing an enduring rivalry than a pair of states that has policy or regime disputes.[26]

---

[22] There are fifty-one dyadic wars (of seventy-nine interstate wars) fought from 1816 to 1997, and of these fifty-one, twenty-six are between neighbors fighting over territory. The next ranked dyadic war between neighbors are fifteen policy wars, see John A. Vasquez and Brandon Valeriano, "A Classification of Interstate War." Paper Prepared for the International Studies Association Annual Meeting, Mar. 21, 2004, Montreal, 14.

[23] Minor states are defined in the post-1945 period in accordance with the Correlates of War project as none of the following: US, USSR, UK, France, China (after 1949), Germany (after 1990), Japan (after 1990). This variable refers to status not to capability.

[24] Vasquez, The War Puzzle, 146–49, 311.

[25] See Diehl and Goertz, War and Peace in International Rivalry, 45; and Diehl, Goertz, and Saeedi in this volume.

[26] Vasquez and Leskiw, "The Origins and War Proneness of Interstate Rivalries," 305–07.

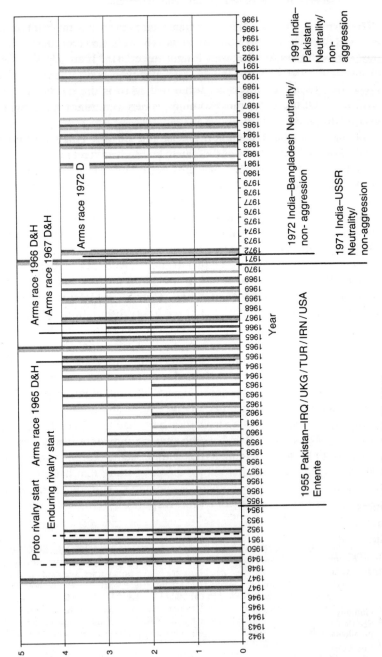

Figure 3.1 India–Pakistan relations, 1947–1991

The disputes and wars fail to produce victory primarily for two reasons: first, each side is relatively equal in status, and, second, international intervention prevents the wars from becoming fights to the finish. Nevertheless, one of the remarkable things about this rivalry from a realist perspective is that the two states, although equal in status, are relatively unequal in capability and that Pakistan persists in pursuing the issue and initiated three of the four wars (if one includes the Kargil armed action as a war) even though it is typically the weaker of the two. This was true early on, as pointed out by Sumit Ganguly, when military hardware was divided on a 30:70 ratio in favor of India, and especially the case after the Bangladesh War, which led to Pakistan's dismemberment.[27] Nevertheless, there are times when this asymmetry is not very large in Kashmir, the main theater of the conflict.[28]

Although much work has been done on the seeming irrationality of such asymmetric conflict,[29] the steps to war explanation can provide a couple of insights. First, it maintains that hardliners push leaders to take more forceful and often more escalatory action. They often prevent leaders from granting concessions and making compromises that might settle the dispute. The Pakistani leadership has certainly felt this pressure at various times, and if we are to take it at least partially at its word, they have even been drawn into MIDs by the actions of nationalist groups not fully under their control. In states with salient territorial disputes, there is always an incentive for leaders to ride to power on a nationalist tiger, but once in power they then have to satisfy that constituency and failure to do so will result in losing power. In Pakistan this simple model will not account for the various leadership changes, which are complex; nevertheless, leaders do feel compelled by their own beliefs and nationalist hardliners not to allow the Kashmir issue to slip off the agenda.[30]

Second, the steps to war explanation maintains that coercive strategies are not abandoned until they fully run their course. Realists and hardliners can always explain why force failed by maintaining that the strategy and tactics were not sufficiently escalatory – they held back, i.e., the state did not go to war or did not fight the war correctly. So long as the existing strategy has not met with success, hardliners feel a more escalatory strategy or a war fought in more favorable circumstances will lead to

---

[27] Ganguly, *Conflict Unending*, 19.
[28] See Paul in this volume, who points out that at times nearly half of India's troops are on the border with China.
[29] For example, see T. V. Paul, *Asymmetric Conflicts: War Initiation by Weaker Powers* (Cambridge: Cambridge University Press, 1994).
[30] For an analysis of how identity and the Kashmir issue are important for framing domestic politics in Pakistan, see Nasr in this volume.

success. There is a reluctance to abandon the coercive realist path until all
the strategies embodied in its logic have been tried. Russell Leng has
shown that this kind of thinking has led crises to become more escalatory
as they repeat; in this way coercion leads to coercion and wars to more
wars.[31]

Leng's definition of "crisis" involves characteristics that make them a
more hostile sub-set of MIDs in general. Nevertheless, the kind of escalatory pattern he describes as taking place across crises is only partially
evident in the India–Pakistan rivalry depicted in Figure 3.1. Rather than a
straight linear relationship, the general pattern is a fairly high level of
severity with a periodic low-level dispute.[32] What is remarkable about the
India–Pakistan case (see Figure 3.1) is how many MIDs reach level four.
This pattern however does not necessarily contradict Leng since the five-
point MID scale is very broad with four being any use of force without
regard to the degree of force other than that it produces fewer than 1,000
battle deaths.[33] Leng does not specify an escalatory trend across wars,
and it is less clear whether there is an upward trend across wars in this
case, although the Bangladesh War can be seen as more severe, especially
in terms of its consequences, than those before, as can the nuclear
posturing in 1998–99.

If a given leader will not try the unused strategies, then domestic
constituencies will push the leader from office or even try the strategies
on their own. Territorial disputes are particularly prone to such tendencies because leaders do not want to give in, and hardliners' constituencies
will not permit them to give in. Some research on Latin America is
informative in this regard in that it shows that even when leaders try to
avoid responsibility for giving in on a territorial issue by turning it over to
an arbitration board, they end up either reneging on the agreement if it
goes against them or being overthrown.[34] Within the India–Pakistan case,
the most recent example of this tendency is the overthrow of Nawaz
Sharif by Musharraf after the Kargil War, although Sharif provoked the
coup by not permitting General Musharraf's airplane to land.[35]
Nevertheless, Sharif felt boxed in by Pakistan's hardliners, especially

[31] Leng, *Bargaining and Learning in Recurring Crises*, 260.
[32] See Diehl, Goertz, and Saeedi in this volume.
[33] See the discussion in the next section on rivalry where research using a more refined
measure provides support for Leng's hypothesis on escalation across MIDs.
[34] Beth Simmons, "See You in Court? The Appeal to Quasi-Judicial Legal Processes in the
Settlement of Territorial Disputes," in Paul Diehl (ed.), *A Road Map to War: Territorial
Dimensions of International Conflict* (Nashville: Vanderbilt University Press, 1999),
205–37.
[35] Strobe Talbott, *Engaging India: Diplomacy, Democracy, and the Bomb* (Washington, DC:
Brookings Institution, 2004), 176.

those in the military, and expressed this concern during his White House meeting regarding Kargil.[36]

What theoretical conclusions can be reached about the India–Pakistan case in light of the above analysis? The analysis maintains that territory is the key to this and most other conflicts between neighbors. Ideological, religious, or cultural rationales, even if believed by actors, may intensify a territorial dispute, but they are not the fundamental cause, especially in terms of determining whether an issue has a high probability of escalating to war. At best these rationales are epiphenomena produced by the natural tendency to infuse territorial stakes with symbolic and transcendent attributes, or, at worse, attempts to rally domestic and external supporters. In this sense, this analysis agrees with Steve Saideman that territory is the key in terms of explaining the rivalry and its wars.[37] Likewise, it agrees with Ashok Kapur, that the religious *vs.* secular state issue is not fundamental.[38] It follows that territory is the key to resolving the rivalry and avoiding future war.

Conflicts between neighbors over territory are seen as both natural and difficult to avoid. In the absence of clear natural borders or a history of an established border, the territorial explanation of war posits that two states will use aggressive displays to establish a border. Given that the British departure did not delineate the borders of the two states and get all sides to recognize them, but instead established a process for creating independent states, disagreement is not surprising. Interestingly, the British did get recognition of existing borders of many individual states. The dispute was not over the border of Kashmir, but the process of determining whether it would adhere to India or Pakistan, or be independent. Despite this concern over legality, the territorial explanation would anticipate that loopholes would be exploited and then lead to conflict when the borders were not mutually accepted.[39]

Having said that territory is a key, it is equally true that some types of territorial disputes are more intractable than others. In particular, ethnic disputes that center on the control of the same territory are highly conflict-prone. The main reason for this, as stated earlier, is that they give rise to hardline constituencies that push for their issue. In doing so, they often

---

[36] *Ibid.*, 164; see also Bill Clinton, *My Life* (New York: Knopf, 2004), 865.
[37] Saideman in this volume.   [38] Kapur in this volume.
[39] Ambiguity in norms for transferring territory usually leads to conflict, as can be seen whenever there was an ambiguity in the norm of dynastic succession (e.g., could succession occur through the female line) or when there is a conflict of norms as between dynastic succession and nationalism; on both these questions, see Evan Luard, *War in International Society* (New Haven: Yale University Press, 1986), 87, 110; Vasquez, *The War Puzzle*, 148–49.

68   John A. Vasquez

infuse territory (which is a concrete material tangible stake that is divisible) with symbolic and transcendent (involving fundamental values) qualities that make it intangible and difficult to divide. The inability of either India or Pakistan to impose their preferred position has meant that they have become long-term rivals, where Pakistan, as the weaker revisionist state, will not give in and/or try to become stronger in order to change the status quo. In such cases, the weaker revisionist state tends to follow the kinds of power politics strategies suggested by realist culture, which simply increase the probability of war.

The role of power politics

In *The War Puzzle* it is stated:

When territorial disputes are not settled, relations with neighbors become a struggle for power. Much of power politics thinking probably derives from such experiences. So long as there is a struggle for power over contiguous territory, then world politics is a struggle for power, but once boundaries are settled, world politics has other characteristics ... This suggests that the very idea of power politics and its practices are derived from an inability to settle territorial questions. Power politics is not the key fact of existence, as the realist paradigm would have us believe, but may simply be an epiphenomenon of territoriality. Realism and the practice of power politics come out of a particular set of struggles and construct a world appropriate to those struggles.[40]

As the quotation above suggests, power politics and strategic thinking are most apt to occur when territorial disputes are at the center of relations. These disputes transform whatever relationship two states might have into one of intense hostility and rivalry. This has been the case with India and Pakistan, as well as other states, that are "born feuding."[41] Power politics are endemic to (an enduring) rivalry. The reason for this, as outlined in the first section of this chapter, is that realist thinking tells diplomats and leaders to increase their power when faced with security issues. The two ways to do that are through the making of alliances and the building up of one's military.

Figure 3.1 denotes when during the history of the India–Pakistan conflict each side has had outside alliances and when they have been engaged in an arms race.[42] The figure demonstrates that all three steps to

<hr/>

[40] Vasquez, *The War Puzzle*, 147–48.   [41] Wayman, "Rivalries," 230.
[42] These data are drawn from the politically relevant alliance data set of the steps to war project (see Senese and Vasquez, "Alliances, Territorial Disputes, and the Probability of War" for a brief description) and from Susan G. Sample's arms race data for minor states in her, "The Outcomes of Military Buildups: Minor States *vs.* Major Powers." My thanks to Susan Sample for sharing her data. "D&H" in the figure refers to whether both the

war have been present in this conflict: recurrent disputes, outside alliances, and arms racing. It is also significant that alliances come early on and arms races later, which is also consistent with work on the steps to rivalry,[43] although India's outside alliance does not come until after the first major period of arms races. The graph does not show the nuclear arms race which we could assume to be occurring at least around 1998, the period of overt nuclear testing and signaling. On the basis of the graph, it can be concluded that the India–Pakistan conflict, on the whole, has all the steps to war listed in Table 3.1. Not every single war, however, especially the first, has been preceded by each step. As can be seen in Figure 3.1, the First Kashmir War has none of the steps, the Second Kashmir War has all the steps, and the Bangladesh War lacks an arms race.

The steps to war explanation assumes that alliance making and military buildups occur in order to increase capability so that one can compete more effectively. These in turn lead to counter-alliances and arms races, which in turn lead to increased hostility and a hardening of positions. There is evidence that this motivation is present in the India–Pakistan case. Pakistan as the weaker state is always hopeful that support from allies, especially the US and Britain, will give it an edge, if not carry the day by providing better equipment or by diplomatic intervention.[44] Likewise, it looks to China as a potential ally after the Chinese–Indian border conflict and war. However, there is a distinct tendency for the Pakistanis to exaggerate the support of potential allies,[45] even though at the UN the US will tilt toward Pakistan, especially before the end of the Cold War. On the Indian side, there are fears that Pakistan's allies, particularly the US and Britain have, from the beginning, supported Pakistan as a way of keeping India down and managing the Indian subcontinent for their own purposes through a policy of divide and rule.[46]

Because Pakistan is continually declining, it feels that time is not on its side and it tries to time its war activities for when it can have the support of outside parties. This is seen in 1965 with China before the Second Kashmir War when Pakistan thought it had the promise of Chinese military assistance should war break out.[47] Pakistan is also bolder when it feels the US needs it, as it did after the Soviet invasion of Afghanistan, a condition again present after September 11.

Diehl and Horn measures of arms races apply, see Sample, "Arms Races and Dispute Escalation" for the definitions. My thanks also to Hilde Ravlo (who worked as my research assistant) for including these two variables on the MID plot.
[43] Brandon Valeriano "The Steps to Rivalry," unpublished Ph.D. thesis, Vanderbilt University (2003).
[44] See Leng, *Bargaining and Learning*, 217, 225, 228. [45] Ganguly, *Conflict Unending*, 27.
[46] Kapur in this volume. [47] Ganguly, *Conflict Unending*, 42–43.

India, as the stronger side, is less in need of a formal ally, particularly since during the Cold War it can rely on the Soviet Union to protect it in the UN Security Council, as it does by either exercising or threatening to exercise its veto on India's behalf. Nevertheless, the US alliance with Pakistan and its tilt toward Islamabad puts domestic pressure on India's leadership to abandon India's non-alignment policy and align with the Soviet Union, which eventually does happen in 1971, finally giving India its counter-alliance. In the interim, it does react to Pakistan receiving support from outside allies, as the steps to war explanation anticipates, by digging in its heels, as Nehru does when he rejects the idea of a plebiscite and fundamentally shifts his view on the role of the UN after the US and Pakistan sign their military pact.[48]

The India–Pakistan conflict provides some insights for the steps to war explanation in that it illustrates, at least for one case, the interactive effect between alliance making and arms races, as well as the impact of these on hardliners in each side. Alliances and informal alignments often result in military buildups, some of which become full-fledged arms races as denoted in Figure 3.1. This linkage, which is probably typical of many minor states, occurs because both Pakistan and India rely on credits from major states to buy very expensive armaments. When Pakistan gets aid from the US, including new weapons systems, this puts pressure on India, which at times complains directly to the US, as when the latter agrees to sell AWACS systems to Pakistan.[49] On the other side, India sees itself as having to rely on the Soviet Union to ensure that it can maintain its edge over Pakistan after the Bangladesh War.[50]

Nevertheless, when all is said and done, what produces the arms race in the first place is the territorial dispute over Kashmir and Pakistan's belief that it cannot change the status quo without increasing its power. This affects India in that if India does not arm, then it can be exploited by Pakistan. This can be seen in 1965: when Ayub Khan thinks Pakistan is more than a match for India after the Rann of Kutch skirmishing, he attacks.[51] Further re-enforcing Pakistan's perception that only an increase in its power will make India negotiate is India's feeling that it is

---

[48] *Ibid.*, 25; see also Escott Reid, *Envoy to Nehru* (Delhi: Oxford University Press, 1981), which is a primary source for Ganguly.

[49] Ganguly, *Conflict Unending*, 83; for an overview, see Dennis Kux, *Disenchanted Allies: The United States and Pakistan, 1947–2000* (Baltimore: Johns Hopkins University Press, 1992).

[50] Ganguly, *Conflict Unending*, 81.

[51] Leng, *Bargaining and Learning in Recurring Crises*, 221, 224–25, 257; see also, Altaf Gauhar, *Ayub Khan: Pakistan's First Military Ruler* (Karachi: Oxford University Press, 1996), 203, 211, cited by Leng, 224–25.

militarily superior and therefore does not need to negotiate. Leng argues that Khan, like Anwar Sadat of Egypt, launches a war not in the expectation that he will necessarily win (although he seems to believe that at times) but that this will lead to mediation where he will have a chance for gains.[52]

Fueling the arms race is the presence of outside rivalries and conflicts, in particular the Chinese–Indian border dispute. After the Sino-Indian War of 1962, India reacts to its defeat with a substantial military buildup, including not only increased procurement of weapons, but also increasing the number of military personnel.[53] This puts more pressure on Pakistan, especially since India is getting aid from the US. The fear in Pakistan is that India, which already has an edge, will now be beyond Pakistan's reach, if nothing is done.[54] At the same time, the conflict with China draws India closer to the Soviet Union, which has its own incipient conflict with China. This bond becomes tighter as China and the US move toward a rapprochement under Nixon.[55]

As would be anticipated by the steps to war explanation, these various military buildups do not lead to one side's conceding to the other; rather they lead to more intense efforts to court allies and gain weapons and to a deterioration of relations, as when American military aid increases toward Pakistan after the Soviet invasion of Afghanistan.[56] It is at this time that India also moves closer to the USSR than it probably wanted to, in order to balance Pakistan's new weapons.

This case also shows that when alliances become unreliable, states turn to their own military buildups as a way of compensating. This is seen most dramatically when the US does little to prevent the breakup of Pakistan during the Bangladesh War (contrast this to Soviet and US intervention to save their allies in the 1973 Yom Kippur War). Some have argued that this realization plays a role, although obviously only a partial role, in Pakistan's attempt to acquire nuclear weapons.[57] Here, we have the idea that with nuclear weapons Pakistan will not have to rely on a reluctant ally in a situation where its very existence might be threatened.[58] Although splits between the military and civilian leadership make the

---

[52] Leng, *Bargaining and Learning in Recurring Crises*, 221. See also Paul, *Asymmetric Conflicts*, ch. 6. Nawaz Sharif attempted a similar strategy during Kargil (see the discussion below), although it is less clear whether the Kargil action was initiated for that purpose or whether Sharif is exploiting the situation after the fact.

[53] Ganguly, *Conflict Unending*, 103. [54] *Ibid.*, 37–38. [55] *Ibid.*, 52, 64–66.

[56] Ganguly, *Conflict Unending*, 82. [57] *Ibid.*, 106.

[58] T. V. Paul maintains that the failure to gain security guarantees from the major states plays an important role in triggering Pakistan's decision to go nuclear, see Paul, *Power versus Prudence: Why Nations Forgo Nuclear Weapons* (Montreal and Kingston: McGill-Queen's University Press, 2000), 133.

current evidence unclear, it seems that even after Pakistan has nuclear weapons, it tries to manipulate its ally by initiating a crisis or war hoping to draw in the US as some sort of intermediary that will force India into serious negotiations. During Kargil the US and Clinton resist such manipulation and insist on Pakistani withdrawal, while simultaneously Clinton moves closer to India.[59] After September 11, the threat posed by al-Queda and the new critical issue of terrorism leads the US to repair its strained relations with Pakistan and Musharraf, again illustrating how outside conflicts can affect the dynamics of the India–Pakistan rivalry.

The repeated crises and the interaction of alliances and military build-ups play a crucial role in orienting both sides toward emphasizing strategic thinking and possible windows of opportunity and vulnerability. As would be expected in a territorial rivalry, states behave in the kind of realist worst-case scenario; contrary to some thinkers, Pakistan and India do jump through windows of opportunity. Thus, every one of the three wars after the First Kashmir War can be seen as being initiated when one side thinks it has an edge that it did not have before, even though in Pakistan's case, in three of the four wars it is clearly weaker. In the Bangladesh War, which India initiates, it takes the opportunity of Bengali resistance and the problem of dealing with a huge number of refugees to support the creation of a separate state that will dismember Pakistan and weaken it even further, while ending the potential threat of a two-front war.[60] The steps to war explanation would expect such strategic thinking to occur in enduring rivalries because of the threat perception and hostility generated by repeated crises and the interaction of alliances and arms races. The steps to war explanation differs from realism, however, in that it sees this kind of behavior as the hallmark of enduring rivalries and not the only kind of relationship that is present in world politics.

In addition, the India–Pakistan rivalry exhibits the kind of escalation across crises and wars that Leng anticipates. Leng finds this to be the case where hostility begets hostility with each crisis leading each side to learn this from the previous crisis.[61] In addition, Valeriano finds that in the India–Pakistan rivalry prior to each of the three major wars the severity of escalation from one MID to the next increases. His data reveal an increased severity level from the time period between the first and sixth MID.[62]

---

[59] Talbott, *Engaging India*, 165; Clinton, *My Life*, 865.
[60] Leng, *Bargaining and Learning in Recurring Crises*, 244.   [61] *Ibid.*, 260.
[62] See Valeriano, "The Steps to Rivalry," for his measure of escalation within rivalries. Severity is taken from Diehl's and Goertz's basic rivalry level (see Diehl and Goertz, *War and Peace in International Rivalry*, 2000, Appendix b).

This underlines the point that intense territorial rivalries are a material source for realist thinking and the practice of power politics. Just because realist folklore and ideas encourage power politics thinking, this does not mean that certain conditions – like territorial rivalries – do not also encourage certain ideas. The use of power politics makes it more difficult for the other side not to reciprocate, especially since such tactics promote the rise of hardliners in each side. A dramatic example of this is the conversion of Nehru, who starts out eschewing power politics and alliances and ends up embracing both. He was particularly affected by the 1962 war with China and later said of his earlier view that "we had been living in a world of unreality."[63]

The acquisition of nuclear weapons has been the latest development in this enduring rivalry. The original acquisition by India may have had more to do with China than with Pakistan, although the book on that is still open.[64] Nevertheless, the acquisition of nuclear weapons by Pakistan seems to fit what the steps to war explanation would posit about military buildups. Pakistan was in a position where its power *vis-à-vis* India was on the decline, with no hope of ever catching up on the demographic, economic, or military dimensions of capability. It had failed to win a single war to date and it lost badly in 1971. Its allies appeared unreliable and reluctant. It seemed that Pakistan could only get weapons and support from the US when the US needed Pakistan, as during the Afghan War and then after September 11.

The lure of nuclear weapons is that they are a quick fix. They can serve two purposes: they can be used as a last resort to protect existing territory and they can be used to play chicken games of nuclear diplomacy that might be a way of making gains on the Kashmir territorial issue.[65] Will they increase or reduce the probability of war in the future? The last section addresses this question in light of classical deterrence theory and the steps to war explanation.

Classical deterrence theory

Classical deterrence theory is based on the notion that nuclear weapons make war unwinnable if both sides have a second strike capability, since either side could utterly destroy the other after absorbing an

---

[63] Quoted in Nayar and Paul, *India in the World Order*, 115–16. My thanks to T. V. Paul for suggesting this theoretical point and pointing me to the quotation.

[64] See Leng, *Bargaining and Learning in Recurring Crises*, 265 on the role of China.

[65] Paul, for example, states, "Acquiring an independent nuclear capability also seemed essential for dealing with India as an equal on Kashmir." Paul, *Power versus Prudence*, 133 (see also note 42 on the same page).

attack.[66] Such Mutual Assured Destruction (MAD) would make it irrational to initiate a war because it could not attain any political objective, and it would destroy the territorial integrity and political sovereignty of the state.

This has led some theorists to argue that the spread of nuclear weapons would increase the prospects for peace because everyone would be subject to the conditions of MAD.[67] Some of this is implied in the idea of a unit veto system, which sees a world of many nuclear states as able to veto the foreign policy goals of any other state by threatening nuclear war.[68] At some level, Pakistan and Israel hope that nuclear weapons will prevent them from being overrun by being able to destroy their opponents if they are going to be destroyed.[69]

Will nuclear weapons bring peace to the India–Pakistan enduring rivalry? Much of the argument in favor of nuclear deterrence and peace rests on the single case of the Cold War and the avoidance of a nuclear war between the US and USSR. Yet many who see this case as evidence in favor of the proposition forget important things about the case. As I wrote as the Cold War was ending, nuclear deterrence did not work alone, but in conjunction with a number of irenic factors.[70] In fact, peace may have been preserved in the Cold War because a number of these factors prevented even the prospects of an all-out conventional war, like that of World War II. What are these irenic factors? There are six.

First, and the main difference between the India–Pakistan conflict and the Cold War is that there was no territorial dispute between the US and the USSR. Their dispute was ideological. The absence of a territorial dispute between the US and USSR made it easier for nuclear deterrence to work. The absence of any territorial disputes between these two parties may also explain why the US and USSR never directly fought a war with each other.[71] Furthermore, the two times the Cold War came closest to

---

[66] Herman Kahn, *On Thermonuclear War* (Princeton: Princeton University Press, 1960); Thomas C. Schelling, *Strategy of Conflict* (New York: Oxford University Press, 1960).

[67] See Kenneth N. Waltz, *The Spread of Nuclear Weapons*, Adelphi Paper 171 (London: International Institute for Strategic Studies, 1981) and John J. Mearsheimer, "The Case for a Ukrainian Nuclear Deterrent," *Foreign Affairs* 72 (Summer 1993), 50–66.

[68] Morton A. Kaplan, *System and Process in International Politics* (New York: John Wiley, 1957).

[69] See Paul, *Power versus Prudence*, 132–41; for an informed review of the nuclear balance between India and Pakistan, see Daniel Geller in this volume.

[70] John A. Vasquez, "The Deterrence Myth: Nuclear Weapons and the Prevention of Nuclear War," in Charles W. Kegley, Jr. (ed.), *The Long Postwar Peace* (New York: HarperCollins, 1991), 205–23.

[71] John Lewis Gaddis, "The Long Peace: Elements of Stability in the Postwar International System," *International Security* 10 (Spring 1986), 99–142. As with Gaddis, I am not counting the 1917 Allied intervention in which the US participated.

war – in Berlin and Cuba – were at the territorial frontiers of the two empires. If deterrence almost failed there, where the homeland territory of neither state was at stake, would it not fail at some point for the more salient and festering Kashmir territorial dispute?

Second, since the Soviet–American rivalry was essentially ideological, both sides learned to live with it, and there developed among both leaders and followers a tolerance of the status quo, best exemplified by the Helsinki Accord.[72] Tolerance of the status quo has been at the heart of the disagreement between India and Pakistan. For more tolerance to occur, one or both sides would have to make major concessions. Pakistan and Muslim nationalists and other non-state actors would have to accept the LoC as the basis of a formal border, and this has been a major obstacle to any peace agreement. Instead, nationalists and hardliners are apt to do whatever they can to keep the issue on the agenda, even if this means taking matters into their own hands. India would have to simply concede the idea of keeping this state if a plebiscite went against the status quo, something that it has not been willing to do, as of yet.

Third, as John Mueller argues, the experience of the two world wars was a deterrent for both the East and the West.[73] No one wanted to fight another war like that in the 1950s or any other time. This restrained both sides. Mueller goes so far as to argue that nuclear weapons were essentially irrelevant to deterrence, and that the experience of the two world wars made both sides perceive the weapons in much more apocalyptic terms than was warranted, especially in the 1950s. Obviously, India and Pakistan have not had similar experiences in their wars with each other. Their experience has not made them see war as something that is abhorrent and must be avoided at all costs.

Fourth, nuclear deterrence stopped giving rise to repeated disputes after the Cuban missile crisis as the US and USSR developed a set of rules of the game. These are best illustrated by détente. India and Pakistan have not yet developed such rules, but as T. V. Paul and others have pointed out, it may take a while after the acquisition of nuclear

---

[72] While this is mostly true for Western and Eastern Europe, sometimes a tolerance of the status quo also occurred in developing areas as the Cold War matured. This was especially true when there was a risk of expanded war. Thus, in the Korean War the US does not accept the status quo, but tries to roll back the communist regime, and in Vietnam, the US explicitly rules out a land invasion of North Vietnam for fear of Chinese intervention; see Yuen Foong Khong, *Analogies at War* (Princeton: Princeton University Press, 1992). Even if one wants to argue that there was not much US–Soviet tolerance of the status quo in the developing world, that tolerance is still higher than anything in the India–Pakistan rivalry.

[73] John W. Mueller, *Retreat from Doomsday: The Obsolescence of Major War* (New York: Basic Books, 1989).

weapons to stabilize relations. In this regard, it is hopeful that attempts have been made to adopt certain confidence-building measures that will help prevent accidental nuclear war – a real concern between two contiguous countries. Similarly, after Kargil there is an attempt to establish a naval hotline. There is also the mutual agreement not to attack each other's civilian nuclear facilities.

Fifth, and related to the fourth factor, is that both the US and USSR learned how to manage crises so as to avoid a war and managed their respective interventions into ongoing wars, like Vietnam and Afghanistan, so as to prevent them from escalating to a conventional war between the two of them. As a result, the US and USSR have experienced more MIDs than India and Pakistan have, but none of them has ended in a war. India and Pakistan have not had this kind of success, and indeed have not so much sought to manage crises to avoid war, but have used them to time their wars for when it is perceived to be an advantageous or strategic opportunity to score some points. One thing we do know about nuclear deterrence from both the Cold War and now the India–Pakistan rivalry is that it does not prevent crises from developing. In fact, the belief that war is impossible because of MAD may lead some decisionmakers to take risks and play chicken games and give rise to the "stability-instability paradox." Some of this sort of thinking may have been going on in Kargil.[74] Indeed, it appears that it was only when the US showed both Pakistan and India the kinds of casualties a limited nuclear exchange might produce and Clinton put pressure on Sharif to withdraw that the threat of escalation at Kargil was defused.[75]

Nevertheless, there are indications that India and Pakistan can and have learned how to manage some of these militarized conflicts along the LoC, as well as terrorist incidents. Likewise, a number of MIDs since the Bangladesh War have not escalated to war and some of these outcomes can be attributed to conscious efforts at crisis management. Having said all of this, however, these efforts still have a long way to go before they reach the level of crisis management and preventive diplomacy achieved by Kennedy and Khrushchev after the Cuban missile crisis.

Sixth, arms control agreements between the US and USSR prevented the arms race from getting out of control. MAD did not just happen, it was

---

[74] See Leng in this volume. Also see Geller in this volume for a discussion of the "stability–instability paradox."

[75] See Talbott, *Engaging India*, 167, particularly on Clinton's concerns about the danger of nuclear war posed by Kargil. For a declassified analysis of casualties resulting from a nuclear exchange, see Robert T. Batcher, "The Consequences of an Indo-Pakistani Nuclear War," *International Studies Review* 6 (2004), 135–62. See also Geller in this volume.

institutionalized and planned. Arms control played a role in limiting threat perception and in that way sought to avoid creating windows of vulnerability. We do not yet have that kind of arms control in the India–Pakistan enduring rivalry, although there have been some recent movements in that direction, which is a hopeful sign given that such measures usually occur once the states become more adjusted to the reality of the destructiveness of nuclear weapons and the dangers of MAD.

Nuclear deterrence during the Cold War worked with all these factors in its favor. Would it work if just one were absent? Would it work if several were absent, as seems to be the case in the India–Pakistan conflict? The point is that we do not *know*. Can we rely on a theory with such a slim base of evidence to preserve the peace when it comes to nuclear war? One of the main problems is that nuclear deterrence must work not only once, but for infinity. One slip and total destruction is the end game.

Deterrence theorists have assumed that nuclear weapons raise the provocation threshold so that what was once a provocation for war is no longer a provocation warranting going to war. There is no question that nuclear weapons have raised the provocation threshold, but have they raised it so high that there could be no provocation whatsoever that would make one side resort to nuclear war?[76] Even during the Cold War, the US abstained from a no-first-use pledge because it said it would use nuclear weapons to defeat an all-out conventional Soviet attack on Western Europe.

These criticisms raise serious questions about the ability of classical nuclear deterrence to prevent war in the India–Pakistan conflict, but they deal primarily with politically conscious decisions about war. In addition, there are still other paths to nuclear war that, even if the above were managed, need to be handled to avoid nuclear war. These involve questions of command and control and nuclear war through accident or miscalculation. It is encouraging that India and Pakistan have made attempts to establish certain rules of the game and to manage crises yet fundamental differences remain between this nuclear rivalry and that of the US and USSR.

A conflict that has had repeated wars with none of the underlying factors that have produced these MIDs being changed is apt to have more MIDs and more wars. Without altering these underlying factors, nuclear deterrence will be working in conditions highly unfavorable to its success. Relying on nuclear deterrence to produce peace is at best a high-risk strategy.

---

[76] On the concept of provocation threshold, see Richard Ned Lebow, *Between Peace and War* (Baltimore: Johns Hopkins University Press, 1981), 277.

If a nuclear exchange is to be avoided, it is important that more aspects of the six factors that helped manage crises and eventually prevent crises between the US and the USSR be implemented by Pakistan and India. The first way to do that is to continue to implement confidence-building measures and other rules of the game and to adopt safeguards for avoiding an inadvertent nuclear war. Yet even with these improvements, the India–Pakistan rivalry still lacks four of the six irenic factors present in the Soviet–American rivalry: no territorial dispute, a tolerance of the status quo, a deep abhorrence of war (brought about by the two world wars), and arms control agreements regulating arms races.

Conclusions

Three major conclusions emerge from this analysis. First, at the heart of this rivalry is a territorial dispute that is seen as both symbolic and transcendent. This makes this case not unique or exotic, but quite typical of dyadic wars that have occurred between neighbors in the modern international system. The birth of these two states without having previously agreed on mutually acceptable borders has led to a series of crises and wars – once they decided to frame and handle this issue in a power politics fashion. Indeed most states that handle territorial issues in a power politics fashion have them recur, and as a result they become enduring rivals.

Why this is the case is due to two factors: (1) the unwillingness to compromise, which is a function of the ability of domestic hardliners to keep the issue on the agenda while simultaneously vetoing any compromise that would lead to peace, and (2) the relative equality of the two states that prevents one from completely defeating the other and unilaterally imposing a solution and a post-war settlement that would keep the defeated party weak or willing to abandon permanently its previous position. The acquisition of nuclear weapons by the parties makes this even less likely, while at the same time re-enforcing the status quo.

In this case, what is present that is often lacking with disputes among major states is that outside parties and allies play a prominent role in intervening to prevent a military settlement. Pakistan as the weaker side has exploited this tendency; yet no major states have been willing to move toward imposing a settlement.

Second, it is clear that the India–Pakistan case fits the steps to war explanation. With the exception of the first war, all the steps are present, and in a rough order that is expected. Territory is the factor driving disputes and the making of alliances and military buildups. The making of an alliance by one side leads to a counter-alliance on the other.

A military buildup by one side leads to an arms race. A classic security dilemma dominates relations.

The unwillingness to accept the status quo leads the revisionist state, in this case Pakistan, to initiate crises, which because of the salience of territory and the relative equality of capability, leads the issue to fester and crises to recur. This happens even with the fairly asymmetric distribution of capability present in this enduring rivalry, which illustrates that only overwhelming preponderance can prevent war – a simple asymmetric distribution cannot. The domestic dynamics of the steps to war model also seem to fit, in that hostile actions by one's opponent lead to an increase in the number and influence of hardliners in the other side, which leads them to take ever more hostile actions, which leads to more hardliners and an upward spiral often ending in war.

Third, classical nuclear deterrence theory may be flawed and is based on inferences derived from a single case. Nuclear weapons may not have been the main factor preventing a nuclear war between the US and USSR during the Cold War, even if it raised the provocation threshold. Instead at least six other factors can be identified as producing that irenic effect. To the extent that several of these factors continue to be absent from the India–Pakistan rivalry, it is risky to think that classical nuclear deterrence will continue to prevent nuclear war *ad infinitum*.

4   The India–Pakistan rivalry: prospects for war, prospects for peace

Daniel S. Geller

Introduction

In a very real sense, the conflict between India and Pakistan constitutes an archetype for an "enduring rivalry." This is true with regard to origins, intensity of violence, failures in both mediation and conflict management, and persistence. Beyond the war-prone dynamics of the rivalry relationship itself, the Indo-Pakistani dyad exhibits a number of structural characteristics that increase the likelihood of large-scale violence. Moreover, the multiple tests of nuclear weapons by both states in May of 1998 have added the possibility of a level of destruction in a future conflict not witnessed since the end of World War II. This chapter will explore the prospects for war and peace within the Indo-Pakistani rivalry.

General patterns of enduring rivalries

As Frank Wayman observes, geographic contiguity or an unresolved territorial dispute are factors common to most rivalries.[1] This pattern has been noted in general studies on war-prone dyads[2] as well as in specific analyses of rivalries.[3] According to Wayman, in his rivalry database covering the years 1816 through 1986, "[a]t least a third of the

---

The author wishes to thank T. V. Paul, John Vasquez, and Manus Midlarsky for their insights and helpful comments on an earlier draft of this chapter.
[1] Frank W. Wayman, "Rivalries: Recurrent Disputes and Explaining War," in John A. Vasquez (ed.), *What Do We Know about War?* (Lanham, MD: Rowman and Littlefield, 2000), 219–34.
[2] Stuart A. Bremer, "Dangerous Dyads: Conditions Affecting the Likelihood of Interstate War, 1816–1965," *Journal of Conflict Resolution* 36 (1992), 309–41; Gary Goertz and Paul F. Diehl, *Territorial Changes and International Conflict* (London: Routledge, 1992).
[3] John A. Vasquez, *The War Puzzle* (Cambridge: Cambridge University Press, 1993); John A. Vasquez, "The Evolution of Multiple Rivalries Prior to World War II in the Pacific," in Paul F. Diehl (ed.), *The Dynamics of Enduring Rivalries* (Urbana: University of Illinois Press, 1998), 191–224; Paul K. Huth, *Standing Your Ground* (Ann Arbor: University of Michigan Press, 1996).

twenty-eight enduring rival dyads are born feuding."[4] Three cases date from the political formation of both states: India–Pakistan, 1947–86; Syria–Israel, 1948–79; and North Korea–South Korea, 1949–86. All three cases involve a contiguous border – and contending territorial claims.

Another factor common to enduring rivalries is an absence of "state learning" across multiple disputes. Goertz and Diehl identify a "basic rivalry level" (BRL) that reflects the severity and duration of disputes that arise between rivals and conclude that "a constant, unchanging BRL describes ... most rivalries."[5] Goertz and Diehl observe that enduring rivals establish conflict levels early in the relationship and that these conflict levels remain relatively stable throughout the term of the rivalry. In other words, there is little evidence of "learning" or conflict management that would be indicated by a "pattern of dispute escalation at the beginning of enduring rivalries or dispute de-escalation at the end."[6] Wayman finds similar results in his analysis of the war behavior of rivals: "If becoming mature consists of learning to find alternatives to war as a way of settling disagreements, then our rivals show little sign of maturity ... [T]here is no upward or downward trend in the tendency to escalate to war."[7] Maoz and Mor also find scant evidence of state learning in the conflict interaction patterns of Middle Eastern rival states,[8] and Leng observes no indication of conflict management in the four Indo-Pakistani crises that he studied in his analysis of bargaining and escalation in rivalries.[9] In short, successful conflict management in enduring rivalries is a rare occurrence.

A similar finding pertains to work in the area of mediation. Preliminary research indicates that international mediation has little effect on the conflict patterns of enduring rivalries. Bercovitch and Diehl examine efforts toward international mediation between rivals and state that the presence or absence of mediation does not appear to have any impact on

---

[4] Wayman, "Rivalries: Recurrent Disputes and Explaining War," 229–30.
[5] Gary Goertz and Paul F. Diehl, "The 'Volcano Model' and Other Patterns in the Evolution of Enduring Rivalries," in Diehl (ed.), *The Dynamics of Enduring Rivalries*, 98–125; Gary Goertz and Paul F. Diehl, "(Enduring) Rivalries," in Manus I. Midlarsky (ed.), *Handbook of War Studies II* (Ann Arbor: University of Michigan Press, 2000), 222–67.
[6] Goertz and Diehl, "(Enduring) Rivalries," 251.
[7] Wayman, "Rivalries: Recurrent Disputes and Explaining War," 232–33.
[8] Zeev Maoz and Ben D. Mor, "Learning, Preference Change, and the Evolution of Enduring Rivalries," in Diehl (ed.), *The Dynamics of Enduring Rivalries*, 129–64.
[9] Russell J. Leng, *Bargaining and Learning in Recurring Crises: The Soviet–American, Egyptian–Israeli, and Indo-Pakistani Rivalries* (Ann Arbor: University of Michigan Press, 2000), 256, 260.

the occurrence of rivalry wars.[10] In a more extensive analysis of the effects of mediation on rivalries, Diehl and Goertz conclude that mediation attempts have little impact on the conflict behavior of rival dyads. At best, mediation might increase the length of the interval between militarized disputes in some rivalries, but does not influence the likelihood of subsequent war.[11]

With regard to the termination of enduring rivalries, Wayman's data supplies some interesting insights. Of the twenty-eight severe rivalries in his set (1816–1986), twelve were still active by the last year in his database. Fifteen rivalries involved minor power dyads and, of these minor power dyadic rivalries, only six had ended. Three of Wayman's rivalry cases terminate in war with the destruction of one of the contending regimes. Issue salience appears to be a strong factor in the duration of rivalries – with territorial disputes a key example of a high salience issue.[12] Hence, rivalries with a territorial component appear among the most persistent and least likely to terminate swiftly.[13]

In sum, the prospects for peace within the Indo-Pakistani dyad are not encouraging when placed within the context of general patterns in enduring rivalries.[14] The origins of this rivalry, its intensity of violence, the failure of both mediation and conflict management, and its persistence all point toward future confrontations. However, structural factors associated with general patterns of war as well as the availability of nuclear weapons also impact the likelihood of future conflict between these states. Any estimate of the probability of another Indo-Pakistani war hinges on the effect of these additional elements.

Indo-Pakistani wars: structural factors

The question of the effect of nuclear weapons on the outbreak of war is an issue in much debate. Some scholars argue that nuclear-armed states will exercise extreme caution in their confrontations, given the potential consequences of war: tactics of intimidation including threats, military alerts,

[10] Jacob Bercovitch and Paul F. Diehl, "Conflict Management and Enduring Rivalries: Frequency, Timing and Short-Term Impact of Mediation," *International Interactions* 22 (1997), 299–320.
[11] Paul F. Diehl and Gary Goertz, *War and Peace in International Rivalry* (Ann Arbor: University of Michigan Press, 2000), 201–18.
[12] Wayman, "Rivalries: Recurrent Disputes and Explaining War," 231–32.
[13] Goertz and Diehl, "(Enduring) Rivalries," 256.
[14] For a detailed analysis and interpretation of the extant research on the patterns of genesis and development of enduring international rivalries, see Ben D. Mor, "The Onset of Enduring Rivalries: A Progress Report," *International Politics* 40 (2003), 29–57.

mobilizations, and even the limited use of force may be employed in contests of nuclear brinkmanship, but neither side will cross the threshold of large-scale armed conflict with its potential costs of escalation to a nuclear exchange.[15] However, other analysts contend that the possession of nuclear weapons provides avenues to both conventional and nuclear war either through escalatory processes from low-level conventional conflicts or through incentives for nuclear preemption in severe crises.[16] The issue of future war between India and Pakistan partially turns on the impact that nuclear weapons possession will have on the conflict interaction of these states.

Of course, a scientific approach toward estimating the likelihood of future Indo-Pakistani conflict would build on established empirical patterns of war,[17] and in this area considerable progress has been made. The systematic quantitative empirical analysis of war has a history extending from the third decade of the twentieth century in the pioneering work of Lewis F. Richardson[18] and, over the ensuing years, a large number of scientific studies of war have produced impressive evidence on the factors and processes leading to violent international conflict. A recent analysis by Geller and Singer[19] identified a series of strong empirical patterns relating to the onset (occurrence/initiation) and seriousness (magnitude/duration/severity) of war drawn from a review of over 500 quantitative

[15] For example, see Glenn H. Snyder and Paul Diesing, *Conflict Among Nations: Bargaining, Decision Making, and System Structure in International Crises* (Princeton: Princeton University Press, 1977); Kenneth N. Waltz, "Nuclear Myths and Political Realities," *American Political Science Review* 84 (1990), 731–45; Kenneth N. Waltz, "More May Be Better," in Scott D. Sagan and Kenneth N. Waltz, *The Spread of Nuclear Weapons: A Debate* (New York: W. W. Norton & Company, 1995), 1–45, 93–113; Bruce Bueno de Mesquita and William H. Riker, "An Assessment of the Merits of Selective Nuclear Proliferation," *Journal of Conflict Resolution* 26 (1982), 283–306.

[16] For example, see Solly Zuckerman, *Nuclear Illusion and Reality* (New York: Viking Press, 1982); Scott D. Sagan, "The Perils of Proliferation: Organization Theory, Deterrence Theory, and the Spread of Nuclear Weapons," *International Security* 18 (1994), 66–107; Scott D. Sagan, "More Will Be Worse," in Sagan and Waltz, *The Spread of Nuclear Weapons: A Debate*, 47–91, 115–36; Scott D. Sagan, "The Origins of Military Doctrine and Command and Control Systems," in Peter R. Lavoy, Scott D. Sagan, and James J. Wirtz (eds.), *Planning the Unthinkable: How New Powers Will Use Nuclear, Biological and Chemical Weapons* (Ithaca: Cornell University Press, 2000), 16–46; and Russell J. Leng and Adil Husain, "South Asian War Games." Paper presented at the Annual Meeting of the Peace Science Society (International), Atlanta, GA, October 26–28, 2001.

[17] Carl G. Hempel, "The Function of General Laws in History," in Patrick Gardiner (ed.), *Theories of History* (Glencoe, IL: The Free Press [1942] 1959), 344–56.

[18] Lewis F. Richardson, "Generalized Foreign Policy," *British Journal of Psychology Monographs Supplements* 23 (1939); Lewis F. Richardson, *Arms and Insecurity* (Pittsburgh: Boxwood Press, 1960); Lewis F. Richardson, *Statistics of Deadly Quarrels* (Pittsburgh: Boxwood Press, 1960).

[19] Daniel S. Geller and J. David Singer, *Nations at War: A Scientific Study of International Conflict* (Cambridge: Cambridge University Press, 1998).

data-based studies on international conflict. These patterns were applied in conjunctive explanations of specific dyadic and multistate wars.

The observation that wars result from a conjunction of conditions or factors is becoming more commonplace.[20] As Vasquez notes, the phenomenon of war is so complex that important variables – while not sufficient conditions for war – may be critical in increasing the probability of war, and it is only when multiple factors that increase the probability of war combine that war actually occurs.[21]

This process of complex conjunctive causality in the occurrence of certain types of social phenomena was described explicitly by Charles Ragin:

> It is the intersection of a set of conditions in time and space that produces many of the large-scale qualitative changes, as well as many of the small-scale events, that interest social scientists, not the separate or independent effects of these conditions ... The basic idea is that a phenomenon or a change emerges from the intersection of appropriate preconditions ... This conjunctural or combinatorial nature is a key feature of causal complexity.[22]

Hirschman makes this argument with regard to the Russian Revolution of 1917[23] and, more recently, Lebow presents a similar thesis dealing with the onset of World War I.[24] However, both Hirschman and Lebow discount the value of quantitative empirical analysis as a method for understanding specific large-scale events involving social change. In contrast, King, Keohane, and Verba note that scientific generalizations are quite applicable to understanding highly unusual events that do not fall within a class of similar occurrences and they argue that probabilistic

[20] For example, see Vasquez, *The War Puzzle*; John A. Vasquez, "Developing a Strategy for Achieving Greater Cumulation in Peace Research," in Stuart A. Bremer and Thomas R. Cusack (eds.), *The Process of War* (Amsterdam: Gordon and Breach, 1995), 241–49; Stuart A. Bremer, "Advancing the Scientific Study of War," in Bremer and Cusack (eds.), *The Process of War*, 1–33; Geller and Singer, *Nations at War*; Russell J. Leng, "Cumulation in QIP: Twenty-Five Years After Ojai," *Conflict Management and Peace Science* 17 (1999), 133–47; Jack S. Levy, "Reflections on the Scientific Study of War," in Vasquez (ed.), *What Do We Know about War?*, 319–27; Richard N. Lebow, "Contingency, Catalysts, and International System Change," *Political Science Quarterly* 115 (2000), 591–616; and Bruce Russett and John Oneal, *Triangulating Peace: Democracy, Interdependence, and International Organizations* (New York: W.W. Norton, 2001).
[21] John A. Vasquez, "What Do We Know about War?" in Vasquez (ed.), *What Do We Know about War?*, 335–70.
[22] Charles C. Ragin, *The Comparative Method: Moving Beyond Qualitative and Quantitative Strategies* (Berkeley: University of California Press, 1987), 25.
[23] Albert O. Hirschman, "The Search for Paradigms as a Hindrance to Understanding," *World Politics* 22 (1970), 329–43.
[24] Lebow, "Contingency, Catalysts, and International System Change," 610.

generalizations can be useful in studying even "unique" events.[25] Indeed, empirically derived generalizations identifying convergent causal conditions have been applied in explanations of the Iran–Iraq War of 1980,[26] World War I,[27] and World War II.[28]

In summary, there is a developing consensus on the need for a scientific explanation of war based on conjunctural causation – war understood in terms of convergent or intersecting conditions. However, it is also frequently maintained that any of several combinations of conditions might produce a given social outcome[29] – that the complexity of certain social phenomena (such as war) is due not only to the conjunctural nature of social causation, but also to the possibility that multiple combinations of factors or conditions may produce the same outcome. This property of certain types of social phenomena is referred to as "multiple causation" or "equifinality."[30] As Ragin argues, it is the conjunctive and often complex combinatorial nature of social causation that makes it so difficult to unravel the sources of major events in human affairs.[31] In fact, if wars occur according to a multiple conjunctural causative mechanism, then the conception of necessary and/or sufficient causation in war may have to be eliminated, since no factor alone may be *either* necessary or sufficient for the onset of war.[32]

The vast mass of accumulated quantitative empirical evidence has shown that the presence or absence of certain structural factors increases the probability of the onset and seriousness of war for units of analysis specified at the state, dyad, region, and international system levels.[33] Indeed, a number of these structural factors have shaped the conflict-ridden relationship between India and Pakistan and will continue to exert a powerful influence on their future interaction. The following analysis discusses these factors within a framework of complex convergent causality and examines their implications for the probability of future war between these states.

---

[25] Gary King, Robert O. Keohane, and Sidney Verba, *Designing Social Inquiry: Scientific Inference in Qualitative Research* (Princeton: Princeton University Press, 1994), 10–12.

[26] Geller and Singer, *Nations at War*.

[27] Vasquez, *The War Puzzle*; Geller and Singer, *Nations at War*; William R. Thompson, "A Streetcar Named Sarajevo: Catalysts, Multiple Causation Chains, and Rivalry Structures," *International Studies Quarterly* 47 (2003), 453–74.

[28] John A. Vasquez, "The Causes of the Second World War in Europe: A New Scientific Explanation," *International Political Science Review* 17 (1996), 161–78.

[29] Ragin, *The Comparative Method*, 25.

[30] King, Keohane, and Verba, *Designing Social Inquiry*, 87.

[31] Ragin, *The Comparative Method*, 26.

[32] King, Keohane, and Verba, *Designing Social Inquiry*, 87; Bremer, "Advancing the Scientific Study of War," 21.

[33] Geller and Singer, *Nations at War*, 27–28.

Contiguity/territorial dispute

The presence of a contiguous land or sea (separated by 150 miles of water or less) border increases the probability of war within a dyad.[34] If the categories of land and sea contiguity are combined, then the probability of war between contiguous states is approximately thirty-five times greater than the likelihood of war between non-contiguous nations.[35] Contiguity not only provides the easy opportunity to use military force (i.e., decreases the requirement of "military reach"), but it may also provide an issue for war – as in a disputed border – or may structure interactions in a way that leads to conflict – as in the dynamic of the "security dilemma."[36] In the case of India and Pakistan, the territorial dispute over the contiguous area of Kashmir has shaped the relationship between these two states since their post-colonial inception in 1947.[37]

Conventional wisdom holds that the root cause of the Indo-Pakistani conflict is to be found in religious – or more broadly – ethnocultural differences. In other words, the distinctions between the Hindu and Muslim religions are so stark that the conflict of Hindu India with Muslim Pakistan can be understood simply as the result of contact and friction between states of different ethnocultural composition. Although such an explanation may seem compelling, it is overly facile and without much empirical support. As Hagerty notes, Hindus and Muslims have coexisted in South Asia without widespread violence for centuries. Despite episodic communal conflict in the history of the sub-continent, "Hindu–Muslim carnage on a massive scale is only a twentieth century phenomenon."[38] In a related discussion, J. David Singer observes more generally that ethnocultural dissimilarities alone are rarely sufficient to produce war.[39]

Recent research[40] indicates that territorial disputes have a particularly high probability of escalating to war. Moreover, a majority of enduring rivalries involve some aspect of territorial conflict.[41] The reasons

---

[34] *Ibid.*, 141.   [35] Bremer, "Dangerous Dyads."

[36] John Herz, *Political Realism and Political Idealism* (Chicago: University of Chicago Press, 1959).

[37] For various perspectives on the territorial dispute over Kashmir, see Robert G. Wirsing, *India, Pakistan, and the Kashmir Dispute: On Regional Conflict and Its Resolution* (New York: St. Martin's Press, 1994); Richard Sisson and Leo E. Rose, *War and Secession: Pakistan, India, and the Creation of Bangladesh* (Berkeley: University of California Press, 1990); and Mushtaqur Rahman, *Divided Kashmir: Old Problems, New Opportunities for India, Pakistan, and the Kashmiri People* (Boulder, CO: Lynne Reinner, 1996).

[38] Devin T. Hagerty, *The Consequences of Nuclear Proliferation: Lessons from South Asia* (Cambridge, MA: MIT Press, 1998), 64.

[39] J. David Singer, "The Etiology of Interstate War: A Natural History Approach," in Vasquez (ed.), *What Do We Know about War?*, 3–21.

[40] See Vasquez in this volume.   [41] See Diehl, Goertz, and Saeedi in this volume.

proffered for the volatility and protraction of territorial disputes include domestic political pressure, symbolic value, economic or strategic interest, and even human genetic structure. Whatever the basis, conflict over territory is a potent source of war.

The territory that currently constitutes the contemporary states of India, Pakistan, and Bangladesh became part of British India during the eighteenth and nineteenth centuries. Subjected to strong Islamic influences beginning in the seventh century, the area combined a mix of Hindu and Muslim populations. The idea of a separate Muslim state was initially raised in the early 1930s and was endorsed in 1940 by the major Muslim political party in India known as the All-India Muslim League. The League won the 1946–47 election, and on August 15, 1947 Britain promulgated the Indian Independence Act, which partitioned the subcontinent into the sovereign states of predominantly Hindu India and Muslim Pakistan. However, the partition of British India was hastily constructed, creating a number of complex territorial problems and disputes, most notably over Kashmir. While India's Muslim majority provinces and princely states were given the option of remaining in India or joining Pakistan, the Hindu maharaja of the predominantly Muslim state of Jammu and Kashmir subsequently acceded to India. Pakistan challenged the action by sending troops into the territory and the following combat between Indian and Pakistani forces was halted by a United Nations ceasefire on January 1, 1949.[42]

The military conflict over Kashmir in 1947–48 resulted in a *de facto* division of the territory into Indian and Pakistani-held sectors. The Indian sector was subsequently incorporated as a separate state within the Indian Union in 1957. Pakistan protested this action, and the issue incited new armed conflict resulting in a second Indo-Pakistani war in 1965.[43] Other incendiary elements in Indo-Pakistani relations beginning in the late 1960s were the policies of both governments to provide support to dissident groups in the territory of the other state. Pakistan supported such elements in the Indian section of Kashmir and permitted the placement of training camps in East Pakistan for Naga and Mizo rebels from India's northeast frontier. For its part, India provided political and material support for dissidents on Pakistan's northwest border.[44] These simmering

[42] Arthur S. Banks and Thomas C. Muller (eds.), *Political Handbook of the World: 1999* (Binghamton, NY: CSA Publications, 1999), 740.
[43] Lawrence Ziring, "The Geopolitics of the Asian Subcontinent: Pakistan's Security Environment," in J. Henry Korson (ed.), *Contemporary Problems of Pakistan* (Boulder, CO: Westview Press, 1993), 147–69.
[44] Sisson and Rose, *War and Secession*, 42–43.

border and territorial disputes, as well as the movement of refugees, led to a third Indo-Pakistani war in 1971 which resulted in the dismemberment of Pakistan and the creation of the Bengali state of Bangladesh. However, as Ziring argues, "Bangladesh . . . was not the root cause of Indo-Pakistani hostility [in 1971] . . . The territorial dispute that keyed their mutual antagonism was the Muslim-majority state of Kashmir."[45]

Now in the twenty-first century, Kashmir persists as an explosive issue in the relationship between these two countries. From May through July of 1999, Indian and Pakistani troops engaged in bloody combat in the Kargil area of Kashmir. Islamabad has supported dissident groups that engage in violence within the Indian sector, while Indian military forces, in pursuit of these rebels, cross into Pakistani territory. Artillery shelling, cross-border raids, and sporadic movement of military forces within and along the borders of Kashmir have become commonplace throughout the last decade. Indeed, the latest confrontation between India and Pakistan involved the mass mobilization of the military forces of both countries (from December 2001 through June 2002) and was directly tied to the attack by Kashmiri-based Islamic militants on the Indian Parliament. In sum, the contiguous border between India and Pakistan with the disputed territory of Kashmir has been a potent factor in the past Indo-Pakistani wars. The possibility of continued conflict over Kashmir must be considered a potential route to future war as well.

Political systems

One of the strongest empirical patterns in international politics involves the "democratic peace" – nations with democratic political systems rarely engage each other in war.[46] Two explanations for this phenomenon have been proffered. One explanation focuses on the non-violent norms for conflict resolution that are inculcated within democratic societies, whereas the other explanation involves the constraining effect of democratic political institutions on war decisions. Compelling evidence has yet to be produced that will permit selection among the alternative explanations of political culture or decisionmaking constraints; but whatever the mechanism responsible for the democratic peace, non-democratic dyads (one or both states non-democratic) are almost fifty times more likely to engage in war than are democratic pairs.[47]

---

[45] Ziring, "The Geopolitics of the Asian Subcontinent," 151.
[46] Geller and Singer, *Nations at War*, 142.
[47] Stuart A. Bremer, "Democracy and Militarized Interstate Conflict, 1816–1965," *International Interactions* 18 (1993), 231–49.

Banks and Muller describe the Indian political system as a parliamentary republic since January 26, 1950.[48] The Polity IV database[49] provides India with consistently high scores on its "democracy" variable. Democracy is conceptualized as the presence of institutions and procedures for the expression of preferences about policies and leaders, guarantee of civil liberties, and constraints on the power of the executive. The Polity IV database gives India consistently low scores on its measure of "autocracy." Autocracy is conceptualized as a system with suppressed or restricted political participation, where chief executives are selected by a political elite who then rule with few institutional constraints. Each of these measures varies between zero (low) and +10 (high) for the attribute in question. By subtracting the autocracy score from the democracy score, a variable representing a democracy/autocracy continuum ranging between +10 and −10 was created. Employing this procedure for the period 1950–99 (the last year coded in Polity IV) produced yearly rankings for India ranging from a high of +9 to a low of +7, indicating a political system strongly characterized by democratic institutions.[50]

Political development in Pakistan presents a much more variegated history. The death of Mohammed Ali Jinnah – the first governor-general and president of the Constituent Assembly of Pakistan – in 1948 created a political vacuum that persisted for years. The subsequent leadership elites could not agree on a constitutional framework and it was not until 1956 that a constitution creating a republic was established.[51] The following decades saw the creation, amendment, abrogation, and restoration of multiple constitutions, including the imposition of a martial law regime that lasted until 1985 following a military coup in 1977, and a second coup and martial law regime imposed in 1999.

The Polity IV database provides Pakistan with variable scores on both its "democracy" and "autocracy" measures for the period 1947–99. High democracy ratings (+7 or +8) were indicated for 1956–57, 1973–75, and 1988–96, with high autocracy scores (+7) for 1958–61 and 1977–84. Employing the same coding procedure as with India for each year for the period 1947–99 (the last year coded in Polity IV) produced

---

[48] Banks and Muller, *Political Handbook of the World: 1999*, 432.

[49] The Polity IV database by Monty G. Marshall and Keith Jaggers, "Polity IV: Political Regime Characteristics and Transitions, 1800–1999." Computer File INSCR (Integrated Network for Societal Conflict Research), Center for International Development and Conflict Management (College Park: University of Maryland, 2000).

[50] See James L. Ray, *Democracy and International Conflict: An Evaluation of the Democratic Peace Proposition* (Columbia: University of South Carolina Press, 1995) for a discussion of this method of producing quantitative estimates of regime type.

[51] Robert LaPorte, Jr., "Another Try at Democracy," in Korson (ed.), *Contemporary Problems of Pakistan*, 171–92.

an average score of +1.4 for the entire 53-year span. This may be considered indicative of a political system that has vacillated between democracy and autocracy to the extent that its average position on the political continuum is midway between the poles of the political authority characteristics.[52]

On October 12, 1999, Prime Minister Nawaz Sharif attempted to remove the chief of the army, General Pervez Musharraf. This action was followed by a bloodless *coup d'état* and the installation of General Musharraf as Pakistan's new chief executive. Within two days of the coup, martial law was declared, the Constitution suspended, and Parliament disbanded. On June 20, 2001, General Musharraf appointed himself president and formal head of state. Although a new federal Parliament was elected in October 2002, General Musharraf has placed his presidency beyond the reach of the elected assembly. He remains the most powerful political figure in the country. He retains command of the army and still wields near-dictatorial powers, including authority to dissolve the Parliament.

The preceding analysis demonstrates that Pakistan is not a democratic polity. Therefore, India/Pakistan is a mixed dyad with regard to political systems and is lacking shared non-violent norms for conflict resolution as well as shared institutional constraints on war decisions. A new crisis impacting this dyad will not benefit from the conflict-dampening effects of the democratic peace.

Economic development

The level of joint economic development also shapes a dyad's propensity toward violent conflict. An examination of quantitative empirical studies in this area[53] concluded that the absence of joint advanced economic systems increases the probability of war for pairs of states.[54] The explanation for this empirical pattern is to be found in the benefits of peace for advanced economies: war disrupts international trade and highly developed economic systems tied to the international economy suffer most heavily from conflict which interferes with the natural function of the market mechanism.

---

[52] This evaluation is mirrored in such discussions of Pakistan's political history as Zulfikar K. Maluka, *The Myth of Constitutionalism in Pakistan* (Oxford: Oxford University Press, 1995); Iftikhar H. Malik, *State and Civil Society in Pakistan: Politics of Authority, Ideology and Ethnicity* (London: Macmillan, 1997); Rasul B. Rais (ed.), *State, Society, and Democratic Change in Pakistan* (Oxford: Oxford University Press, 1997).

[53] Geller and Singer, *Nations at War*, 145.

[54] Bremer, "Democracy and Militarized Interstate Conflict, 1816–1965," calculates that wars are five times more likely to originate in economically underdeveloped dyads than in developed dyads.

Agriculture employs about 70 percent of Indian workers. Moreover, due to economic policies emphasizing protectionism, government intervention, and import-substitution, India's percentage of world trade declined between the 1950s and late 1980s, resulting in trade imbalances and high inflation rates. Faced with economic stagnation and decline in foreign investment, the government of P. V. Narasimha Rao (1991–96) attempted a radical restructuring of the Indian economy, including such measures as the acceptance of control by foreign firms of domestic companies, and the lowering of government constraints on market activity. Annual growth in Gross Domestic Product (GDP) was substantially increased, giving India the fifteenth largest economy in the world by 1997 and, in the first five years of the twenty-first century, high-technology sectors within the Indian economic system have become integrated within the global economy. Nevertheless, according to World Bank calculations, the per capita income level of India places it in the 102nd position in the world with one-third of its population subsisting below the national poverty line.[55]

Pakistan presents an analogous picture. Agriculture employs about half of the working population, with industry accounting for less than one-fifth of the labor force. GDP growth for Pakistan averaged over 4 percent a year for the period 1990–98, largely the result of economic reforms leading to liberalized trade policies and increased privatization of banking, utilities, and industry. By 1999, Pakistan had completed new loan arrangements with the International Monetary Fund, the World Bank, and the Asian Development Bank, as well as rescheduling and restructuring debt payments to Western creditors. The most serious obstacle to sustained progress is the Pakistani population growth rate – one of the highest in Asia. Currently, about one-third of the population in Pakistan subsists below the national poverty line.[56]

In sum, the negative economic effects of war on states with advanced economies may not enter the decisional calculus of leaders in India and Pakistan. Given low levels of economic development, the use of force may appear to be a foreign policy instrument with minimal economic repercussions.

Capability balance

Conventional military capability There is a strong empirical pattern linking an unstable conventional military balance within a dyad to

---

[55] Banks and Muller, *Political Handbook of the World: 1999*, 433.   [56] *Ibid.*, 739, 740.

92 Daniel S. Geller

an increased probability of the onset of war.[57] Conceptually, dynamic capability balances can be divided into two categories: shifts (capability convergence or divergence) and transitions (a reversal of relative capability position). Intricate explanations as to why capability shifts may lead to conflict can be found in works by Levy[58] and Wayman.[59] Most simply, however, either the possibility of advancing national interests or a growing perception of threat to those interests may be generated by convergence, divergence, or transition in relative capabilities among states.

India's military forces totaled 1,263,000 active personnel in 2001. The army comprised 1,100,000 of that total. Equipment levels for that year included 3,414 main battle tanks, 157 armored personnel carriers, 4,175 towed artillery pieces, and 1,795 surface-to-air missiles. Naval resources for 2001 included 53,000 personnel, 16 submarines, and 27 principal surface combatants including one aircraft carrier and eight destroyers. The air force in that year was composed of 110,000 personnel, 738 combat aircraft, and 22 armed helicopters.[60]

Pakistan's military forces totaled 620,000 active personnel in 2001. The army comprised 550,000 of that total. Equipment levels for that year included 2,300 main battle tanks, 1,150 armored personnel carriers, 1,467 towed artillery pieces, and 1,400 surface-to-air missiles. Naval resources for 2001 included 25,000 personnel, ten submarines, and eight principal surface combatants – all of which were frigates. The air force in that year was composed of 45,000 personnel, 353 combat aircraft, and no armed helicopters.[61]

Standard methods of capability measurement employed by the Correlates of War (COW) Project involve the computation of capability indices. Estimates of the relative conventional capability balance between India and Pakistan from 1947 through 2001 were created by the use of one of these indices. The COW National Capability data set encompasses six measures covering three dimensions of national power in yearly entries for every state in the world from 1816 to 1993. Two of these measures involve military capabilities:

[57] Geller and Singer, *Nations at War*, 147; Daniel S. Geller, "Material Capabilities: Power and International Conflict," in Vasquez (ed.), *What Do We Know about War?*, 259–77.
[58] Jack S. Levy, "Declining Power and the Preventive Motivation for War," *World Politics* 40 (1987), 82–107.
[59] Frank W. Wayman, "Power Shifts and the Onset of War," in Jacek Kugler and Douglas Lemke (eds.), *Parity and War: Evaluations and Extensions of The War Ledger* (Ann Arbor: University of Michigan Press, 1996), 145–62.
[60] International Institute for Strategic Studies, *The Military Balance 2001/2002* (London: Oxford University Press, 2001), 161–64.
[61] *Ibid.*, 167–68.

Military Personnel: number of active troops
Military Expenditures: amount of financial resources allocated for
                             military purposes; collected in native currency,
                             then expressed in one common currency for
                             purposes of comparison (pounds sterling
                             1816–1913 and US dollars 1914–93).

In addition, the United States Arms Control and Disarmament Agency
(US ACDA) published a yearly database, *World Military Expenditures and*
Arms Transfers (WMEAT), which includes entries for military expenditures and armed forces (military personnel). A statistical comparison of
these two measures with the COW Project military capability variables
has demonstrated that they are virtually indistinguishable.[62] Combining
the COW and WMEAT databases provides entries on military expenditures and military personnel for India and Pakistan from 1947 through
1999. Data on these two variables from *The Military Balance* were used
for 2000 and 2001.

To measure relative military capabilities for India and Pakistan, a Mil.
Cap. score for each nation was developed by first obtaining the sum of the
values on both capability variables for the dyad for every year from 1947
to 2001. A Mil. Cap. score indicating the yearly percentage share possessed by each nation of the total military capability pool of the dyad was
then computed.[63] The "stability" of the power balance over time was
estimated by the use of two sets of measures. A "stable" or static balance
was defined as a consistent threshold differential of 20 percent in the
periods from 1947 (war) to 1965 (war) to 1971 (war) to 1999 (war) to
2001. An "unstable" or dynamic balance involving a power shift was
defined as a change in relative capabilities of 20 percent or more in the
periods 1947–65, 1966–71, 1972–99, and 2000–01.

By these measures the capability balance between India and Pakistan
from 1947 (the year of their first war) to 1965 (the year of their second

---

[62] Correlates of War Project mimeo (August, 1998). In 1999, ACDA was dissolved within
the US Department of State; however, WMEAT data through 1999 have been made
available by the Bureau of Arms Control, US Department of State. United States Arms
Control and Disarmament Agency, *World Military Expenditures and Arms Transfers*
1995–1996 (Washington, DC: US Government Printing Office, 1997); United States
Department of State, *World Military Expenditures and Arms Transfers 1998* (Washington,
DC: http://www.state.gov, 2001).

[63] Compare with Zeev Maoz, "Resolve, Capabilities, and the Outcome of Interstate
Disputes, 1816–1976," *Journal of Conflict Resolution* 27 (1983), 195–229; Charles
S. Gochman, "Capability-Driven Disputes," in Charles S. Gochman and Alan N. Sabrosky
(eds.), *Prisoners of War? Nation-States in the Modern Era* (Lexington: Lexington Books,
1990), 141–59; Daniel S. Geller, "Power Differentials and War in Rival Dyads,"
International Studies Quarterly 37 (1993), 173–93.

war) is unstable. The first two shifts occur in 1950 and 1956. A third shift occurs in 1963 with war following two years later. A fourth shift takes place in 1970, the year immediately preceding the third India–Pakistan war. From 1972 until 1981 the military balance between India and Pakistan is stable. However, between the years 1981 and 2001, shifts in relative capabilities occur in 1982, 1988, 1992, and 1998. The shifts in 1988 and 1992 are followed by military engagements between India and Pakistan involving the limited use of force, and the shift in 1998 preceded by five months of the Kargil War in 1999.

In sum, the conventional military balance for the India/Pakistan dyad exhibits chronic instability with shifts in relative capability generally followed by wars or lower-order military engagements. Instabilities in the conventional military balance cannot be ruled out as a factor contributing to future conflict.

Nuclear capability The net effects of nuclear weapons possession on conflict interaction between India and Pakistan are more difficult to estimate. For two decades, Kenneth Waltz has argued that the gradual spread of nuclear weapons will promote peace and reinforce international stability due to the devastating consequences associated with the use of such weapons in war.[64] Other analysts, such as Scott Sagan, maintain that strategic and operational doctrine in many new nuclear weapon states will be influenced heavily by their military organizations, and that the biases, routines, and parochial interests of these organizations will result in deterrence failures and unauthorized or accidental usage of nuclear weapons.[65]

In May of 1998, India set off five underground nuclear explosions – adding to the one it detonated in 1974. Within a matter of days, Pakistan responded with six of its own underground nuclear tests. Information on the numbers of nuclear weapons and quantities of weapons-grade fissile material in the Indian and Pakistani stockpiles is classified. Open source estimates of the size of the current Indian and Pakistani nuclear weapons inventories vary enormously. In a sophisticated analysis, Jones states that India easily could have accumulated enough plutonium (Pu) from dedicated facilities (the CIRUS and Dhruva reactors) to have constructed about 133 nuclear weapons by the year 2000.[66] The projected annual rate of increase from these facilities is about seven weapons annually.

[64] Waltz, "Nuclear Myths and Political Realities"; and Waltz, "More May Be Better."
[65] Sagan, "The Perils of Proliferation"; Sagan, "More Will Be Worse."
[66] Rodney W. Jones, "Minimum Nuclear Deterrence Postures in South Asia: An Overview," *Final Report to the Defense Threat Reduction Agency* (Reston, VA: Policy Architects International, 2001), 8–13.

By extrapolation, India could have produced 168 nuclear weapons by 2005. Jones also estimates that Pakistan may have constructed about 43 nuclear weapons by 2000, primarily using highly enriched uranium (HEU) from its gas centrifuge enrichment facilities. Including the fissile material (plutonium) from the Khushab heavy water reactor that began operation in 1998, Pakistan's projected annual rate of nuclear weapons production, using both uranium and plutonium, is also about seven weapons per year. By extrapolation, Pakistan could have produced 78 nuclear weapons by 2005. Given probable supplies of weapons-grade materials (year 2000) of 485 kilograms of plutonium for India and 830 kilograms of highly enriched uranium for Pakistan, these nuclear arsenal numbers are roughly within the boundaries of estimated requirements – 4.5 kilograms of Pu and 18 kilograms of HEU – for the production of a 20-kiloton fission weapon at low levels of technology.[67]

Both India and Pakistan have aircraft and ballistic missiles for nuclear weapons delivery capable of reaching virtually all of the opposing nation's territory. India possesses 16 Sukhoi 30K/MK multirole fighters (combat radius of 1,500 kilometers), 63 MiG-29 fighters (combat radius of 630 kilometers), 84 Jaguar S(I) deep-penetration strike aircraft (combat radius with external fuel tanks of 1,408 kilometers), 135 MiG-27 ground attack aircraft (combat radius with external fuel tanks of 540 kilometers), and 40 Mirage 2000H fighters (combat radius with external fuel tanks of 1,852 kilometers) – all of which are nuclear-capable. These aircraft have the range to effectively cover Pakistan.[68] Pakistani nuclear-capable aircraft are limited to 32 F-16 A/B fighters (combat radius with external fuel tanks of 1,371 kilometers), although 122 Mirage fighter-bombers (combat radius of 500 kilometers) could be adapted to nuclear missions.[69]

---

[67] For lower estimates of nuclear weapons stockpiles, see W. P. S. Sidhu, "Asian Nuclear Testing," *Jane's Intelligence Review* (July 1998), 23–27. For calculations on available weapons-grade materials, see Thomas B. Cochran and Christopher E. Paine, "The Amount of Plutonium and Highly Enriched Uranium Needed for Pure Fission Nuclear Weapons" (New York: Natural Resources Defense Council, 1994); Frederic S. Nyland, "Quantitative Aspects of Growth in Nuclear Warhead Stockpiles," R-131, US Department of State, Bureau of Arms Control, Office of Technology and Analysis, 1999; and Jones, "Minimum Nuclear Deterrence Postures in South Asia," 8–13, 45–49.

[68] Under certain conditions, these aircraft could reach most of urban China as well, including the east coast cities of Fuzhou, Nanchang, Hangzhou, Shanghai, Nanjing, Tianjin, and Beijing. However, the combat radii of the Jaguar and Mirage are roughly between 1,400 and 1,800 kilometers. The maximum range for these aircraft between 2,800 and 3,600 kilometers is attainable only if India attempted a suicide mission by sending the aircraft on a one-way bombing run. To reach most of the cities listed above would require maximum-range one-way missions.

[69] See the International Institute for Strategic Studies, *The Military Balance 2001/2002*, 164, 168; and Sidhu, "Asian Nuclear Testing," 23–24, 26.

The only nuclear-capable ballistic missile in the current Indian arsenal is the Prithvi, a single-stage, liquid-propellant, mobile, short-range missile. There are two operational versions of the Prithvi, an SS-150 (single warhead 1,000 kilogram payload) ballistic missile with a range of 150 kilometers and an SS-250 (single warhead 500 kilogram payload) ballistic missile with a 250 kilometer range. A third version (SS-350) with a range of 350 kilometers is in development. The current size of the Prithvi force is estimated to be about 100 missiles. In addition, India has under development (since 1979) an intermediate-range, surface-based, solid-propellant, single warhead ballistic missile called the Agni. On January 9, 2003, India tested the Agni I tactical short-range (700 kilometer) ballistic missile. The missile can carry a 1,000 kilogram nuclear warhead and is designed to be launched from mobile platforms that can operate on railway tracks or roads. The Agni II (or Agni-plus) is a two-stage missile using solid fuel in both stages. It is believed that the warhead section carries a 1,000 kilogram payload. The range of the Agni II is estimated to be between 2,000 and 2,500 kilometers. The Agni III is a three-stage mobile missile using solid fuel with inertial navigation. It is projected to have a range of 3,000 to 3,500 kilometers and to carry a 1,000 kilogram payload.[70] India is working on at least two indigenously produced variants of a submarine-launched missile, the Danush, a naval version of the Prithvi ballistic missile, and the Sagarika, a submarine-launched short-range cruise missile. India is also ready to introduce the short-range Russian Klub cruise missile to its new Kilo-class submarines.

Pakistan has a number of nuclear-capable ballistic missiles in its inventory. For battlefield use, Pakistan has developed the Hatf-1 (500 kilogram payload with a 100 kilometer range) and Hatf-2 (500 kilogram payload with a 300 kilometer range). In the late 1980s, China transferred M-11 (CSS-7/DF-11) short-range, road-mobile, solid-propellant, single warhead (800 kilogram payload) ballistic missiles to Pakistan. The Hatf-2 is believed to be based on the Chinese M-11. In 1997, Pakistan test-fired the Hatf-3, a missile with a 500 kilogram payload and a range of 800 kilometers. The Hatf-3 can reach important strategic installations and military targets in western and central India. On October 4, 2002, Pakistan successfully tested the nuclear-capable Shaheen I – also known

[70] The Agni II and III are most likely to be directed against China. Assuming the upper range of 2,500 kilometers and deployment as far east as Assam, the Agni II could reach six cities in China with populations of over 500,000 – Kunming, Lanzhou, Guiyang, Nanning, Changsha, and Zhengzhou – and six cities – Chengdu, Chongqing, Guangzhou, Wuhan, Xi'an, and Taiyuan – with populations over 1 million. See International Institute for Strategic Studies, *The Military Balance 2003/2004* (London: Oxford University Press, 2003), 131.

as the Hatf-4. This missile is believed to be a derivative of the Chinese M-9 with a range of 750 kilometers and a 500 kilogram payload. Pakistan also has nuclear-capable ballistic missiles with North Korean lineage. In April 1998, Pakistan conducted a test of a ballistic missile that Pakistani authorities called the Ghauri; however, it is believed that the missile is actually a North Korean Nodong-2. The Nodong-2 is an intermediate-range, ground-mobile, liquid-propellant, single warhead (700 kilogram payload) ballistic missile that can cover a distance of roughly 1,500 kilometers. This missile can reach all major Indian cities, nuclear facilities, and strategic installations. Pakistan is also reported to be working on derivatives of the North Korean Taepodong-1 (2,000 kilometer range) and Taepodong-2 (3,000 kilometer range) ballistic missiles, both with 1,000 kilogram payloads. The size of the Pakistani missile force is estimated at approximately 12 Ghauris, a combined number of 18 Hatf-1s and Hatf-2s, and 30 Hatf-3s.[71]

W. P. S. Sidhu describes India's nuclear use doctrine as follows:

India developed a *de facto* doctrine of deterrence ... based on the premise that India would first use its conventional capability to counter military threats from either China or Pakistan. If these countries threatened or launched a nuclear attack, however, India would respond with its own nuclear weapons in a second strike ...[72]

In a speech delivered to the Indian Parliament on December 15, 1998, Prime Minister Atal Bihari Vajpayee declared that his government "will maintain the deployment of nuclear weapons, continue development of ballistic missiles and reserve the right to produce more bomb-grade material." This declaration marked the first public statement that India may have deployed nuclear weapons. The prime minister noted that he was asserting India's sovereign rights in rejecting any externally proposed restraints on weapons deployment, missile development, and production of weapons-grade fissile material, and that such strategic defense decisions are not subjects open to negotiation. A senior Indian official commenting

---

[71] For information on Indian and Pakistani ballistic missiles, see Jane's, "Strategic Weapon Systems" (Surrey, UK: Jane's Information Group, Inc., Nov. 1997); Jane's, "Missiles and Rockets" (Surrey, UK: Jane's Information Group, Inc., May 1998); Sidhu, "Asian Nuclear Testing," 24, 27; Zafar I. Cheema, "Pakistan's Nuclear Use Doctrine and Command and Control," in Peter R. Lavoy, Scott D. Sagan, and James J. Wirtz (eds.), *Planning the Unthinkable: How New Powers Will Use Nuclear, Biological, and Chemical Weapons* (Ithaca: Cornell University Press, 2000), 158–81; *The Military Balance 2000/2001* (London: Oxford University Press, 2000), 158; *The Military Balance 2003/2004* (London: Oxford University Press, 2003), 131.

[72] W. P. S. Sidhu, "India's Nuclear Use Doctrine," in Lavoy, Sagan, and Wirtz (eds.), *Planning the Unthinkable*, 125–57.

ón the remarks by the prime minister stated that "India's short-range Prithvi missile ... [is] a battlefield weapon ready for nuclear duty."[73] Cheema[74] discusses Pakistan's prospective use of nuclear weapons as follows:

Pakistan has not formally announced a nuclear doctrine. In practice, however, it is pursuing a doctrine of minimum deterrence and conventional defense ... Pakistan's rejection of India's suggested bilateral "no-nuclear-first-use" pledge suggests, however, that nuclear weapons are integral to its defense and deterrent doctrine ... Pakistan's political and military leaders might opt for preemption rather than be the victims of an Indian preemptive attack.[75]

Estimated flight times from Indian and Pakistani missile launch sites to Islamabad and New Delhi are about four to five minutes.

As Siverson and Miller note, little systematic quantitative research has been conducted on the effects of nuclear weapons possession on dyadic-level conflict interaction.[76] Geller[77] analyzed the 393 militarized disputes that occurred between 1946 and 1976 utilizing Correlates of War Project data and concluded that conflict escalation probabilities are significantly affected by the distribution of nuclear capabilities: dyads with nuclear capabilities exhibit higher escalation probabilities (0.238) than either directional mixed dyads (0.147/0.018) or non-nuclear dyads (0.032). Hence, the findings pertaining to escalation patterns between nuclear states are consistent with the "competitive risk-taking" or brinkmanship theses of Kahn, Schelling, Osgood and Tucker, and Snyder and Diesing.[78] They indicate an actual raising of the provocation threshold for war and an expansion in the use of coercive tactics – threats, military displays, and force short of war – for achieving political objectives in disputes between nuclear powers.

---

[73] Kenneth J. Cooper, "India Rejects Some Weapons Restraints," *The Washington Post*, Dec. 16 (1998), A37.

[74] Cheema, "Pakistan's Nuclear Use Doctrine and Command and Control," 175–78.

[75] The views presented by Sidhu, "India's Nuclear Use Doctrine," and Cheema, "Pakistan's Nuclear Use Doctrine and Command and Control," on Indian and Pakistani nuclear strategies, doctrines, and postures are consistent with the more detailed analysis provided by Jones, "Minimum Nuclear Deterrence Postures in South Asia," 24–35.

[76] Randolph M. Siverson and Ross A. Miller, "The Escalation of Disputes to War," *International Interactions* 19 (1993), 77–97.

[77] Daniel S. Geller, "Nuclear Weapons, Deterrence, and Crisis Escalation," *Journal of Conflict Resolution* 34 (1990), 291–310.

[78] Herman Kahn, *Thinking About the Unthinkable* (New York: Avon Books, 1962); Herman Kahn, *On Escalation: Metaphors and Scenarios* (New York: Praeger, 1965); Thomas C. Schelling, *The Strategy of Conflict* (Oxford: Oxford University Press, 1960); Robert E. Osgood and Robert W. Tucker, *Force, Order, and Justice* (Baltimore: Johns Hopkins University Press, 1967); and Snyder and Diesing, *Conflict Among Nations*.

In fact, both the May–July 1999 military engagement between India and Pakistan over Kashmir and the crisis of December 2001–June 2002 after the terrorist attack on the Indian Parliament mirrored the conflict escalation pattern for nuclear-armed states. Each side initiated troop mobilizations and general military alerts, coupled with the evacuation of civilians from border-area villages. However, the outcome of future confrontations for India and Pakistan may not adhere to the pattern established by other nuclear dyads. Elements are present in this dyad that were largely absent between other nuclear-armed antagonists and that make the escalation to war more probable. Among those factors are the presence of a contiguous border between India and Pakistan, a history of multiple wars, and an ongoing territorial dispute. These factors, among others,[79] increase the likelihood that an Indo-Pakistani dispute will turn violent and that the violence will escalate to war irrespective of the presence of nuclear weapons.

There exist a number of speculative but plausible avenues along which a nuclear war between India and Pakistan might begin. For example, one scenario involves escalation, beginning with the use of conventional military forces in a struggle over Kashmir. Such a military engagement could escalate to the nuclear level if one side found itself losing the war on the conventional battlefield. The introduction of battlefield nuclear weapons could be a tactic for manipulating risk or be pursued as a last, desperate means of avoiding defeat. A second possibility involves crisis-generated preemption. In the case of a crisis, one side, fearing a first strike by the other during the confrontation, launches a preemptive attack on its opponent's nuclear forces thereby hoping to minimize damage to itself. A third scenario involves preventive war. A "bolt out of the blue" attack could be initiated by either side not as the result of some provocation or crisis, but rather as the outcome of an expectation that war will inevitably occur at some future date, and, given a calculation that war now – under current circumstances – is preferable to war later under circumstances which may be less favorable, a decision is made to strike against the opponent's ungenerated forces.

It should be noted that all of these war scenarios (escalation, crisis-generated preemptive attack, and preventive war) were considered plausible, to varying degrees, by the US and USSR during the Cold War. Moreover, neither India nor Pakistan has yet instituted secure command and control systems for their nuclear forces. Under such conditions, the possibility of the accidental or unauthorized use of nuclear weapons cannot be ruled out.

---

[79] See Leng, *Bargaining and Learning in Recurring Crises.*

Of course, these are merely possibilities. Whether the joint nuclear capability possessed by India and Pakistan serves to deter conventional and nuclear conflicts between these states – or only increases the amount of destruction in a future war to unprecedented levels – remains to be determined.

Enduring rivalry Current empirical work suggests the importance of a subset population of dyads (within the set of all nation-dyads) defined by long-term conflicts. These conflict-prone dyads, or "enduring rivals," account for a disproportionately large amount of the violence which occurs in the interstate system. It has been noted that the presence of an enduring rivalry increases substantially the probability of war within a dyad.[80] Analyses by Goertz and Diehl estimate that long-term rivals are responsible for almost half of the wars, violent territorial changes, and militarized disputes that have occurred in the last two centuries.[81] Accordingly, a growing number of studies have focused on these dispute-prone dyads in an effort to gain a better understanding of the factors associated with a large proportion of interstate conflict (e.g., how arms races, capability balances, and deterrence conditions operate within the rivalry context). For instance, Gochman has argued that shifts in relative capability might be expected to have a particularly strong effect on the interaction of rival states with a history of violent conflict.[82]

However, Goertz[83] has argued that enduring rivalries not only provide a context for the analysis of the dynamics of capability balances[84] and deterrence conditions[85] on war but also operate as an independent contributing factor toward war. In reaching this conclusion, Goertz examines the distributions and probabilities of conflict for rival and non-rival

---

[80] Geller and Singer, *Nations at War*, 150–54.

[81] Gary Goertz and Paul F. Diehl, "The Empirical Importance of Enduring Rivalries," *International Interactions* 18 (1992), 151–63; Gary Goertz and Paul F. Diehl, "Enduring Rivalries: Theoretical Constructs and Empirical Patterns," *International Studies Quarterly* 37 (1993), 145–71.

[82] Gochman, "Capability-Driven Disputes," 147.

[83] Gary Goertz, *Contexts of International Politics* (Cambridge: Cambridge University Press, 1994).

[84] For example, see Gochman, "Capability-Driven Disputes"; Geller, "Power Differentials and War in Rival Dyads"; Daniel S. Geller, "Relative Power, Rationality, and International Conflict," in Jacek Kugler and Douglas Lemke (eds.), *Parity and War: Evaluations and Extensions of The War Ledger* (Ann Arbor: University of Michigan Press, 1996), 127–43; Geller, "The Stability of the Military Balance and War among Great Power Rivals" in Paul F. Diehl (ed.), *The Dynamics of Enduring Rivalries* (Urbana: University of Illinois Press, 1998), 165–90; Wayman, "Power Shifts and the Onset of War."

[85] For example, see Paul K. Huth and Bruce Russett, "General Deterrence Between Enduring Rivals: Testing Three Competing Models," *American Political Science Review* 87 (1993), 61–73.

dyads: his findings indicate that between 1816 and 1976 approximately 40 percent of all non-war militarized disputes occur within enduring rivalries, 47 percent of all wars during the same period take place within enduring rivalries, and that the probability of a dispute escalating to war is eight times higher for an enduring rivalry than for a non-rival dyad.[86]

Employing standard time/density dispute criteria with the Militarized Interstate Dispute database, it is calculated that the India/Pakistan dyad constitutes an enduring rivalry from 1947 through 2001 (the last year in the data set). Over the period of fifty-five years between 1947 and 2001, India and Pakistan engage in forty-three militarized disputes. Thirty-four of these disputes involve the use of force by at least one state. Thirty of these disputes involve the use of force by both states. Four of these disputes are classified as wars.[87] Given the continuing rivalry between India and Pakistan, the likelihood of future war for this dyad must be considered high.

Conclusion

On the basis of general patterns in enduring rivalries, the prospects for peace between India and Pakistan are not encouraging. The origins of this rivalry, its intensity of violence, the failure of both mediation and conflict management, and its temporal persistence suggest that the relationship between India and Pakistan is not likely to change absent a "political shock" of substantial magnitude.

Moreover, the conflict between India and Pakistan is shaped by the complex conjunction of a number of structural factors that increase the probability of violent interaction. The ongoing territorial dispute over Kashmir and the opportunity to exercise military force are directly related to the contiguous border; the absence of paired democratic regimes means that non-violent norms for conflict resolution as well as shared institutional constraints on war decisions are lacking; the low levels of economic development for both states mean that the use of force may

---

[86] Goertz, *Contexts of International Politics*, 208–12.

[87] The original coding for the South Asia component of the MID 3 database was done by the author and his research group during 2000–03. The Kargil conflict of 1999 met all of the COW Project criteria for classification as a war – including the battle death threshold of 1,000 for regular military personnel. According to the tallies maintained by the research group, Indian battle deaths totaled 410 with Pakistani battle deaths numbering 698. This total of 1,108 collected by the MID 3 South Asia group is almost identical to the total of 1,174 battle deaths (474 for India and 700 for Pakistan) released by the Indian government (*Report of the Kargil Review Committee*, New Delhi: Government of India, March 2000. Executive Summary, 10, 75). The other Indo-Pakistani wars were fought in 1947, 1965, and 1971.

appear to be a foreign policy instrument with minimal economic consequences; shifts in the conventional military balance may create incentives to exploit a transient advantage, and the addition of nuclear capabilities without secure second-strike systems may create pressures for preemption in a crisis; lastly, the classification of the dyad as a current enduring rivalry with a history of chronic military interaction places the probability of future war for these states well beyond the mean probability for all nation-pairs. Of course, the onset of war ultimately turns on decisions. Structural forces influence and shape those decisions, but do not determine them entirely. In this sense, the conditions conducive to war may be present, but due to the element of human choice, the last step remains indeterminate. Unfortunately, the conjunction of structural forces in the India/Pakistan dyad is heavily weighted toward war, and the presence of nuclear weapons may well have little effect in deterring future violence that now holds the potential for catastrophic destruction.

5   Realpolitik and learning in the India–Pakistan rivalry

Russell J. Leng

Introduction

The India–Pakistan rivalry has been punctuated by recurring militarized crises, four of which have resulted in wars.[1] The enormous costs of this dysfunctional relationship have been obvious since the blood-letting that accompanied partition; today there is the added risk of a nuclear catastrophe. Why cannot the two sides learn to manage their disputes without the risk of war? Will they ever be able to transform their relationship from a competition to achieve relative gains to obtain the absolute gains of peace? Learning, whether functional or dysfunctional, lies at the heart of the answers to these questions. This chapter examines what the parties have learned and have failed to learn over the course of the rivalry. Then it concludes with some thoughts on the requirements for building a more peaceful relationship.

The evidence indicates that, insofar as the peaceful management of disputes and progress toward the termination of the rivalry are concerned, the lessons drawn by both sides have been largely dysfunctional. Experiential learning that has occurred during the course of the rivalry most often has reinforced behavior that has encouraged the recurrence of crises and wars. Vicarious learning from the Soviet–American rivalry regarding the avoidance of nuclear war may prove to be an exception. At first glance, the Kargil crisis and war of 1999, and the border crisis of 2001–02, suggest otherwise. That the crises occurred at all, as well as the bellicose rhetoric that accompanied them, raises serious doubts about the prospects for peace and stability on the subcontinent. But the Kargil hostilities were kept limited, and the border tensions of 2001–02 were defused without hostilities. Two years later, the two sides had entered into bilateral talks on a wide range of issues, including nuclear

---

[1] Militarized interstate crises are disputes between members of the interstate system in which both parties threaten, display, or use military force. See Russell J. Leng and J. David Singer, "Militarized Interstate Crises: The BCOW Typology and its Applications," *International Studies Quarterly* 32 (1988), 155–73.

confidence-building measures and Kashmir. Is it possible that, like the subjects in repeated plays of Prisoner's Dilemma Games, the parties finally have begun, albeit with the help of third party pressure and the threat of nuclear war, to learn the benefits of cooperation? Or are we observing simply another of the diplomatic interludes that have been interspersed among the recurring crises and wars?

Dysfunctional learning is neither a necessary nor a sufficient cause of recurring crises. So, before turning to a discussion of learning, it is important to consider some of the other variables that have been associated with the persistence of the rivalry, beginning with the central issue of Kashmir. Unresolved competing territorial claims lie at the heart of most enduring rivalries, and the India–Pakistan rivalry is no exception. Kashmir is the essential bone of contention between India and Pakistan.

Both states consider control of Kashmir to be vital to their security. Kashmir's high mountain passes dominate both states, and its rivers irrigate their farmlands. But Kashmir's importance extends beyond strategic considerations. Control of Kashmir has become symbolic of the *raison d'être* of both states. Pakistan was created to unite Muslim majority regions in an independent state that would not be dominated by India's Hindu majority. Three-quarters of Kashmir's population are Muslims. Conversely, for India retention of Kashmir is considered essential to its conception of a pluralist secular state.[2]

When United Nations mediation finally achieved a ceasefire in the First Kashmir War, the armistice called for a plebiscite to determine Kashmir's future. The plebiscite has never been held, and, since 1949, India has been engaged in solidifying its control over two-thirds of Kashmir, while Pakistan has been attempting to reverse the process. More specific, or immediate, precipitants to crises have occurred when Pakistan's leadership has perceived a strategic opportunity to shift the status quo in Pakistan's favor; when the Indian leadership has perceived an immediate threat to the status quo; and when the Pakistani leadership has perceived that India is succeeding in stabilizing the status quo in its favor.

Pakistan found strategic opportunities in the Muslim unrest in Kashmir following partition in 1947; in the combination of improved military capabilities and favorable fighting terrain in the Rann of Kutch in 1965; in more unrest in Kashmir in 1965; in a Sikh insurgency in Punjab that led to the Brasstacks crisis in 1987; in the Kashmiri independence movement and insurgency, which led to a crisis in 1990; and in a new nuclear deterrent capability that encouraged its military leaders to seize

---

[2] For a more detailed examination of Kashmir's central role in the rivalry, see Saideman in this volume.

a strategic opportunity in the Kargil in 1999. In each of these instances, India responded more or less cautiously to Pakistani challenges, but all of India's responses were essentially military. None of the challenges led to any significant changes in the goals of either side.

According to proponents of prospect theory,[3] individuals accept greater risks to avoid losses than to achieve gains. Most of the Pakistani opportunities noted above were coupled with perceived risks of loss in the ongoing struggle over Kashmir's future. In 1947, Pakistan faced the risk that the Hindu maharaja of Kashmir would accede to India; the Rann of Kutch and 1965 Kashmir crises came after an Indian declaration of Presidential Rule over Indian-occupied Kashmir; the Kargil incursion came at a time when India appeared to be gaining control over the insurgency movement in Kashmir. India's military actions have been responses either to perceived threats to its control of Kashmir, as in the 1947, 1965, 1990, and 1999 crises, or to threats to India proper. East Pakistan's war of secession in 1971, which led to the Bangladesh crisis and war, offered India a strategic opportunity to dismember Pakistan. But India's decision to enter the conflict militarily was also encouraged by threats to its own economic and social stability, which were generated by the more than 8 million refugees who fled into India to escape the civil war. India's Brasstacks exercise in 1987 was in response to Pakistan's assistance to insurgents in Punjab, and its show of force in the 2001–02 border crisis followed an attack on the Indian Parliament by Pakistani terrorists.

Among the factors that have influenced how the two rivals have responded to opportunities and threats of losses are: changes in capabilities, including the acquisition of nuclear capabilities; changes in government; domestic pressures; relationships with other states, most notably the United States, Soviet Union, and China; and changes in the international environment. These factors are discussed at length in other chapters, so I will not rehearse them here.[4] No less important, however, are each party's perceptions of the other, particularly perceptions of the other's intentions and capabilities, and of the most effective means of dealing with the other. Learning plays an important role in forming these perceptions.

---

[3] Daniel Kahneman and Amos Tversky, "Prospect Theory: An Analysis of Decision under Risk," *Econometrica* 47 (1982), 263–91.

[4] On the superpowers and the Indian–Pakistani rivalry, see Russell J. Leng, *Bargaining and Learning in Recurring Crises: The Soviet–American, Egyptian–Israeli, and Indo-Pakistani Rivalries* (Ann Arbor: University of Michigan Press, 2000), ch. 5.

Learning in rivalries

Learning as it is used in this chapter refers to changes in beliefs derived from observation and interpretation of experience, either through direct experience, or vicariously through observation of the behavior of others. The beliefs of interest are those relating to the attributes of the rival state, particularly its intentions and capabilities, and what constitute the most effectives means of interacting with that state. What is learned may or may not be accurate or effective. The lessons that policymakers draw from experience may be dysfunctional insofar as the management of the rivalry, or the fulfillment of state interests is concerned.

Levy makes a useful distinction between two types of learning: causal and diagnostic.[5] Causal learning refers to changes in beliefs regarding the consequences of actions. Diagnostic learning refers to changes in one's beliefs regarding attributes of the other party, such as its capabilities, intentions, and resolve. Most of the diagnostic learning that has occurred in the Indo-Pakistani rivalry has been related to changing views of comparative military capabilities, particularly following India's decisive defeat of Pakistan in the Bangladesh War in 1971, and more recently with the development of nuclear capabilities by both states. Each party's beliefs regarding the hostile intentions of the other have been reinforced over the course of the rivalry.

There has been causal learning. Most of it, driven by realpolitik beliefs, has been dysfunctional, as both sides have associated the prospects for success with the demonstration of resolve, as opposed to a search for common ground. Pakistan's military success in the Rann of Kutch hostilities in 1965 encouraged its Kashmir incursion a few months later. The prevailing view in India that its government had not acted with sufficient resolve in the Rann hostilities prompted a military response to the Kashmir incursion that led to a general war. India's decisive victory in the Bangladesh War in 1971 provided a realpolitik lesson for both sides regarding the asymmetry in military capabilities. Pakistan's response was not to adjust its goals, but to revise its military and paramilitary strategies. For its part, a self-confident India became even more intransigent on the defining issue of Kashmir. Global geopolitical changes in the late 1980s and 1990s, as well as the development of nuclear capabilities by both sides, have been followed by new militarized crises and more inflammatory rhetoric.

---

[5] Jack S. Levy, "Learning and Foreign Policy: Sweeping a Conceptual Minefield," *International Organization* 48 (1994), 279–312.

A second useful distinction can be made between levels of learning, specifically between learning about *means*, that is, strategy and tactics, as opposed to learning that leads to a shift in *goals*.[6] The distinction is germane to consideration of the prospects of terminating an enduring rivalry, which ultimately requires a shift in goals. Goals, however, are more resistant to change than beliefs about means,[7] and the Indo-Pakistani rivalry has been no exception to the rule. Changes in the political environment, including changed perceptions of comparative military capabilities, have resulted in shifts in strategies and tactics, but the aspirations of the two parties with regard to the central issue of the rivalry have not changed. Both parties remain determined to control Kashmir.

Belief systems, realpolitik, and learning

There is an inevitable difference between the environment in its totality and that part to which our attention is drawn. How we frame a given situation is dependent on our beliefs regarding what is, and what is not significant. To maintain cognitive balance, we give greater weight to information that is consistent with our existing beliefs, and less weight to information that is contrary to our expectations. The political belief systems of state policymakers frame their understanding of foreign policy problems so that policymakers are predisposed to give greater salience to certain actions over others, and to evaluate them in particular ways. The perceived saliency of events influences whether they will be remembered. How they are evaluated influences what lessons will be drawn from them.[8]

The belief systems of policymakers in rival states influence what changes in the political environment, events, or attributes of their political rivals are perceived as most salient, how they are evaluated, the intensity with which they are remembered, and how they affect future behavior with the rival state. Belief systems do not determine what lessons policymakers draw from particular events and situations, but they do predispose them to draw certain lessons rather than others.

---

[6] George W. Breslauer and Phillip E. Tetlock (eds.), *Learning in US and Soviet Foreign Policy* (Boulder, CO: Westview Press, 1991), 8–10.
[7] Phillip E. Tetlock, "In Search of an Elusive Concept," in Breslauer and Tetlock (eds.), *Learning*, 27–31.
[8] On observation and learning, see Albert Bandura, *Social Learning Theory* (New York: General Learning Press, 1971); Bandura, *Aggression: A Social Learning Analysis* (Englewood Cliffs, NJ: Prentice-Hall, 1973).

When it comes to issues affecting national security, the belief systems of state policymakers are formed within an international political culture of practical realism, that is, a shared informal understanding of interstate relations as driven by considerations of power and interest.[9] The realist culture encourages foreign policies based on realpolitik, that is, a policy directed solely at serving state interests in an environment that is viewed as essentially competitive. At their best, realpolitik relationships are based on reciprocal cooperation that serves the interests of both sides. At their worst, they are based on deterrence and war, that is, the demonstration of power and the willingness to use it. Enduring rivalries encourage the latter approach.

The lessons that policymakers in rival states draw from past crises are important to foreign policy decisionmaking because of a tendency on the part of policymakers to evaluate current situations by drawing analogies to similar circumstances in the past. Which analogies are selected depends on their ease of recall, which favors particularly memorable, or dramatic situations observed by the recaller.[10] These analogies influence causal inferences regarding the rival state's motivation, intentions, and reactions to different types of influence attempts.[11] In the rivalry between India and Pakistan, the most memorable events have been militarized crises and wars, and the leaders of the two states have drawn realpolitik lessons from those events.

Empirical research on the behavior of states in recurring crises offers support for what I have called "realpolitik experiential learning (REL)."[12] The REL hypothesis posits that policymakers draw realpolitik lessons from preceding militarized crises to guide their behavior in current crises. They also are likely to draw a causal link between the outcome of a crisis and the influence strategy of their own state. Consequently, policymakers are likely to repeat influence strategies associated with success and to change strategies that were associated with failure. When policymakers do change their influence strategies, they are likely to move to more coercive tactics. That is because realpolitik beliefs encourage policy-makers to assume that a lack of success was a function of a failure to

[9] Russell J. Leng, *Interstate Crisis Behavior, 1816–1980: Realism versus Reciprocity* (Cambridge: Cambridge University Press, 1993), 1–10; Leng, *Bargaining and Learning*, 8–9.

[10] Daniel Kahneman and Amos Tversky, "Availability: A Heuristic for Judging Frequency and Probability," in Daniel Kahneman, P. Slovik, and A. Tversky (eds.), *Judgment under Uncertainty: Heuristics and Biases* (Cambridge: Cambridge University Press, 1982).

[11] Leng, *Bargaining and Learning*.

[12] *Ibid.*, 296–300; Russell J. Leng, "When Will They Ever Learn? Coercive Bargaining in Recurrent Crises," *Journal of Conflict Resolution* 27 (1983), 379–419.

adequately demonstrate resolve. Leaders of previously successful states similarly are likely to assume that it was their own demonstration of power and the willingness to use it that allowed them to prevail. When states that were unsuccessful in one crisis switch to a more coercive strategy in the next crisis, the other party is likely to respond in kind. Thus each successive crisis is likely to be more contentious and more likely to end in war. Among the cases for which there is empirical evidence to support the REL proposition are the four crises between India and Pakistan between 1947 and 1971.[13]

Psychological influences on learning

Each successive crisis or war leaves behind a residue of antipathy and distrust, which affects diagnostic learning.[14] Over the course of the Indo-Pakistani rivalry, the recurring crises and wars have reinforced each side's inclination to assume the worst possible motives on the part of the other. The process also encourages attributional distortion. That is, hostile actions by the other party are likely to be attributed to dispositional causes, whereas cooperative actions are attributed to circumstantial constraints.[15] For example, the Indian victory in the Bangladesh War, which led to the loss of East Pakistan, encouraged the view among some Pakistani leaders that India's leadership would use any future escalation of hostilities over Kashmir as a pretext for a war to reunite the subcontinent under Hindu control, a view that has been reinforced by inflammatory rhetoric from India's Hindu nationalist party, the BJP.[16] For their part, Indian leaders are inclined to see the hand of the Pakistani government in every insurgency or terrorist event in Kashmir or India proper.

Learning in the India–Pakistan rivalry

The following discussion of learning in the India–Pakistan rivalry begins with an overview of types and levels of learning by each of the rival states over the course of the rivalry. Then it turns to a consideration of how

---

[13] Leng, *Bargaining and Learning*, ch. 5.

[14] See Leng, *Interstate Crisis Behavior*, 10–18, for a fuller discussion.

[15] Thomas Hayden and Walter Mischel, "Maintaining Trait Consistency in the Resolution of Behavioral Inconsistency: The Wolf in Sheep's Clothing," *Journal of Personality* 44 (1976), 109–32.

[16] Altaf Gauhar, *Ayub Khan: Pakistan's First Military Ruler* (Karachi: Oxford University Press, 1996), 211; K. S. Hasan, *The Kashmir Question* (Karachi: Pakistan Institute of International Affairs, 1966), 440, 452; Richard Sisson and Leo E. Rose, *War and Secession: Pakistan, India, and the Creation of Bangladesh* (Berkeley: University of California Press, 1990), 44.

lessons drawn from the past combined with recent environmental changes affected the behavior of the two parties in the 1999 Kargil crisis and war, and in the border crisis of 2001–02.

India

Diagnostic learning The recurring crises, wars, and continuing Pakistani efforts to destabilize the situation in Indian-controlled Kashmir have reinforced Indian distrust of Pakistani intentions. The distrust has led India, on occasion, to overestimate the hostile intentions of Pakistan. The Pakistani incursion across the Line of Control (LoC) between the Indian and Pakistani sectors of Kashmir in 1965, for example, was designed to add to unrest in Kashmir in an attempt to "defreeze the Kashmir problem, weaken Indian resolve and bring her to the conference table," but it was interpreted by Indian leaders as the beginning of an attempt to seize the Indian-controlled sector of Kashmir by force.[17] Over the past decade and a half, the participation of Pakistani mujahidin "volunteers" in the Kashmiri insurgency, plus the Kargil incursion, and terrorist attacks in India, have only reinforced India's distrust of Pakistan.

With regard to the capabilities of the two sides, the outcome of the 1971 Bangladesh War unequivocally demonstrated India's military superiority. Pakistan's inferior bargaining power was further underscored by the unwillingness of the United States or China to intervene militarily or diplomatically on Pakistan's behalf in 1971 or in 1999. In sum, the evolution of the rivalry has reinforced the Indian leadership's aversion to the risks attendant on seeking a peaceful settlement and reinforced its confidence in being able to attain its goals in Kashmir through unilateral means.

Levels of learning India's goals have not changed over the course of the rivalry. Its behavior has been consistent with the REL hypothesis: states that find themselves in recurring crises with the same adversary are likely to continue strategies that have been successful in previous crises, and to turn to more coercive strategies when they have been unsuccessful.[18] India's cautious, and relatively unsuccessful, response to Pakistani incursions in the Rann of Kutch conflict was followed by an aggressive military response to the Pakistani infiltration into Kashmir a few months later. After being criticized at home for its slow and uncertain response to the Kargil incursion in 1999, India swiftly moved troops to the

---

[17] Gauhar, *Ayub Khan*, 216.
[18] Leng, *Bargaining and Learning*; Leng, "When Will They Ever Learn?"

Indo-Pakistani border in December of 2001 following the terrorist attack on the Indian Parliament. In the latter instance, the Indian leadership was influenced also by lessons that it drew from the American response to the September 11, 2001 attacks on the United States.

Following the attacks on the World Trade Center and the Pentagon, the United States held the government of Afghanistan responsible for harboring the al-Queda terrorists. Then it invaded Afghanistan when the Taliban failed to apprehend the terrorists and surrender them to the United States. The forceful American action resonated with an Indian government that suspects Pakistan of turning its back on, if not actively encouraging, the movement of terrorists from and through Pakistan to attack Indian targets, including the attack on the Indian Parliament that December. Whether the analogical link to the United States' 9/11 response was based on vicarious learning *per se*, or it was drawn because the American action provided a handy justification for India's response to the December attack on the Parliament, is an open question. In either case, it demonstrates how existing beliefs create a disposition to draw analogies from prominent analogous situations that are consistent with those beliefs.

The lessons that Indian leaders have drawn from the rivalry have reinforced their belief that India's interests are best served by responding in a resolute and uncompromising manner to what they view as an implacably hostile rival. India's decisive conventional military superiority, the coopting of the insurgency movement in Kashmir by Islamic militants from Pakistan, and an international environment conducive to proactive responses to terrorists and the states that provide them with safe havens, add to the rationale for India's realpolitik approach.

Pakistan

Diagnostic learning The rivalry has reinforced Pakistani perceptions that not only is India intent on attaining permanent accession to the two-thirds of Kashmir that India controls, but that India remains a threat to seize the Pakistani-occupied third of Kashmir (*Azad Kashmir*) as well. A number of Pakistani leaders, especially within the military, believe also that India's leaders harbor a long-term goal of reuniting the subcontinent under Hindu control. To them, there has been nothing in India's behavior since 1949 to cast doubt on the first assumption. India has refused adamantly to negotiate any reduction in its control over Indian-occupied Kashmir, while it has continued political and military efforts to solidify its control. Pakistani fears of more expansionist Indian goals were reinforced by India's intervention in the Bangladesh civil war in 1971, and, more recently, by bellicose rhetoric from the BJP party. As for its relative capabilities *vis-à-vis* India, attributional distortion has contributed to a Pakistani belief in its inherent military superiority. For example, Pakistani President Ayub Khan attributed Indian caution in the Rann of Kutch conflict to Hindu passivity, rather than the logistical and operational advantages afforded to Pakistan in the Sind-Kutch theatre.[19] Pakistani leaders have attributed India's measured responses in more recent crises to a combination of Indian cautiousness and Pakistan's nuclear deterrent capability.

Levels of learning Even from a realpolitik perspective, the growing gap in military superiority, and in bargaining power more generally, should cause the Pakistani leadership to reassess its goals. But as the rivalry has evolved and intensified, the reputational importance of the Kashmir issue has grown. Therefore, learning by Pakistan's leaders has been at the level of means. Moreover, that learning has been distorted by the psychological effects of the enduring rivalry, domestic pressures, and the few options available to a revisionist state facing a stronger status quo power. Over the course of the rivalry, India's unwillingness to negotiate or to accept mediation of the Kashmir issue has left Pakistan with four options: (1) reduce its aspirations by accepting the status quo in Kashmir; (2) force a change in the situation through unilateral military action; (3) alter the situation sufficiently to persuade India to view the status quo as unsatisfactory; or (4) create a regional crisis that will lead to the diplomatic intervention of concerned major powers. Pakistani leaders have ruled out simply accepting the status quo, and, since the Second Kashmir War, they have recognized that the second option is not feasible. Instead they have followed a two-pronged strategy that combines the third and fourth options. Since the start of the rivalry Pakistan has encouraged and supported opposition movements in Kashmir and, on occasion, in India. The objective has been to promote sufficient instability, either to cause India to reconsider its unyielding stand on Kashmir, or to induce powerful third parties, who would otherwise remain aloof, to intervene diplomatically.

Action by one party to create a shared risk of war to convince the other to negotiate is commonly referred to as "brinkmanship." The Cuban missile crisis, for example, is an archetypical brinkmanship crisis. There was an element of brinkmanship in the Rann of Kutch crisis in 1965, with Pakistan's immediate calls for negotiation following incursions across the

---

[19] Gauhar, *Ayub Khan*, 203.

border.[20] But it was third-party mediation and, ultimately, arbitration that Pakistan sought and obtained in the spring of 1965, and the Rann of Kutch approach became the model for the Pakistani behavior that led to the Second Kashmir War. In what could be called a "demonstration crisis," the intent is to engage the attention and involvement of otherwise disinterested powerful third parties, in the hope that they will intervene diplomatically to force a mediated reconsideration of the status quo. Pakistan was moderately successful in employing this approach in the Rann crisis. The issue of the Sind-Kutch border was reopened through the diplomatic intervention of Great Britain and settled by a panel of arbitration, albeit with little tangible gain to Pakistan.

When Ayub Khan's government launched Operation Gibraltar, by sending disguised Pakistani irregulars into Indian-controlled Kashmir a few months later, he had three objectives in mind: to add to the instability in Kashmir that had been created by India's invocation of martial law and the arrest of independence advocate Sheikh Abdullah; to generate a guerrilla conflict within Kashmir that would encourage India to reconsider negotiations over the future of Kashmir; and to create sufficient regional instability to obtain the diplomatic intervention of powerful third parties.[21] If the conflict escalated to direct hostilities, the Pakistani leadership was convinced that Pakistan would have a military advantage fighting in Kashmir with new weapons supplied by the United States, and that the Indian caution demonstrated in the Rann of Kutch conflict would keep the hostilities limited to India. When India responded to the incursion by sending its regular forces into *Azad Kashmir* and threatening Pakistani control of the headwaters of the Indus River, as well as all of *Azad Kashmir*, the hostilities escalated to full-scale war.

The war that ensued achieved Pakistan's last objective in the form of Soviet mediation, but the Tashkent Agreement brought no change in the Kashmir issue. Ayub was willing to accept the cost of a short, limited war to break the diplomatic deadlock over Kashmir in 1965, but that was no longer an option after Pakistan's decisive defeat at the hands of India in 1971.[22] With India's obvious military advantage,

---

[20] Leng, *Bargaining and Learning*, 217–20.   [21] *Ibid.*, 235; Gauhar, *Ayub Khan*, 216.

[22] That a crisis might lead to war is not, in itself, sufficient grounds to avoid a demonstration crisis. Egypt's Nasser was encouraged to accept the risk of war with Israel in 1967, despite his awareness of Egypt's military inferiority, because of his memory of the superpower intervention to save Egypt in the 1956 Sinai War. Nasser's successor, Anwar Sadat, initiated a war with Israel in 1973 in order to obtain superpower diplomatic intervention to break the impasse over Israel's occupation of the Sinai. See Leng, *Bargaining and Learning*, ch. 4. The Argentine invasion of the Falkland Islands in 1982 was undertaken in the expectation that the United States would block a British military response and reopen the stalled negotiations over the future of the islands. (See Richard Ned Lebow,

brinkmanship was no longer an option for Pakistan either. Nor could Pakistan expect that a demonstration crisis would lead to major power intervention to save it from a crushing military defeat. Following the Bangladesh War, there were no militarized crises or wars until the Brasstacks crisis of 1987.

Shortly after the 1971 war, Pakistan's President Zulfikar Ali Bhutto launched a nuclear weapons program in an attempt to redress the military imbalance.[23] During the Brasstacks crisis of 1987, a Pakistani general stated for the first time that Pakistan now had the nuclear capability to defend itself.[24] By the end of the 1980s a number of changes in the political environment also encouraged a more proactive strategy by Pakistan: American military aid to Pakistan had been re-established following the Soviet invasion of Afghanistan in 1979; increasing religious fundamentalism in both countries, but especially in Pakistan, intensified the religious component of the Kashmir dispute; and the independence movement in Indian-controlled Kashmir had escalated to an insurgency, which opened the door to the infiltration of armed Islamic militants from Pakistan and Afghanistan.

Kargil crisis and war, 1998–1999

The Kargil crisis had its antecedents in an ongoing dispute over the location of the LoC as it passes through the Siachen glacier, one of the highest and most inhospitable heights in the Himalayas. Kargil is situated on Highway 1-A from Srinagar to Leh, which is the only land route to supply Indian troops on the glacier. Controlling the high ground over Kargil would allow Pakistan to cut off the Indian supply route. Sporadic low-level hostilities began in 1984 and continued into the late 1990s. Beginning in the fall of 1998, Pakistani light infantry troops, accompanied by mujahidin volunteers, infiltrated undetected across the LoC to establish positions on the Himalayan peaks, which Indian troops regularly abandoned during the harsh winter months. When returning Indian troops discovered the Pakistani emplacements the following May,

---

"Miscalculation in the South Atlantic: The Origins of the Falklands War," in Robert Jervis, Janice Stein, and Richard Ned Lebow (eds.), *Psychology and Deterrence* (Baltimore: Johns Hopkins University Press, 1989), 108–15. For the diplomatic calculations of weaker challengers, see T. V. Paul, *Asymmetric Conflict: War Initiation by Weaker Powers* (Cambridge: Cambridge University Press, 1994).

[23] See Sumit Ganguly, *Conflict Unending: India–Pakistan Tensions since 1947* (New York: Columbia University Press, 2001), 105.

[24] *Ibid.*, 87.

the ensuing fighting led to "a short, sharp, war."[25] India's attempts to dislodge the Pakistani troops led to high casualties and little success until Indian air strikes, coupled with strong American diplomatic pressure, led to a Pakistani withdrawal.

The Kargil crisis surprised Indian leaders because it occurred just a few months after a summit meeting between Sharif and Vajpayee at Lahore had led to a relaxation in tension. Why the Pakistani government undertook such a provocative action during a period of relative détente has been the subject of much speculation. The most likely explanation is a combination of domestic pressures, fragmented decisionmaking, recent changes in the military leadership, strategic opportunity, and, not least, the prospect of loss on the central issue of Kashmir.[26] During the late 1990s Islamic militants were becoming an increasingly potent force in Pakistani domestic politics at the same time that India was gaining the upper hand in quelling the Kashmiri independence movement. As Tremblay and Schofield note in Chapter 10, Sharif's decision was influenced both by pressures from fundamentalist parties demanding action, and from military leaders who were determined to reverse Indian gains in Siachen. But two other factors also influenced Pakistan's Kargil challenge, as well as the Indian response: the addition of a nuclear component to the rivalry, and the "spirit of Lahore" itself.

The nuclear factor The immediate reaction to the 1998 nuclear tests by military officers on both sides was that full-scale conventional war had become unthinkable.[27] But, from the Pakistani perspective, the nuclear tests had led to a significant shift in the military equation, a shift that, in their view, reduced the risk that limited military hostilities would escalate to a general war. The paradox of nuclear crises is that mutual recognition that all-out war could be catastrophic for both sides can encourage greater risk-taking because each side assumes that the other's fear of escalation to nuclear war will raise its tolerance of coercive behavior. In fact, there is empirical evidence that nuclear

---

[25] Indian Government, *From Surprise to Reckoning: The Kargil Committee Report* (New Delhi, Thousand Oaks, CA, and London: Sage, 1999). The Kargil hostilities meet the widely accepted Correlates of War inter-state war criteria of over 1,000 battle-connected deaths.

[26] See P. R. Chari, *Nuclear Crisis, Escalation Control, and Deterrence in South Asia*, H. L. Stimson Working Paper (Washington, DC: Henry L. Stimson Center, 2003), 18–20; Ashok Krishna and P. R. Chari (eds.), *Kargil: The Tables Turned* (New Delhi: Manohar Press, 2001).

[27] See John Burns, "On Kashmir's Dividing Line, Nuclear Fears Enforce Calm," *New York Times*, June 8, 1998; Steve Coll, "The Force of Fear in South Asia," *The Washington Post National Weekly Edition*, June 8, 1998.

crises do escalate to higher levels without war than conventional crises.[28] This "stability-instability paradox" can be extended to limited conventional war. The shared fear that a general war could lead to a nuclear war reduces the risk that the other party will escalate a limited engagement to a general war; therefore the shared risk encourages nuclear states to undertake limited wars.[29] Based on this line of reasoning, the new environment created by the nuclear tests in 1998 encouraged Pakistan to launch the Kargil operation on the assumption that India would not respond by attacking across the LoC at a strategically more favorable location. India, they assumed, would be restrained by fear of triggering a full-scale conventional war, which, in turn, could escalate to nuclear war.[30] The Indian government's Kargil Review Committee described the Pakistani operation as "a typical case of salami slicing," a Cold War phrase referring to attempts to achieve small territorial gains that would not be sufficient to prompt the other side to risk a military escalation that could lead to a general war that could become nuclear.[31]

Some leading figures in Pakistan have asserted that Pakistan's nuclear capacity played a role in deterring India from using its advantage in conventional forces on three earlier occasions: a preventive attack on Pakistani nuclear facilities in 1984; a planned Indian cross-border attack in conjunction with the Brasstacks exercise in 1986–87; and in 1990, when India was purported to be considering air attacks on mujahidin camps in *Azad Kashmir*.[32] There is no solid evidence that any of the three assumptions regarding the military plans of the Indian government are accurate. But such arguments gain currency because of a predisposition on the part of Pakistani leaders to assume the worst in Indian intentions. That predisposition has been reinforced by over five decades of recurring crises and wars. Thus, in a classic example of attributional distortion, it is presumed that the fact that India did not launch an attack on any of those

---

[28] See Daniel Geller, "Nuclear Weapons, Deterrence, and Crisis Escalation," *Journal of Conflict Resolution* 34 (1990), 291–310.

[29] On the stability–instability paradox applied to South Asia, see Paul Bracken, *Fire in the East: The Rise of Asian Military Power in the Second Nuclear Age* (New Delhi: HarperCollins India, 1999); P. R. Chari, "Nuclear Restraint, Nuclear Risk Reduction, and the Stability–Instability Paradox," in Michael Krepon and Charles Gagne (eds.), *The Stability–Instability Paradox: Nuclear Weapons and Brinkmanship in South Asia* (Washington, DC: Henry L. Stimson Center, 2001).

[30] See Chari, *Nuclear Crisis, Escalation Control, and Deterrence*, 19. The Indian government's subsequent review of the Kargil conflict quotes Musharraf's comment during the crisis that while the likelihood of a general conventional war was virtually zero, limited hostilities were possible (*Kargil Committee Report*, 1999).

[31] *Kargil Committee Report*, Feb. 25, 2000.

[32] Aga Shahi, Zulfiqar Ali Khan and Abdul Sattar, "Securing Nuclear Peace," *The News International* (Pakistan), Internet version, Oct. 5, 1999.

occasions can be explained only by a situational constraint, namely Pakistan's nuclear deterrent capability. More important, this reasoning encourages the belief that Pakistan's nuclear capabilities have redressed the military imbalance sufficiently to allow it to pursue low-intensity conflict, such as its support of insurgency movements in Kashmir, and even limited conventional hostilities, such as in Kargil, without running the risk of triggering a general war.

On the other hand, the *apparent* risk of escalation to nuclear war reopens the possibility that a demonstration crisis will lead to forceful diplomatic intervention by the international community, most notably the United States. There is no direct evidence that Sharif or his advisors planned the Kargil operation for the express purpose of obtaining American diplomatic intervention. But Pakistani leaders learned early in the rivalry that only outside pressure could move India to discuss any alteration of the status quo in Kashmir, and that outside pressure could be obtained only through creating sufficient instability on the subcontinent to threaten international security. The Pakistani leadership had observed how in the 1987 and 1990 crises, the United States, mindful of the risk of nuclear war, played a proactive role in defusing tensions and preventing the outbreak of war.[33] The Kargil crisis did lead to diplomatic intervention by the United States, but the US did not use its diplomatic leverage to reopen the Kashmir issue. Instead, US President Clinton devoted his efforts to pressuring Pakistan to withdraw its troops, while refusing Sharif's plea to mediate between India and Pakistan.[34]

India did respond cautiously to the Kargil incursions. Its leaders were willing to accept heavy casualties by attempting to scale the Himalayan peaks under heavy fire, rather than extending the war horizontally by attacking at a more favorable point along the LoC. Whether India would have continued to demonstrate restraint had its air force, coupled with American diplomatic pressure, not forced the intruders to retreat is an open question. But following the nuclear tests of 1998, Indian Home Secretary Advani had offered the view that India's second-strike capabilities would allow it to respond to Pakistani incursions, or support of terrorism, with "hot pursuit" across the LoC without fearing a Pakistani nuclear response.[35]

---

[33] See Devin Hagerty, "Nuclear Deterrence in South Asia: The 1990 Indo-Pakistani Crisis," *International Security* 20 (1995/96), 79–144.
[34] President Clinton quoted by Reuters in *Times of India*, June 2, 2001.
[35] *New York Times*, May 22, 1998.

The "Spirit of Lahore" and Kargil One of the more intriguing questions about Pakistan's Kargil incursion is why it was undertaken when the rivalry appeared to be in remission. The Lahore Agreement, with Vajpayee's dramatic "bus diplomacy" and the agreement on confidence-building measures, occurred as violence was waning in Kashmir. But peace and stability favor the continuance of the status quo. With India solidifying its hold on most of Kashmir, and the international community turning its attention elsewhere, Pakistan needed to find a means of reigniting the flames of the rivalry. In fact, a period of relative peace is not an unusual precursor to a challenge from the revisionist party in a continuing rivalry. The Argentine attempt to seize and hold the Falkland Islands in 1982, for example, came just a month after cordial negotiations with Great Britain. As in the Kargil War, there were a number of factors precipitating the Argentine action, including domestic pressures and strategic opportunity – Britain had ended its naval patrols off the islands – but a contributing factor was the realization that the status quo was becoming more comfortable for their adversary.

Egypt's Sadat faced an analogous situation when he launched his limited war against Israel in October of 1973 to regain Sinai territory occupied by Israel. Sadat held out no hope of regaining all of the Sinai. The 1973 war, like Kargil, was undertaken partly to achieve a limited success that would strengthen morale. But also it was a demonstration crisis designed to create the risk of escalation to general war that would engage the superpowers.[36] More specifically, Sadat wanted to persuade the United States to bring pressure to bear on Israel to reconsider its unyielding position *vis-à-vis* the status quo.

In all three instances, albeit for different reasons, the only member of the global community with the capability to shift the balance in bargaining power was the United States. In 1973, Sadat was able to convince US Secretary of State Kissinger to restrain Israel and to obtain an outcome that ultimately led to a negotiated return of the Sinai to Egypt. In 1982, US Secretary of State Haig attempted to mediate the Falklands crisis, but he was unable to restrain Britain from going to war. In 1999, Pakistan's Sharif tried to persuade President Clinton to mediate the Kargil War and the Kashmir issue; instead Sharif was pressured by Clinton to withdraw Pakistani troops and mujahidin irregulars from their positions across the LoC. Sharif and his advisors failed to remember the diplomatic lessons of the Bangladesh War when the United States' half-hearted efforts to restrain India failed. Even in 1971, the United States was beginning to

[36] See Leng, *Bargaining and Learning*, 192–83.

have doubts about its Cold War support of Pakistan, particularly in light
of Pakistan's friendly relationship with China, and the global support for
the Bengali independence movement that followed the Pakistani army's
brutal actions in East Pakistan. By 1999 the Cold War was a distant
memory; India's economic importance to the United States had grown
substantially; Pakistan was impoverished and facing US economic sanctions. Pakistani leaders underestimated the United States' desire to maintain good relations with India, and they overestimated American
bargaining power *vis-à-vis* India, particularly with regard to Kashmir.

   Kargil and realpolitik learning It is not hard to imagine a different
scenario having resulted from the Kargil crisis and war. Frustrated by its
inability to dislodge the Pakistani troops from their positions on the peaks in
the Kargil area, India could have launched an attack across the LoC into
Azad Kashmir at a more favorable location. Ensuing combat with Pakistan's
regular army could have escalated to general war. Then, if India's superior
forces crossed into Pakistan and threatened a major city, say Lahore,
Pakistan's leadership might have concluded that it was faced with an immediate threat to survival that required launching a preemptive nuclear strike.
   The Kargil War was the first Indo-Pakistani war since the Indian
victory in the Bangladesh War of 1971, and the first war over Kashmir
since 1965. Unlike the two previous wars, Kargil was short, and limited in
scope and intensity. Had the two sides learned something about crisis
management in the ensuing decades? A comparison of the behavior of the
two sides in 1999 and 1965 Kashmir crises is instructive. Both crises
began with the infiltration of mujahidin irregulars across the LoC into
Indian-controlled Kashmir. In both instances, the Pakistani challenge
came during a period when India was strengthening its control over
Kashmir – presidential rule in 1965, a series of elections and the waning
of the resistance movement in the mid to late 1990s – and the Pakistani
leadership was feeling increasing pressure from hardline factions to take
action. In both instances Pakistani military leaders were convinced that
they could create a *fait accompli* – a shift of the LoC in their favor – and
defend it in a short, limited war.[37] In each instance the success of the
strategy was dependent on a cautious Indian response, and, ultimately,
diplomatic intervention by the UN or major powers that would lead to
reopening negotiations over Kashmir's future. In 1965, India responded
to Pakistan's incursion by sending regular troops into Azad Kashmir, and
Pakistan responded with "Operation Grand Slam," a full-scale armored

[37] See Paul, *Asymmetric Conflict*, 111.

attack that led to a general war. The stalemated war was costly for both sides and it settled nothing. In 1999, India reacted in a more measured manner, and the hostilities remained limited to the Kargil area.

Pakistan's failure in 1965 and its decisive defeat in 1971 should have warned it against attempting a military *fait accompli* in 1999. Conversely, India's previous military successes would seem to have prescribed a more forceful response in 1999. One explanation for the Pakistani action, aside from domestic factors, is that it was prompted by the shift in the strategic environment created by the shared risk of nuclear war. Pakistan's Musharraf claimed that India's cautious response confirmed the validity of that perception. But another explanation is the poverty of imagination that has been endemic in the Pakistani leadership's narrow realpolitik approach to the rivalry, particularly within the highly influential military establishment.[38] The goodwill nurtured by Lahore was quickly discarded when it appeared to Pakistani military leaders that there was a window of opportunity to achieve a strategic gain along the LoC. The success of the highly risky operation depended on assumptions regarding likely Indian and American responses, which were based on faulty diagnostic learning regarding Indian resolve and American interests. India did not respond to the Pakistani incursion by geographically expanding the war. But that may be only because it was unnecessary to do so. Indian air power and American diplomatic pressure were sufficient to force a Pakistani retreat.

The rhetoric of the two sides indicated that their goals had not changed. The causal learning that grew out of the Kargil conflict, at least that which appeared in public statements, was dangerously hawkish. After the war, Musharraf claimed not only that Pakistan's nuclear deterrent had restrained India, but that the crisis achieved its primary purpose by diplomatically re-engaging the United States.[39] For senior Pakistani military officers, the stability–instability paradox became part of a new strategic doctrine, with low-intensity warfare the "fashion of the day."[40]

Kargil intensified the deep Indian distrust of Pakistan, which Indian leaders now characterized, in the jargon of the day, as a "rogue state." India's Prime Minister Vajpayee, who expended a good deal of political capital on the Lahore summit, complained that he had been "stabbed in the back."[41] The Kargil experience could not help but reinforce the

[38] See Tremblay and Schofield in this volume.
[39] Interview quoted in *Dawn* (Pakistan), Internet version, Aug. 19, 2000.
[40] Based on interviews conducted by Adil Husain, reported in Russell J. Leng and Adil Husain, "South Asian War Games: Game Theory and the Likelihood of an Indo-Pakistani Nuclear War" (Middlebury, VT: Middlebury College Center for International Affairs, 2001).
[41] Harjinder Sidju, "Ansari Arrest Proves Pak Hand: PM," *Hindustan Times*, Feb. 11, 2002.

Indian view that the only way to deal with Pakistan was through the application of force, a perspective reflected in the *Kargil Review Committee Report*.[42] Applying a different twist to the stability–instability paradox, Indian strategists had their own low-intensity warfare strategy, which included covert operations by special forces in Pakistan, "hot pursuit" of Pakistani militants across the LoC, and degrading Pakistan's military capabilities through a war of attrition.[43] If hostilities escalated to general war, Pakistan, they argued, would be restrained from a nuclear response by India's second-strike capabilities. Thus neither the Kargil experience, nor the nuclear cloud that hung over the crisis, produced changes in goals for either side. Like the seven militarized crises before it, Kargil deepened mutual hostility and reinforced each side's determination to demonstrate its resolve in any future crisis. Whatever learning occurred remained within the bounds of realpolitik assumptions about inter-rivalry relations.

The border crisis of 2001–2002

Political fall-out from the 9/11 attacks in the United States added to the rationale for hawkish strategies on both sides. The US need for Musharraf's assistance in the campaign against the Taliban and al-Queda appeared to provide new diplomatic leverage for Pakistan. For the first time since the end of the Cold War, the United States needed Pakistan's assistance. Perhaps the United States would be more sympathetic to Pakistan in a future crisis over Kashmir. On the other hand, the US "war against terrorism," with its doctrine of "preemptive war" against states that harbor or support terrorists, provided legitimacy for not only a more proactive Indian anti-terrorist strategy in Kashmir, but also for extending operations to attack terrorist camps in *Azad Kashmir*, and within Pakistan.[44]

Pakistani terrorists attacked the Indian Parliament on December 13, 2001. The attack came a little over a month after a terrorist attack on the Jammu and Kashmir Legislative Assembly took twenty-nine lives, and a little over three months after 9/11. India's Union Cabinet echoed the

---

[42] *The Kargil Review Committee Report, 1999*. See also Rajesh M. Basrur, "The Lessons of Kargil as Learned by India," unpublished manuscript (New York, Columbia University, 2003), 13.

[43] See Chari, "Nuclear Restraint, Nuclear Risk Reduction," 19.

[44] The American strategic doctrine is more appropriately described as "preventive war." Preemption occurs when one party believes that another is preparing an imminent attack. Therefore it strikes first to beat the other to the punch. A preventive war is launched to eliminate the prospect that the other party might attack at some time in the future, or assist others in doing so.

American government's response to 9/11, and its "preemptive war" doctrine, in a resolution that promised to "liquidate the terrorists and their sponsors wherever they are, whoever they are ... "[45] India ordered mobilization of its forces on December 18, and the government warned Washington that it was considering striking terrorist training camps in *Azad Kashmir*.[46] When India moved 800,000 troops to the Indo-Pakistani border, Pakistan responded in kind. A military stand-off ensued, with the armed forces of both sides placed on high alert. Despite diplomatic pressure from Britain and the United States, India refused to enter into bilateral or mediated talks with Pakistan until all cross-border terrorism ceased. Under diplomatic pressure from the United States, Musharraf promised, in January, to crack down on militant Islamic organizations in Pakistan. Tensions relaxed somewhat, only to flare up again in May when Islamic terrorists attacked an Indian army compound in Kashmir. When Vajpayee declared that India was ready for war, Pakistan responded defiantly with three missile tests. With both sides facing intense diplomatic pressure to retreat from the brink of war, tensions gradually subsided. Musharraf restated his intentions to put an end to infiltration across the LoC. In October of 2002, India began to withdraw its troops.

Realpolitik learning and crisis bargaining When both parties approach a militarized crisis from a realpolitik perspective, bargaining becomes a competition in risk-taking, with each party determined to demonstrate superior resolve. During the course of the border crisis, leaders on both sides indulged in provocative rhetoric to demonstrate their resolve in the face of the risk of nuclear war. At the peak of the crisis, Vajpayee declared that India was ready for a "decisive battle with Pakistan," and Musharraf answered that Pakistan would give "a fitting reply" if India attacked. Indian Defense Minister Fernandes asserted that, if the crisis did escalate to a nuclear exchange, India had the capability to survive a first strike and then destroy Pakistan.[47] After the crisis was over, Pakistan's Musharraf claimed that if a single Indian solider had crossed the border into Pakistan, Pakistan would have responded with "unconventional war."[48] And so on.

---

[45] Quoted on http://www.rediff.com/2001/dec/13/parl29.htm.
[46] See J. K. Baral and J. N. Mahanty, "The US War on Terrorism: Implications for South Asia," *Strategic Analyses* 26 (Oct.–Dec. 2002), 508–18.
[47] George Fernandes, "India Could Take a Strike and Survive, Pakistan Won't," *Hindustan Times*, Dec. 30, 2001.
[48] Chari, *Nuclear Crisis, Escalation Control*, 22. See Chari for a more complete account of the rhetoric surrounding the border crisis.

The rhetoric must be balanced by the actual behavior of the two sides, which was more restrained. Nonetheless, nuclear crises carry a high risk of inadvertent war through a preemptive attack borne of misunderstood behavior or misperceptions regarding the other's intentions. Early in the crisis, Indian Lieutenant General Vij, who commanded troops on the border with Pakistan, was replaced, partly at US insistence, after he exceeded his orders with provocative armor movements along the border.[49] The risk created by Lieutenant General Vij's behavior bears some resemblance to when the United States and Soviet Union were brought to the brink of war in the Cuban missile crisis. A lower-level Soviet commander on the island took it upon himself to order the downing of an American U-2 surveillance plane at the height of the crisis. US leaders, however, speculated that the action was a deliberate escalation of the crisis that had been ordered by the Kremlin.[50] The resulting confusion over Soviet intentions and, from the Soviet side, speculation regarding the likely American response, brought the two sides to the brink of nuclear war. War was averted partly because the two sides remained in communication with each other through the course of the crisis. By the time the U-2 incident occurred, each party had signaled to the other its understanding of the catastrophic consequences of a nuclear war. Nevertheless, the Cuban missile crisis was replete with misunderstandings and misperceptions in a situation that the leaders on both sides felt was virtually out of control.[51] Forty years after the crisis, following several meetings with the 1962 Soviet and Cuban leaders, Kennedy's defense secretary, Robert McNamara, concluded, "We lucked out! It was luck that prevented nuclear war!"[52]

The lessons that have been drawn from the Cuban missile crisis by its participants – the high risks of losing control of the situation, the risk of inadvertent war, misperceptions of the other's intentions that can lead to premature preemption – run counter to the realpolitik admonition that success in crisis bargaining depends on demonstrating superior resolve. But the nuclear rhetoric of Indian and Pakistani leaders is consistent with the realpolitik mindset that has dominated whatever learning has occurred over the course of the rivalry. In a relationship that has been contaminated by the residue of decades of recurring crises and wars, the

---

[49] Girja S. Kaura, "Orders from PMO: Gen. Vij Moved after Powell Took Up Issue," *The Tribune* (India), Jan. 22, 2004.
[50] See Ernest R. May and Philip D. Zelikow (eds.), *The Kennedy Tape: Inside the White House During the Cuban Missile Crisis* (Cambridge: Cambridge University Press, 1997), 572, 597.
[51] See Leng, *Bargaining and Learning*, 85–90.
[52] *Fog of War*. Dir. Errol Morris. Interview with Robert McNamara, Sony Pictures, 2003.

public assertion of such views only adds to mutual distrust, and the likelihood that, in a future crisis, one side or the other will be tempted to preempt.

Nuclear learning Since the nuclear tests conducted by India and Pakistan in 1998, a number of American specialists have traveled to India and Pakistan to meet with leaders to discuss the lessons that have been drawn from the Cuban missile crisis, and the Soviet–American nuclear rivalry more generally. During the 2001–02 crisis, American and British representatives played key roles in mediating and attempting to advise the leaders of both sides. To the extent that the United States, by recounting its own nuclear crisis experience, can encourage vicarious learning by the leaders of India and Pakistan, or can use its influence to moderate the behavior of the protagonists in escalating crises, it can play a stabilizing role in the now nuclear environment of the Indo-Pakistani rivalry.

But the prospect of American mediation can be destabilizing when it encourages demonstration crises to trigger the active involvement of the United States in the rivalry. The potential for nuclear war makes the United States more sensitive than ever to the risks associated with militarized crises on the subcontinent. For most of the rivalry, it has been Pakistan that has employed demonstration crises in an attempt to bring its Kashmiri claims to the center of global attention. But now India faces a similar temptation. If India responds forcefully against mujahidin terrorists, and against Pakistan for harboring them, it is responding in a manner consistent with American policy in its war against terrorism. That the terrorists are Islamic fundamentalists strengthens the link to the American campaign, with the two states sharing an interest in pressuring the Pakistani leadership to take firmer action against radical Islamic groups. By responding to terrorist attacks or guerrilla incursions by creating a demonstration crisis with Pakistan, India can trigger American diplomatic intervention in a way that is consistent with Indian objectives. That is what happened in the Kargil War and in the 2001–02 crisis. The realpolitik lesson did not escape notice by Indian leaders.[53]

---

[53] See Siddharth Varadarajan, "Nuclearisation and Decision-Making: Some Lessons from the India–Pakistan Crisis of 2001-2." Paper presented at SSRC Workshop on Understanding South Asia's Nuclear Crisis Behavior, Washington, DC, Jan. 16–18, 2004; Rajesh M. Basrur, "Coercive Diplomacy in a Nuclear Environment: The December 13 Crisis," in Rafiq Dossani and Henry S. Rowan (eds.), *Prospects for Peace in South Asia* (Stanford: Stanford University Press, 2004).

Conclusion

Despite their rhetoric, the governments of India and Pakistan are aware of the costs and risks associated with nuclear war on the subcontinent. In all three of their post-nuclear crises – 1990, 1999, and 2001–02 – India and Pakistan have restrained their military behavior. In fact, even in those crises that ended in war, the forces of the two sides have shown remarkable restraint on the battlefield, as they have avoided attacking cities and other civilian targets. What the two sides have been either unable or unwilling to do, is to draw useful diplomatic lessons from their own behavior. P. R. Chari, in an excellent overview of Indo-Pakistani crisis behavior, compares the leadership of the two states to the eighteenth-century Bourbons in learning nothing and forgetting nothing over the course of the rivalry.[54] It is an apt but incomplete description. The two sides have been learning, but they have been predisposed by their realpolitik beliefs to draw only certain types of lessons from their behavior. Each successive crisis raises the reputational stakes for both sides, and each success or failure is attributed to the state's ability to demonstrate superior resolve. Coercive bargaining strategies and tactics have created a self-fulfilling prophecy.

The realpolitik culture that pervades Indo-Pakistani relations constricts the range of actions available to their leaders, colors their historical memories, and narrows their collective identities. If one views the realpolitik rules of the game in interstate politics as immutable, there is little room for creative learning. Moreover, a realpolitik perspective predisposes leaders to remember some things and to forget others. The historical analogies from which leaders draw lessons to inform their decisions are those consistent with their realpolitik beliefs, most notably their behavior in militarized crises and wars. The lessons themselves focus on military strategy, rather than diplomacy. More harmonious past relations between Hindus and Muslims, either before partition, or within India, are forgotten or presumed to be exceptional. The competitive relationship presumed by a realpolitik approach accentuates Hindu–Muslim differences and masks cultural and historical commonalities in the identities of Indians and Pakistanis. Vicarious learning, drawn from events like the Cuban missile crisis, or the US response to the 9/11 attacks, focuses on those aspects of the situation that are consistent with realpolitik.

The Indo-Pakistani rivalry will not be terminated until the leaders of the two sides are able to move their relationship beyond the bounds of

[54] Chari, *Nuclear Crisis, Escalation Control*, 23.

realpolitik. Even without the termination of the rivalry, the management of future crises will require more balanced diagnostic learning. In their determination to demonstrate resolve during the 2001–02 nuclear crisis, both sides engaged in nuclear saber-rattling. Such rhetoric encourages diagnostic learning that reinforces the other side's worst fears regarding one's intentions. It also raises the risk of a preemptive attack. In the Soviet–American crisis over Cuba in 1962, more than anything else, it was the communication by Khrushchev and Kennedy of their mutual recognition that nuclear war would be catastrophic for *both* sides that provided each of them with some reassurance against a first strike by the other. A critical first step toward stability in Indo-Pakistani relations would be for the leaders of the two sides to move away from nuclear saber-rattling to a public recognition of the obvious, that a general war, with its high probability of nuclear war, would be a shared catastrophe. Each side needs to communicate to the other that it recognizes that in a nuclear war on the subcontinent there would be no relative gains, only absolute losses.

The termination of the rivalry itself would require learning at a higher level, that is, a shift in goals as well as means. A significant reduction in the mutual distrust that infects Indo-Pakistani relations requires that both sides publicly disavow hostile goals. Pakistan would have to give up the goal of attempting to achieve control over all of Kashmir. India would have to renounce any intention of seizing *Azad Kashmir*, or of harboring any long-term goal of reuniting the subcontinent under Indian control. It is not enough to change goals; the changes must be communicated to the other side in a manner that leads to trust in the other's intentions. Ultimately, diagnostic learning would have to extend to empathy, that is, an understanding of the interests of the other party, and the constraints under which it operates. Without mutual trust and empathy, there is little likelihood of reaching a lasting settlement of the Kashmir issue and terminating the rivalry. Witness the fate of the many peace plans designed to bring an end to Israeli–Palestinian rivalry. Only when the parties develop some trust in each other's intentions will it be possible to move away from contentious bargaining to a problem-solving approach to the issue of Kashmir's future.

What I have suggested is a tall order given the bitter residue of over half a century of recurring crises and wars. Recently, however, there have been some hopeful signs. The 2001–02 border crisis between India and Pakistan led to renewed efforts at confidence-building measures, and to an agreement to conduct bilateral talks that would include Kashmir on the agenda. Two years later, Pakistani President Musharraf promised to put an end to the use of Pakistani territory by guerrilla or terrorist groups crossing into Kashmir or India proper.[55] As this is being written, an unprecedented number of bilateral talks are under way on issues ranging from trade, cross-border travel, and narcotics control, to nuclear and conventional ballistic missile confidence-building measures, the Siachen border, and Kashmir. There is no doubt that these moves, not unlike the Soviet–American détente that began in the 1960s and 1970s, have been influenced by the addition of a nuclear dimension to the relationship between the two rivals. The improvement in Soviet–American relations began with diagnostic learning in the form of confidence-building measures. But movement beyond diagnostic learning to a shift in goals did not occur until one side, the Soviet Union, was driven by economic necessity to seek a cooperative relationship with its long-term rival. It is not inconceivable that we are witnessing the beginning of a comparable process in the Indo-Pakistani rivalry, with Pakistan finding itself in the position of the former Soviet Union.

To choose to accept the risks of peace in a rivalry saturated with distrust and hostility requires extraordinary leadership skills and great personal courage. The requisite leadership skills include not only the vision to see beyond the realpolitik boundaries of the rivalry, but also the ability to impart that vision to the rest of the nation. If the Indo-Pakistani rivalry now resembles the Soviet–American rivalry in its nuclear dimension, it also shares the seemingly intractable territorial dimension that lies at the heart of the Middle East rivalry. The two leaders most notable for taking a risk for peace in the Middle East rivalry, Anwar Sadat in the 1970s, and Yitzhak Rabin in the 1990s, were unable to impart their visions to enough of their countrymen, and they paid for their efforts with their lives. That rivalry, now primarily between Israel and the Palestinians, drags on with both sides emotionally and morally exhausted, but with no end in sight. The Indo-Pakistani rivalry currently is in remission, but it remains to be seen if the leaders of India and Pakistan possess the courage and vision to enable their nations to move beyond the bounds of realpolitik.

[55] *New York Times*, Jan. 7, 2004.

Part III

Roots of the India–Pakistan conflict

6   Major powers and the persistence of the India–Pakistan conflict

Ashok Kapur

Introduction

The India–Pakistan rivalry remains both a protracted conflict and an enduring rivalry as discussed in many chapters of this volume.[1] This chapter argues that the great powers' involvement in the India–Pakistan rivalry has helped to prolong and institutionalize the conflict; it intensified the polarization rather than help to moderate and negotiate an end to the rivalry. This chapter takes a challenging look at the role of the great powers in institutionalizing South Asia's enduring rivalry. The discussion is based on the historical record rather than abstract theorizing about India and Pakistan and regional conflict. The main claim, that until recently, and especially during the period of Nehru and the Nehruvians, the outside powers (Pakistan, UK, US, China in particular) were primarily interested in reducing India's power and influence and in building up Pakistan as the challenger to India, will be contested by Western readers. Subtle points will be made that the West (particularly UK–US) joined forces with Pakistan because of the perceived external threat to its security posed by India; that their military and diplomatic aid was meant to make the Indo-Pakistani competition evenhanded and that Cold War policy shaped the formation of the US–Pakistan military pact. Our argument is that Western policy, whose strategic principles emerged in the experiences of the British Raj before 1947, were extended by the development of a UK–US–Pakistan nexus with common interests that

The author would like to acknowledge the SSHRC for its support and research assistance by Marta Nestaiko, and T. V. Paul, Michael Brecher, and an anonymous reviewer for their critical comments.

[1] For definitions of "protracted conflicts," please see Edward E. Azar *et al.*, "Protracted Social Conflict: Theory and Practice in the Middle East," *Journal of Palestine Studies* 8 (1978), 50; Saira Khan, *Nuclear Proliferation Dynamics in Protracted Conflict Regions: A Comparative Study of South Asia and the Middle East* (Chippenham, UK: Antony Rowe, 2002), 42; and Jacob Bercovitch and Patrick M. Regan, "The Structure of International Conflict Management: An Analysis of the Effects of Intractability and Mediation," *The International Journal of Peace Studies* 4 (1999), 1–16.

required the buildup of Pakistan and the adoption of an anti-India stance in diplomatic and military affairs. It will be shown by reviewing the declassified documents and secondary Western and Pakistani sources that Washington and Beijing were pro-Pakistan and anti-India; these biases originated during the Cold War era and continued after the end of the Cold War. It will be argued that while America has gone to lengths to assert a policy of balanced relations with both India and Pakistan, the realities were different. For a brief period, America tried to build up India as a Western strategic partner but Indian non-alignment policy came in the way. In the 1950s and the 1960s, America played up Indian democracy as an alternative model to Chinese authoritarianism in Asia but this buildup of India existed as long as America was engaged in a Cold War with China. Pakistan was built up as a strategic partner because of American strategic interests in the Middle East (oil politics that required a check against Iranian nationalism, as an anti-Soviet base, as a moderate Muslim leader of the Arab world, as a counter to the appeal of Indian non-alignment and nationalist politics in the area) where Pakistan's strategic location placed it in the inner circle of Western defense. Pakistan was built up also to check Indian ambitions and power by promoting a situation of military and diplomatic parity so that Indian power could be neutralized. The India–China democracy versus communism in Asia topic was cultivated as a part of the ideological campaign but strategic interests, not demo-cratic values, drove the Anglo-US–Pakistani and Chinese coalition where democratic values were unimportant but the strategic needs of each player were as in the Bangladesh War.

The claim is that without massive external assistance to Pakistan and external pressure against India in several crucial areas the India–Pakistan rivalry would not have been so prolonged. The premise is that Indo-Pakistani rivalry is not inevitable; it is negotiable. It is not Pakistan's destiny to compete with India without the support of its major external partners. It may be argued that Pakistan sought nuclear weapons to be able to compete with India without American help. The chapter argues that Pakistani nuclear and missile capability does not reduce Pakistani dependence on outside powers to balance India because Pakistani nuclear and missile capability is based on extensive transfers by China and North Korea and Western European suppliers and the dependence is not ended with the exposure of the A. Q. Khan affair. The chapter examines the strategic principles that brought together the UK–US–Pakistan–China coalition against India from the 1950s through the 1990s, and shows how this coalition went nuclear as a result of Western and Chinese policies. The West and China practice a policy of selective tolerance and support of nuclear and missile proliferation for their friends, and conversely a policy of selective opposition of nuclear and missile proliferation for their enemies. There are, therefore, two Western and Chinese non-proliferation regimes, and the adoption of the one or the other regime was based on strategic calculations under the prevailing circumstances of the 1980s and the 1990s.

This chapter is not a historical account but rather focuses on the development of the argument starting with the pre-1947 setting that became the basis of post-1947 policies. Of course, the regional and international circumstances differed from the pre-1947 situation in the subcontinent and in world politics. Our interest is to see how American policies in Indo-Pakistani affairs, despite the American claim that it is not a colonial power, acquired imperial characteristics and an affinity for British strategic calculations; the power in play was American but the political guru was initially London, and later Beijing shaped the attitudes and policies of American leaders like Nixon and Kissinger.

Conflict resolution literature suggests that third parties can reduce conflict or help resolve it. I argue that the resolution of the India–Pakistan conflict has not been the primary motive in the policies of major powers that have been heavily involved in the area. The interventionist character of their diplomatic and military postures was driven by a desire to maintain a situation of manageable instability (prevent outbreak of war, secure a ceasefire if war broke out, support Pakistan against India, and sustain Pakistan in war and peace). These policies shaped their actions in the subcontinent between 1947 and 2000. The US, Pakistan, and China preferred a great-power-centric approach to India–Pakistan issues which sought to diminish India's diplomatic and military space in the subcontinental and international sphere while building up Pakistan as the challenger. In this respect, the convergent Pakistani, American, and Chinese policies institutionalized the Indo-Pakistani conflict. The common cause was to contain India, widely seen as the potential regional hegemon in the 1950s.[2] Until India liberated itself from the unilateral constraint of not exercising its nuclear weapons option, the great powers' norm was to maintain Indo-Pakistani polarity and parity. The USSR supported India diplomatically at the UN Security Council on Kashmir in the 1950s, using its veto often on India's behalf, and later it helped India militarily by giving it valuable and timely military aid and equipment. But Moscow

---

[2] US government documents on Asia in 1949 recognized the danger of several hegemons, principally the USSR, but also China, Japan, and India. See "The Position of the United States with Respect to Asia," Dec. 23, 1949 (top secret, declassified), in T. H. Etzold and J. L. Gaddis, *Containment: Documents on American Policy & Strategy, 1945–1950* (New York: Columbia University Press, 1978), 252–53.

Table 6.1 *Great power interests in India–Pakistan conflict during the Cold War*[a]

US	USSR	China
1. In late 1940s, India- Pakistan conflict had a low priority	1. South Asia was geographically important for several reasons:	1. China has continually sought India's weaknesses by attacking its prestige in the region and internationally through war, by seeking India/Pakistan arms balance and by pursuing an active anti-India policy with India's neighbors during the Cold War and thereafter
2. The US was not interested in pushing the USSR out of the region; the US regarded the Soviet presence in the region as helpful; the US–USSR's interests were convergent	a. India–China rapprochement against USSR would affect Soviet interests	
	b. the spread of Chinese influence in the Middle East through Pakistan could hurt Soviet position in the area	
3. During mid-1960s, US policy changed; South Asia became an area of convergence of US/Chinese interest to limit Soviet and Indian Power – i.e., to convince India to give up its aim to become an independent power and to remain a weak, non-aligned state	c. like other great powers, Moscow was interested in limiting the growth of Indian military and nuclear capabilities	
	d. the 1971 Bangladesh was a contest between India and Pakistan and between two combinations: US/China/ Pakistan *vs* India/USSR	

[a] This table draws on the work of M. S. Rajan and Shivaji Ganguly (eds.), *Sisir Gupta, India and the International System* (New Delhi: Vikas, 1981), 154–55, 157–58, 177–78, 181–83, 186–89.

too wanted to contain India's nuclear development, to maintain a situation of manageable instability in the region and Indian–Pakistan polarity, and to compete with other great powers for regional influence (see Table 6.1). I will focus most of my analysis on the great power relationships with Pakistan, as without them Islamabad would not have been able to sustain the challenge to India which has now lasted more than half a century.

My chapter is located in the context of a significant prehistory of external intervention in the military, economic, and political affairs of the Indian subcontinent. This is outlined below. First, the history of India in the past millennium has a rich record of external interventions starting in the eleventh century leading to the Mughal rule, 1526–1857 onwards, followed by the rise of the influence of the East India Company and then the British crown. European rivalries involving the Portuguese, French and British India, and the Dutch in India's neighborhood (Ceylon now Sri Lanka, and Indonesia) directly affected the political and economic fortunes of the Indian subcontinent. They show the vitality of the classical realpolitik tradition, which cherished intervention, balance of power, and imperialism. In the post-1947 period, these experiences formed the basis of the great powers' conduct in relation to the India–Pakistan rivalry.

The second contextual element is a constant in Indo-Pakistani affairs since 1947 and it relates to the character of the Pakistani state and its skilled development of ties with the great powers. Pakistan's ruling elite has always been ambitious and possesses strong political skills, even though the state has been economically weak, its political institutions and conventions lack legitimacy, it is a nation divided along ethnic lines, there is asymmetry in the distribution of internal political and economic power in favor of the Punjabis, and the state was nurtured on the basis of a two-nations theory which highlighted the importance of religion and the Hindu–Muslim divide in South-Asian politics. Pakistan's geostrategic location was important in terms of East–West competition and the strategic aims of the great powers during the Cold War period. Pakistan was able to function effectively as the gateway for the policies of the US and China in relation to the USSR and India.

The third contextual factor relates to the character of India's political system. It is a democracy and the system possesses legitimacy but the state has had weak institutions, the domestic political class is divided and ridden with ongoing power struggles, it is economically challenged, its political philosophy has been divided between peace and disarmament and national security ideologies, and finally, its foreign policy decision-making process has been dominated by a small number of elites who are closed, secretive, and vulnerable to external inputs and manipulation.

Further, Indians have been confident in their destiny as a great power and sought to manage their interests and their internal challenges through peaceful economic and political change. Pakistan's strategy, on the other hand, has been to relieve internal stresses by externalizing conflict and by borrowing international power through aid and alliance activity, and by using its strategic location as the selling point in a region where great power interests were intertwined.

The great powers who are active in South Asia, particularly the US and China, have their respective strategic agendas and, until recently, they did not facilitate regional conflict resolution. Between the 1950s and 1990s, their agenda largely converged with Pakistan's strategic agendas. Pakistan's strategic agendas were driven primarily by its military elite, who saw themselves as guardians of Pakistan's sovereignty against Indian domination, and as guardians of Islam in South Asia. Moreover, Pakistan sought to expand its strategic and ideological space in Afghanistan, Indian Punjab, Bangladesh, Kashmir, and India's northeast.

My supposition is that the Indian–Pakistan polarity does not rest on the territorial dispute over Kashmir alone. There is a deep-seated conflict between the two countries based on their differing visions of nationhood. From Pakistan's point of view, there are two nations in existence, based on religion. The conflict, therefore, concerns the role of religion in defining Pakistan's identity, and its desire to provide a sense of Pakistani separateness from India. Beyond Kashmir, Pakistan has another strategic aim: to seek diplomatic and military parity with India by increasing Pakistan's military strength, by borrowing power through alignments with external powers and by promoting Islamic militancy in strategic Indian border provinces. The 1980s and the 1990s gave Pakistan an opportunity to expand its strategic and ideological presence into Afghanistan by its policy of building up and collaborating with the Taliban and al-Queda.

The great powers have prolonged the Indo-Pakistani conflict because they joined forces with the revisionist state Pakistan, allegedly the weaker challenger to India's alleged hegemony. The US tried an evenhanded approach to mediation of the Kashmir dispute in the 1947–54 period and saw India as a democratic alternative to Communist China. At the time, the UK and the State Department showed a sensitivity to Indian concerns. But the decision to form a military pact in 1954 with Pakistan was the end of an evenhanded policy. Vice President Nixon's view: 'Pakistan is a country I would like to do everything for ...' summed up the dominant US government attitude.[3] In 1971 President Nixon,

---

[3] R. J. McMahon, "United States Gold War Strategy in South Asia: Making a Military Commitment to Pakistan, 1947–54," *Journal of American History* 75 (Dec. 1988), 837.

Henry Kissinger, and Chou-en-lai carried this attitude forward to an official tilt toward Pakistan and against India.[4]

In reality, Pakistan has been the challenger but it was not necessarily the weaker party because Pakistan had enjoyed near-parity in the military sphere with India in the 1950s as a result of its military ties with the US. In 1947–48 it used an asymmetric strategy of tribal invasion to take Kashmir by force, despite India's bigger size. Since the mid-1950s Pakistan has bridged the power asymmetry by aligning first with the US and later on with China. Since the 1960s the region has been significantly penetrated (in the Himalayas) by Chinese power and in Pakistan by the power of the US and China. Pakistan was militarily and economically weak but politically it was skilled; it used the US and China (and later Saudi Arabia) to reduce the asymmetry with India. India, although territorially bigger, did not under Nehru have a policy to make relations with Pakistan an area of power politics because Nehru shunned *realpolitik*. By referring the Kashmir issue to the UN, Nehru helped to internationalize it, and helped introduce great power politics into the Kashmir arena. This way India became progressively dependent on the great powers in dealing with Kashmir and Indo-Pakistani issues. Thus Nehru's policies inadvertently offered Pakistan and the great powers an opportunity to prolong the Indo-Pakistani rivalry.

There thus lies a difference between Pakistan's and India's use of the great powers in support of their positions. Initially, Pakistan used the great powers to advance its strategic agenda of making South Asia the arena of great power politics and to protect Pakistan's security and territorial integrity. Only after Nehru offered the great powers a role in the settlement of the Kashmir issue (through the involvement of the UN Security Council) did India turn to Moscow for support. But the India–USSR coalition merely balanced/offset the Pakistan–US–China coalition. This way the regional polarity became part of the prevailing international polarity despite changing asymmetries in the distribution of power involving these states. In sum, Pakistan used the US and China, while India used the USSR, but from two different vantage points; Pakistan was the proactive challenger to India; the latter was reactive and defensive under the Nehruvians (1947–98).

However, during the 1990s, a number of significant changes altered the structure of the South Asian conflict and opened up the prospects of a negotiated Indo-Pakistani settlement. First, India shed its Nehruvian

[4] See Washington Special Action Group (WSAG) meeting on India/Pakistan, Dec. 3, 1971 (summary) (extracts) in K. Arif (ed.), *America–Pakistan Relations*, vol. II (Lahore: Vanguard Books, 1984), 165.

dislike of militarized power politics and decided to use coercive diplomacy in regional crises. Second, the acceleration of economic reforms increased India's economic profile along with China's, and made it a point of attraction for international market forces. Third, the emergence of Pakistan and Afghanistan as the hub of international terrorism diminished Pakistan's appeal as a moderate Muslim country. Fourth, changes in the US strategic outlook under the Bush administration enhanced India's position as a strategic partner of the US (as well as Israel) in Asia. Finally, China saw a threat to its border areas by Islamic warriors trained in Pakistan. It recognized a need to build its ties with India in the context of an emerging anti-China alignment of the US, India, and Japan in Asia. Thus, a changed strategic environment created conditions to tone down the Indo-Pakistani conflict and to distance the US and PRC from giving wholehearted support to Pakistan as in the past.

The historical process dates back to the institution of the India–Pakistan rivalry, which was based on a Hindu–Muslim division. This rivalry was formed by the link between Mughal India and British India (1526–1947). This connection served as the elemental force in subcontinental politics thereafter. The Cold War brought about a convergence of American and Pakistani interests. It produced a strategic triangle of UK–US–Pakistan power against India. Subsequently, the USSR joined the triangle. Chinese and Pakistani interests converged in the mid-1950s and China too joined the UK–US–Pakistan coalition in opposing India in the 1970s. Pakistani-Chinese-North Korean missile and nuclear trade links in the 1980s and 1990s gave the coalition a broad international character. These links had a historical foundation. Britain, the key Western authority in the region before 1947, was aligned with Indian Islam and both sought to contain political Hinduism. They succeeded because historically Hinduism was a defensive and reactive force. The great powers' alignment with Pakistan maintained this historical, ideological and strategic triangle. By rejecting power politics, and by insisting on the primacy of moral imperatives in Indian foreign affairs Nehru's India left the field open to great power interventions in the subcontinent.

Only with the defeat of the Nehruvians in Indian politics did the new political class in India build the third side of the triangle. They did so by developing India's internal economic and military strength, and by proactive economic, military, and diplomatic actions. They indicated that India was here to stay, that India would immunize itself to regional and international pressures, that India's political class would reoccupy the decisionmaking space concerning Indian and subcontinental strategic affairs. This is the post-1998 story that is germane to the examination of a process for a possible end to the India–Pakistan conflict.

The scope and the rate of change in Indian policies since 1998 have been revolutionary by Indian standards. From Gandhian non-violence and Nehru's peace diplomacy, India has moved to a position of relying on military force and nuclear capability for its security. From Nehru's faith in socialist planning and strong state intervention in economic affairs, India has slowly moved toward a freer enterprise system and economic liberalization. Indian policies achieved a new regional power formation in the sense that India has learned to anticipate and deal with likely contingencies against a coalition of external powers.

In the 1950s, the distribution of military power between India and Pakistan favored Pakistan because of the American military and economic aid. By the 1990s, it favored India though Pakistan received extensive Chinese and North Korean supplies of conventional armament, and financial aid from Saudi Arabia. This asymmetry could change if China were to join Pakistan in a war. However, the pattern of China's behavior indicates that it was not willing to fight for Pakistan in the 1965 and 1971 wars. China gave small arms to insurgents in India's northeast and modern arms to Pakistan, but it has been unwilling to joining the India–Pakistan military fight directly. America too discovered in 1971 and in 1998 the limits of its coercive power *vis-à-vis* India. Its historical policy to contain India eventually failed. On the other hand, despite its history of a reactive military policy and a defensive diplomatic posture, Indian policies have achieved "stable conflict formation" in the region. India has shown that it can initiate conflict and bring it to a successful conclusion as in 1971. The contemporary Indo-Pakistani military situation is not a stalemate because India retains the capability through ongoing military modernization and economic growth, and the confidence to manage and if necessary, to escalate conflict against Pakistan. India has emerged as a catalyst for change in the subcontinent because it has developed a war policy as well as a peace policy in relation to Pakistan and China.

The historical evolution

The India–Pakistan relationship of conflict has a long pedigree involving great powers and regional actors. It ought to be studied as part of strategic and ideological triangles that formed in the subcontinent. Ideologically, there is a triangle between Pakistani Islam (with Wahhabi overtones since the 1970s), political Hinduism, and Western support of religion as the basis of subcontinental politics. On the strategic plane, India–Pakistan relations are located in the context of triangles such as: India versus the UK–US–Pakistan combination in relation to the Kashmir dispute (1947–50s) and Indo-Pakistani military and diplomatic affairs (1950s–present).[5] When the UK–US–Pakistan link appeared shaky in the early 1960s, a new combination emerged to create the Pakistan/China coalition versus India. These post-1947 developments were a buildup on the pre-1947 history, and to a discussion of this aspect I now turn.

Pre-independence history

The pre-independence history set the stage for great power intervention in the subcontinent after 1947. It had two features: (1) the British rulers played with religion and used it as a divisive element in Indo-Pakistani and Hindu–Muslim politics; (2) the robust nature and extensive influence of British–Mughal linkages led to the development of a subsidiary alliance system between the imperial power, the Mughals, and the native rulers. The first stimulated the British divide and rule policy. To the second were added the politics of oil, Cold War politics, and opposition to the rise of regional hegemons such as Soviet Russia, China, India, and Japan in Western strategic thought. After 1947, great power interventions in the subcontinent rested on two aims: to sustain and deepen the subsidiary alliance system between the UK, US, and Islamic Pakistan; and to maintain the polarity between India and Pakistan. Three Western experts tell the story.

Percival Spear explains the British–Mughal organic link:

British India was deeply indebted to Mughal India on one hand, and Mughal India was a characteristic Indian entity on the other in a way not realized by any other regime during the previous thousands of years. In many ways, British India saw the development of trends already existing in Mughal India and it is certain that British India would have been a very different place had the Mughals never ruled before them.[6]

Karl E. Meyer adds:

Building on a practice pioneered by their Mogul predecessors, the makers of British India evolved what became known as the subsidiary alliance system.

---

[5] Although Western governments state that the Kashmir dispute is a matter to be settled between India and Pakistan, and China no longer speaks in terms of Kashmiri self-determination, various Kashmiri study groups in London and Washington project a Pakistan/India/Kashmiri triangle which requires third-party mediation or intervention.

[6] Percival Spear, *A History of India* (London: Penguin Books, 1970), 13.

Native rulers could only keep their thrones as long as they contributed taxes and soldiers to the Raj and discreetly heeded the British Residents posted to their courts.[7]

Meyer brings out the systematic practice of divide and rule policy. In 1905, Lord Curzon, viceroy of India, divided Bengal. The reasoning was as follows:

Bengal united is a power, one of them counseled. "Bengal divided will pull several ways: That is what the Congress leaders feel; their apprehensions are perfectly correct and they form one of the great merits of the scheme ... One of our main objects is to split up and thereby weaken a solid body of opponents to our rule."[8]

Indian Muslims nourished the organic link. Meyer recalls Nirad Chaudhuri's view that from 1906, "The Muslims were coming over quite openly in favor of partition and on the side of the British."[9] Sir Olaf Caroe, the last British governor of North West Frontier Province and an early mentor of the US State Department, advocated Pakistan's importance in the Anglo-American strategy to secure Middle East's oil, to contain the USSR and to check India's ambitions.[10]

Finally, American scholar and practitioner Owen Lattimore delivers his damning judgment about the use of religion by British imperialism:

The fact that Pakistan separated from India on the issue of religious politics reveals one of the effects of British rule that nationalism has not yet been able to submerge. Encouragement of political organization within the framework of religion had, after the First World War, become the principal British device for splitting the onslaught of a united nationalism. British official and semi-official literature persisted in referring to a supposed Hindu Congress long after the All-India Congress had made it a major policy to stress the union in nationalism of people of different religious faiths. Mohammed Ali Jinnah developed the momentum of his political career by turning this British policy to his own advantage.[11]

This pre-history was the foundation of the great powers' attitudes towards Pakistan and India after 1947.

The great powers after 1947

Typically, the literature looks at the issue of the Indo-Pakistani conflict and its endurance in terms of "big India and her smaller neighbors." I stress that due to the support given by the US and China to Pakistan, the India–Pakistan power asymmetry has been reordered, or it became

---

[7] Karl E. Meyer, *The Dusk of Empire* (New York: Century Foundation, 2003), 17.
[8] *Ibid.*, 89–90.   [9] *Ibid.*, 90.   [10] *Ibid.*, 107.
[11] Owen Lattimore, *The Situation in Asia* (Boston: Little Brown, 1949), 185.

"truncated" as argued by T. V. Paul in the introductory chapter. Because of this support from the great powers, Pakistan had little reason to compromise and settle its dispute with India.

The argument I present here is based on the work of the late Professor Sisir Gupta. It operates at two levels. First, at the interstate level, Pakistan reacted aggressively to India's power and policies. The core Pakistani assumption was that India was the big fish which was likely to swallow the smaller Pakistani fish. Against this danger, the Pakistani shield required a strong military, the mobilization of Islam, and ties with the West, and later with China. When the pre-1947 two nations theory was married to the post-1947 theory of India's hegemonic threat to Pakistan, the state ideology and policy required the exacerbation of differences with India. Second, Pakistani domestic politics shaped its external policies. There are deep-seated linguistic and regional differences among Pakistanis. Moreover, there is a history of competition for political power between "Indian Muslims" who migrated to Pakistan, and the indigenous Punjabi Pakistanis who had local roots and who did not participate in the partition movement under Jinnah and the Muslim League. After Jinnah's death and the first Prime Minister Liaqat Ali Khan's assassination in 1948, the Punjabi elite successfully hijacked Pakistani politics. Without the cementing influence of Islam and anti-Indianism Pakistan would likely have degenerated into civil war among the Punjabis, Baloochs, Pushtuns, and Sindhis. So it was essential for Pakistan to differentiate itself from India and to minimize India's pull in terms of power asymmetry as well as political culture.[12] Muslims were different, and therefore Muslim separatism was justified. This theory was effective as a bargaining strategy. It secured an independent homeland, Pakistan, in a short span (1930s to 1947), and it secured a third of Kashmir by force (1947–48). Before 1947, the two-nation theory shaped a constitutional struggle against the Congress Party where the British–Pakistani theory of the threat of the Hindu majority and the importance of religion in politics led to the partition. This triangle between allegedly "weaker Muslim Pakistan," allegedly "stronger Hindu India," and allegedly "impartial West" remained in force after 1947.

Three orientations dominate the Indo-Pakistani story. (1) Pakistan's ceaseless internal power struggles. Pakistan's political class has been at war with "Hindustanis," first against the "Hindu dominated Indian Congress Party," and then against Indian Muslims including Jinnah and Liaqat Ali Khan. With the death of Jinnah and the assassination of Khan,

---

[12] M. S. Rajan and Shivaji Ganguly (eds.), *Sisir Gupta, India and the International System* (New Delhi: Vikas, 1981), 193, 9, 94, respectively.

the political power of Indian Muslims in Pakistan faded but internal power struggles continued. Later, Pakistan's political-military rulers were at war with the East Pakistani (Bengali) Muslims. Neither partition nor the creation of Bangladesh settled the internal power struggle between Indo-Islamists ("Hindustanis") and the Mohajirs (Indian refugees who live in Karachi) and Pakistan's dominant political and military class (Punjabis) and hardline Islamists. (2) Great power support for Pakistani policy against India delayed Indo-Pakistani conflict resolution as well as settlement of internal power struggles in Pakistan. The great powers helped deflect Pakistan's internal struggles into external Indo-Pakistani controversies but this postponed the need to address the real causes of Pakistan's internal political, economic, and social problems. (3) Pakistan's political class had the motive and skills to bargain in the international sphere with the great powers as long as it played into the strategic agendas of its external patrons.

Pakistan's bargaining strategy with the West, and an aggressive policy toward India were facilitated by four elements. First, the Cold War made Pakistan a pivotal actor in Anglo-American policy. The USSR's atomic testing, and Iranian nationalism and oil politics under Mossadeq, showed the importance of Pakistan's strategic location. Until recently, India–Pakistan issues were dealt with by the Bureaus of the Middle East and South Asia in various US government departments. Not surprisingly, American preoccupations in the Middle East dovetailed with its Indo-Pakistani policies, i.e., the importance of oil, the search for moderate Muslim allies, the repression of Arab and Indian nationalism, and the containment of Soviet ambitions and diplomatic/military/economic influences in the region. America's faith in a military approach to the Cold War, and the politics of the Middle East and Asia, made Pakistan a part of the inner perimeter in its strategic policy; and India became a part of the outer perimeter.[13]

Second, while Pakistan could not exert its power beyond its borders in the early 1950s, it could offer a valued territorial base to America. Its location was a bargaining tool. Given its irredentist claims against India, and its limited capacity to intervene against India, Pakistan became an active player in great power politics, and its alliance with the US and China reduced the power differential between Pakistan and India. In other words, the great powers – especially the US and China – along with Pakistan had a determining role in shaping the structure of South Asian international relations up to 1998.

---

[13] This orientation is well captured in Olaf Caroe, *Wells of Power: The Oil Fields of South-Western Asia: A Regional and Global Study* (Westport, CT: Hyperion Press, 1976).

Third, Pakistan's strategic partners shared a concern to contain Nehru's appeal in the Third World, and to cut him and India down to size by diplomatic and military pressures. Initially, the US tried to build up Nehru and India as a democratic model in contrast to the communist powers; and Nehru's India was closer to the UK and US than to the USSR.[14] But by the early 1950s, the US policy and attitude toward Nehru and India changed completely. With growing Indo-US controversies on policies on Pakistan, Kashmir, Korea, and China, the US tilted toward Pakistan as early as August 1949. President Truman's assistant wrote: "It would be prejudicial to American interests in the Middle East and Far East to develop an Indian policy without taking into account Pakistan's legitimate interests."[15] Nehru recognized "a concerted attempt to build up Pakistan and build down ... India."[16] President Truman told a US legislator that Nehru's Korea policy sold the US down the river, and Nehru recognized the growth of Pakistani, US, and UK pressures on India in Kashmir.[17] Gupta outlines America's (and China's) anti-Indian approach as follows:

Although China and the United States shared the belief that India could be kept under check through Pakistan, the reasons for their doing so might have been different. In the case of America, the underlying assumption behind many of its foreign policy postures was in its supreme confidence in itself. There was consequently a broad Western stance of siding with the so-called weaker Powers in regional contests, e.g., Malaysia against Indonesia, Pakistan against India, Israel against the Arabs.

There was also a highly biased and distorted image of India and its problems in the United States. Partly because of the British propaganda before Independence and partly because of the experiences of individual Americans based on superficial observation of the Indian scene, the United States had begun to regard India as incapable of asserting its rightful status. There was a visible American confidence in Pakistan, which was greatly strengthened after the army came to power in that country. Finally, the United States had a deep distrust of Indian politics and an equally healthy respect for Pakistani public life.

In the case of China ... its geo-political stakes in preventing India from becoming a major Power were so high that it began to perceive a great deal of interest in the ability of Pakistan to act as a check on India.[18]

Finally, Nehru's initial diplomacy on Pakistan and Kashmir was tied closely to British thinking. Lord Louis Mountbatten shaped Nehru's (and India's) policy. Both rejected a policy of general war with Pakistan,

---

[14] S. Gopal, *Jawaharlal Nehru*, vol. II, *1947–1956* (Cambridge, MA: Harvard University Press, 1979), 57.

[15] *Ibid.*, p. 60, note 82.   [16] *Ibid.*, 63.   [17] *Ibid.*, 109, 113 respectively.

[18] Rajan and Ganguly (eds.), *Sisir Gupta, India*, 188–89.

emphasized friendship with Pakistan, referred the Kashmir dispute to the UN Security Council, and accepted the principle of self-determination (plebiscite) in Kashmir. These were Mountbatten's proposals to Nehru. These positions facilitated Pakistani as well as Anglo-American activism in the Kashmir issue and in Indo-Pakistani relations because the issue was held on the UN agenda as a "threat to international peace."[19]

These factors collectively gave a powerful second wind to Pakistan's pre-1947 politics, which had yielded a rich dividend in the formation of Pakistan and the acquisition of a third of Kashmir by force. According to Gupta, Pakistan had three major options: (1) to hope for military victory in Kashmir; (2) to unfreeze the bilateral military and political situation in Kashmir and in the subcontinent by having the international community, and especially the West, weigh in on India; and finally (3) to accept the ground realities and seek a new relationship with India. Great power (the US, UK, China) policies facilitated the first and the second Pakistani options; the great powers (the US and China) reinforced Pakistan's aggressive strategy against India. Pakistan had no reason to compromise and to settle its political dispute with India.[20]

Great powers' interests and policies towards India and Pakistan do not fit into the bipolar mold because there was constant interaction among the three powers (the US, UK, and USSR), and there was competition between two communist powers (USSR and China) in their relations with India and Pakistan and with the US. Table 6.1 outlines the nature of the great powers' interests and policies in India–Pakistan relations during the Cold War and their effect in delaying a bilateral India–Pakistan settlement (the third option). The following pages show the parameters of the US's Pakistan policy in the 1950s, the parameters of US–China's Pakistan policy from the 1960s to the 1990s, and the parameters of China–Pakistan–Saudi Arabian policies in the region. This chapter will conclude with a discussion of the emergence of India's counter-strategy and its effect in changing the policies of the US–China–Pakistan coalition. Here, India the victim of great power coalition policies in the 1950–60s emerges as an active player and catalyst of regional change. India has played two types of games. It first brought the USSR on its side and played off the three great powers against each other. This was the Nehru game based on political diplomacy. But it failed because the ability of the great powers to intervene in South Asian affairs was greater than

---

[19] The issue of Kashmir was referred to the UN Security Council under Article 37 of the UN Charter. For Mountbatten's influence on Nehru's Kashmir policy, see H. V. Hodson, *The Great Divide* (Karachi: Oxford University Press, 1969, 1985), ch. 25.

[20] Rajan and Ganguly (eds.), *Sisir Gupta, India*, 152–53.

Nehru's ability to manipulate the great powers. Since 1998, India's game is to reposition itself through creative diplomacy based on military and economic strength and to turn around stalemated relations with the US, PRC, and Pakistan. Now India is playing two connected games – to escalate the threat of violent conflict and to seek a negotiated settlement. The emergence of the third option in Pakistani behavior, and the shifts in US–China policies, are largely the result of India's counter-strategy since 1998.

Parameters of US policies toward Pakistan and India: 1947–1950s[21]

A dominant reason for the endurance of the India–Pakistan rivalry lies in the support that the US and later China, along with other arms suppliers, have extended to Pakistan, the regional challenger involved in the regional dispute. Pakistan was in competition with India since 1947 but it recognized the need for external military and diplomatic aid to sustain its rivalry with India. It could not sustain the rivalry alone, i.e., without borrowing external power to its side. Some argue that Pakistan likes nuclear weapons because they reduce dependence on outside powers for balancing India. This misses a crucial point: Pakistan's nuclear and missile capacity is based on European imports, China's nuclear test data, Chinese and North Korean missile aid, and Saudi financing. Pakistan is dependent on outside powers for its conventional and nuclear armament.[22] In this respect, it is instructive to outline the attitudes and policies of the US toward Pakistan and the anti-India biases in the US assessments *vis-à-vis* the region.

According to US government documents, US policy in South Asia had several distinct characteristics. (1) Pakistan was one of the largest Muslim countries in the world, occupying "one of the most strategic areas in the world," in the view of Secretary of State, George C. Marshall. From the military point of view, Pakistan had strategic value in the view of the joint chiefs of staff. (2) In 1951, the US government adopted an aggressive anti-India diplomatic stance. The agreed conclusions and recommendations of American missions in South Asia were as follows:

We should suggest to Governments associated with us in the North Atlantic Pact and the Hemisphere Defence Pact that they instruct their diplomatic and consular

---

[21] This part relies on K. Arif (ed.), *America–Pakistan Relations: Documents*, vol. I (Lahore: Vanguard Books, 1984), 3, 15–16, 23–24, 30–31, 25, 38, 10, 61.

[22] For details, see Ashok Kapur, "Pokhran II & After," in A. Shastri and A. J. Wilson (eds.), *The Post-Colonial States of South Asia* (London: Curzon Press,), 345–46.

representatives in South Asia and elsewhere, and their representatives to the United Nations, to point out on every appropriate occasion to the officials of the Governments of Middle Eastern and Asian countries the fallacious basis of the present foreign policies of India, and the dangers to Asia and to world peace inherent in those policies.

(3) Pakistan was deemed worthy of American support because of its potential to lead a strong Muslim bloc to counter Pakistani fear of "Hindu imperialism" and to provide a balance of power in Asia. The US officials also had a view about Indian imperialism and the importance of Pakistan in shaping the South Asian balance of power. To quote:

With regard to Pakistan's endeavor to assume leadership of a Middle East Muslim bloc, it may be in time become desirable critically to review our concept that Pakistan's destiny is or should be bound with India. There is increasing evidence that Pakistan is a viable state ... Moreover, the vigor and methods which have characterized India's execution of its policy of consolidating the princely states, and its inflexible attitude with regard to Kashmir, may indicate national traits which in time, if not controlled, could make India Japan's successor in Asiatic imperialism. In such a circumstance, a strong Muslim bloc under the leadership of Pakistan and friendly to the US, might afford a desirable balance of power in South Asia.

(4) Pakistani and American practitioners saw value in Islam in Pakistani and American policies in the Middle East and South Asia. Thus the interview of Assistant Secretary of State McGhee and Pakistani finance minister Ghulam Mohammed (December 12, 1949 dispatch) notes the following:

Again and again, he reverted to the importance of the fight which Pakistan was making for independence, both political and economic, and insisted the new Middle East grouping was essential in Pakistan's fight with India.

The record of informal US–UK discussion (September 18, 1950) registers McGhee's attitude about the positive role of Islam in American policy.

(5) Finally, American statements show their appreciation of the UK's primary role in South Asian affairs – to maintain international peace and security in South Asia; the UK's role was judged to be in the American interest. American strategy was to remain "impartial" in Pakistan–India disputes, to wish for close and friendly UK–Pakistan ties, and to avoid any US action which might weaken them (July 1, 1951, State Department policy on Pakistan).

Seven themes in the US's India–Pakistan policies revealed the US's pro-Pakistan and anti-India biases. (1) Pakistan was strategically important in the context of the US's Cold War and Middle Eastern policies.

(2) Indian non-alignment was a threat to Asia and world peace. (3) Indian domestic policies revealed imperialist traits which if unchecked could make India a successor to Japan's Asiatic imperialism. (4) Pakistan was a check to Indian imperialism. Pakistan could be used to balance India in the region. (5) Pakistan, a moderate Muslim state, could be the leader of a Muslim bloc in the Middle East. (6) On the basis of Islam, a new Middle Eastern bloc could be crafted by the US with Pakistan's help. (7) The US favored the UK's friendly role in Pakistan, and this was in the US's interest. Preventing the spread of communism in the subcontinent was a concern in the 1940s but it was used as a cover to build up Pakistan and the US–Pakistan military relationship; by the 1950s, the US–Pakistan military tie-up brought the USSR into subcontinental politics as critics of the US–Pakistan military pact had warned. Avoiding an India–Pakistan war was a concern, but the concern was to avoid a regional war that could lead to a superpower confrontation rather than to reduce Indo-Pakistani polarity. The biases in US policies were evident in the 1950s, well before the infamous Nixon–Kissinger–Chou en-Lai tilt was revealed in the 1971 Bangladesh War (see notes 3 and 4). These themes reveal an intensity of the US engagement with Pakistan, India, USSR, and the Middle East at three levels: global politics, regional politics, and Indian domestic politics (i.e., US views about Indian policies toward princely states and their integration into the Indian union).

US policies in the 1950s sought to contain India's influence in South Asia and in Asia, and to enlarge Pakistan's role in the Middle East and Asian politics. By projecting Pakistani Muslim separateness and the positive role of religion in international politics, the US government was undermining secularism in South Asia and the Middle East; and there was no inclination to facilitate Indo-Pakistani confidence building and conflict resolution. Rather, US policies and attitudes in the 1950s reinforced Indo-Pakistani polarization even further. In other words, the pre-1947 British–Muslim organic link grew stronger with the addition of a US tilt to the UK–Pakistan alignment in the 1950s.

The following section shows how and why China, and later Saudi Arabia, joined the UK–US–Pakistan coalition. Communist (anti-religious) and revolutionary China surprisingly had no difficulty in embracing in practice the seven UK–US–Pakistani policy themes. As well, China saw Pakistan as a line of pressure against India and as a gateway to promote China's influence in the Middle East. In the 1950s, Pakistan was attractive to China in the context of its global competition with the USSR and the US. Pakistan was the weak link in the anti-China coalition of SEATO and CENTO and it was a strategic gateway to the USSR's southern underbelly and a counter to US influence in the Middle East.

Parameters of US–China–Pakistan policies: 1971–2000

These biases and themes were intact when East Pakistan revolted in 1971 and India and Pakistan went to war. This crisis revealed the worst features of Pakistani militarism because it led to genocidal behavior against Muslim Bengalis in East Pakistan. At the same time, US interest in building a strategic link with China (and vice versa), to support Pakistan and to curb India and the USSR created a strategic alignment between Nixon, Kissinger, and Chou en-Lai. The result was a major US–China tilt against India in regional politics and against the USSR in global politics.[23] This alignment between Pakistani militarism and the US–China balance of power coalition increased the Indo-Pakistani polarity. Repeated US calls for a UN-sponsored ceasefire prolonged the India–Pakistan conflict because US–China–Pakistani policies lacked credibility in India. The 1971 war ended in a humiliating defeat of the US–China–Pakistan coalition but there was neither learning nor adaptation in US, Chinese, or Pakistani behavior as a result of India's victory and Pakistan's breakup. The surrender of the Pakistani army to India in December 1971 was a compromise peace for Pakistan. It was not a turning point towards a peace dialogue or a settlement because the Pakistani army's defeat created a motive for revenge against India. Furthermore, it reinforced the convergence between American, Chinese, and Pakistani policies of the 1960s (see Table 6.1). The 1971 defeat was followed by the 1972 nuclear decision when Zulfikar Ali Bhutto in the famous January 1972 meeting authorized Pakistan's nuclear weapons development. India's 1974 nuclear test reinforced Pakistan's 1972 decision.

As a result of the 1971 outcome, Pakistani strategy developed several layers of thought and action and the India–Pakistan polarity was sharpened. First, Hindu–Muslim ideological polarity was reinforced. Second, from 1972 onwards on the strategic plane, a new layer emerged in the form of a nuclearized rivalry. This was a new layer because Pakistan committed itself to the development of nuclear weaponry for the first time. Earlier in the 1950s and the 1960s, it had explicitly rejected the development of an indigenous Pakistan nuclear weapons option even though India was known to have one. Third, after its defeat in 1971, the Pakistan military sought to regroup and re-plan the liberation of

---

[23] Dennis Kux, *The United States and Pakistan, 1947–2000* (Baltimore: Johns Hopkins University Press, 2001), ch. 7; F. S. Aijazuddin, *From a Head, Through a Head, To a Head* (Karachi: Oxford University Press, 2000); and F. S. Aijazuddin, *The White House and Pakistan: Secret Declassified Documents 1969–1974* (Karachi: Oxford University Press, 2002), Preface xiv–xv.

Kashmir by force. This was an old layer but it was reinforced by the policies of Pakistani Generals Zia ul-Haq, Aslam Beg, and Hamid Gul. It had the institutional support of Pakistani intelligence and military services. The Chinese government provided conventional armaments as well as nuclear and missile aid to Pakistan. The US tolerated this supply because Pakistan was a frontline state in the fight to eject Soviet forces from Afghanistan in the 1980s. This frontline status provided cash and modern arms to Pakistan to supply the mujahidin in Afghanistan. However, the US lacked control over the disposition of its deliveries, and in the hands of the Pakistan military and intelligence services, the arms and funds were also available for use in Kashmir and Indian Punjab.[24] The new Pakistani rationale was to expand Pakistan's strategic space by a policy of coercive intervention in Afghanistan, Indian Punjab, and Indian Kashmir. This was based on an old policy, i.e., to build India–Pakistan parity and to challenge India's primacy. The aim was to unfreeze the Kashmir situation through military action combined with the alliance support of the US and China. The Pakistan elite's idea was to induce a change in Indian policy under external pressure. Note that the policies of the US and China against the USSR generally, and particularly in Afghanistan, had a negative fallout on India. It enhanced Pakistan's capacity and motivation to intervene against India, and it enlarged the geographical sphere of Pakistani intervention from Kashmir to Indian Punjab to Afghanistan. The Pakistan–US–China coalition also helped to contain India in the nuclear sphere, to unbalance it by pressure in its border areas, and to build Pakistan into a military and a diplomatic counterforce to check India. The liberation of Kashmir by force or by international diplomatic action was no longer the sole aim of Pakistani policy. It was also to support the rise of Khalistan in the Indian Punjab, which has never been disputed territory, and to change the security and politics of India's northeastern provinces through support of militancy and illegal Muslim migration into India from Bangladesh.

The late 1970s also marks the entry of Saudi Arabia as an ally of Pakistan. Riyadh funded the setting up of thousands of madrassas (religious schools) in Pakistan to promote Wahabism and the export of radical Islam into Afghanistan, Kashmir, Central Asia, and Southeast Asia.[25] The Saudi princes also relied on the Pakistani army to protect them from internal enemies. With such a cast of international patrons, the

---

[24] For CIA–ISI–Saudi–Taliban/jihadi links, see Ahmed Rashid, *Taliban* (New Haven: Yale University Press, 2001), 72, 80, 85, 129; Peter L. Bergen, *Holy War Inc.* (London: Phoenix edition, 2002), 67–71, 58, 32.

[25] Rashid, *Taliban*, 90.

Indo-USSR alignment was kept off balance by the US–China–Saudi–Pakistani coalition, and the India–Pakistan rivalry endured.

Parameters of the Pakistan–China–Saudi connection: 1980s–present

Here, the nature of this connection and its effects on the Indo-Pakistani rivalry are outlined. China's involvement in Pakistan should be viewed in the context of China's Middle East policy as well as China's India policy. For China, Pakistan is a gateway for both regions: the Middle East and South Asia. The Pakistan–China–Saudi connection is an important ideological and strategic triangle, which developed on the basis of mutual interests between these countries. The issues include the following:

- China has supplied conventional and nuclear armaments, including missiles, to Pakistan, in support of its special ties with Pakistan, to maintain it as a line of military and diplomatic pressure against India, and as a gateway to the Middle East region.
- China assisted Pakistan to develop a deep sea port in Gwadar, with a view to developing a Chinese naval presence at a strategic point close to the Persian Gulf and the sea lanes in the Arabian Sea.
- China has provided long-range missiles to Saudi Arabia in exchange for access to Saudi oil. China's energy needs are growing and Saudi Arabia fills them; and China fills Saudi military needs as the US–Saudi relationship is changing.
- Saudi Arabia has funded religious schools in Pakistan as the agency to export Saudi Wahabism. These schools are a training ground for Islamic warriors in Afghanistan, Kashmir, the Caucasus region, and in South East Asia (Indonesia and the Philippines).
- Pakistan has been involved in providing security to the Saudi royal family by supplying its armed forces.
- According to recent press reports, Saudi Arabia is becoming a *de facto* military power and there is a convergence of links between China, Pakistan, and Saudi Arabia in the military arena.[26]

Following the September 11, 2001 terrorist attacks and allegations of Saudi complicity in al-Queda's activity, Saudi Arabia's insecurity would dictate a need for a close strategic relationship with Pakistan and China.

---

[26] Thomas Woodrow, "The Sino-Saudi Connection," *China Brief*, vol. II, issue 21, Oct. 24 (Washington, DC: The Jamestown Foundation, 2002); A. de Borchgrave, "Pakistan–Saudi Arabia Deal on Nuclear Technology for Oil," *South Asia Tribune*, 64, Oct. 26–Nov. 1, 2003; E. MacAskill and I. Traynor, "Saudis Consider Nuclear Bomb," *The Guardian*, Sept. 18, 2003.

Turning the conflict around

This chapter argued that historically India–Pakistan polarity has been embedded in Pakistan's internal character and in great power policies, which sought to reduce India–Pakistan power asymmetry and strengthen Pakistan as a counterweight against India's regional and international influence. The two-nation theory required continued differences with India to maintain Pakistan's Islamic identity and to manage the power asymmetry. Until recently, conflict and its management, not conflict resolution, was the desired norm in Pakistani politics and external affairs. The norm was to facilitate Pakistani interventions against India, and to curb Indian military action against Pakistan by the UK–US sponsored ceasefires through the UN if India responded to Pakistan action by force. The chapter pointed to a tie-up between the ideological and strategic nature of the India–Pakistan conflict and the nature of the international system. The regional conflict provided an opportunity for the great powers to intervene for two main reasons; first, to manage their competition with other great powers, and second, to keep India in check. Two themes were thus in play in Pakistan–US–Chinese–Saudi alliance activity. The first, practiced by the pro-Pakistan international coalition, was to balance India. The second was for Pakistan to export its internal strains by creating avenues in Kashmir, Afghanistan, and India, and to promote the strategic aims of Pakistan's military, intelligence, and diplomatic services. Their success was essential to maintain the dominance of these services in Pakistani politics and the integrity of Pakistan's international alignment and regional position. One must not underestimate the importance of externalizing internal tensions in Pakistan's case because it lacks legitimate constitutional and political arrangements to accommodate internal conflicts.

The imperatives of Pakistan and the international coalition were a natural fit in the 1950s–80s because the international system was bipolar and it was driven by Cold War calculations as well as by the regional interests of the great powers. Checking Soviet expansion was the primary declared American aim, and checking Indian power and assertiveness was the secondary undeclared American aim at the time. Both aims converged with Pakistani and Chinese policies.

But checking Indian power remained an American goal even after the end of the Cold War and after the Indo-Soviet special relationship faded following the USSR's collapse. The end of the Cold War is, therefore, not a defining point in the Indo-Pakistani case. Great power involvement in the Indo-Pakistani conflict increased following the end of the Cold War because the restraining hand of Moscow was no longer in the picture.

There was a sense in American, Pakistani, and Chinese thinking that India was isolated and hence vulnerable to international pressure on arms control, Kashmir, and Indo-Pakistani issues. In other words, the structure of protracted Indo-Pakistani ideological and strategic conflict was formed and institutionalized during the Cold War. Thereafter, the international retreat of Soviet power, the USSR's defeat in Afghanistan, volatility in Indian politics, China's rise, and the aggressive Saudi export of Wahabism and monies for the holy cause, reinforced the Cold War structure of India–Pakistan polarity. From the 1980s, it became a hurtful stalemate for India. This situation suited American, Chinese, Pakistani, and Saudi interests. The imperial idea of divide and rule continued to appeal to the great powers and, in the context of decolonization in South Asia, it became divide and cancel the other's power by tying India to a debilitating fight with Pakistan. In other words, the post-colonial practice of the great powers was to stimulate local/regional power rivalries and to provide diplomatic and material support to the weaker challenger.

Nehru's India went along with the aforesaid pattern of great power interests and policies. Despite her military action in Bangladesh (1971) and the first nuclear test in Pokhran (1974), Indira Gandhi was not able to alter the pattern of great power intervention in India–Pakistan affairs as well as the politics of the local elites. Pakistan and the great powers remained the primary catalysts of change in subcontinent international relations. India remained on the defensive and in a reactive mode.

Between the 1950s and late 1990s, India adapted to the pattern of aggressive behavior by Pakistan and its international partners. India failed because it had a peace policy or a policy of making peace-oriented declarations as the basis of international diplomacy. This was the Nehru tradition. It did not have a war policy. Both are necessary and one alone is not sufficient. The twinning of the two, with plans and knowledge about when to strike and when to negotiate is required to meet the test of "necessary and sufficient" ingredients of national policy. A war policy without a peace process is a prescription for militancy and instability; a peace policy without a war policy is feel-good rhetoric but it is ineffective in the face of an aggressive opponent. Both are needed to secure stability and safety through negotiated restraint.

India became a catalyst for regional and international change when it demonstrated its ability to militarily join the conflict process in the vast subcontinental region which extended from Afghanistan to the Indian Ocean area and included the entire Himalayan belt and Myanmar. It was taken seriously by the Pakistan–US–China–Saudi coalition when it showed a determination to escalate the fight by war and war preparations in a number of crises between 1997 and 2002, and to hold its own against pressure from China and Pakistan as well as insurgents who were fighting India's military in key border areas including Kashmir and the north-east.

The contrast with the Nehru's policies was striking. Nehru sought friendship with Pakistan and avoided general war. By involving the UN in the Kashmir dispute, he internationalized the dispute. His policy was to develop the nuclear option but not to exercise it. His was an anti-military, anti-balance-of-power thinking and anti-coercive diplomacy. Nehru wanted to reduce East–West tensions and to serve the world as a bridge-builder. By the late 1990s, Indian strategic practitioners had abandoned the Nehruvian framework, and chose instead the path of coercive diplomacy. India used coercion in 1971, and it showed restraint in 1999 and again in 2001–02; 1971 was not typical Indian practice of coercive diplomacy because it did not entail the *skilled use* and *skilled non-use of force and threats* to secure a peace settlement, or a durable India–Pakistan peace process. That is, in 1971 India had a war policy but no peace process with Pakistan, as it did after 1998. Post-Nehruvian policy required the assertion of the right, and the development of an ability, to increase international tensions through military escalation and to use this method to seek change in the enemy's behavior about war and negotiations. The decisions to test nuclear arms in 1998, to adopt a nuclear weapons policy, to reject the Comprehensive Test Ban Treaty, and to repeatedly practice coercive diplomacy with Pakistan in several crises were signs of the new Indian orientation. India had learnt to walk on both legs – of war making or war preparation and peacemaking. Despite the practice of crises making in 2001–02, Prime Minister Vajpayee also sought repeatedly to develop a peace process with Pakistan. He also sought to turn the diplomatic relationship with China into a cooperative one even though the military relationship was based on strategic rivalry and mistrust. The Indian pattern of behavior showed a combination of escalation and negotiation. This duality was revealed in India's policies towards the US, China, and Pakistan after 1998.

Following the 1998 tests, India negotiated nuclear restraints with America. After declaring China potential enemy number one, India sought to enhance diplomatic and economic links with China. After the military crises with Pakistan, India started a peace process. India became a catalyst for changing the behavior of Pakistan and its allies when it showed a capacity to unilaterally escalate and then to negotiate bilaterally with these countries.

Thus the chapter ends on an optimistic tone. It implies that the protracted India–Pakistan conflict may become a turnaround story as the US and China distance themselves from Pakistan's challenge to India, as Pakistan's elite and public opinion re-think Pakistani options, and as

India's strength and skills grow. However, the optimism should be tempered because the process of peacemaking has just begun and it is likely to be prolonged. It took India and Pakistan over fifty years to go through a number of stages: chaos (1947–48 Kashmir War, millions of refugees, and weak or non-existent local authorities), instability, conflict, and arms racing (1950s–70s), and finally, regional power and conflict formation (1970s–90s) in India's favor. On the Indian side, there is a commitment to a peace process along with Indian military preparations, economic development, and mobilization of non-traditional allies (US, Israel, Iran, and lately to an extent China) in addition to traditional ones (France and Russia). On the Pakistani side, it requires a re-assessment of Pakistani options when the history of war indicates that the Pakistani military and intelligence services have not won a single war even with the support of their international coalition partners. The continued challenge to the regional order by Pakistan has not yet resulted in a territorial reorganization of the Indian subcontinent.

7 Nuclear weapons and the prolongation of the India–Pakistan rivalry

Saira Khan

Introduction

The India–Pakistan enduring rivalry has survived the twentieth century, and demonstrates little signs of termination in the foreseeable future. While many other rivalries have ceased to exist owing to external or internal shocks,[1] this rivalry continues to be prolonged, even though the international system has transformed from a bipolar to a near unipolar system while substantial changes have occurred in many regions of the world. What explains the prolongation of this rivalry? Is this a unique case in world politics? Under what conditions would the enduring rivalry witness changes in the relationship between the parties with the potential to terminate the conflict? These salient questions need addressing for a better understanding of the rivalry and its resolution possibilities.

The dimensions of the India–Pakistan rivalry are many, as is the case with most long-running rivalries, and there may not be one answer to the question why its termination has been so difficult compared to some other enduring rivalries in the world. Nonetheless, one of the crucial factors contributing to the continuation of the rivalry is the possession of nuclear weapons by the dyad. A rivalry can end with a war or a thaw in the relationship for diplomacy to take precedence over coercion, which can be stimulated by external pressures from great powers. It may be difficult for any of these to occur in the presence of nuclear weapons. Ironically, while nuclear weapons are generally acquired with the intention to deter wars and maintain stability in an enduring rivalry, they help generate severe crises, which negatively affect the prospects of rivalry termination. Nuclear weapons are notable equalizers and as such the weaker power with nuclear arms in the dyad is much more confident in the military sphere and can trigger crises to make possible short-term tactical gains. The stronger

---

[1] Garry Goertz and Paul F. Diehl argue that shocks, exogenous or endogenous, can terminate enduring rivalries. See Garry Goertz and Paul F. Diehl, "The Initiation and Termination of Enduring Rivalries: The Impact of Political Shocks," *American Journal of Political Science* 39 (Feb. 1995), 31–32.

power would not compromise because it is already placed at a position of strength. The frequency of crises, usually generated by the weaker power in the dyadic rivalry, increases in a situation where full-scale war is unlikely to occur because military escalation would be controlled. The creation of such a crisis-prone environment has adverse effects on terminating the enduring rivalry. As the level of hostility and rivalry is elevated, it becomes more entrenched; thus, paths to termination remain unexplored. Such a situation is more common between asymmetric conventional power dyads and nascent nuclear rivals. With the passage of time, these states could become mature nuclear states that may learn how to utilize the non-war situation in thawing the rivalry and eventually terminating it through dialogue, negotiations, and compromise.

The purpose of this chapter is not to undermine the significance of other factors analyzed in this volume that may have impacted the continuation of the India–Pakistan conflict, but to underscore the salience of nuclear weapons in the prolongation of the rivalry. The following section provides a theoretical discernment on the role of nuclear weapons in an enduring rivalry. The framework portrays the advantages and disadvantages of states in enduring rivalries possessing nuclear weapons, while discussing how the disadvantages impact the rivalry in terms of its entrenchment. The following pages test the theoretical arguments against the India–Pakistan case. The impact of the absence or presence of nuclear weapons on crises is explicated and the stability–instability paradox in South Asia in the nuclear period is examined. Following that the connection between instability – an aspect of the stability–instability paradox – and conflict resolution initiatives taken by the leaders of India and Pakistan is discussed. These peace endeavors highlight the difficulties of initiating and continuing a peace process in a crisis-prone environment. Finally, the conclusion discusses the conditions under which the rivalry may be terminated. A durable peace process requires a non-crisis environment in order to eliminate hatred and misunderstandings between the contending parties.

Nuclear weapons in an enduring rivalry

An enduring rivalry represents "competition between the same pair of states as a result of well-entrenched causes and represented in severe and repeated conflicts over an extended period of time. It involves six or more militarized disputes between the two states over a period of twenty years."[2] An enduring rivalry is similar to a protracted conflict where hatred is

[2] *Ibid.*, 31–33.

embedded, crisis is ingrained, and high probability of war commands the relationship. Since each rival considers the other as its "principal opponent,"[3] most enduring rivals face chronic security threats and endeavor to match the capabilities of the adversary. Because the outbreak of war remains a high probability between them, actors make efforts to acquire defensive and offensive weapons to ward off possible attacks so as to be prepared to fight back in case of an attack. In the nuclear age, most enduring rivals have either decided to obtain the guarantee of a power capable of providing them with a nuclear umbrella to deter wars with their adversary, or have taken the task of developing the weapons upon themselves. Nuclear weapons have attracted enduring rivals at the systemic and subsystemic levels because of their deterrent value. When wars are more probable in a conflict setting, which is the case with most enduring rivals, rivals tend to attach more importance to the acquisition of nuclear weapons for war-avoidance purposes.[4] However, once acquired, they fall into a trap of an unending cycle. The acquired deterrent capability produces a special kind of insecurity because the rivalry could become entrenched with the possession of nuclear weapon by both sides. Although deterrence is achieved in terms of preventing full-scale wars in the presence of nuclear capabilities due to their devastating effects, the actors are unlikely to perceive an urgency to negotiate because a degree of parity is achieved between them. The power asymmetry in the relationship, if there was one, is generally reduced, as nuclear weapons tend to be "great equalizers"[5] for the weaker state. This environment means the revisionist actor is tempted to entertain low-to-medium-intensity crises to make short-term gains. The weaker rival could take advantage of the situation because it understands that its chances of achieving its goal by other means are slim. The stronger or the initially preponderant power may also consider undertaking coercive actions to counter the attacks of the weaker side and empower it with new strategies to confront the new security environment.

In the absence of full-scale wars, the eruption of low-to-medium-intensity crises generates instability. Low-to-medium-intensity violence may include all severe violent military conflict short of all-out war. In South Asia, low-intensity violence includes border clashes and skirmishes, and some low-level fighting along the Line of Control (LoC) in Jammu and Kashmir. Medium-intensity violence generally erupts with intensive border battles

---

[3] William R. Thompson, "Principal Rivalries," *Journal of Conflict Resolution* 39 (June 1995), 201.

[4] See Saira Khan, *Nuclear Proliferation Dynamics in Protracted Conflict Regions: A Comparative Study of South Asia and the Middle East* (Aldershot, UK: Ashgate Publishing, 2002), 35–57.

[5] See Paul in this volume.

and confrontation between the armed forces of the adversaries. They remain non-war crises when armed forces do not cross the international border.

Where crises occur frequently in a war-free conflict between nuclear dyads, the conflict faces instability because absence of war is not sufficient to generate stability. Stability is a function of absence of war (large-scale, all-out, conventional, and nuclear) and absence of crisis (heated, non-violent, or violent). While crisis scholars consider war to be an integral part of a crisis, this is inapplicable in a nuclear situation.[6] Between nuclear dyads, the probability of war is almost zero, even though the probability of low-to-medium-intensity violence remains high.

A crisis-prone environment deteriorates the already-hostile environment between the adversaries. The continuity of this environment is non-conducive to rivalry termination, especially through dialogue. A ceasefire may be established from time to time and rivals may retreat from their defined positions, but these are temporary solutions to de-flame heated situations which need not generate an atmosphere to explore paths to rivalry resolution. A bold leader of one of the states may attempt to change the environment by taking unilateral and conciliatory moves, but such initiatives need not last long because the other side may exploit the situation to change it in its favor by initiating a crisis.

A change in the rivalry can emerge if leaders of both states realize how iniquitous the game is and make moves to alter the situation for mutual gains. Mature nuclear states having experienced this process may come to this realization. The end of the Cold War exemplifies this. Additionally, great powers may compel the rivals to mitigate their differences through negotiation. The great powers must have a vested interest in convincing the parties to negotiate. This may not be easy in general, but may be possible in a hegemonic world where one power enjoys the authority and power to dictate to smaller states.

Absence and presence of nuclear weapons impacting crises

The India–Pakistan enduring rivalry, which started in 1947 over the issue of Kashmir, has continued for more than five decades. Three major

[6] Michael Brecher and Jonathan Wilkenfeld, *A Study of Crisis* (Ann Arbor: University of Michigan Press, 1997), 3–4, 8–11; Brecher, *Crises in World Politics* (Oxford: Pergamon Press, 1993), 3; Glenn H. Snyder and Paul F. Diesing, *Conflict Among Nations: Bargaining, Decision-Making and System Structure in International Crises* (Princeton: Princeton University Press, 1977), 7; Snyder, "Crisis Bargaining," in Charles F. Hermann (ed.), *International Crises: Insights from Behavioral Research* (New York: Free Press, 1972), 217.

wars – in 1947–48, 1965, and 1971 – have erupted between the two proximate rivals in four decades. The last of these wars was not over Kashmir, but was the most salient one because it disintegrated Pakistan and the intensification of the rivalry reached its peak during and after the war. Both countries have paid special attention to the acquisition of nuclear weapons in the post-1971 period and by the late 1980s they had the capability to produce nuclear arms. In 1998, India and Pakistan finally tested their nuclear weapons.

Dyadic crises in the rivalry

The rivalry has experienced eleven interstate crises from 1947 until 2004.[7] Only three of these crises escalated to wars – 1947–48, 1965, and 1971. It is notable that during this period the rivals did not possess nuclear weapons or were not nuclear-weapons-capable states. Four severe dyadic crises erupted after India and Pakistan became nuclear-weapons-capable states in the late 1980s. The Brasstacks crisis (1987), Kashmir crisis (1990), Kargil crisis (1999),[8] and the Parliament attack crisis (2001–03) were all intense, having the potential for military escalation. The Brasstacks crisis involved one of the largest military exercises, comparable to NATO or Warsaw Pact exercises. Many in the West believe there was a growing risk of a miscalculated nuclear war between India and Pakistan during the Kashmir crisis.[9] The Kargil crisis is notable because Pakistani forces acted as Kashmiri mujahidin and infiltrated into India, while the Indians, for the first time since the Bangladesh War of 1971, used air power in this medium-intensity crisis. The most recent crisis in the rivalry erupted when the Indian Parliament was attacked by terrorists in December 2001. The two countries were almost on the brink of war. The remarkably heavy deployment of forces by both sides along the LoC is just one indicator of how serious the crisis was.

---

[7] Brecher and Wilkenfeld list nine interstate crises between 1947 and 1990, including two serious crises in the nuclear period – the Brasstacks crisis and the 1990 nuclear crisis. The first seven crises occurred in the pre-nuclear period, while the last two erupted when both were nuclear weapons states. Two other severe crises occurred after 1990, the Kargil crisis (1999) and the Parliament attack crisis (2001) after India and Pakistan tested their nuclear weapons. Thus, there were eleven interstate crises between India and Pakistan in the last fifty-six years. See Brecher and Wilkenfeld, *A Study of Crisis*, 164.

[8] Although some of the contributors to this volume count the 1999 crisis as a war, I discount it because it was a limited engagement confined to a pocket in Kashmir. War is a declared armed conflict between the military forces of two or more states. Kargil was not a war in this sense, because there had been no acknowledgment from Pakistan that its forces were involved in the fight with their Indian counterparts.

[9] Seymour M. Hersh, "On the Nuclear Edge," *New Yorker*, Mar. 29, 1993, 56–67.

The rivalry encompasses two periods: pre-nuclear and nuclear. The first period lasted for thirty-nine years, 1947–86, and seventeen years of the second period, 1987–2004, have already passed. The two periods are different in terms of the number of crises, frequency of crises per fifteen years, intensity of crises, and strategies employed in crises. In terms of numbers, India and Pakistan have had seven interstate crises in the first thirty-nine years when nuclear weapons were not introduced in the region. After nuclear weapons became a factor in the India–Pakistan rivalry, in the seventeen years from 1987 to 2004 there have been four interstate crises. Thus, the frequency and number of crises increased in the nuclear period compared to the pre-nuclear era. Additionally, since 1987, the frequency of crises per fifteen years has also increased. The first thirty-nine years of the pre-nuclear phase consists of three periods, two fifteen-year periods and one nine-year period – 1947–62, 1963–78, and 1979–86 – because after 1986 the dyads became nuclear-weapons-capable states. During the first fifteen years, between 1947–62, there were four crises.

The first decade of the enduring rivalry witnessed the largest number of interstate crises. The three crises of the 1940s include Junagadh (1947–48), Kashmir I (1947–49), and Hyderabad (1948). In the 1950s Punjab War Scare I (1951) was the only crisis between the dyads which did not escalate. However, in the second fifteen-year period, 1963–78, the number of interstate crises decreased to three; two of those crises led to wars. In the third non-nuclear period, 1979–86, there was no dyadic crisis in the India–Pakistan conflict. This demonstrates the gradual decrease of dyadic crises between India and Pakistan in the pre-nuclear era. Contrary to that, in the nuclear era, in the first fifteen years, 1987–2002, the dyads have had four major crises. The last crisis of 2001 ended in spring 2003, making the beginning of the second fifteen-year nuclear period, 2003–18, crisis-prone from the start. The seven interstate crises that occurred in South Asia during the first thirty-nine years were distributed in the 1940s, 1950s, 1960s, and 1970s. In other words, in every decade there was one or more crisis. The two crises of the 1960s were Rann of Kutch (1965) and Kashmir II (1965–66). The second one led to a full-scale war. Finally, in the 1970s there was only one crisis, in 1971, which led to the Bangladesh War.[10]

Although there were three crises in the 1940s, which is normal in the initial phase of an enduring rivalry, between the fourth and the fifth crises there was a gap of fourteen years. In the nuclear period, there was no such gap and, in essence, within a period of fifteen years the rivals generated

[10] Brecher and Wilkenfeld, *A Study of Crisis*, 164.

four intense crises. In terms of intensity, although there were three wars in the pre-nuclear era, making three of the seven interstate crises severe, the other four crises were low-intensity ones. In the nuclear period, all four crises were severe in terms of intensity and escalation potential. Although there was an absence of wars in all of them, these were all medium-intensity crises. Additionally, one of them – the Parliament attack crisis – lasted 18 months and was the longest crisis the rivalry had witnessed.

The strategies employed by India and Pakistan in the pre-nuclear period also changed in the nuclear period. In the first era, both states used war as a crisis management mechanism. Thus, the use of regular forces was the norm. The nuclear period witnessed the usage of terrorism, proxy wars, and low-to-medium-intensity violence by Pakistan. The Indians also changed their strategies from full-scale war to limited war – even though India was prepared to widen the Kargil conflict if it had been unable to evict Pakistani forces with limited means. Unlimited war may erupt where one side wants to keep the conflict limited but the other side has the ability to escalate it. Nuclear weapons created a permissive condition in offering a variety of coercive strategies to the challenger and allowing the defender to overcome that by adopting tougher postures. Table 7.1 demonstrates these points.

In the pre-nuclear age, wars occurred readily with little hesitation, leading to instability in the relationship. The 1965 war demonstrates rapid escalation of a crisis to war in the pre-nuclear period. Contrary to that, the nuclear period had more stability due to absence of wars, but it also had more instability due to the frequent eruption of crises. Thus, the conflict witnessed a stability–instability paradox in the nuclear period, which is analyzed below. A comparative analysis of the crisis situations in the pre-nuclear and nuclear periods follows for a better understanding of the escalation and non-escalation policies that were adopted by both states in pre-nuclear and nuclear periods respectively.

Crisis escalation and non-escalation patterns In September 1965,[11] the Pakistan army infiltrated the ceasefire line in Kashmir, which led the Indians to cross the international border. For India, the crisis began when Pakistanis infiltrated into Kashmir to create a massive uprising against Indian control of the state of Kashmir. When India responded by sending several thousand troops across the 1949 ceasefire line, Pakistan perceived

[11] I use only the 1965 war and compare it with four crises of the nuclear period because only these crises in the rivalry had the potential to escalate. The 1947–48 and 1971 wars could not be used for comparison because the first erupted right after India and Pakistan acquired independence and the second one was not over Kashmir.

Table 7.1 *India–Pakistan crises in pre-nuclear and nuclear periods*

	Periods	
Crises	Pre-nuclear 1947–1986 = 39 years	Nuclear 1987–2004 = 17 years
Total number	7	4
Frequency per 15 years	1947–62 = 4 1963–78 = 3 1979–86 = 0	1987–2002 = 4 2003–2004 = 0 (the last crisis of 2001 continued till the spring of 2003)
Intensity	High due to wars in 1947–48, 1965, and 1971; low in all other non-war crises	Medium in all non-war crises: 1987, 1990, 1999, and 2001
Strategies employed	War; use of regular force	No full-scale war, limited war; use of terrorism, proxy war, and low-to- medium-intensity violence

a crisis. The armies of India and Pakistan faced each other across the Punjab border, occupied each other's territory, and violated the ceasefire agreement, triggering an all-out war. The war ended within four months in January 1966 with the Tashkent Declaration. This crisis highlights how little restraint both India and Pakistan have shown in crossing the cease-fire line drawn in 1949 and in using war as a central crisis management technique. Since none of the contending parties possessed nuclear weapons at that time, crisis was escalated to the war level without hesitation. Such crisis management strategies changed as soon as nuclear weapons capabilities were introduced into the rivalry. Indian defense analyst K. Subrahmanyam compared the 1965 crisis leading to a war to the medium-intensity crises of the 1990s in South Asia. He posited that when Pakistan sent 5,000 armed forces into Kashmir in 1965 it triggered the Indian army to cross the ceasefire line and that escalated to a war. However, even though Pakistan had acted in an almost similar manner for many years in the 1990s, India did not cross the ceasefire line and this new Indian strategy was employed due to Pakistan's acquisition of nuclear weapons capability.[12] P. R. Chari maintains that after the nuclear tests of India and Pakistan, the former was deterred in crossing the LoC to attack

[12] Personal interview with K. Subrahmanyam, New Delhi, Jan. 28, 1997.

Pakistani operational bases in Skardu.[13] Adversaries employed prudent crisis non-escalation strategies in more severe and intimidating crises.

Four major crises of the nuclear period – the Brasstacks crisis of 1987, the Kashmir crisis of 1990, the Kargil crisis of 1999, and the Indian Parliament attack crisis of 2001 – did not escalate to wars. Thus, a general level of stability at the war level was maintained between India and Pakistan in the nuclear period. In 1986, the Indian army under the leadership of General Sundarji conducted a massive military exercise in the Rajasthan desert, which triggered a crisis for Pakistan. As part of its action-reaction policy, Pakistan deployed its armed forces and India responded by occupying defensive positions, turning the situation into an international crisis, known as the Brasstacks crisis of 1987.[14] In terms of manpower, equipment, the use of air force, and the placing of additional ammunition close to the exercise area near the Pakistan border, this was an intense crisis in the rivalry. Nonetheless, the crisis did not escalate to war, and the leadership of the two countries managed "to de-escalate without violence."[15] This begs the question why such a crisis did not escalate.

By 1987, even though the Pakistanis knew about the Indian nuclear capability, India was still unsure whether or not Pakistan possessed a nuclear capability. During the crisis, however, the Indian journalist, Kuldip Nayar, was contacted by Mushahid Hussein, the editor of the Pakistani newspaper, *The Muslim*, and was permitted to interview Pakistan's chief nuclear scientist, Abdul Qadeer Khan. This event took place on January 28, 1987, which was the peak period of the Brasstacks crisis. In that interview Khan stated, "Nobody can undo Pakistan or take us for granted. We are here to stay and let it be clear that we shall use the bomb if our existence is threatened."[16] Indian leaders understood that this was a nuclear signal to bring an end to the crisis. Hussein claimed that "the message given by A. Q. Khan ... is directed against those detractors of the Islamic bomb. To the Indians, it was a 'hands-off' message at a time when New Delhi has been carrying out massive warlike exercises all along our eastern border."[17] In a world where nuclear weapons acquisition was

---

[13] P. R. Chari, "Indo-Pakistan Relations: Uncertain Future," in Major General Ashok Krishna and P. R. Chari (eds.), *Kargil: The Tables Turned* (New Delhi: Manohar, 2001), 261.

[14] For a detailed discussion on the Brasstacks crisis, see Kanti Bajpai, P. R. Chari, Pervaiz Iqbal Cheema, Stephen P. Cohen, and Sumit Ganguly, *Brasstacks and Beyond: Perception and Management of Crisis in South Asia* (New Delhi: Manohar, 1995).

[15] C. Raja Mohan and Peter Lavoy, "Avoiding Nuclear War," in Michael Krepon and Amit Sevak (eds.), *Crisis Prevention, Confidence-Building, and Reconciliation in South Asia* (New York: St. Martin's Press, 1995), 32.

[16] Kuldip Nayar, "We Have the A-Bomb, Says Pakistan's Dr. Strangelove," *The Observer*, London, Mar. 1, 1987.

[17] "Bomb Controversy," *The Muslim*, Islamabad, Mar. 3, 1987.

shrouded with secrecy, statements of this nature were used to communicate to the adversaries about the possession of nuclear capabilities and
intent to use them if needed.

In 1990, some Western journalists and analysts argued that South Asia
was on the verge of nuclear war during a crisis over Kashmir.[18] Seymour M.
Hersh wrote that according to a reliable intelligence report to Washington,
the army chief of Pakistan, General Aslam Beg, had authorized the techni-
cians at Kahuta Research Laboratories to assemble nuclear weapons to use
them at the proper time. As the Kashmir crisis intensified because of India's
buildup of conventional forces in Kashmir and Rajasthan, Pakistan,
"openly deployed its armored tank units along the Indian border and,
secretly, placed its nuclear-weapons arsenal on alert."[19] General Beg, however, stated that Pakistan was definitely not mobilizing its aircraft and
nuclear capabilities during the crisis.[20] South Asian scholars and decisionmakers contend that this crisis was one of the best proofs of nuclear
deterrence in the subcontinent before Kargil. Pakistan had already
acquired nuclear weapons capability before this crisis,[21] and the weapons
were ready for assembly at short notice; India was well aware of this
development through various sources, which included the media, scholarly
publications, and the condemnation of the international community, especially, the US. Devin Hagerty argues: "Indian leaders perceived Pakistan to
be an aspiring nuclear weapon state in 1987, but an actual nuclear weapon
state in 1990."[22] Indians understood the message that Pakistan could drop
nuclear weapons with their F-16 aircraft and that they could retaliate if
India began a conventional war against Pakistan. Pakistan would use its
nuclear weapons as a last resort, a message that was conveyed to the Indians
through the press.[23] Indian nuclear capability had also advanced qualitatively by then. Neither state could contemplate war in the presence of
nuclear capabilities.

---

[18] Hersh, "On the Nuclear Edge," 56–67; William E. Burrows and Robert Windrem,
Critical Mass: The Dangerous Race for Super-weapons in a Fragmenting World (New York:
Simon and Schuster, 1994), 61–82; James Adams, "Pakistan 'Nuclear War Threat,'" *The
Sunday Times*, London, May 27, 1990.

[19] Hersh, "On the Nuclear Edge," 56.

[20] Personal interview with General Aslam Beg, Islamabad, Feb. 13, 1997.

[21] For more information on the Kashmir crisis, see Michael Krepon and Mishi Faruqee
(eds.), *Conflict Prevention and Confidence-Building Measures in South Asia: The 1990 Crisis*,
Occasional Paper 17 (Washington, DC: Henry L. Stimson Center, 1994); Sumit
Ganguly, *The Crisis in Kashmir: Portents of War, Hopes for Peace* (New York: Cambridge
University Press, 1997).

[22] Devin T. Hagerty, *The Consequences of Nuclear Proliferation* (Cambridge, MA: MIT Press,
1998), 166.

[23] Personal interview with Ross Masud Hussein, Islamabad, Feb. 13, 1997.

The May 1998 nuclear tests by India and Pakistan removed the opacity encircling nuclear weapons acquisition. Just one year after their tests, Pakistan intruded into the heights of Kargil in the spring of 1999 by employing an entirely different strategy – from low-intensity operations to a medium-intensity conflict. Although Pakistan's intention was to capture the Kargil heights without a fight and present India and the international community with a *fait accompli*, Pakistan was ready for a medium-intensity operation – the outcome of Kargil operations.

In Kargil, professional military personnel acted as mujahidin and moved on to Indian territory. Pakistan's intrusion and seizure of the Kargil heights on the Indian side of the LoC in Kashmir resulted in the worst fighting between Indian and Pakistani regular armed forces since the 1971 war. Pakistan had waited till the nuclear tests were completed for the Kargil crisis to start even though it had devised such an operational strategy in the late 1980s.[24]

In the escalation phase of the crisis, the Indian air force used combat air power in the high mountain ranges above 15,000 feet altitude. Pakistan deployed large numbers of surface-to-air missiles and air defense weaponry in the battlefield across the LoC on the Indian side. As tensions rose, the military confrontation in Kargil could have rapidly escalated into a full-scale war. However, the Indian army did not cross the LoC. It is believed that the Indian government made the decision not to cross the LoC because it feared that the conflict could escalate to the nuclear level.[25] By July 1999, following President Clinton's intervention, Pakistan's prime minister, Nawaz Sharif, had ordered the army to withdraw from Kargil for fear of a full-scale war involving nuclear exchange.[26] Jasjit Singh argues that nuclear weapons had possibly eliminated the probability of a full-scale war where the contestants were willing to risk escalation just short of a nuclear exchange.[27] The crisis was exceptional because of Pakistan's usage of a new strategy to make gains on a surprise attack short of war and India's decision to unleash its air power as part of its retaliation strategy, yet not crossing the crisis threshold. Stephen P. Cohen calls it "a classic limited war between two nuclear-weapons states ... It is war by other means – diplomacy, public relations, terrorism and limited use of air power."[28]

---

[24] Leng in this volume.
[25] "Indian Envoy Rules Out Full-scale War," *Dawn*, May 18, 1999.
[26] *Hindu*, July 6, 1999.
[27] Jasjit Singh, "Pakistan's Fourth War," *Strategic Analysis* 23 (Aug. 1999), 685–702.
[28] Quoted in Sandand Dhume, "Limited War," *Far Eastern Economic Review*, Aug. 26, 1999, 24.

On December 13, 2001, terrorists attacked the Indian Parliament, which triggered a serious crisis for India. India deployed heavy forces, about 800,000 troops, along the border, and Pakistan responded by similar deployments, creating intense hostility between them that prevailed for more than 18 months. South Asia was considered a nuclear flashpoint because the belligerents were unwilling to budge from their positions for an extended period. India insisted that Pakistan must stop supporting the terrorists, and troop pullout would be a function of that. Pakistan maintained that it was innocent, but was prepared for an eventual military confrontation. However, war was avoided and the crisis deescalated without any major conflict. This was a cautious political decision taken by key Indian policymakers. On December 19, the Indian prime minister told Parliament: "There can be no hasty decision in choosing between war and peace. We must be patient and take a comprehensive view of all options,"[29] and based on this, on December 21, 2001, he decided to recall the Indian high commissioner from Pakistan and stop transportation links between the two states.[30] Non-war options were chosen because, as the former Chief of Army Staff General Shankar Roy states, "There is a limit to which the counter terrorist operations can be intensified. The government will have to understand that this could lead to horizontal escalation and a full-blown conventional conflict."[31] The main apprehension was that Pakistan could turn it into a nuclear war. This crisis also exemplifies the fact that the outbreak of war (a probability) was avoided for fear of nuclear escalation.[32]

The four crises of the nuclear period indicate that wars have been intentionally avoided in the region. Although threats and counter threats from both sides have been common since the late 1980s and have become more frequent since the 1990s, none has actually crossed the crisis threshold. The most recent long-drawn-out crisis after the Indian Parliament attack also demonstrates that the Indians, who were serious about undertaking a hardline policy against Pakistan, decided to exhaust other diplomatic and non-violent means of crisis management before undertaking the last option – a war. Such prudent decisions would not have been taken

---

[29] Bhavdeep Kang, "Tempers Tempered," *Outlook*, Dec. 31, 2001, 24.
[30] V. Sudarshan, "It's War, Put Diplomatically," *Outlook*, Dec. 31, 2001, 32.
[31] Raj Chengappa and Shishir Gupta, "In Cold Pursuit," *India Today*, Dec. 24, 2001, 37.
[32] Other important factors of war avoidance include the strong role the US played in urging India not to attack, India's consideration not to agitate the US by attacking Washington's ally in the war on terror, and the slowness of the Indian forces to get into proper fighting positions when Pakistani forces had taken strong defensive positions and were ready for counter-attack.

if nuclear weapons did not factor into the calculations of both states. Thus, even though academic debates continue over South Asian stability, this is perhaps the only region in the world that has proved more than once that an acute crisis can also deescalate without a war when crisis actors possess nuclear weapons. However, stability at the war level generates instability at the lower levels of the conflict.

Stability breeds instability in the nuclear era

Stability at the war level in nuclear South Asia does not necessarily indicate the maintenance of peace. Pakistan's bomb maker, Abdul Qadeer Khan once said that he considers "nuclear weapons as weapons of peace."[33] This begs the question: Is peace equivalent to a condition of no war alone? Although nuclear weapons may have kept wars between India and Pakistan at bay, the four crises discussed in the previous section also demonstrate that serious and medium-intensity crises have been integral parts of the India–Pakistan rivalry in the nuclear period. Looking at the enduring rivalry from this perspective, it seems that a nuclear South Asia did not experience comprehensive stability. Instability is a product of changes in strategies employed by both India and Pakistan, due to the acquisition of nuclear weapons capabilities in the late 1980s.

The frequency and intensity of crises have changed in the nuclear era; so have the strategies employed by India and Pakistan. Since 1987, after Pakistan's President Zia ul-Haq stated that Pakistan could virtually make a nuclear bomb whenever it wanted,[34] Islamabad became a much more confident actor. Having possessed nuclear weapons capability, Pakistan's strategies pertaining to Kashmir underwent substantial changes. Pakistan, being a conventionally weaker power in the rivalry, felt much more assured in the military sphere and triggered a series of crises because of its expectation that escalation would be controlled. It started taking advantage of the nuclear situation and employed strategies such as terrorism, proxy wars, and low-to-medium-intensity violence in the post-1987 period. South Asian security analyst Michael Krepon states that Pakistan's "support for separatism and militancy has notably coincided with its acquisition of covert nuclear weapons" and that the overall tensions and crises between India and Pakistan had increased since both tested their nuclear weapons.[35]

---

[33] Raj Chengappa, "N-Arms Weapons of Peace," *Hindu*, Aug. 26, 2002.

[34] Edward W. Desmond, "Knocking at the Nuclear Door," *Time*, Mar. 30, 1987, 14–16.

[35] Michael Krepon, "Stability–Instability Paradox, Misperceptions, and Escalation Control in South Asia" (Washington, DC: Stimson Center, May 2003), 3.

In addition to proxy wars, Pakistan introduced terrorist tactics in the late 1980s, which heightened in the 1990s and early 2000s. The 1980s was also a period when autonomy sentiment grew among the Kashmiris. Pakistan, which refrained from exploiting the Kashmir issue in the 1970s after the Bangladesh War, exploited this unrest in its own favor. In the 1990s the Hindu nationalist party, the BJP rose to power after decades of Congress' rule and this elevated the threat level of the Kashmiri Muslims. Demands such as the destruction of the Babri Mosque in Ayodhya in 1992 were used by the BJP during its election campaign. The BJP also used its anti-Muslim and anti-Pakistan discourses to mobilize support.[36] Within this context, Pakistan realized that the Kashmiris would have no choice but to seek its support in a Hindu-dominated India. Given this, it provided assistance to the Kashmiri militants and *madrassas* proliferated to indoctrinate Kashmiri Muslims with jihad-inducing inflammatory religious ethos. The crises in the 1990s and after were mostly generated by Pakistan with the support of the Kashmiris. While the objectives for triggering those crises may have been justified to the Pakistanis, the strategies employed to attain the objectives were unacceptable to the international community in general and India in particular. According to the Pakistanis, in Kargil "the idea was to put pressure on India to come to the negotiating table."[37] However, the Indians believe that Pakistan wanted to internationalize the Kashmir issue through this conflict. In other words, if India could be provoked to retaliate, "the issue would automatically get internationalized."[38] Regardless of the objectives, the strategy used to accomplish the goals only proved that Pakistan did not have any apprehension in launching such a major offensive on India.

The fearlessness the Pakistanis demonstrated in the Kargil crisis proves the point that only nuclear weapons acquisition could give them the confidence to launch such an offensive against India. P. R Chari believes that Kargil revealed that proxy wars and "sub-conventional conflicts" or support for cross-border terrorism and militancy were common in the India–Pakistan conflict due to the presence of nuclear weapons. He further argues that Pakistan "could with impunity, indulge in 'salami slicing' to capture small pieces of territory under the rubric of nuclear deterrence, and in the confidence that India would not find it possible to escalate the conflict lest it approach the nuclear level."[39] On the general

---

[36] Nasr in this volume.
[37] Interview with Niaz Naik, former foreign secretary of Pakistan, Apr. 23, 2003.
[38] D. Suba Chandran, "Why Kargil? Pakistan's Objectives and Motivation," in Krishna and Chari (eds.), *Kargil: The Tables Turned*, 33.
[39] Chari, "Indo-Pakistan Relations: Uncertain Future," 261.

level of militant insurgency and terrorism across the LoC and their connection with nuclear weapons acquisition, Sumit Ganguly argues that in
the 1990s Pakistan aided the insurgents in Kashmir although it knew fully
well that there could be Indian military escalation. This is because, on the
one hand, the Pakistanis saw an excellent opportunity to "impose significant material and other costs on India at little cost to themselves," and
on the other hand, because India's conventional edge over them had been
neutralized as they had achieved nuclear parity.[40]

India's strategies pertaining to the India–Pakistan conflict also changed
in the nuclear period. Indians started to believe that a full-scale war in the
conflict was unlikely to occur because nuclear weapons have a profound
impact on the nature of war. Within this setting, they have also undertaken bold military actions short of full-scale war against Pakistan. For
example, Indians would not have resorted to air power in Kargil, if they
did not think that fighting would be localized. The Indians realized that
military escalation would be controlled should its new strategy prove too
risky. This belief was attributed to K. K. Nayyar's argument when he said
that the nature of war in the conflict had changed and that only minor
wars are likely to occur in the India–Pakistan conflict.[41]

Kargil demonstrates primarily that a war of a limited nature is likely to
occur even though both India and Pakistan are nuclear states. Jasjit Singh
states that "war is an armed conflict between two military forces" and that
Kargil was a war from that perspective. However, "two militaries fought
in a localized region" and thus, "a limited war" occurred. He further
argues that one of the flaws in Pakistani assumptions is that a conventional response will not occur in conventional crises.[42] It is important to
note here that Pakistan in reality did not expect that Kargil would turn out
to be a limited war. Its intention was not to have even a limited military
confrontation with India. Shirin Mazari argues that "Kargil was blown
out of proportion. India opted for military escalation in Kargil."[43]
Although this suggests that Pakistan's intentions in Kargil may not have
been what India believed them to be, it also shows that Islamabad's new
proxy war strategy would not have been employed if the acquisition of
nuclear weapons did not factor into the calculus. Additionally, it implies
that Pakistan was not expecting India to respond by using air power, a
shift from its traditional strategy. The decision to use air power was a

---

[40] Sumit Ganguly, *Conflict Unending: India–Pakistan Tensions since 1947* (New York:
Columbia University Press, 2001), 92.
[41] Interview with Vice Admiral K. K. Nayyar, Dec. 27, 2001.
[42] Interview with Air Commodore Jasjit Singh, New Delhi, Dec. 29, 2001.
[43] Interview with Shirin Mazari, director general, Islamabad Institute of Strategic Studies,
Islamabad, Apr. 22, 2003.

turning point because it marked a significant change from previous Indian attempts to deal with Pakistani intrusions along the LoC.[44]

The medium-intensity crisis in Kargil precipitated the development of a limited-war strategy in India. India is now better prepared to face Pakistan in this new strategic environment. It is devising strategies to fight a limited conventional war against Pakistan. One of those strategies, according to Ganguly, is to attack "a wide band along the border without making deep incursions into Pakistan's territory," and the goal would be to gain as much "captured land" as possible, which would then be used as bargaining chips for Pakistan's concessions in Kashmir.[45] In the realm of the limited-war strategy, T. V. Paul argues that India also focused on a limited-war strategy in 2002 after the Parliament attack, to target the terrorist camps on the Pakistani side without escalating into a war.[46] S. D. Muni maintains: "We assume that hitting a few terrorist camps will not generate into a nuclear war."[47] In a similar vein, but addressing why India needs to devise a bolder strategy, Muchkund Dubey states that the military preparations were taken by India after the Parliament attack to give a new signal to the Pakistanis. The Indian government's position has been that Pakistan should feel that its action of facilitating infiltration has heavy costs.[48] With a massive mobilization of forces, India tried to demonstrate its military readiness to face off the Pakistanis and not give in to the terrorist tactics used by its rival in a nuclear environment. K. Subrahmanyam argues that taking military moves against Pakistan would be counter-productive, but that Indian troop mobilization was required to put pressure on Pakistan.[49] Such strategies were not designed during the initial periods of the India–Pakistan conflict, especially in the post-1965 period, when Pakistanis continued to infiltrate into India. Today, India's strategies have changed with the new strategies employed by Pakistan over Kashmir.

On the strategies used by India and Pakistan in the nuclear period, Michael Krepon argues that both have resorted to brinkmanship over Kashmir and that the difference was in how they used brinkmanship. India resorted to brinkmanship "by mobilizing and threatening war" and "Pakistan by initiating the Kargil incursion and by its continued commitment to a Kashmir policy that relies on militancy to punish India and to leverage favorable outcomes."[50] They have basically changed their strategies on how to demonstrate their resolve. Such strategy changes continue

---

[44] Ganguly, *Conflict Unending*, 117.   [45] *Ibid.*, 126–27.   [46] Paul in this volume.
[47] Interview with S. D. Muni, South Asia specialist, New Delhi, Jan. 4, 2002.
[48] Interview with Muchkund Dubey, former Indian foreign secretary, New Delhi, Dec. 27, 2001.
[49] Interview with K. Subrahmanyam, New Delhi, Jan. 6, 2002.
[50] Krepon, "The Stability–Instability Paradox," 10.

to generate more tension and hostility in the rivalry. They have negative consequences on the conflict because Indians now believe in the exaggerated resolve of the Pakistanis[51] and Pakistanis believe that nuclear weapons acquisition has provided India with a newfound strength, which enables it to flex its muscles.[52] Regrettably, misunderstandings abound in the rivalry, and serious crises erupt frequently, generating instability in the conflict.

Conflict termination in a crisis-prone environment

For obtaining comprehensive stability in the India–Pakistan rivalry, peace initiatives must be taken to resolve the conflict, which can only happen if the recurrent pattern of crises ends. Peace resulting from special endeavors does not generally last due to the eruption of a new crisis. Two peace initiatives and a crisis after each initiative in the nuclear period highlight a new pattern of peace and crises in a nuclear environment.

War tends to be the ultimate instrument resorted to by states to bring an end to many conflicts in the past. As war may no longer remain a tool to terminate the India–Pakistan conflict in a nuclear environment, other mechanisms of rivalry termination must be employed. Means such as dialogue and diplomatic negotiations can be used only if there is a non-crisis environment in the conflict.[53] However, a conflict has a slim chance of being settled by the parties if crisis is a constant factor in the relationship. Where crises erupt frequently, the parties are constantly engaged in some form of violence and are never "free from the psychological legacy of an ongoing conflict."[54] Because war is not an option, Pakistan's policy is to bleed India and India's is to bleed the Kashmiris and to hit Pakistan when possible.[55] The chronic, intense, and long drawn out crises institutionalized the distrust that India has of Pakistan and vice versa, and this is reflected in official statements, policies, and the moves taken to correspond to the policies.

While the conflict most often experiences a medium degree of intensification because medium-intensity crises occur frequently, its degree of

---

[51] Raja Menon, *A Nuclear Strategy for India* (Thousand Oaks, CA: Sage Publications, 2000), 152.

[52] Interview with Shirin Mazari, Islamabad, Apr. 22, 2003.

[53] Richard Ned Lebow argues that a crisis could also be used to coerce one's adversary into making a conciliatory move. This is a high-risk strategy where the essence of the strategy is to manipulate the shared risks of violence. Although an interesting strategy, it may not be applicable in South Asia because coercion has never had positive effects on the India–Pakistan relationship. See Lebow, *Between Peace and War* (Baltimore: Johns Hopkins University Press, 1981).

[54] Michael Brecher, "Crisis Escalation: A New Model and Findings," in Frank Harvey and Ben D. More (eds.), *Conflict in World Politics* (London: Macmillan, 1997), 125.

[55] Eqbal Ahmed, "A Kashmiri Solution for Kashmir," *Himal* (South Asia), 1997.

intensification fluctuates and at times low intensity is experienced when a crisis is terminated. However, policymakers cannot seize the opportunity and start a negotiating process because of the adverse legacy of a prior crisis. Additionally, before a peace process can be institutionalized, another crisis erupts. Consequently, peace initiatives are jeopardized by new and more heated crises.

After the May 1998 nuclear tests of India and Pakistan, the hostility level between them got elevated because a new round of a nuclear arms race had begun. Nevertheless, in less than a year, unexpectedly, Indian Prime Minister A. B. Vajpayee took a bold initiative to thaw the conflict. He believed that time was ripe for conflict resolution and stated that there was no option to them except peace.[56] His bus trip from Delhi to Lahore was part of a confidence-building measure. Pakistan's Prime Minister Nawaz Sharif reciprocated the Indian move. Remarkable progress in the nuclear and missile realm was made with the signing of the Lahore Declaration in February 1999. India and Pakistan agreed to take steps to reduce the risks of accidental or unauthorized use of nuclear weapons, undertake a unilateral moratorium on nuclear tests, and made a commitment to give advance notice to each other when conducting ballistic missile tests.[57] These agreements spelled out a set of confidence-building measures required for achieving a durable peace in South Asia. Diplomatic negotiations seemed to be successful with the establishment of rules and procedures to regulate dyadic relations on certain levels, triggering optimism for conflict termination on both sides of the border.

The peace process, however, ended up being a prelude to the Kargil crisis. Pakistan's Kargil incursion, just a few months after the peace process was initiated, turned the temporary cordial relationship into one in which exchange of fire became a norm in the rivalry once again. Trust between the rivals could not be institutionalized during the peaceful period they had enjoyed between the signing of the peace process and the beginning of the Kargil crisis. On the contrary, during the Kargil crisis, the Indians suspected the Pakistanis of playing dual roles – peacemaking and war-planning simultaneously. After Kargil, the Indians were angry and frustrated.[58] The Indian government could not put up with Pakistan's deceiving tendencies and it doubted Pakistan's ability and intention to have peace with India. New Delhi did not only focus on changing its strategies to deal with Islamabad, but also developed a new understanding about its rival's thinking. Thus, with Kargil, the hatred between India and Pakistan resurfaced again and continued with renewed

[56] *Hindustan Times*, Feb. 22, 1999. [57] *The Hindu*, Feb. 22, 1999.
[58] Interview with Air Commodore Jasjit Singh, Dec. 29, 2001.

intensity. Dialogue – essential for conflict resolution – between leaders requires trust, and Kargil destroyed any trust that India tried to build in the relationship. P. R. Chari questions: "How do you have dialogue if you have mutual suspicion?"[59] The stage on which trust could be built disappeared with Kargil. Hopes of conflict resolution that were up due to the Lahore Peace Process had virtually been inert by then.

Low-intensity violence continued between India and Pakistan after the crisis ended with the retreat of Pakistani troops from the Kargil region. The Pakistan army was displeased with the outcome of the conflict and the Pakistan military's withdrawal from Kargil under foreign pressure was not acceptable to them.[60] With the military in power in Pakistan since October 1999, cross-border firing, infiltration, and Pakistan's support for the Kashmiri militants increased. Relations between the two states sunk to their lowest level in decades. It is notable that a crisis can be developed easily by people who become heavily involved in an interstate conflict such as in South Asia because powerful individuals on opposite sides of the Kashmir border have their agenda and fighting can continue even without the consent of the two governments. For example, in 2000 when India announced a unilateral ceasefire and Pakistan reciprocated, insurgent groups such as Lashkar-i-Taiba and Hiz-ul-Mujahideen did not accept it and the levels of violence in Kashmir did not decline.[61] Although sometimes it may be difficult to know why violence continues, identifying the initiator of a crisis is not difficult. After the introduction of nuclear weapons into the rivalry, Pakistan realized that in the absence of war and where India depends on its military superiority to defend its status quo, only crisis can bring diplomatic intervention,[62] which was always Pakistan's priority but was vehemently opposed by India.

After more than a year and seeing no military solution to the Kashmir problem, in December 2000 India launched a new peace process by declaring a unilateral ceasefire offer. Pakistan offered a truce along the LoC and both completed substantial troop pullback along the borders of Kashmir. As the border areas calmed, in the summer of 2001 the Indian prime minister invited Pakistani president Pervez Musharraf for a summit meeting in Agra, which was accepted by the Pakistani leader. Two years had already passed since Kargil and there was no dyadic crisis between India and Pakistan during this period. Thus, a new environment conducive to peace emerged. While the summit did not produce satisfying results,[63] both parties expressed their interest in continuing the dialogue

[59] Personal interview with P. R. Chari, Jan. 7, 2002.
[60] *Times of India*, Oct. 13, 1999.   [61] Ganguly, *Conflict Unending*, 135.   [62] *Ibid.*, 122.
[63] See, "The Highway Beyond Agra," *Strategic Analysis*, Special Issue 25 (Oct. 2001).

and having more discussions in the future. The effort Musharraf made to visit India and his willingness to rule out a military solution to the Kashmir issue demonstrate that hybrid regimes may also have peace-making interests in a conducive environment.

Within five months, terrorists attacked the Indian Parliament and India took no time in blaming Pakistan for having a role in the attack. This attack led the two countries to deploy their forces along the LoC and almost sever diplomatic ties. A nuclear war was feared as the standoff worsened on a daily basis. While prudent policies were undertaken in order not to escalate the crisis, after more than a year, the two countries decided to pull out their heavy forces from the borders. Many in India are not only dissatisfied with the Pakistani government, but are also dissatisfied with their own government for being extremely patient with Pakistan.[64] Similarly, Pakistanis are exasperated because Pakistan is blamed for every internal crisis in India. The problem is, even if peace initiatives are taken with good intentions, trusting the adversary becomes difficult because a new crisis could jeopardize the essence of peace endeavors. Rivals go back to their war-prone mentalities, hatred resurfaces, and the rivalry is prolonged further. After the Indian Parliament attack, Uday Bhashkar stated that Indians are concerned about President Musharraf's ability to deliver on the promises that he makes to the Indian demands and that "international relations is full of surprises."[65] These surprises make the conflict rocky and new surprising moves are taken under the nuclear shield.

Despite these complications in the India–Pakistan relationship, since the summer of 2003 both states have made efforts to break the impasse and move toward resolving the outstanding issues that prolonged the rivalry. By fall 2003, a limited withdrawal of Indian forces positioned on the international border in the aftermath of the December 2001 Parliament attack started, which was reciprocated by Pakistan. The new peace process started with a ceasefire, followed by the withdrawal of heavy forces. Resumption of transportation links and exchange of diplomats followed. Additionally, Vajpayee took a major step by attending the 12th South Asian Association for Regional Cooperation (SAARC) Summit in Islamabad to thaw the tensions further. It is premature to draw any conclusion on the new developments pertaining to the peace initiatives taken by both governments, but signs are quite encouraging

---

[64] Brahma Chellaney, "Patience Overstretched," *Hindustan Times*, Oct. 2, 2002.
[65] Personal interview with Uday Bhashkar, deputy director, Institute for Defense Studies and Analysis, Jan. 5, 2002.

because the new Indian prime minister and Pakistan's president have both shown strong interest in discussing the outstanding issues, including Kashmir.

The possession of nuclear weapons has generated a *de facto* no-war zone, particularly with regard to Kashmir, and both New Delhi and Islamabad have come to the conclusion that a military solution just does not exist. After five years into the game in the nuclear period, Pakistan now realizes that none of its new military strategies – proxy wars, terrorist attacks, or low-to-medium-intensity conflict – will allow it to attain its objectives. Similarly, India understands that it cannot win the battle militarily with a conventionally weaker Pakistan that possesses nuclear weapons. It has to negotiate and be prepared to compromise on issues that have kept this rivalry ongoing. Without mutual understanding and dispute settlement, South Asia can never prosper on economic and social levels, unlike other regions. Although both India and Pakistan have moved forward to give non-military options an opportunity to resolve their long-standing differences, there is room for pessimism. The possession of the nuclear bomb did not make them forthcoming negotiators. The facilitator of the thaw in 2004 was the US. Since President Clinton's visit to South Asia in 2000, Pakistan has been under tremendous pressure from the US to change its strategies pertaining to terrorism in general and South Asia in particular. After 9/11, India and the US have shared a common interest in eliminating terrorism and pressures on Pakistan have mounted since then. Thus, Pakistan had to give in to US pressure and crack down on terrorism, which created a better environment for generating a thaw in the conflict. However, the success of this new process will certainly depend on the commitment of the leaders of the two states, the Kashmiris, and the facilitator of the peace process, the US.

Conclusion

While the enduring rivalry between India and Pakistan compelled the rivals to acquire nuclear weapons, nuclear weapons possession has generated a prolongation of the rivalry. Although with the acquisition of these weapons the rivals intended to avoid wars between them, the absence of war has had a negative impact on the conflict. With the understanding that a full-scale war is unlikely to occur, both India and Pakistan have become much less interested in making compromises with a view to terminating the rivalry. On the one hand, Pakistan is much more confident in the nuclear period about its position *vis-à-vis* India and sees no need to make unilateral concessions to obtain peace with its rival; on the other hand, India does not perceive the need for compromise under pressure. In the absence of a traditional war possibility in the rivalry, there is no pressure on the parties to compromise.

To make matters worse, the almost continuous low-to-medium intensity violence and irregular warfare in the rivalry – both functions of nuclear weapons acquisition – have generated a situation where each side views the other as intensely hostile; thus, embittering the conflict further. The nuclear period under investigation witnessed frequent and intense crises compared to the non-nuclear period. Additionally, strategies of both India and Pakistan have changed with the introduction of nuclear weapons into the rivalry. While Pakistan has used terrorism, proxy wars, and low-to-medium intensity violence in the nuclear period, India has also responded with a limited war strategy to deal with the new environment. A real crisis-free environment has not been present in the relationship from the late 1980s since both acquired nuclear weapons capabilities. The general instability in the conflict – a product of the stability–instability paradox – creates a non-conducive environment for substantial dialogue, which is often instrumental in terminating a rivalry. Thus the presence of nuclear weapons has helped to prolong the South Asian enduring rivalry.

8   National identities and the India–Pakistan conflict

Vali Nasr

Introduction

Enduring rivalries pose particularly interesting theoretical questions for both international relations and comparative politics.[1] Here it is not only the causes of the conflict that matter, but also the reasons for their persistence. These conflicts tend to have both deeper roots in and more directly impact domestic politics. In fact, neither the persistence nor the ultimate resolution of these rivalries can be explained without taking domestic political factors into consideration.

The case of Pakistan–India rivalry sheds much light on the dynamics of enduring rivalries, more so because it involves the question of identity. Identity here refers not only to ethnic or linguistic attachments, but more to how the nature of politics, purpose of the state, and its underlying values and interests are understood by key political actors and their respective constituencies. These notions can be defined in terms of overarching worldviews that are drawn from a religion or political ideology. The Pakistan–India rivalry in particular has involved questions of national identity – in fact, it has helped forge and change those identities on both sides. The rise of Islamism and Hindu nationalism and their role in shaping state ideology and national identities in Pakistan and India has played an important role in the endurance of the rivalry between the two countries. However, what is not immediately clear is if the impact of religious identity has been the same in the two countries, and if that impact has entrenched and intensified the rivalry. At face value the sacralization of politics in the two countries can be construed as a source of increased tensions. However, the historical evidence does not necessarily support this conclusion. Islamic and Hindu identities have polarized positions, but they have not intensified conflict. In fact, to the contrary, it has provided for greater maneuverability and opened new doors for

---

[1] For a thorough analysis of the relevant theoretical literature on these conflicts, see Paul˙ Diehl, Gary Goertz, and Daniel Saeedi's chapter in this book.

compromise. This chapter will examine the manner in which religious identity plays a role in the rivalry between Pakistan and India, and assess the impact it has had.

Some six decades have lapsed since the partition of the Indian subcontinent. In this time period India and Pakistan have fought three major wars, and numerous border skirmishes – involving the conflict in Kashmir – which over the course of the past two decades nearly escalated to major confrontation, the first nuclear conflict between two developing countries. Most recently, continued attacks on Indian targets in Kashmir by militant fighters trained in Pakistan, and the Kargil incident in 1999, raised the specter of conflict.

In many regards, Kashmir has become the fulcrum of conflict in the region. The centrality of the Kashmir conflict to Pakistan and India's enduring rivalry has less to do with the geostrategic or economic significance of the small province, and more with the symbolic value that it holds for dominant perceptions of national identity in the two countries. The greatest difficulties in resolving the India–Pakistan conflict have to do with overcoming the directives of national identities and how they shape politics in each country – and more so in Pakistan. However, identity has been particularly central to Pakistan's politics and, more important, Pakistani identity has largely evolved not in terms of any indigenous cultural or civilizational values but in contradistinction to the idea of India.

In India too, identity mattered, especially after the rise of the Bharatiya Janata Party (BJP) to prominence in the 1990s. However, India does not depend on identity for legitimacy, stability, and survival in the manner that Pakistan does. Moreover, Indian identity is not dependent on Pakistan. Therefore the implications of identity for conflict and peace are somewhat different in the two countries; and identity plays a more central role in Pakistan than it does in India.

Identity and politics in Pakistan

Pakistan was the product of the Muslim communalist/separatist discourse of power. That discourse emerged in defiance of the anti-imperialist thrust of Indian politics during the interwar years. It therefore early on underlined Muslim identity in lieu of a common Indian identity. It did not view the struggle against the British to be the paramount concern of Muslims, and remained apprehensive about the prospects of the Muslim minority in a predominantly Hindu India.[2] This was not an approach that was

---

[2] Mushirul Hasan, *Islam and Indian Nationalism* (Delhi: Manohar, 2000).

sanctioned by the directives of the Islamic faith. In fact, leading Muslim intellectuals of the time, men like Abu'l-Kalam Azad (d.1958, later India's minister of education) or Zakir Husain (d.1969, later India's president), and the bulk of the Indian ulama (Muslim religious leaders), rejected Muslim communalism. The leading ulama organization of the time, Jam'iat-i Ulama-i Hind (Society of Indian Ulama, JUH) supported the Congress, and its leader Mawlana Husayn Ahmad Madani (d. 1958) wrote a tract defending Indian identity – *Islam awr Mutahhidah Qawmiyat* (Islam and Composite Nationalism). The bulk of JUH's ulama remained in India after Pakistan was created.[3]

The political predilections of Islamic identity were therefore not the same as those of Muslim identity. The former was reliant on Islamic values and saw no threat to those values from Indian nationalism. Islamic institutions merely sought to protect Islamic values and make available to Muslims the public space needed for them to practice their faith. They saw no reason why this would not be possible in a united India. In fact, their goal would be achieved by participating fully in Indian society. The latter was based on Islam as an identity marker. It was not concerned with protection of Islamic values or the space needed to practice Islam, but with the upward mobility of Muslims in a society in which Muslims did not hold power. Muslim identity therefore did not look to inclusive nationalism as a solution, but as a problem. This was very much a minority community's discourse of power. The tendency to define Muslim identity in contradistinction to the Hindu one was a facet of the Muslim nationalist discourse of power. It continues to persist in Pakistani political thinking. Pakistan's approach to India continues to be conditioned by the need to justify Muslim communalism.

Muslim communalism as a form of nationalism, as perceived by Mohammad Ali Jinnah (d. 1948), was a manifestation of the fear of loss of social and political status.[4] Indian nationalism, as is expected of a movement of its kind, was essentially a force for emancipation and liberation.[5] However, as it began to employ Hindu symbolisms – in articulating its political agenda as well as in dress and outward

---

[3] On this issue see, Yohanan Friedmann, "The Attitude of Jamiyyat-i 'Ulama-i Hind to the Indian National Movement and the Establishment of Pakistan," in Gabriel Baer (ed.), *The 'Ulama in Modern History* (Jerusalem: African and Asian Studies, Israeli Oriental Society, VII, 1971), 157–83; and Ishtiaq Husain Qureshi, *Ulema in Politics: A Study Relating to the Political Activities of the Ulema in South Asian Subcontinent from 1566–1947* (Karachi: Ma'aref, 1972).

[4] Liah Greenfeld, "Transcending the Nation's Worth," *Daedalus* 122 (Summer 1993), 47–62.

[5] Liah Greenfeld, *Nationalism: Five Roads to Modernity* (Cambridge, MA: Harvard University Press, 1992), 10.

appearances – especially after Gandhi appeared on the scene, that link to pluralism and democracy in the eyes of Muslims like Jinnah and his followers became weaker. They were propelled into action by their distrust of the Congress Party, and by the belief that Indian democracy, infused with Hindu symbolism, far from safeguarding their interests, would in fact marginalize them.[6]

The Muslim discourse was not necessarily directed at separatism.[7] It rather sought to use identity to safeguard Muslim interests – demanding special constitutional rights and privileges that it believed would be lost as Muslims sublimated their identity into the Indian one. However, in the end, despite its initial intent, Jinnah's gambit led to separatism.[8] The impact that this development had on Pakistan was to ensconce the notion of separatism into Pakistani politics. Jinnah's discourse would serve as a model for minorities to maximize interests. Hence, Muslim communalism, contrary to the Muslim League's hopes, did not become a one time affair, but rather an ongoing discourse. It was Jinnah's methods rather than ultimate objective that became the mantra for Pakistani politics. As a result, the problematic facing Pakistan was how to manage the discourse of identity that had produced it – using it to legitimate the creation of Pakistan – but prevent other communities from carrying the process of fragmentation further. For Pakistan, India is central to this problem. For, in 1971 India facilitated the secession of Bangladesh. Therefore, Pakistan's trials and tribulations with stability and national integration are tied to its rivalry with India and account for its persistence over time.

The challenges facing Pakistan from the outset have been considerable. However, once Muslim separatism produced the new country the tables were turned. Islam no longer paraded as an ethnicity, but was charged with the task of containing it. Muslim separatism had been popular in those Indian provinces where Muslims had been a minority, fearing Hindu domination most: Bihar, Hyderabad, and the United Provinces, to name the most important. Pakistan, however, was created in the Muslim majority provinces of North Western India – Punjab, North-West Frontier Province, Sind, Baluchistan, western Kashmir – and East Bengal. While all of these provinces were predominantly Muslim, ethnic, linguistic, and cultural distinctions set them apart from one another, and from the Muslim populations of the Muslim minority provinces.

---

[6] Farzana Shaikh, *Community and Consensus in Islam: Muslim Representation in Colonial India, 1860–1947* (Cambridge: Cambridge University Press, 1989).
[7] Ayesha Jalal, *The Sole Spokesman: Jinnah, the Muslim League, and the Demand for Pakistan* (Cambridge: Cambridge University Press, 1985).
[8] On Jinnah, see Stanley Wolpert, *Jinnah of Pakistan* (New York: Oxford University Press, 1984).

The language of the Muslim minority provinces was Urdu, which had very little following in Sind, Baluchistan, or even Punjab. Hence, language immediately distinguished Muslims from Bihar, Hyderabad, or the United Provinces from those in Sind, Baluchistan, or Bengal. Nor did Sindhis, Punjabis, Bengalis, or Biharis and Hyderabadis follow the same customs and mores; they were different people who, save for their religious faith, shared more with their Hindu neighbors than with Muslims of other provinces.

Yet, as Islam dominated the struggle for independence in India, Muslims from disparate ethnic backgrounds, following different cultures, and conversant in different languages, were thrown together. The bulk of the leadership of the ruling party, Pakistan Muslim League (PML, originally All-India Muslim League), were born and raised in provinces which had remained in India, and hence had no political base in their new country. The influx of the newcomers, and their domination of politics, seen in such measures as declaring Urdu the national language, raised the ire of the "sons of soil" and precipitated ethnic tensions.[9]

The Kashmir issue complicated this problem. For, Kashmir was an "unfinished part" of the separatist struggle. Whereas in Pakistan the communalist/separatist discourse had to be halted, the Kashmir struggle was legitimated very much on the basis of that discourse. Pakistan has seen Kashmiri identity as an extension of the Pakistani one – a component of the discourse that produced Pakistan – and not as a separate identity (what Kashmiris call *Kashmiriyat*).[10] Hence, Kashmir prevented the Pakistan identity from quickly metamorphosing from an "ethnic" separatist one into a "national" one.

Given these problems, Islam was mobilized, this time as a religious force to override the differences between "sons of soil" and migrants (Muhajirs [Muslim migrants from India to Pakistan]), and between the provinces and the country's leadership. Islam thus became the main legitimating force in Pakistan's politics, underlying the viability of the federal unit.[11] The more the state was challenged, by war or internal conflict, the more Islam was mobilized to sustain it.[12] Islam was not,

---

[9] Hamza Alavi, "Ethnicity, Muslim Society and the Pakistan Ideology," in Anita M. Weiss (ed.), *Islamic Reassertion in Pakistan* (Syracuse: Syracuse University Press, 1986), 21–48; K. K. Aziz, *The Making of Pakistan: A Study in Nationalism* (London: Chatto & Windus, 1967); Astma Barlas, *Democracy, Nationalism, and Communalism: The Colonial Legacy in South Asia* (Boulder, CO: Westview Press, 1995).

[10] On this issue, see Ashutosh Varshney, "India, Pakistan, and Kashmir: Antinomies of Nationalism," *Asian Survey* 31 (Nov. 1991), 997–1007.

[11] Leonard Binder, *Religion and Politics in Pakistan* (Berkeley: University of California Press, 1961).

[12] See Kahlifa Abdul Hakim, *Islamic Ideology* (Lahore: Institute of Islamic Culture, 1951).

however, allowed a free rein, which somewhat impeded its ability to legitimate the state. For instance, the secularization policies of the afore-mentioned rulers, above and beyond their appeal to religious sentiments, weakened the Islamic basis of the state, opening the door for the resurgence of ethnic politics, which culminated in the secession of East Pakistan.

The problematic of identity became most evident during the civil war of 1969–71, which culminated in the war with India and separation of Bangladesh.[13] East Pakistan was where the discourse of communalism/separatism confronted the discourse of unity – the first defined in ethnic terms and the latter in Islamic ones. The implication of the debacle of East Pakistan was that the Islamic discourse of unity had failed, and it had done so pursuant to the Indian intervention. This fact intensified the competition between the discourses of communalism/separatism and unity, and also made the Indian threat more central to this debate.

In the end, the separation of Bangladesh acted to Islamize Pakistan's politics. Islamic identity, promoted by the state to contain separatist tendencies, now drew on the more strident ideology of Islamism to define Pakistani identity. Pakistan moved from being a homeland for Muslims to being the embodiment – and also guarantor – of the Islamic ideal as defined by the ideology of Islamism. The notion of a Muslim homeland had been both the culmination of Muslim separatism in India and the brake before Pakistan's integration along ethnic lines. Yet, in East Pakistan it had proven to be an inadequate concept. The East Pakistan debacle therefore had a cathartic effect.[14] It weakened the original conception of Pakistan and strengthened a new Islamic definition of it. The ideal of the Muslim homeland thus became that of the Islamic paragon. Interestingly, General Musharraf is once again looking back to that failed pre-1971 conception of identity.

The growing prominence of Islamism in Pakistan's politics eventually culminated in the Islamization regime of General Zia ul-Haq (1977–88). An alliance between the military and Islamist parties provided a cadence between domestic and the regional politics. In Islam the state found a powerful means to shore up its domestic authority and also to project power regionally, not only to contain Islamic challenges to its authority,

[13] Rounaq Jahan, *Pakistan: Failure in National Integration* (New York: Columbia University Press, 1972); Philip Oldenburg, "A Place Insufficiently Imagined: Language, Belief, and the Pakistan Crisis of 1971," *Journal of Asian Studies* 44 (1985), 715–23; and Vali Nasr, "The Negotiable State: Borders and Power Struggles in Pakistan," in Ian Lustick, Thomas Callaghy, and Brendan O'Leary (eds.), *Rightsizing the State: the Politics of Moving Borders* (New York: Oxford University Press, 2001), 168–200.

[14] Nasr, "The Negotiable State," 168–200.

but also to make the Pakistan state stronger.[15] Islam increased Pakistan's regional power by opening new foreign policy possibilities before Islamabad, most notably in using *jihadi* activism to deal with developments in Afghanistan and Kashmir.[16]

The ideology of Islamism is anti-Indian in that it rejects both the secularism and Hindu cultural and political domination of post-partition India. However, unlike the communalist/separatist discourse of Jinnah it is not preoccupied with the "Hindu question" and is not concerned with the need to legitimate Pakistan as a negation of the idea of a united India. Islamism is first and foremost concerned with the Islamic nature of Pakistan. The country's legitimacy comes from embodying and protecting the Islamic ideal. Before independence, the prominent Islamist thinker Mawlana Mawdudi (d. 1979) observed that if Pakistan was to be secular then what was the point of separating from India?[17] Pakistan, he argued, should exist as an Islamic ideal and not as merely a negation of Hindu authority. For him the secularism of Indian nationalism was the nemesis and not its Hindu underpinnings. An Islamic Pakistan would therefore provide a new conception of state and society – one that although anti-Indian was not preoccupied with distinction from India.

In addition, an important segment of Pakistan's Islamism is associated with the ulama of the Deobandi school and their party, Jam'iat-i Ulama Islam (Society of Ulama of Islam, JUI).[18] JUI was formed by a small breakaway faction of JUH on the eve of partition, and was initially led by Muhajir ulama in Karachi and Punjab, and therefore shared the position of the Pakistan Movement. Since the early 1970s the JUI has been dominated by Pashtun Deobandi ulama from NWFP and Baluchistan, who trace their intellectual lineage to the JUH in India, and are especially devoted to Mawlana Husayn Ahmad Madani – who was and continues to be widely popular among Pashtuns in NWFP and Baluchistan – as well as in Afghanistan. Many of the *madrassas* there were close to JUH before

---

[15] Seyyed Vali Reza Nasr, *The Islamic Leviathan: Islam and State Power* (New York: Oxford University Press, 2001).

[16] Marvin Weinbaum, *Pakistan and Afghanistan: Resistance and Reconstruction* (Boulder, CO: Westview Press, 1994); Rasul B. Rais, *War Without Winners: Afghanistan's Uncertain Transition after the Cold War* (Karachi: Oxford University Press, 1994); Olivier Roy, *Islam and Resistance in Afghanistan*, 2nd ed. (New York: Cambridge University Press, 1990); Sumit Ganguly, *The Crisis in Kashmir: Portents of War and Hopes of Peace* (New York: Cambridge University Press, 1997).

[17] On Mawdudi, see Seyyed Vali Reza Nasr, *Mawdudi and the Making of Islamic Revivalism* (New York: Oxford University Press, 1996).

[18] On the Deoband, see Barbara D. Metcalf, *Islamic Revival in British India: Deoband, 1860–1900* (Princeton: Princeton University Press, 1982).

partition. For instance, the famous Dar ul-Ulum Haqqaniyah in Akora Khattak, wherefrom many of the Taliban hailed, was inaugurated by Husayn Ahmad Madani in 1937. The most eminent leaders of JUI, such as Mufti Mahmoud (father of current leader Mawlana Fazlur Rahman) and Mawlana Sami‘ ul-Haq (associated with the Taliban) were devotees of Madani.[19] As a result, this wing of JUI – which was indigenous to the territories that became Pakistan – was not committed to Pakistan at the outset, and most likely had a hand in NWFP resistance to joining Pakistan in the elections of 1946–47.

The change in the JUI's leadership has been an important development. During Pakistan's early years Islamism was closely associated with the Muhajir community. Islamist ideologues, such as Mawlana Mawdudi and his party, the Jama‘at-i Islami, and even the leadership of JUI at the time, were deeply rooted in the Muhajir community.[20] The Muhajirs had also been the one Pakistani community that was closest to the communalist/separatist discourse of Pakistan. Hence, the nexus between Islamism and the Muhajir community made Islamism relevant to Pakistan's use of identity politics in managing its relations in the region. However, in the 1970s the leadership of JUI passed from Muhajir ulama in Karachi to Pashtun ulama in NWFP and Baluchistan – from the pro-partition group to pro-JUH stalwarts.

This change in JUI leadership was all the more important, as JUI emerged in the 1970s as a powerful force in Islamic politics.[21] That power has continued to grow both in the proliferation of *madrassas* and *jihadi* groups and at the ballot box – where JUI swept Pashtun areas in the last national elections. The prominence of Pashtuns in JUI, and JUI in Islamic politics has therefore changed Islamist attitudes toward Pakistan's identity and its relations with India. Deobandi politics has been interested more in *jihad* than in legitimating Muslim communalism/separatism. Its interest in India is in the context of its vision of *jihad* and not because it subscribes to the communalist/separatist discourse of Muslim separatism. That since 1970s Islamism has ceased to be a Muhajir issue (in fact Muhajir politics has become distinctly ethnic rather than Islamic), and increasingly a Pashtun one, has separated Islamic

---

[19] On these issues, see Seyyed Vali Reza Nasr, "The Rise of Sunni Militancy in Pakistan: The Changing Role of Islamism and the Ulama in Society and Politics," *Modern Asian Studies* 34 (January 2000), 139–80.

[20] Seyyed Vali Reza Nasr, *Vanguard of the Islamic Revolution: the Jama‘at-i Islami of Pakistan* (Berkeley: University of California Press, 1994).

[21] Sayyid A. S. Pirzada, *The Politics of the Jamiat-i-Ulema-i-Islam Pakistan, 1971–1977* (Karachi: Oxford University Press, 2000).

186   *Vali Nasr*

identity from the India–Pakistan rivalry in important ways, and created a far more complex relationship between the two.

This is a trend that is evident in other Islamist groups as well. For instance, the Jama'at-i Islami that was initially led by a Muhajir leadership is today led by a Pashtun, Qazi Husayn Ahmad, who comes from a Deobandi ulama family, and is named after Husayn Ahmad Madani.

However, the full impact of the ascendance of Pashtuns and JUI became clear only through the convergence of identity and state interest in the Zia period. It was then that Islamism joined hands with the one Pakistani institution that is most closely associated with the Pakistan–India rivalry – and defender of the communalist/separatist discourse and India-centered definition of Pakistan's self-perception – the military. The military–mullah alliance defined a strongly Islamic identity for Pakistan. The alliance provided Islamism with regional perspectives and encouraged them to use the doctrine of *jihad* to propagate their ideals – which were identified as Pakistan's interests now that the country was Islamic. This trend found its most clear expression through the Afghan war.

It is important to note that the Islamist views on identity resonate in the Pakistan military. To begin with, the military in Pakistan has been a bastion of nationalism, which has been defined in opposition to India. The military's definition of Pakistani nationalism is premised on the same assumptions that have animated Islamist views of Pakistan's interests and identity. In the 1970s and the 1980s pro-Islamist journals such as *Takbir*, *Urdu Digest*, and *Qaumi Digest* had a great following in the military – creating common perspectives between Islamists and military officers over domestic as well as international issues. It is for this reason that after the military became open to Islamism after 1977 it was able to quickly build alliances with Islamist forces in Afghanistan and Kashmir.

Moreover, since the late 1960s, the military has been recruiting its rank-and-file from the lower middle classes.[22] This segment of Pakistani society is also the social base of Islamism in Pakistan. As a result, with the new recruits who have consistently moved up the ranks over the past four decades, much of the political worldview of Islamism – at times secularized and shorn of its religious language – has been ensconced in the military as well. Although the military continues to espouse its own corporatist interests and define national security and identity in accordance with its own strategic thinking, it nevertheless has found itself in agreement with Islamist perspectives on these subjects.

[22] Stephen P. Cohen, *The Pakistan Army* (Berkeley: University of California Press, 1984).

Islam and "strategic depth"

The Afghan war opened new strategic vistas for Pakistan.[23] Since its creation Pakistan had faced irredentist claims by Afghanistan against its northwestern territories. Pashtun nationalism had continuously posed challenges to the consolidation of the Pakistani state. Throughout the 1960s and much of the 1970s Pakistan had used its close ties with Iran to offset what it viewed as the pincer challenges of the Afghan–Indian alliance. The Daoud regime's Pashtun nationalism in the context of Kabul's closer ties with India in the late 1970s, in particular, threatened Pakistan. In Pakistan's eyes the ties between Kabul and Delhi constituted a serious threat to the country's national security.

This threat grew with the communist coup in Kabul in 1978 and later with the Soviet invasion of Afghanistan. The Soviet Union's close ties with India during Mrs Gandhi's rule meant that its growing control of Afghanistan would sandwich Pakistan between a tight alliance between Delhi and Kabul. Interestingly, the prospect of a similar axis between Kabul and Delhi following the fall of the Taliban haunts Islamabad and animates its policy toward the Karzai regime in Kabul.

Pakistan saw an opportunity in the Afghan war to undo the Afghan–Indian alliance. The Islamic ideology of the war was conveniently anti-communist, and as such would challenge communism for ideological dominance in the region, thus weakening Delhi's position, which was close to the Soviet Union. Moreover, the war had brought the mujahidin fighters, most of whom were Pashtun tribesmen under Pakistan's military control. In fact, for a time, Pakistan looked to the mujahidin commander Gulbidin Hikmatyar to also control Pashtun nationalist politics. The Islamic tenor of the war conveniently sublimated Pashtun nationalism under the banner of Islam, which was now controlled by Pakistan owing to its own Islamization.

Throughout the Afghan war Pakistan sought to divide and rule mujahidin groups as it promoted Islamic ideology among them.[24] Gradually an interest in containing and controlling Pashtun nationalism gave place to the goal of controlling Afghanistan in order to provide Pakistan with "strategic depth." This concern became more important after the Kashmir conflict flared up in the late 1980s and the war in

---

[23] Marvin Weinbaum, "War and Peace in Afghanistan: The Pakistani Role," *Middle East Journal* 45 (Winter 1991), 71–86.

[24] Barnett Rubin, *The Fragmentation of Afghanistan: State Formation and Collapse in the International System* (New Haven: Yale University Press, 1995); Roy, *Islam and Resistance in Afghanistan*; and Steve Coll, *Ghost Wars: The Secret History of the CIA, Afghanistan and Bin Laden, from the Soviet Invasion to September 10, 2001* (New York: Penguin, 2004).

Afghanistan wound down after 1988.[25] Pakistan's military was particularly interested in providing Pakistan with a safe backyard, which would also enable Pakistan to better absorb an Indian blitzkrieg.

This aim led Pakistan to look beyond rolling back Soviet gains in Afghanistan to controlling Kabul. By 1994 it was clear that the mujahidin were unable to control Afghanistan. The growing power of the Tajik mujahidin commander Ahmad Shah Masud and his Northern Alliance troops seriously challenged Pakistan's position in Afghanistan. After the Tajik alliance of Burhanuddin Rabbani and Masud sidelined Hikmatyar it became clear that Pakistan was losing its control over Afghanistan, and potentially over Pashtun nationalism. In addition, the ferocity of infighting between Afghan groups was placing a great burden on the Pakistani military, and was causing Pakistan to lose control over one of the factions, thus providing an opening to India to enter the fray. The possibility of using the Afghan–Pakistan corridor to open Central Asian riches to the world further added to the need to control the scope of the war in Afghanistan.

It was in this context that in 1994 Pakistan turned to the Taliban – who represent the most militant expression of Islamic identity.[26] Although the Taliban were initially organized to open trade routes and bring law and order to Afghanistan – what foreign investors and ordinary Afghans hoped for – Pakistan looked to the Taliban to protect Pashtun interests and preserve Pakistan's position in Afghanistan.[27] The Taliban, however, held the promise of fully Islamizing Pashtun nationalism, and then making it subservient to Pakistan's interests. Through the Taliban Pakistan would first divert the attention of Pashtuns away from ethnic nationalism to religion, and then contain it within Pakistan's relations with Afghanistan. To achieve this, however, Pakistan had to bring the role of Islam in its own society and politics into greater alignment with changes that were afoot in Afghanistan.

Hence, during the 1994–96 period, the Pakistan government was also instrumental in organizing militant Sunni *madrassa* students into the Taliban and Harakat ul-Ansar (Movement of Companions of the Prophet, HUA)/Harakat ul-Mujahedin (Movement of Mujahedin, HUM) – which later became Jaiesh Muhammad (Muhammad's Army)

---

[25] Ganguly, *The Crisis in Kashmir*; and Robert Wirsing, *India, Pakistan, and the Kashmir Dispute* (New York: St. Martin's Press, 1994).

[26] Ahmed Rashid, *Militant Islam, Oil, and Fundamentalism in Central Asia* (New Haven: Yale University Press, 2001); and Larry Goodson, "Foreign Policy Gone Awry: The Kalashnikovization and Talibanization of Pakistan," in Baxter and Kennedy, *Pakistan 2000*, 151–81.

[27] Interview in Pakistan 1997.

units for Pakistan-backed operations in Afghanistan and Kashmir.[28] This change in strategy also meant that domestically the Deobandi and sectarian extremist groups that were closely tied to the Taliban replaced the Jamaʿat-i Islami and mainstream Islamism as the main allies of the military – its Islamic arm. According to a Pakistan government report 800 militant sectarian fighters active in anti-Shiʾi violence in Punjab were receiving training at HUA/HUM's Khalid Bin Waleed military training camp in Afghanistan in 1998–99.[29]

The proliferation of *madrassas* across Pakistan was also important in defining Pakistani identity. In 1947 there were 137 *madrassas* in Pakistan; today there are just as many in small divisions of Punjab.[30] The number of *madrassas* rose most quickly after General Zia's assumption of power and the onset of the Afghan War.[31] The proliferation of *madrassas* meant that growing numbers of Pakistanis, especially in rural areas and small towns, were receiving their early socialization and education in *madrassa* settings. Islamist notions of identity and attitudes toward Islam and politics were thus increasingly proliferating in the broader society. The graduates of the *madrassas* often created new *madrassas*, became preachers in mosques, or joined municipal government services. As such, they helped disseminate and entrench the underlying message of *madrassa* education regarding national identity and security issues.

This trend bolstered the military's strategy. The military from the late 1970s onwards co-opted Islamism and directed its drive to the utopian Islamic ideal to achieve its strategic goals which reflected the fundamental directives of the communalist/separatist discourse. The military continued to understand Pakistan's identity in contradistinction to India, and to be preoccupied with maintaining national unity – i.e., balancing the demands of the communalist/separatist discourse that it saw validated Pakistan – and continues to legitimate Pakistan's position on Kashmir – with the imperative of halting that discourse's impact on continued disintegrative tendencies in Pakistan.

The military used the growing militancy of Islamist groups and their greater interest in *jihad* to divert their attention from building an Islamic state in Pakistan to regional conquest and the strengthening of the Pakistan state – especially *vis-à-vis* India. However, whereas for the

---

[28] *Far Eastern Economic Review*, Mar. 9, 1995, 24.
[29] *The News International*, Mar. 4, 1999, 1 and 4.
[30] *The News* (Islamabad) (Mar. 2, 1995), 1.
[31] "Pakistan: Madrasah, Extremism and the Military," International Crisis Group, Report Number 36 (Islamabad/Brussels: July 29, 2002), 2; and Nasr, "The Rise of Sunni Militancy," 142.

military the issue of Kashmir was the unfinished last chapter of partition, for militant *jihadis* it was merely a stage in their outward regional expansion. The collapse of the Congress Party's strategy in Kashmir in the late 1980s provided the *jihadi* groups with an opening to exploit the civil strife in Kashmir to put forth an Islamist strategy for pressuring India on the Kashmir issue.

For so long as the Taliban prevailed in Afghanistan the military–mullah alliance persisted, directing the sharp edge of the politics of identity in the direction of Kashmir. The events of September 11, 2001, however, changed the dynamics of identity politics in Pakistan. The collapse of *jihadi* warfare in Afghanistan has created a wide chasm between the military and Islamists. The military has been compelled to endorse Operation Enduring Freedom and the War on Terror and publicly dissociate its campaign against India from *jihadi* activism. Mainstream Islamist forces have responded by focusing on building an Islamic state in Pakistan and have distanced themselves from the Kashmir issue. Only fringe groups such as Jaiesh Muhammad or Lashkar-i Tayiba (Army of the Pure) – which had been under the military's control – have remained active in the Kashmir *jihad*. During his recent visit to India, JUI leader Mawlana Fazlur Rahman commented that "India has nothing to fear from the mullahs, it has to fear the generals."[32] The new diplomatic line put forth by Fazlur Rahman has facilitated the thaw in relations between Delhi and Islamabad, which culminated in a new round of diplomacy between the countries in 2002. First, it has suggested a backing away of mainstream Islamists from *jihadi* activism; and second, it has provided religious cover for General Musharraf to pursue normalization of relations with Delhi. Furthermore, it has suggested that as Islamists pursue power in Islamabad they are likely to promote more pragmatic foreign policy positions.

The coming apart of Pakistani identity as it was defined during the Zia period has occurred at a particularly difficult time for Pakistan. The country is under international pressure to move away from Islamic identity. It has lost strategic depth in Afghanistan, and the concordat between the generals and the mawlvis that created stability domestically has now fallen apart – opening the door for new approaches to Pakistani identity which are more forthcoming regarding resolution of conflict with India. More interesting, these changes in Pakistan have come about during a time of ascendance of identity politics in India.

---

[32] Personal interviews, Oct. 2003.

Islam and martial rule

Since 1977 Islam has been important to legitimating military rule in Pakistan. In 1984 General Zia ul-Haq turned a plebiscite on his regime into a referendum on Islamization. The efficacy of Islamic identity for furthering the political interests of the military requires that the military maintain an Islamic image, but more important, that there exist a cadence between the military's geostrategic vision and the directives of Islamic identity. In short, the military needs Islamic identity to maintain its commanding position in Pakistan's politics – which in turn is necessitated by the imperative of defending Pakistan in its rivalry with India.

The military has also justified its own power by highlighting the rivalry with India. The military's budget and size have been justified by the Indian threat, as has the military's need to keep the civilian political order in check. As such, the rivalry between India and Pakistan is central to the corporate interests of the military. Hence, it is the military that has pushed Islamic identity in the direction of supporting its position in the Pakistan–India rivalry, and not Islamic identity that has stoked the fires of that rivalry. For instance, since the 1980s the military and its intelligence wing have been supportive of the Urdu press's jingoistic rhetoric on Kashmir, and some of the leading anti-Indian Islamist journalists, such as Muhammad Salahuddin of the *Takbir*, enjoyed close ties with General Zia. That relationship has continued during the post-Zia period with the popular Urdu press supporting the military's position on the uprising in Kashmir after 1988.

Since the mid-1990s newspapers associated with *jihadi* groups such as Lashkar-i Tayibah have printed their own newspapers, some of which have notable circulation. In 2003 Lashkar's *Da'wah* had a circulation of 100,000, providing the small organization with a broad audience. Deobandi papers, once exclusive to NWFP and Pathan areas of Baluchistan now have broad readership in Karachi and Punjab. Extremist Deobandi publications, such as *Zarb-i Mo'mim* and *al-Hilal* sell very well in Islamabad and Rawalpindi – urban areas that are associated with the government and the military.[33] These publications have propagated the military's line on Kashmir far more emphatically than has the Urdu press. Hence, Islamic identity's importance lies in the domestic and not in shaping the structure of the rivalry. There, the Pakistan military and its geostrategic views continue to set the tone.

[33] Hassan Abbas, *Pakistan's Drift into Extremism: Allah, the Army, and America's War on Terror* (Armonk, NY: M. E. Sharpe, 2005), 222–23.

The saffron wave and Pakistan

For much of the post-independence period identity did not play an important part in India's attitude toward Pakistan. India was conceived as a secular state with a strong sense of national identity that was forged through the crucible of the struggle for independence.[34] That identity was rooted in Indian history and civilization and to the extent that it was defined in contradistinction to any other conception of India, it was that of the British Raj. Indian nationalism was moreover inclusive, and in this it was the obverse of the discourse that had produced Pakistan. The idea of Pakistan drew on the notion that Muslims and Hindus could not happily coexist in the same polity – at least not to the satisfaction of Muslims. Hence, whereas Pakistan rejected the idea of an Indian society and polity, India embodied exactly that ideal.[35]

For much of its history Indian identity has been far from uniform. The democratic environment provided for contestation between different conceptions of India: secular, religious, liberal democratic, socialist, and rooted in politics of class. In the early 1990s during the premiership of V. P. Singh competition for defining India's identity and polity became particularly intense. With the failure of the Singh administration to define India's politics and the gradual decline of the Congress Party and its failure to produce strong national leadership, the picture began to change. Secularism, socialism, and liberal democracy began to lose ground to Hindu nationalism and the ascendance of the BJP in the 1990s. Hindu nationalism has diverse roots, some of which go back to the colonial period.[36] It is also tied to the vicissitudes of India's fissiparous caste and ethnic politics. Here, Hindu nationalism has performed the same function that Islam has in Pakistan, namely, the ideological glue that diverts attention from disintegrative ethnic tendencies.[37] Finally, Hindu nationalism has captured the frustration of the Brahmin castes with India's preferential treatment system and quotas that favored the untouchable, and which became an issue just before the BJP's meteoric

---

[34] T. N. Madan, "Secularism in its Place," *Journal of Asian Studies* (1987), 747–60; and Ashis Nandy, "The Politics of Secularism and the Recovery of Religious Tradition," *Alternatives* 13 (1988), 177–94.

[35] Jim Messelos, *Indian Nationalism: A History* (Delhi: South Asia Books, 1998) and Sunil Khilnani, *The Idea of India* (New York: Farrar Straus & Giroux, 1999).

[36] Kenneth W. Jones, *Arya Dharm: Hindu Consciousness in Nineteenth-Century Punjab* (Berkeley: University of California Press, 1976); and William Gould, *Hindu Nationalism and the Language of Politics in Late Colonial India* (Cambridge: Cambridge University Press, 2004).

[37] See in this regard, for instance, Sikata Banerjee, *Warriors in Politics: Hindu Nationalism, Violence, and the Shiv Sena in India* (Boulder, CO: Westview Press, 1999).

rise to power when the Janata Party government sought to expand them in the early 1990s.[38]

Still, it was the "Muslim question" and Pakistan that energized Hindu nationalism and facilitated its rapid rise to power.[39] First, Hindu nationalism had been critical of Indian secularism and hence the special protections that Muslims enjoyed under the Indian constitution.[40] The BJP proved adept at capitalizing on the outcome of the Shah Banu Case (1986), which problematized those privileges. That those anti-Muslim sentiments proved so effective in mobilizing support for the BJP – although Hindu nationalism also drew on ethnic feelings and frustrations for Brahmin youth – was of great significance.

If the Shah Banu case led to a rejection of Muslim separateness within India in the form of empowerment of Hindu nationalism, the Kashmir issue played the same role regionally. In other words, Hindu nationalism also was animated by rejection of Muslim separateness in Kashmir.[41] The growing tensions in the Vale of Kashmir in the late 1980s raised the specter of the continuation of the Muslim communalist/separatist discourse that produced Pakistan. Hindu nationalism emerged to definitively reject that possibility, and to do so by altering the balance of power between Hindus and Muslims that had persisted since partition – within India as well as regionally.

As a result, the BJP grew in power through mobilizing the masses around anti-Muslim and anti-Pakistan themes – in many regards tying the Indian Muslim community to Pakistan. Hence, campaigns such as the destruction of the Babri Masjid in Ayodhya in 1992 became the hallmarks of the BJP campaign for power.[42]

[38] On these quotas, see Myron Weiner, "The Political Consequences of Preferential Policies," reprinted in Myron Weiner and Ashutosh Varshney, *The Indian Paradox: Essays in Indian Politics* (Beverly Hills, CA: Sage, 1989), 152–75; and Ashutosh Varshney, "Is India Becoming More Democratic?" *Journal of Asian Studies* 59 (Feb. 2000).

[39] On this issue see Peter van der Veer, *Religious Nationalism: Hindus and Muslims in India* (Berkeley: University of California Press, 1994); Chritophe Jaffrelot, *The Hindu Nationalist Movement in India* (New York: Columbia University Press, 1998); Thomas Blom Hansen, *The Saffron Wave* (Princeton: Princeton University Press, 1999); Thomas Blom Hansen and Chritophe Jaffrelot, *The BJP and Compulsions of Politics in India* (Delhi: Oxford University Press, 2000); Bruce D. Graham, *Hindu Nationalism and Indian Politics: The Origins and Development of the Bharatiya Jana Sangh* (Cambridge: Cambridge University Press, 1990).

[40] Tapan Raychaudhuri, "Shadows of the Swastika: Historical Reflections on the Politics of Hindu Communalism," *Contention* 4 (Winter 1995), 141–62.

[41] Ashutosh Varshney, "Contested Meanings: Hindu Nationalism, India's National Identity, and the Politics of Anxiety," *Daedalus* 122 (Summer 1993).

[42] On Ayodhya, see the various articles in the special issue of the *Asian Survey* on the topic; *Asian Survey* 33 (July 1993).

The impact of the BJP's rise to power on Pakistan–India rivalry was complex. First, it suggested that India was now more overtly interested in achieving a new balance of power in the region, one that would clearly establish the primacy of India and Hinduism *vis-à-vis* Pakistan and Indian Muslims. Second, that the partition era paradigms of identity and politics that had continued to define regional politics long after 1947 were now defunct. Third, as far as Pakistan was concerned the rise of the BJP and its anti-Muslim rhetoric and actions were vindication for the communalist/separatist discourse that had produced Pakistan. The suppression of Indian Muslims showed that secular India could not be trusted to protect their rights and that Hinduism was bent on "destroying" Islam and the Muslims. As a result, the BJP animated a great deal of emotion in Pakistan's politics, which the military used to mobilize public support – particularly among Islamically inclined voters and parties.

However, the impact of the BJP's policies was not to inflame Islamic fervor and mobilize Islamists against India. Those elements of Islamism that were most at odds with India were militant groups that were committed to *jihad* in all arenas, and were moreover reflecting the military's thinking on India. Beyond initial reactions to the Ayodhya incident – which were strongest among muhajirs – Islamist reaction was relatively muted. In fact, the Islamically oriented parties would from the mid-1990s onwards provide the new opening in India and Pakistan relations. Meetings between JUI chief, Mawlana Fazlur Rahman, and RSS and BJP leaders in India in 2003 are of great symbolic significance.

Although the BJP rose to power by manipulating anti-Muslim sentiments, once in power its politics has moderated in response to the political requirements of managing its coalition governments, and the need to create a stable environment in order to support India's economic growth. Prime Minister Vajpayee was instrumental in instilling pragmatism in the BJP's policies. The trend towards pragmatism on the BJP's side was gradually matched by Islamists in Pakistan. Since 1999 they have witnessed diminishing returns to *jihadi* activism, and have understood the need for pragmatism if they are to lay a claim to the political center in Pakistan. The strong showing of Islamists in the elections of 2002 in Pakistan has presented them with the potential to serve as contenders for power in Islamabad. To achieve that goal they have backed away from the rhetoric of militancy to portray themselves as responsible power brokers able to formulate viable national policies. The growing political prominence of both the BJP and Pakistani Islamists – more than any change in their notions of identity – has had a moderating influence on their views. The extent to which these forces will contribute to continuation or cessation of the India–Pakistan conflict is likely to be a function of how the requirements of the exercise of power in the domestic political arena will force pragmatism on them. This trend first became manifest in 1999 with the Lahore Summit, and since 2002 has gained greater momentum with General Musharraf's meetings with Indian Prime Minister Vajpayee and Prime Minister Manmohan Singh.

The Vajpayee–Nawaz Sharif model

The Lahore Summit of 1999 between Prime Minister Vajpayee and Prime Minister Nawaz Sharif represented a significant thaw in the relations between Pakistan and India, one that was rooted in mutual interests of the governments and was directed at measured steps towards deescalation of tensions.[43] What is notable is that the rapprochement occurred between two leaders who represented identity politics in their countries. For Vajpayee, the Lahore Summit was a means of bringing stability to India's domestic political environment – both in terms of reducing tensions within the ruling coalition and providing encouragement to foreign investors who were wary of the prospects of war in the region. Vajpayee was also motivated by his personal desire to end his career with a legacy of peace.

For Nawaz Sharif, the Lahore Summit was an attempt to reduce tensions with India in order to provide the requisite climate for Pakistan's economy to grow out of its isolation. Sharif was responding to the demands of the business community in Pakistan and also the imperative of dealing with Pakistan's mounting international debt. Moreover, Sharif sought to deal with the pressure of maintaining parity with India not through the conflict in Kashmir, but by growth in Pakistan's economy. The Lahore Summit was a first step in that regard.

Whereas Vajpayee had risen to power as the leader of the BJP, Nawaz Sharif had gradually consolidated control over the Islamic vote bank throughout the 1990s. This trend became evident first in the 1993 elections. Nawaz Sharif's PML did not win the elections, but it did win the Islamic vote.[44] A leading claimant to the Islamic vote, the Jama'at, which had positioned itself as the third force in the elections to represent the Zia legacy against both the PML and PPP, performed poorly. The result suggested the emergence of a strong right-of-center party that would

---

[43] Robert Wirsing, *Kashmir in the Shadow of War: Regional Rivalries in a Nuclear Age* (Armonk, NY: M. E. Sharpe, 2003), 25–36.

[44] Tahir Amin, "Pakistan in 1993," *Asian Survey* 34 (Feb. 1994), 195.

also represent the Islamic vote – rendering Islamist parties irrelevant. This was the first time in the Muslim world that democratic process had produced a brake on Islamism. The military, however, was less concerned with limiting Islamism and more with constricting democratic parties.

The military was shocked by these results. They had expected that the Jama'at would limit the PML's electoral success, and that without Islamist allies Nawaz Sharif would fail to gain favor with the public. The result was a military–Islamist alliance that enjoyed little prominence on the political scene, and an increasingly independent right-of-center party that portended to take away control of Islamism from the military.

The PPP government of Prime Minister Benazir Bhutto that ruled between 1994 and 1997 was allied with the JUI, and sought to counter Sharif's Islamic base of support by investing in militancy. Its success in doing so enticed Sharif's other nemesis, the military, to also look to *jihadi* activism to both counter Sharif's Islamic base of support and revitalize the use of identity politics in pursuing regional interests.

In 1994 the PPP government, led by its secular minister of interior, General Nasirullah Babur, and the JUI's leadership, turned to the *madrassas* and *jihadi* fighters to form the Taliban to undermine Nawaz Sharif.[45] The growing prominence of the Taliban and their Deobandi allies in Pakistan soon led the military to look to them as serious partners for managing Afghanistan and later as a model for escalating the Kashmir conflict. This in turn necessitated greater support of the institutional basis of Deobandi ascendancy – the *madrassas* – and the network that recruited and supported these forces and projected their power, and which extended from Afghanistan into Kashmir.[46]

General Babur and the military also looked to the Taliban to replace Hikmatyar as Islamic spokesman for Pashtun nationalism. Hikmatyar's failure at Kabul had proved that he and his brand of Islamism – and that of its main Pakistani ally, the Jama'at – cannot contain Pashtun nationalism in the long run. The Taliban, however, held the promise of fully Islamizing Pashtun nationalism, and then making it subservient to Pakistan's interests. Through the Taliban, Pakistan would first divert the attention of Pashtuns from ethnic nationalism to religion and then contain it within Pakistan's relations with Afghanistan. To achieve this, however, Pakistan had to bring the role of Islam in its own society and politics into greater alignment with changes that were afoot in Afghanistan.

---

[45] Abbas, *Pakistan's Drift into Extremism*, 154–55.
[46] Goodson, "Foreign Policy Gone Awry," 151–81.

Hence, during the 1994–96 period, the Pakistan government was instrumental in organizing militant Sunni *madrassa* students into Taliban and HUA/HUM (later renamed Jaish Muhammad) units for Pakistan-backed operations in Afghanistan and Kashmir.[47] This change in strategy also meant that domestically the Deobandi and sectarian extremist groups that were closely tied to the Taliban replaced the Jamaʿat-i Islami and mainstream Islamism as the main allies of the military – its Islamic arm. In fact, it was after the advent of the Taliban that HUA/HUM Islamist extremism and militancy became more prominent. These links have become increasingly entrenched, creating organizational ties as well as ideological ones. It was reported that militant activists who were responsible for a number of attacks on Shiʾi targets as well as an attempt on Nawaz Sharif's life were trained in HUA/HUM camps.[48] Increasingly young activists turned to the Taliban as a model. Hence, between 1993 and 1997 the most radical element of Islamism was associated with the military and the secular PPP, and not with the mainstream Islamism of Nawaz Sharif and PML. Islamism did not play an independent role in determining the direction of Pakistan's thinking on regional issues. It was not identity that was driving the Pakistan–India rivalry, but the rivalry that was driving the identity. Moreover, there existed more than one Islamist message in the political arena. Between 1997 and 1999 the mainstream message under the PML's direction would serve as the foundation for a new approach to the Pakistan–India rivalry.

In 1997 Nawaz Sharif and PML came back to power, and sought to chart a new path for Pakistan to follow.[49] The elections of 1997 were the first since 1988 to give a party a clear mandate to rule. The PML led by Nawaz Sharif won the majority of seats (63 percent) in the National Assembly. The elections produced the smallest contingent of Islamist representation in parliament on record (a sharp contrast with the elections of 2002). The results permitted Nawaz Sharif to vie for control of Pakistan's politics, defining the relationship between civilian rule and Islam, and creating a tenable relationship between Islam and the state – the first since the Zia period. To achieve this he openly fashioned the PML as simultaneously a modern democratic party that was committed to the development of Pakistan, and the champion of the cause of Islamization. The PML's claim was bolstered by the fact that it had taken over seats that were once held by Islamist parties and had defeated

---

[47] *Far Eastern Economic Review*, Mar. 9, 1995, 24.
[48] Owen Bennett Jones, *Pakistan: In the Eye of the Storm*, 2nd edn (New Haven: Yale University Press, 2003), 22–23; and Abbas, *Pakistan's Drift into Extremism*, 209–10.
[49] Nasr, *Islamic Leviathan*, 154–56.

those Islamist candidates who had participated in the elections. It argued that it could better serve the interests of the Islamic vote bank.

Sharif was perhaps the first Pakistani leader since General Ayub Khan (1959–69) to be responsive primarily to the demands of the business community, and also to understand that Pakistan's geostrategic interests lay in economic development and not regional adventurism or the quest for military parity with India. Sharif's vision was one of changing Pakistan's economic profile, and only by so doing to alter the balance of power in Pakistan–India rivalry. Hence, Sharif was keen to temper Pakistan's commitment to *jihad* in Afghanistan and Kashmir, and to normalize relations with India in order to facilitate more rapid economic development in Pakistan.

The Sharif administration, however, was saddled with two problems: first, growing corruption, and second, creeping authoritarianism.[50] Although the military was in part responsible for creating an environment in which civilian politicians felt the need to accumulate war chests and to use strong-arm tactics with opponents in order to preempt the military and the judiciary in impending struggles for power, the Sharif government bears the responsibility for mismanaging its opportunity in office. The growing popular frustration with corruption and the heavy-handedness of the prime minister in dealing with parliament, the judiciary, and ultimately the military damaged his standing and helped grease the skids for his fall from power.

The military under General Pervez Musharraf had all along viewed Nawaz Sharif's gambit as a threat. First, Sharif had succeeded in establishing a viable right-of-center and Islamist coalition he would have dominated the middle ground in Pakistan. Moreover, with this success it would have been a democratic party rather than the military that would have defined and controlled the nexus between Islam and the state.

Second, the military opposed normalization of relations with India, and, more important, the change in strategic outlook away from *jihad* in Afghanistan and Kashmir toward economic growth. During this time period the main political force attached to Islamic identity – and heir to Jinnah's party – favored a reduction of tensions with India, and it was the secular political forces that favored continued tensions.

The military – led by General Musharraf – opposed the Lahore Summit. The military even asked Sharif to limit Prime Minister Vajpayee's moves to the Governor's House in Lahore. When Sharif defied the military request to hold a state dinner at the Lahore Fort, militant

---

[50] Abbas, *Pakistan's Drift into Extremism*, 159–77.

thugs smashed the cars of all the guests. Having failed to prevent the Summit, the military then sought to undermine it through heightening tensions in the region, first through fresh missile tests and ultimately through the Kargil adventure.[51]

It was in this context that between 1997 and 1999 the military turned to extremist forces to also undermine Sharif and the PML government. By encouraging increasing radicalization of the Islamist discourse, and supporting the extremist forces, the military sought to destabilize relations between the PML and its Islamist constituency, and more generally to radicalize Islamism to the extent that a viable center-right coalition would not be feasible. The military also used extremist forces in Kashmir to undermine the Sharif–Vajpayee rapport, most notably in Kargil in 1999 when an incursion by militants into Indian-held Kashmir brought the two countries to the brink of war and greatly weakened Nawaz Sharif.

The growing tensions between the military and the PML government eroded Sharif's authority, and eventually led to the military coup of 1999. The new regime was based on an untenable relationship between a secular-leaning military elite that promised secular development and Islamist extremist forces. The military sought to manage this situation by encouraging Islamist extremism to spend its energies in Afghanistan and Kashmir. Keen to ride the tiger of radical Islam at a time when the military's ideological cadence with Islamism was waning, the military was hard pressed to react to the fact that the Afghan campaign was producing Islamic radicalism more rapidly than the military could handle. By encouraging the Afghan jihad to extend to Kashmir the military was not only hoping to utilize the successful Afghan strategy to change the balance of power in Kashmir, but also to find a new preoccupation for the growing radicalism.

The events of September 11, 2001 forced a change of perspective on Pakistan. First, international pressure compelled General Musharraf to increasingly distance the state from *jihadi* forces. This process was further accelerated after attempts on Musharraf's life in December 2003, and on the life of his prime minister, Shawkat Aziz, in July 2004. Second, the imperative of maintaining parity with India and addressing the requirements of the IMF to reduce Pakistan's debt burden led the general to arrive at the same conclusion as Nawaz Sharif had: namely, Pakistan had to invest in its economy in order to maintain its regional position. Growth

---

[51] *Ibid.*, pp. 169–75; Shireen Mazari, *The Kargil Conflict, 1999: Separating Fact from Fiction* (Islamabad: Institute for Strategic Studies, 2003); Jasit Singh (ed.), *Kargil 1999: Pakistan's Fourth War for Kashmir* (Delhi: South Asia Books, 1999).

in the economy in turn required reducing the influence of *jihadi* forces and the threat of war with India. Hence, three years after scuttling the Lahore Summit, the Pakistan military embarked on a rapprochement with India, putting in place a framework for reducing tensions between the two countries and taking measured steps toward peace.

Since 2002 Pakistan and India have been engaged in dialogue directed at lessening tensions between the two countries. US pressure brought to bear on both South Asian nuclear powers, the imperatives of the War on Terror, which requires winding down *jihadi* activity in Kashmir, combined with economic and military incentives given to Pakistan, have helped maintain momentum in the talks. However, there are no changes evident in the understanding of national interest and strategic requirements in Delhi and Islamabad to suggest that either India or Pakistan is likely to make the kind of compromises that are required for a resolution to the conflict. That Pakistan today feels more vulnerable to Indian hegemony in the region than at any other time since 1988, when Afghanistan became a vassal of Pakistan, and that the United States is not likely to address Pakistan's strategic needs, means that Islamabad is not likely to make any bold moves on Kashmir in the short run.

The role that identity will play in this process is not likely to be markedly different than in the 1980s and the 1990s. In India the return of the Congress Party to power in 2004 is indicative of a palpable decline in identity politics in that country. However, although Congress will be less "Hindu" in its orientation, it will nevertheless respond to the residual identity posturing that exists in Indian polity, especially with regard to Kashmir and Pakistan.

In Pakistan, the Musharraf government is secular in orientation. However, the Islamic and nationalist identity politics that pervaded the political arena and the ranks of the military over the past two decades has not weakened. Pakistan today has a secular government ruling over a religious society, and the tensions between the state and society are entrenching Islamic consciousness in various social strata. This means that attitudes toward India – insofar as they stemmed from identity politics in Pakistan – have not changed. However, since the Musharraf government faces an "Islamic" deficit with the population, it is not able to speak for the Islamic constituency, and to give concessions in their name. This is also true of the Congress Party. As a result, Musharraf and Manmohan Singh will be more hard pressed to push for peace in the face of the reality of identity politics in their respective countries. Peace in Kashmir will therefore remain hostage to fundamental changes in India and Pakistan that can reduce the dominant position of identity in the political process.

Conclusion

Identity has played a complex role in the India–Pakistan rivalry. This role has changed over time as both countries have become far more reliant on religious ideology than was the case at independence. However, identity has not played a clearly negative role in determining the tempo of the rivalry. Rather, religious identity has provided existing dynamics of the rivalry with new ideological direction and political opportunities. In India the rise of Hindu nationalism has strengthened attitudes that existed toward the question of Pakistan even during the secular era. However, in India Hindu identity has not been the tool of any state actor or political institution with a vested interest in the Pakistan–India rivalry.

In Pakistan, on the other hand, the impact of Islamism is far from uniform. Islamism has strengthened Pakistan's identity, but has not necessarily strengthened the communalist/separatist discourse that legitimated the rivalry. In recent years new trends in Pakistan's Islamism have led to new approaches to India, and most notably, in the 1997–99 period under PML leadership it supported a new opening to India. Ultimately, in Pakistan, the military has successfully used Islamic identity to defend its own political position and interests in the Pakistan–India rivalry. Religious identity therefore has not as yet acted as an independent variable, but as a veneer for the military's agenda.

9   At the heart of the conflict: irredentism and Kashmir

Stephen M. Saideman

Introduction

The enduring conflict between India and Pakistan may be moving towards a period of détente. The leaders of both countries met at the outset of 2004, essentially agreeing that the Kashmir conflict should be handled peacefully. This might be a cause of great optimism. One of the key sources of conflict in their relationship – Pakistan's irredentism and India's resistance – may be declining. However, at the same time, there have been repeated efforts to assassinate General Pervez Musharraf by forces that oppose moderation. The simultaneity of these two sets of events is suggestive – that there are grave domestic costs for making peace, and that Musharraf, if sincere, may be following Anwar Sadat more closely than he would like. This brings us to a key shortcoming of the enduring rivalry literature – domestic politics matters but is undertheorized.[1] That is, domestic politics seems to do a lot of the work of causing, prolonging, and ending rivalries, but most scholars in this debate treat it in an *ad hoc* fashion. By focusing on the largely domestic dynamics that drive irredentism, we can get a better idea of under what conditions many rivalries will begin, worsen, and perhaps even end.

Not all enduring rivalries have irredentism as a core dynamic, but many do, including the Koreas, Somalia and Ethiopia, and China and Taiwan. Further, irredentism may separate the more severe and conflict-prone rivalries from the less problematic ones. India's rivalry with Pakistan, in its length and in some of the issues, parallels its rivalry with China. India fought wars and shares contested boundaries with both. However, the level of conflict with Pakistan has been consistently higher. One key difference between the two dyads is that one is characterized by irredentism and the other is not. While China and India have claims to the same

I am grateful to David Lehman for his valuable research assistance and suggestions and to the Canada Research Chair Program for funding his work.
[1] For more on enduring rivalries, see Diehl, Goertz, and Saeedi; and Vasquez, in this volume.

territory, this dispute is not central to the domestic politics of either as the contested regions are not populated by politically relevant groups. On the other hand, Kashmir's population and their claims do play a significant role in Pakistan's domestic politics, resulting in recurrent conflict, despite repeated failures.

The tensions between India and Pakistan over Kashmir have been extraordinarily costly to both sides due to diverted spending, lost opportunities for mutually enriching economic activities, and, of course, lives lost in wars and combat short of war. While the two countries have many differences and there are many sources of conflict, unrealized irredentism is at the core of the rivalry. Pakistan has, through a variety of methods, sought to "regain" the "lost" Muslim-majority territory of Kashmir. India has consistently resisted Pakistan, while inadvertently stoking the fires of irredentism through its policies in Kashmir. The irredentist dynamic in this rivalry may appear to be puzzling because it has lasted so long without resolution and is certainly counter-productive to the long-term interests of both states and the population of the contested territory, Kashmir.

However, this would not be the first case of states pursuing self-destructive foreign policies in the name of unification. Armenia, Croatia, and Serbia are all, arguably, worse off for their efforts to unify territories inhabited by their ethnic kin. Germany and Hungary paid dearly for their efforts to unify peoples speaking their languages during World War II. Somalia is still paying the price today for its failed efforts in the 1970s to annex a Somali-inhabited portion of Ethiopia. Thus, irredentism's role in prolonging conflict and delaying economic and political progress in South Asia is not surprising. By considering what we know about irredentism, we can make sense of some of the dynamics driving the costly conflict between India and Pakistan.

Irredentism often refers to one of two processes: the effort by states to annex territory considered theirs based on ethnic or historical grounds;[2] or the effort by groups to be joined with the mother country. In the India–Pakistan dyad, analysts consider Pakistan to be irredentist, as it seeks to bring together Kashmir with the rest of its territory into a single country. Scholars generally code India as a status quo state, seeking to keep what it has, rather than expanding its territory.[3] The trickier problem is determining which groups in Kashmir desire union with

---

[2] Most analyses focus on ethnic irredentism – where a country seeks to reclaim territory inhabited by ethnic kin.

[3] The focus here is not on blaming one country or the other for the conflict, despite labeling Pakistan as irredentist. Rather, as will become clear, the irredentist dynamic is driven by political processes within both countries.

Pakistan and which seek independence. These two dynamics are related, as irredentist states can encourage or perhaps even create groups within the targeted territory to seek unification; and the existence and activities of irredentist groups can influence the politics of the mother country.[4] To start an analysis of irredentism, it makes sense to consider these dynamics separately, but the next step is to investigate how they interact.

In this chapter, I first consider why groups might want to be unified with the mother country, including as key factors the policies of the mother and host countries. Next, I discuss the conditions under which states might engage in irredentist foreign policies, focusing on the debate about the importance of international constraints and domestic pressures. I then consider how these concepts and arguments translate to South Asia. I examine the politics of Kashmir, first within the state itself, and then in the context of India as a whole. I then consider the domestic dynamics within Pakistan that cause it to engage in dangerous foreign policies. Ultimately, I argue that domestic political dynamics drive both sides of the irredentist equation, with international concerns largely secondary.

When will groups want (re)union?

It is hard to say that irredentism has caused a conflict if there is no group seeking to be reunited with its homeland. Saddam Hussein claimed Kuwait as a lost province, perhaps true historically, but it did not resonate anywhere since there was no significant group in Kuwait seeking union with Iraq. The existence and activities of the potentially irredentist group matter for a variety of reasons. Their condition shapes the salience of the irredentist cause in the homeland, and the irredentist movement may be the focus or the instrument of the homeland's foreign policy. Finally, without any organized effort within the targeted territory to foster union, the irredentist state must engage in war or do nothing. If a group seeks union, then the mother country has a variety of options available.

So, under what conditions will groups desire union? There has been relatively little work addressing this question,[5] as scholars have tended to

---

[4] The mother country refers to the potentially irredentist state that could lay claim to the territory inhabited by the ethnic kin, while host country refers to the state where the group in question resides. For instance, the mother country in this case is Pakistan and the host state is India.

[5] The exceptions include Myron Weiner, "The Macedonian Syndrome," *World Politics* 23 (1971), 665–83; Thomas Ambrosio, *Irredentism: Ethnic Conflict and International Politics* (Westport: Praeger, 2001); and David Carment and Patrick James, "Internal Constraints and Interstate Ethnic Conflict: Toward a Crisis-Based Assessment of Irredentism," *Journal of Conflict Resolution* 39 (Mar. 1995), 82–109.

focus on another form of separatism – secession.[6] Scholars of secession have disagreed over the importance of economic advantage or discrimination,[7] but have concluded that secession is the culmination of a process of frustrated political mobilization. Members of an ethnic group opt for secession if they have lost autonomy and/or if the state has repressed previous efforts to engage in dissent.[8] These factors should breed irredentism as much as secessionism. So, a key question for the case study below will be how India's policies have encouraged groups to pursue separatism or discouraged such efforts.

The differences between secessionist and irredentist inclinations seem to be the existence of a nearby mother country and whether the group is concentrated.[9] Essentially, these factors determine a group's options – a group cannot hope for union if their kin do not reign in a nearby country; and a group cannot hope to secede unless they are relatively concentrated. If a group is concentrated and resides near a country where their kin govern, what is a group to do? This is particularly important for understanding Kashmir, because both goals are in play here. In Kashmir, groups can choose either secession or irredentism, being both concentrated and adjacent to a mother country, and there exist a multitude of groups that have chosen one, the other, or both.

Three factors matter most in shaping a group's aspirations towards independence or union: the group's relationship with the mother country; the destiny of the group's leadership in either situation; and the relative situation of the group as a whole in the alternative futures. First, and most obviously, rebel organizations created and funded by the mother country are most likely to call for union. Generally, one would expect an organization in the pocket of the homeland to be more likely than others to seek union.

Second, leaders of a group are likely to seek an outcome that puts them in positions of influence. Successful secession would give them key positions in the new state. Successful irredentism may or may not lead to elites within the territory gaining powerful offices in the newly united entity.[10]

---

[6] Stephen M. Saideman and R. William Ayres, "Determining the Sources of Irredentism: Logit Analyses of Minorities at Risk Data," *Journal of Politics* 62 (Nov. 2000), 1126–44.

[7] Donald Horowitz, *Ethnic Groups in Conflict* (Berkeley: University of California, 1985); Peter Gourevitch, "The Reemergence of 'Peripheral Nationalisms': Some Comparative Speculations on the Spatial Distribution of Political Leadership and Economic Growth," *Comparative Studies in Society and History* 21 (January 1979), 303–22.

[8] Ted Gurr, *Peoples Versus States: Ethnopolitical Conflict and Accommodation at the End of the 20th Century* (Washington, DC: US Institute of Peace Press, 2000).

[9] Saideman and Ayres, "Determining the Sources of Irredentism."

[10] An additional calculation would be whether secession or irredentism is more likely to be successful.

This depends upon the political system of the mother country, including its institutions and balance of groups at home. For instance, in the Somali case, the Ogaden clan within Ethiopia had hopes of mattering politically in Somalia since their kin were already in positions of power.[11]

Third, it may be hard to convince the group to join with the mother country if that is seen as worsening the group's situation. Elites may want to pursue an irredentist course, but have to compromise on secession if they cannot get support for the former. Moldova might be an example of this phenomenon since there was limited appeal for uniting with Romania after the Soviet Union's collapse.[12]

Thus, the activities and condition of groups in Kashmir matter for Pakistan's politics; and India has some ability to influence these through its policies and actions. The irredentist cause is more likely to matter in Pakistan if the groups in Kashmir are active and if their plight seems genuinely tragic. In turn, the groups in Kashmir are more likely to be irredentist if Indian policies frustrate and antagonize the population of the region. There is a key interactive dynamic between Pakistan, India, and the various groups in the contested territory. Below, I consider how things played out to show how domestic politics within the three key sets of actors (Pakistan, India, and Kashmir) exacerbated the conflict. This discussion should provide some indications for why this has been a chronic problem, enduring over the course of more than fifty years.

How do states handle potentially separatist groups?

Due to space limitations, I shall not go into detail about the dynamics of the host state. However, a few critical aspects matter. In dealing with separatist groups, countries face two sets of choices: to let the region go or not; and if not, then how to address the grievances. Most countries simply cannot allow a separatist region to depart. While the contagiousness of conflict from one country to another may be overrated, separatism can spread from one portion of a country to another.[13] The departure of one not only sets a precedent for others, but also changes the domestic distribution of power, increasing the relative strength of some groups at

---

[11] Stephen M. Saideman, "Inconsistent Irredentism? Political Competition, Ethnic Ties, and the Foreign Policies of Somalia and Serbia," *Security Studies* 7 (Spring 1998), 51–93.

[12] Charles King, *The Moldovans: Romania, Russia and the Politics of Culture* (Stanford: Hoover Institution Press, 2000).

[13] Stephen M. Saideman, "Is Pandora's Box Half-Empty or Half-Full? The Limited Virulence of Secession and the Domestic Sources of Disintegration," in David A. Lake and Donald Rothchild (eds.), *The International Spread of Ethnic Conflict: Fear, Diffusion, Escalation* (Princeton: Princeton University Press, 1998), 127–50.

the expense of others. Therefore, countries facing multiple potential separatist groups are much less likely to let any one of them go.[14]

Therefore, the focus is on how governments treat ethnic groups that might seek to separate. The primary dynamic is elite competition for control of the government. Politicians may not be able to offer compromises to soothe an ethnic group's complaints if such efforts can be successfully outbid by a competing party.[15] For instance, in Sri Lanka, moderation was punished and extremist policy stances towards the Tamils were rewarded in large part because the political system gave huge majorities to whichever party gained a plurality of the Sinhalese votes.[16] We need to know whether politicians are in a relatively strong position and can resist the efforts by others to paint them as traitors to their ethnic group, whether they have incentives to play to multiple ethnic groups, or whether they are vulnerable to outbidding, causing them to support policies that make the situation worse.

The key question is what does it take to get into and stay in power? If politicians need the support of members of the separatist group, in addition to their own,[17] then they will be compelled to seek policies that accommodate that group. On the other hand, if the incumbents face a nationalist party that can suck away constituents, then moderation will be unlikely. Ironically, the relatively extreme nationalist parties are more likely to be able to negotiate and make concessions. Parties with robust credentials for defending the majority group's interest are less vulnerable to charges that they are selling out their ethnic group. Sri Lanka provides an example as the Tamil Tigers, having ruthlessly eliminated moderate opponents, are in a better position to make concessions as part of a peace process.[18]

A second factor is the degree to which the agents on the ground do what the central government wants. This refers not only to the agency problem – will agents do what the principals seek – but also a competency problem – can the agents do their job. Regardless of whether the elites at the center try to accommodate the ethnic group or repress it, the implementation of

---

[14] Monica Duffy Toft, *The Geography of Ethnic Conflict: Identity, Interests, and the Indivisibility of Territory* (Princeton: Princeton University Press, 2003).

[15] Joseph Rothschild, *Ethnopolitics: A Conceptual Framework* (New York: Columbia University Press, 1981).

[16] Donald L. Horowitz, *Ethnic Groups in Conflict* (Berkeley: University of California, 1985).

[17] This assumes that the politicians at the center are not of the same ethnicity as the potentially separatist group, as the group is less likely to secede or join the mother country if it has a powerful stake in the system.

[18] Mia Bloom, *Dying to Kill* (New York: Columbia University Press, 2005).

these efforts ultimately depends on the local law enforcement authorities and bureaucrats.

Thus, the impact of the host state on the ethnic group is shaped by the incentives of politicians at the center and the abilities of the implementing agents at the local level. Obviously, there is more going on, but these two dynamics are likely to be critical.

What is an irredentist state to do?

Irredentism is inherently risky when compared to most other foreign policies. To make territorial demands upon a neighbor is tantamount to inviting war. Indeed, some scholars argue that states will only engage in irredentism when there is an available opportunity to act with relative impunity.[19] Others (such as myself) argue that domestic politics drives irredentism to such an extent that states will engage in foreign policies that are truly awful for the country. This is a critical debate – if states are responsive to international opportunities and dangers, then other states have leverage; if domestic politics compels states to engage in self-destructive foreign policies, there may be little that the international community can do.

International constraints

Ambrosio argues that "the more permissive the international system is to irredentist claims, the more likely it is that they will be forcibly made; the more static or rigid the international system, the less irredentism."[20] States are more likely to engage in irredentism if they expect that their efforts will be tolerated. His book focuses entirely on the international side of the equation.

The key problem for such arguments is that countries have engaged in irredentist foreign policies under varying international conditions – when the balance of power favored them, and when it did not. While Somalia is often cited as acting opportunistically in the mid-1970s, launching an irredentist war at a time of Ethiopian weakness, this same country engaged in irredentist efforts against all three of its neighbors in the early 1960s, when it was clearly weaker relative to the others.[21] In the past decade, Armenia, Croatia, and Serbia have joined Somalia as countries that have engaged in self-destructive irredentist foreign policies.

---

[19] Ambrosio, *Irredentism.*   [20] *Ibid.*, 5.   [21] Saideman, "Inconsistent Irredentism?"

Thus, international pressures and opportunities certainly play a role in how successful an irredentist state may be, but we need to know more about domestic politics to understand why states engage in such risky endeavors in the first place.

The domestic politics of self-destruction

Instead of considering international constraints, some scholars have focused on domestic political imperatives. The general notion is that what is best for the country may not be driving the country's foreign policy. While one could argue that national identity drives countries to engage in unsound foreign policies,[22] the focus here is the political incentives elites face as they make foreign policy. Politicians may choose or be compelled to engage in dangerous foreign policies to stay in power. What is rational for the decisionmaker may be unwise for the state.

So, under what conditions will domestic political dynamics produce irredentism? Elsewhere, I have argued that political competition is more important than international constraints.[23] Specifically, when politicians are competing for the support of those having kin in the territory to be redeemed, they will be more likely to support irredentist policies. Competition plays out differently, depending on regime type, but regime type by itself does not say much directly about whether a state is irredentist or not. Politicians need some kind of support and, therefore, face some sort of competitive pressures in any kind of system. So, we cannot say that democracies are more or less irredentist than authoritarian regimes, and, indeed, Somalia was irredentist both when it was democratic and when it was not. However, the dynamics may vary as regime type determines the size of the audience politicians play towards, the means by which they can get support, and most importantly, the audience or electorate itself.

In a democracy, votes and campaign contributions matter, politicians rely on larger constituencies (though not necessarily majorities), and so the preferences of voting blocs matter. The key dynamic that might drive irredentism in a democracy is ethnic outbidding, where two or more politicians or parties compete with each other to be the best nationalist, the best defender of the ethnic group's interests. These circumstances punish moderation as the more extreme politicians accuse others of being traitors to the nation. Ethnic outbidding is likely where relatively small changes in support can lead to significant changes in who governs.

---

[22] See Nasr, this volume, as well as Ashutosh Varshney, "India, Pakistan, and Kashmir: Antinomies of Nationalism," *Asian Survey* 31 (Nov. 1991), 997–1019.
[23] Saideman, "Inconsistent Irredentism?"

The paradigmatic case is Sri Lanka of the 1950s–70s, where whoever won the plurality of the Sinhalese vote would gain large majorities of seats in the parliament. In authoritarian regimes, those who carry the guns, monopolize information, and engage in repression are the key actors, as their loyalties determine who governs.[24] Such governments vary in how much politicians rely on the army, secret police, or a single party (such as the Communist Party). They also vary in how much of that loyalty is gained through ideology, corruption/patronage, or ethnic ties. These factors combine, ultimately, to determine the fragility of the regime and the strategies authoritarian elites use to maintain their rule. Tremblay and Schofield, in their chapter, show how regimes in between democracy and autocracy develop dynamics that produce counter-productive foreign policies. This chapter departs from theirs as I argue that the pattern of interests drive foreign policy, although regime type shapes that to a degree, whereas they argue that a specific type of regime is more conflict-prone.

For the argument here, the relevant questions are who supports the irredentist cause and who opposes such efforts. Supporters of irredentism would include those with direct ethnic ties to the inhabitants of the territory to be redeemed as well as those who would benefit from a poorer relationship with that neighbor and other states. Those with ethnic ties want irredentism for both obvious and less obvious reasons. They genuinely care about the plight of their kin and figure that the kin will be better off if unified with the host state. Further, reunion will increase the relative political power of the united group, compared to other groups within the irredentist state, as a successful union will both bind the group together and increase the group's size. Others may favor the irredentist project as it is likely to offend not only the neighbor but the international community. Those who profit by a dangerous international environment, such as those depending on military budgets or secrecy,[25] and those who may be harmed by economic reform and integration will view this as a good thing. For instance, Slobodan Milosevic developed a constituency consisting of those who genuinely cared about the nationalist cause and those who would be hurt economically by greater integration into the international economy.[26]

---

[24] Barbara Geddes, *Paradigms and Sand Castles: Theory Building and Research Design in Comparative Politics* (Ann Arbor: University of Michigan Press, 2003).

[25] In *Myths of Empire*, Jack Snyder discusses the importance of log-rolling among different groups, each having a common interest in aggressive foreign policies but for different reasons. Jack Snyder, *Myths of Empire: Domestic Politics and International Ambition* (Ithaca: Cornell University Press, 1993).

[26] V. P. Gagnon, Jr., "Ethnic Nationalism and International Conflict: The Case of Serbia," *International Security* 19 (1994–95), 130–66; Saideman, "Inconsistent Irredentism?"

Opponents of irredentism are likely to include beneficiaries of increased or continued engagement with neighbors and the international community and also those who would be weakened by a successful reunion. Those who profit from transnational economic activities should oppose irredentism since aggressive foreign policies are likely to disrupt economic flows. Further, the other costs of aggression – military spending, refugees, etc. – may be borne by those without an interest in irredentism. Moreover, unification will not only strengthen some groups, but it will also weaken others. In Somalia, irredentism aimed towards Ethiopia would have strengthened one clan and one clan-family, but would have weakened other clans. So, there was much less unity about the irredentist project than was generally believed.[27]

In sum, politicians will do what is necessary to stay in power even if it means supporting policies likely to hurt the country. The key is to consider upon whom leaders depend for support and what their supporters want. If their supporters want aggressive aid for kin in the neighboring countries, and if they can switch their support to someone else, you are likely to see irredentism as politicians compete with each other to be the best nationalist – the same outbidding process discussed above. If elites depend upon those who would be hurt by aggressive foreign policies, irredentism is less likely. If supporters are a mixture of pro- and anti-irredentists, then you may see a set of inconsistent policies – enough support to antagonize the neighbor but not enough to sacrifice engagement with the rest of the world – what I like to call the Hungarian strategy.[28] The balance of interests in irredentism is subject to change as the mix of supporters and opponents changes and, as events on the ground in the targeted territory develop. Irredentism depends in part on whether the group inhabiting the key slice of territory wants unification or not.

Understanding the Kashmir conflict

In an irredentist conflict, there are three discrete sets of actors, whose behavior interacts to reinforce that of the others. Without a disgruntled group, there would be no irredentist conflict – we would be calling it something else and applying different concepts. India's efforts to govern

---

[27] Saideman, "Inconsistent Irredentism?"

[28] Stephen M. Saideman, "Inevitable Irredentism? Considering the Surprising Lack of Ethnic Aggression in Eastern Europe in the 1990s," Paper Presented at the Central and East European International Studies Association/International Studies Association Convention, June 26–28, 2003, Budapest, Hungary.

Kashmir can create more or less tension, which, in turn, can energize or demobilize the groups in the region. In turn, Pakistan can increase or decrease its support for rebel groups in Kashmir, which can then provoke an Indian reaction. Below, I discuss each of these sets of actors and dynamics, and show how their interactions can cause conflict to spiral.

Politics in Jammu and Kashmir

To understand the irredentist conflict, we need to know who the actors on the ground are and what they want. This is quite difficult as there are many organizations competing for the support of the residents of Jammu and Kashmir with varying aims, ranging from greater autonomy to secession to union with Pakistan. As should be expected, India and Pakistan play crucial roles in the interests and efforts of the Kashmiris.

The state of Jammu and Kashmir breaks down into three regions,[29] each with its own mix of ethnic/religious groups. Jammu is primarily Hindu and Sikh; Ladakh is split largely between Shia Muslims and Buddhists; and Sunni Muslims dominate the Valley or Vale of Kashmir. Separatist sentiment is strongest in the Valley, as Muslims there feel most alienated from the Indian government and closest to the Kashmiris on the other side of the international line of control – Azad Kashmir – in Pakistan and to Pakistanis more generally. Geography – extreme mountainous terrain – has limited the Kashmiris' ethnic bonds with their neighbors, producing a distinct language and unique cultural practices, leading to a somewhat contested identity of *Kashmiriyat*.[30] Perhaps the strongest bond unifying Kashmiris on both sides of the border is religion – sharing Islam but differing in other ethnic markers. These ethnic divisions matter, weakening the potential support for an independent Kashmir since not all Muslims in the region consider themselves to be Kashmiri. Moreover, the demographic preponderance of the Valley means that groups from other districts fear the potential hegemony of the Valley in an independent Jammu and Kashmir.

Before partition, Kashmiris divided their support between pro- and anti-Pakistani parties. Partition caused the pro-Pakistani elites to flee to Azad Kashmir, leaving behind Sheikh Abdullah and his National

---

[29] Only the Indian-controlled portions of Jammu and Kashmir are under consideration here. In this analysis, the Pakistan-occupied territories (Azad Kashmir) are, for the sake of simplicity, treated as part of Pakistan. This is analytically clearer and is not inappropriate, considering the integration of Azad Kashmir into the Pakistani political system.

[30] On the subject of *Kashmiriyat*, see Leo E. Rose, "The Politics of Azad Kashmir," in Raju G. C. Thomas (ed.), *Perspectives on Kashmir: The Roots of Conflict in South Asia* (Boulder, CO: Westview Press 1992), 235–53.

Conference Party to pursue a relatively ambiguous pro-independence platform. Over the years, Abdullah fell in and out of favor with the Indian government, landing him in jail in 1953 for five years. He came to power again in 1977, after perhaps the first essentially free elections in the region, doing very well in the Valley. Abdullah continued to hold an opaque position on the independence issue up to his death in 1982. His son, Farooq Abdullah, replaced him as leader of the National Conference, but was less successful in negotiating the conflicting currents.

Farooq's missteps, along with meddling by New Delhi (see below) helped to spur political mobilization, as Kashmiris increasingly protested corruption and the poor economy. The Jammu and Kashmir Liberation Front (JKLF), which has espoused secessionist rather than irredentist aims, was formed at this time. JKLF mobilization along with the flawed election of 1987 caused Kashmiris to seek a more violent course of action, having tried the democratic route.[31] Isolated attacks on government outposts escalated to the December 1989 kidnapping of the home affairs minister's daughter. Having made democratic participation seem futile, the Indian government appeared now to reward violent political expression when it submitted to the JKLF's demands in order to secure the release of their captive. Violence increased the next month, resulting in the placement of the state under Governor's (Federal) Rule.[32]

This escalation coincided with the ending of the war in Afghanistan and the rise of political Islam elsewhere in the world. These developments mattered for a few reasons. First, it fostered a proliferation of Islamic parties in Kashmir, with most preferring union with Pakistan.[33] Second, as discussed below, elements of the Pakistani military became very competent at supporting insurgency,[34] and these skills translated well to the Kashmir context. Third, the end of the war produced an influx of foreign fighters (as well as arms), mujahidin, who provided much of the core insurgent effort.

Two umbrella groups – the United Jihad Council, which consists of militant groups, and the All-Party Hurriyat Conference, which consists of political parties – include groups with varying aims. Parties and organizations range from the vociferously irredentist Jamaat-i-Islami to the more independence-minded People's Conference to the clearly secessionist

---

[31] Iffat Malik, *Kashmir: Ethnic Conflict, International Dispute* (Karachi: Oxford University Press, 2001), 283.

[32] Robert G. Wirsing, *India, Pakistan and the Kashmir Dispute: On Regional Conflict and its Resolution* (New York: St. Martin's Press, 1994), 113.

[33] Malik, *Kashmir*, 273–74.   [34] Wirsing, *India, Pakistan and the Kashmir Dispute*, 115.

JKLF. The groups with the strongest ties to Pakistan would be most interested in irredentism, while those based on ideas or coalitions that differ significantly from Pakistan would seek independence. The Hizb-ul-Mujahideen (the most significant of irredentist groups, which include Al-Jehad, Al Barq, Ikhwan ul-Musalmeen, and Al Umar Mujahideen) is a fundamentalist Islamic group and prefers union with Pakistan, as it shares common cause with key actors in Pakistan, including the Inter-Services Intelligence (ISI) Directorate.[35] Due to this support, it is the most feared separatist organization.[36] The JKFL is secular, which sets it apart from tendencies within Pakistani politics. Therefore, it logically should not seek union with Pakistan, and, indeed, it does not, as it has been avowedly secessionist. Consequently, Pakistan has supported the Hizb-ul-Mujahideen and the other like-minded irredentist groups at the expense of the JKLF.

There is significant doubt about the indigenous component of some of these groups, which seem to be largely foreign mujahidin rather than Kashmiris. The Laskar-i Tayyiba is a case in point – the US Department of State considers this group to be essentially foreign. It may be the case that as Kashmiris tired of the conflict, having borne the brunt of its costs, outsiders were needed to continue the insurgency. Despite avowedly fighting for the Kashmiris, the various militant groups are not entirely popular. In addition to causing India to retaliate against the local population, the various groups themselves have been quite brutal in their interactions within Kashmir, engaging in rape and murder.[37] Interestingly, the greed versus grievance debate in the civil war literature[38] plays out on the ground, as there is now much resentment toward the criminal enterprises associated with the separatist movements.[39]

The general course of politics in Kashmir fits the general pattern of separatism. Groups seek to pursue their goals through normal politics, but when they are repressed or otherwise denied their goals, they then pursue separatism. Separatism grew in the 1980s and early 1990s, responding to changes in India's politics – the decline of the Congress Party, the rise of the Bharatiya Janata Party (BJP) – as well as to the various interventions into Kashmir politics by New Delhi, to the success of the JKLF, and perhaps also to Abdullah's death. Since then,

[35] Sumit Ganguly and Kanti Bajpai, "India and the Crisis in the Kashmir," *Asian Survey* 34 (May 1994), 401–16; Wirsing, *India, Pakistan and the Kashmir Dispute*, 132–33.
[36] Wirsing, *India, Pakistan and the Kashmir Dispute*, 132.   [37] *Ibid.*, 137.
[38] Paul Collier, "Rebellion as a Quasi-Criminal Activity," *Journal of Conflict Resolution* 44 (Dec. 2000), 839–53.
[39] Wirsing, *India, Pakistan and the Kashmir Dispute*, 137.

indigenous separatism appears to have declined as the costs of violence spiraled and as India has worked to regain its legitimacy in Kashmir. Instead, the insurgent movement became increasingly dependent upon and driven by Pakistan and by foreigners based in Pakistan.[40] The divisions within the Kashmiris are quite important as they significantly complicate any effort to build a lasting peace, as revealed by events in 2004, particularly the bilateral talks between Pakistan and India that exclude Kashmiri parties.[41]

Indian policies in Kashmir

Motivated by its secular ideology[42] and a concern that allowing one territory to leave would cause a chain of secessionist efforts, India has tried a variety of strategies to keep Kashmir in the fold. Therefore, the focus is not on whether, but how; what has India done to govern Kashmir and how have these efforts shaped separatism within the contested territory?

India initially promised significant autonomy to Kashmir and an eventual plebiscite on its future. Article 370 of India's constitution gave the state of Jammu and Kashmir a special status, with greater autonomy than other federal units. However, from the mid-1960s onward, India sought to integrate Jammu and Kashmir more tightly into the rest of the country.[43] These efforts may have provoked Pakistan in 1965, causing the outbreak of a second war between the two countries. There is little support for a referendum on the issue: "Will Indian public opinion allow any government to carry through a plebiscite now or in the foreseeable future? A widespread Indian view is that it will not and that any government seriously committed to such an option will fall. There is no sign that any Indian leader or party today has the courage and persuasive powers to change the public's mind..."[44]

During the 1970s, India pursued a more accommodative set of policies, perhaps as the Pakistani threat receded in the wake of the secession of Bangladesh. However, the temptation to meddle in Kashmiri politics, as in the rest of India, was too much. During the 1980s, the Congress Party began to collapse. Indira Gandhi both accelerated this trend and worsened the situation in Kashmir by trying to recentralize, weakening and replacing governors of several states.[45] Many scholars point to the

---

[40] *Ibid.*, 134.   [41] *The Economist*, Aug. 21, 2004.
[42] See Sumit Ganguly, *Conflict Unending: India–Pakistan Tensions since 1947* (New York: Columbia University Press, 2001).
[43] *Ibid.*, 35.   [44] Ganguly and Bajpai, "India and the Crisis in the Kashmir," 413.
[45] Varshney, "Antinomies of Nationalism," 1015.

216 *Stephen M. Saideman*

1987 election in Kashmir as a key turning point.[46] The Congress Party formed a coalition with the National Conference, tainting the latter in the eyes of many Kashmiris. Further, the election was apparently marred by vote rigging. After these events, significant mobilization occurred, leading to greater support for separatism both within Kashmir and from Pakistan.

Hindu nationalism in the form of the BJP began to rise in part due to resentment about concessions given to ethnic minorities throughout India.[47] This made it increasingly difficult for Indian elites to pursue moderate policies and increased the sense of threat and alienation perceived by Muslims in Kashmir and elsewhere in India. Things worsened in Kashmir as newly elected Prime Minister V. P. Singh, relied on a coalition that included the BJP. Its first steps were moderate, but produced a backlash. As a result, his government then took harder positions on Kashmir.[48]

"It was New Delhi's mistaken response, its understanding of Kashmir as a law-and-order problem to be dealt with by 'brute force,' that enabled separatism to gain real headway in 1990. Pakistan's success ... came *subsequent* to India's failure."[49] Wirsing goes on to document the counter-insurgency strategies India pursued, which might have been effective at preventing the conflict from escalating further, but also increased the sense of grievance felt by Kashmiris.[50] Efforts to provide greater oversight, such as the appointment of human rights activist George Fernandes to the post of Minister for Kashmir Affairs, were short lived, in large part due to BJP opposition.[51]

Indeed, the BJP used the issue of Kashmir to increase the salience of the Hindu–Muslim divide in Indian politics, including a "unity caravan" that traveled to the region in late 1991 and early 1992, as this played well to wider audiences than previous symbols/issues. This escalated into efforts to undermine Article 370 and to recruit Hindu militias to fight the Kashmiri militants. The Congress Party was constrained in this competition, as any effort to gain more Muslim votes by being more sympathetic to the Kashmiris was likely to be offset by the loss in Hindu votes.[52]

[46] Ganguly and Bajpai, "India and the Crisis in the Kashmir"; Reeta Chowdhari Tremblay, "Elections in Kashmir: A Question of Pragmatism," in Ramashray Roy and Paul Wallace (eds.), *Indian Politics and the 1998 Indian Election: Regionalism, Hindutva and State Politics* (New Delhi: Sage Publications, 1999), 309–39; Reeta Chowdhari Tremblay, "Kashmir Conflict: Secessionist Movement, Mobilization, and Political Institutions," *Pacific Affairs* 74 (Winter 2001–02), 569–77. Wirsing disagrees, arguing that flawed elections were hardly new in India, *India, Pakistan and the Kashmir Dispute*, 115.
[47] Varshney, "Antinomies of Nationalism," 1002.   [48] Ganguly, *Conflict Unending*, 93.
[49] Emphasis in original, Wirsing, *India, Pakistan and the Kashmir Dispute*, 115.
[50] *Ibid.*, ch. 5.   [51] Malik, *Kashmir*, 287.
[52] Wirsing, *India, Pakistan and the Kashmir Dispute*, 164–66.

After a series of short-lived governments, the Congress (I) Party regained power, holding it for nearly five years (1991–96). At first, this government was distracted by other events in and outside of India. The Rao government eventually launched a series of initiatives and sought to restart the electoral process.[53] The government felt that people in Kashmir were tiring of on-going mobilization and conflict.[54] Because human rights violations gained the attention of the international community, India increased its oversight over the various agencies operating in the region. This went alongside an effort to improve the electoral process. The 1996 elections were flawed within Jammu and Kashmir, but did produce significant support for Farooq Abdullah, ending President's Rule. "India's strategy of repression followed by national and local elections has largely undermined the driving forces behind the insurgency."[55]

In the years that followed, violence diminished, tourism developed again, and there was a relaxation of tensions in the region. The 1998 elections saw relatively high turnout in Jammu and Kashmir and were seen as relatively free and fair.[56] Indeed, Pakistan may have initiated the Kargil conflict to derail India's successes and prevent these gains from being institutionalized. However, just as the previous governments engaged in fewer compromises because of an extremist coalition partner, the BJP was constrained by more secular coalition partners. Still, the BJP as leader of a coalition was better positioned to compromise than other parties, and this may have played a role in the recent reduction in tensions until the party's defeat in the 2004 elections.

Pakistan's failed quest

Pakistan's behavior is the key, as it has initiated at least two wars and one nuclear crisis while supporting multiple groups in Kashmir. Without Pakistani involvement, India would still have problems in this region, but the situation would be entirely different. The irredentist threat would be minimal, and the secessionists would be weaker. So, what has Pakistan done and why? The first question is easier to answer than the second. Pakistan has provided all kinds of support to insurgents in Kashmir: verbal encouragement, diplomatic cover, money, arms, personnel, bases, indirect

---

[53] Malik, *Kashmir*, 322.   [54] Schofield, *Kashmir in the Crossfire*, 257.
[55] Summit Ganguly, "An Opportunity for Peace in Kashmir?," *Current History* 96 (Dec. 1997), 414.
[56] Tremblay, "Elections in Kashmir."

fire (artillery), and, ultimately, war.[57] Infiltration has continued at varying levels ever since the boundary was drawn. Rather than merely happening in Pakistan, elements of the government, especially the army and the ISI, have played a leading role in coordinating these efforts. "Kashmiri Muslim militants themselves have given countless testimonials of the Pakistan Army's assistances; and the circumstantial evidence – even when one discounts the inevitable distortion and exaggeration coming from the Indian side – seems pointed overwhelmingly in this direction."[58]

Pakistan has also not been random in its assistance. Just as it has consistently rejected independence as an option in any eventual plebiscite, Pakistan has supported groups seeking union. "Pakistan's opposition to Kashmiri independence has influenced its role in the insurgency. Islamabad has been highly selective in its support of militant groups, encouraging groups that are fighting for Kashmir's accession to Pakistan, and discouraging those fighting for independence."[59] Further, Pakistan, either directly or through the groups it supports, has used violence against Kashmiri groups seeking independence.[60] Indeed, the fractionalization of the Kashmiri groups may actually be intended, as many, smaller groups may be easier to manipulate.[61]

Only recently has Pakistan seemed to reduce support for Kashmiri irredentists. Pakistan President Pervez Musharraf met in January 2004 with Indian Prime Minister Atal Bihari Vajpayee, agreeing to talks about the Kashmir dispute. At the time this chapter was being revised, little substantive progress had been made, but India had started reducing its force levels in Kashmir. This new peace effort seems to be the product of a dramatic shift in Musharraf's domestic political strategies.

Potential explanations

How can we make sense of this high degree of intervention given the high costs these efforts impose on Pakistan? One cannot lay the blame solely

---

[57] Peter Chalk "Pakistan's Role in the Kashmir Insurgency," *Jane's Intelligence Review*, September 1, 2001, http://www.rand.org/hot/op-eds/090101JIR.html (retrieved Nov. 20, 2003); Daniel L. Byman, Peter Chalk, Bruce Hoffman, William Rosenau, and David Brannan, *Trends in Outside Support for Insurgent Movements* (Santa Monica, CA: Rand Corporation, 2001), 112; Wirsing, *India, Pakistan and the Kashmir Dispute*, 119.

[58] Wirsing, *India, Pakistan and the Kashmir Dispute*, 118–20.

[59] Malik, *Kashmir*, 229. Also, see Wirsing, *India, Pakistan and the Kashmir Dispute*, 121–23.

[60] Sumatra Bose "Kashmir: Sources of Conflict, Dimensions of Peace," *Survival* 41 (Autumn 1999), 155.

[61] South Asia Terrorism Portal, "Terrorist Groups: An Overview," Institute for Conflict Management, http://www.satp.org/satporgtp/countries/india/states/jandk/terrorist_outfits/terrorist_groups_j&k.htm (retrieved Feb. 10, 2004).

on regime type, as democratic leaders of Pakistan have pursued irredentism as strongly as, if not more strongly than, military rulers. In both recent democratic periods, Pakistan became quite aggressive in its support for (or manipulation of) the insurgents in Kashmir. During her government, Benazir Bhutto was apparently compelled by political competition to take a strong stand in favor of Kashmiri separatism. "As the conflict in Kashmir intensified, opposition parties continued to outbid Benazir on the question of Kashmir, leading her to ratchet up her inflammatory political rhetoric."[62] The Kargil crisis, it should be noted, occurred during the most recent elected government of Nawaz Sharif.

To be clear, political competition within Pakistan does not force only democratic governments to engage in irredentist foreign policies. The military has been one of the forces pushing for assertive efforts to unite Kashmir with Pakistan.[63] One could argue that the military seeks an aggressive solution to the Kashmir crisis because it would solve key strategic problems *vis-à-vis* India. Specifically, holding Jammu and Kashmir would simplify the defense of Pakistan and help in Pakistan's quest for maintaining parity with India. However, the cure may be worse than the disease – efforts to unify the territories have endangered Pakistan far more than if the *status quo* had not been contested.

A second explanation of the military's efforts toward Kashmir is bureaucratic self-interest. The Kashmir issue increases the power, prestige, and resources that the Pakistan military can command. As long as the issue is alive, the military plays a decisive role in budgetary decisions and in foreign policy. On the other hand, given India's military superiority, even without Kashmir, the Pakistani armed forces would have a sizable claim to the budget and to security policy. What this does suggest, however, is the potential for a logrolling of those genuinely interested in irredentism with those who benefit from the side-effects of antagonistic relations – a larger, more influential military.[64]

The nuclearization of South Asia may explain the increased irredentism of the 1990s. Ganguly argues that the joint development of nuclear weapons by India and Pakistan may have freed up the latter to engage in more aggressive foreign policies.[65] This is the stability–instability paradox – that nuclear deterrence at the strategic level allows for greater flexibility and aggression at lower levels. The problem with this argument is that it

[62] Ganguly, *Conflict Unending*, 92

[63] The account here does not necessarily conflict with the arguments posed in this volume by Tremblay and Schofield, as their focus on hybrid regimes may clarify the nature of political competition in mixed systems.

[64] Snyder, *Myths of Empire*.   [65] Ganguly, *Conflict Unending*, 88.

does not answer the question of why Pakistan should act aggressively at all. The nuclear balance does not compel Pakistan to seek to control Kashmir or engage in conflict – it simply makes it possible, since Pakistan would not face nuclear retribution for its efforts.

A second dimension of the nuclear arms race may have played a role in the assertive irredentism of the 1990s – lowering the financial penalties and changing the domestic balance of interests. In potentially irredentist states, groups favoring greater international economic opportunities may oppose the forces of irredentism. Firms seeking foreign investment or access to markets may want less controversial foreign policies to avoid sanctions. However, Pakistan's development of nuclear weapons and the end of the war in Afghanistan meant that sanctions were already in effect. These only deepened (at least temporarily) after both India and Pakistan tested their nuclear weapons. Thus, one of the likely counter-balances to irredentist parties, those with ties to the global economy, had little incentive or power to block policies that would risk deeper estrangement.

Pakistan's identity and ethnic politics

A different argument focuses on Pakistan's national identity and its ethnic politics.[66] Because Pakistan defines itself as a Muslim country, Kashmir plays a vital role in its self-image. It could be the issue upon which all Pakistanis agree.[67] Most Pakistanis share religious ties, broadly defined, with the Muslims of Kashmir. Most Pakistanis and most of the population of the Kashmir Valley are Sunnis, though neither population is entirely homogeneous in the form of Sunni Islam they follow. This matters, but not necessarily because Pakistanis inherently identify with the plight of Kashmir. Instead, it may matter because politicians can either use the Kashmir issue to prove their Islamic credentials, or key groups that are devoutly interested may have enough sway to push politicians to take a strong stand. Indeed, Gaborieau has argued that the politics of religion can be "characterized as outbidding: by putting the stakes higher and higher, the religious groups compelled the modernizing elites to concessions on the religious nature of the state."[68] As politicians are pushed to take strong stands on Islamic issues domestically, they may also be pushed to aggressive support on behalf of the Kashmiris.

---

[66] See Nasr in this volume.   [67] Malik, *Kashmir*, 226.
[68] Marc Gaborieau, "Religion in the Pakistani Polity," in Soofia Mumtaz, Jean-Luc Racine, and Imran Anwar Ali (eds.), *Pakistan: The Contours of State and Society* (Oxford: Oxford University Press, 2002), 45.

However, not all groups in Pakistan have a shared interest in unifying Kashmir. There is evidence that Pakistani Sindhis and Balochs, who stand to lose from both the continued tension with India and in the event of the accession of Kashmir, generally reject Pakistan's Kashmir policy. The Sindhis may be more interested in better relations with India than in the Greater Pakistan project.[69] Indeed, Sindhis have in the past had a rival irredentist project in mind – the creation of an independent Sindhi state from Indian and Pakistani territories. The Baloch are not in favor of the irredentist effort either.[70] These groups have no ethnic ties to the contested territories and compete with Punjabis and Pushtuns for state resources.

So, the key question is: why do the Punjabis and Pushtuns care about Kashmir? Given the electoral importance of Punjabis, any serious politician must appeal to their priorities, which include acquiring Jammu and Kashmir. Punjabis have ethnic reasons to care about Kashmir.[71] First, Punjab is the closest part of Pakistan to Kashmir, leading to increased contact and overlapping settlement patterns. This has apparently led to a shared sense of a "blood relationship," where they see each other as kin.[72] Further, many of the soldiers who died in the struggle for Kashmir were from Punjab,[73] deepening the emotional investment in irredentism. Shah relates the following as evidence of Punjabi interest in Kashmir:

Nawaz Sharif exhibits the most hawkish of Punjabi attitudes to Pakistan's national and international affairs and is constantly accusing Benazir Bhutto of selling out the Kashmiris to India. Although at one stage, in 1991, he supported the idea of an independent Kashmir, he now never speaks of Kashmir in such terms. To maintain her diminishing popularity in central Punjab, Benazir Bhutto attempted to outbid Nawaz Sharif in her opposition to the same idea. Thus, most Punjabis, on the left and the right, do not support the idea of an independent state . . .[74]

Pushtuns also play a key role as they are heavily represented in the military and the civil service. Their religious ties to the Muslims of Kashmir are not contradicted by other competing interests, as in the case of the Balochs and Sindhis. In the Pushtun case, geography, bureaucratic interests, and religious ties all push in the same direction.

What is abundantly clear is that the military and particularly the ISI have had a strong and continuing interest in irredentism. While I

---

[69] Mehtab Ali Shah, *The Foreign Policy of Pakistan: Ethnic Impacts on Diplomacy, 1971–1994* (London: I. B. Taurus & Co., 1997), 83.
[70] *Ibid.*, 107.
[71] Additionally, Punjab depends on water flowing through Jammu and Kashmir – Pakistani control of these territories would reduce vulnerability to India. Malik, *Kashmir*, 208.
[72] Shah, *The Foreign Policy of Pakistan*, 145.
[73] *The Economist*, Mar. 13, 2004.   [74] *Ibid.*, 156.

addressed the bureaucratic politics of this above, religious politics may be more important in influencing their behavior, particularly for the past twenty years. While religion has always played a significant role, a fundamentalist variant became more important over time, particularly as the war in Afghanistan developed and became defined as an Islamic war. General Zia ul-Haq "was skilful in encouraging and expanding the base of religious groups ..." within important sectors of the polity.[75] Through these efforts and its role in the war in Afghanistan, the Inter-Services Intelligence Directorate became deeply involved in the region's religious politics. Further, the current government has strong ties to these policies. The current president, Pervez Musharraf, was the Army chief of staff during the Kargil Crisis. The prime minister fired Musharraf in the aftermath of the conflict; he responded by leading a successful coup.

Two new dynamics seem to be causing a shift in both Musharraf's domestic political strategy and Pakistan's foreign policy: increased dependence on US support and the development of a domestic interest group desiring better relations with India. Musharraf has faced greater pressure from outside to moderate Pakistan's policies in the aftermath of 9/11.[76] He has faced a critical dilemma – whether to support the US and its war against al-Queda, which has ties to the ISI and Islamic parties in Pakistan and Kashmir, or to continue to rely upon fundamentalist parties and segments of the military. For much of the time since September 2001, it seems that Musharraf has tried to have it both ways – supporting the US in its Afghan campaign but continuing support for the insurgents in Kashmir. This strategy has been unsustainable, as it has had two effects: increasingly violent opposition from within Pakistan and deepening the role of the United States in Pakistan.

The second change is within Pakistan's domestic politics. Until recently, there may have been no real alternative constituency that would benefit from and lobby for decreased irredentism. As discussed above, politicians have to consider the makeup of their constituencies – whether their supporters are genuinely irredentist, have common cause with the irredentists, are opposed to irredentism based on ethno-political calculations, or oppose irredentism because it endangers other interests, such as economic concerns. In the past few years, Pakistani business leaders have apparently shifted their outlook significantly, realizing that irredentism and economic development were a tradeoff – they could have one but not the other.

---

[75] Saeed Shafqat, "Democracy and Political Transformation in Pakistan," in Mumtaz, Racine, and Ali (eds.), *Pakistan: The Contours of State and Society*, 222.

[76] This pressure has come from China as well, due to its own problems with separatists supported by groups related to al-Queda, *The Economist*, Mar. 13, 2004.

Indeed, the peace dividend could be quite substantial, potentially producing pipelines and other infrastructure linking these two countries to each other and to the rest of the neighborhood.[77] Op-ed sections of Pakistani newspapers have articulated this realization, as the opportunity costs of lost trade have become obvious.[78] Recent efforts to develop an Asian free trade area have excluded Pakistan, due to India's insistence.[79] Consequently, better relations with India not only imply better access to India's market[80] but also to the rest of Asia as well. The best evidence linking Kashmir and free trade is that the meeting of the South Asian Association for Regional Cooperation to create the South Asian Free Trade Agreement occurred on January 4, 2004, at the same time as Pakistan and India agreed to reduce tensions over Kashmir.

Musharraf seems to be changing his strategy, relying increasingly on less religiously oriented constituents. This seems to be the result of two separate trends that have reinforced each other – US pressure to fight the war on terrorism has antagonized fundamentalists, forcing Musharraf to seek political support elsewhere. At the same time, there seems to be a rising consensus among business groups that they would have much to gain if tensions with India were reduced. Thus, the domestic politics of irredentism has changed moderately, with the relative decline in power of pro-irredentist forces and the increased articulation of anti-irredentist interests.

This gamble, Musharraf shifting his political base from the more extreme elements to the more cooperation-minded, may help to explain recent events – the steps to reduce tensions with India, the surprising agreement on a South Asian Free Trade Agreement, and the attempts to assassinate Musharraf.

This delicate balancing act[81] provides further evidence that any politician in Pakistan faces extremely difficult choices as there continues to be strong pressure to support the cause of uniting Kashmir with Pakistan.

---

[77] Toufiq A. Siddiqi, "An India–Pakistan Détente: What it Could Mean for Sustainable Development in South Asia and Beyond," *Asia Pacific Issues* 75 (East-West Center).

[78] For example, see *Dawn*, 13 Mar. 2003.

[79] Shahid Javed Burki, "Keeping Out Pakistan?," *Dawn*, Oct. 21, 2003, www.dawn.com/2003/10/21/op.htm.

[80] The existence of significant illicit trade, as well as circular trade (trade between India and Pakistan routed through third parties) suggests that there is considerable interest in greater economic cooperation, *PakistanLink*, www.pakistanlink.com/headlines/Jan04/13/09.html. Also, see "Unofficial Pakistan–India Trade Thrives," Al-Jazeerah, aljazeerah.info/News%20archives/2003%20News%20archives/May%202003%20News/22%20n/Unofficial%20Pakistan-India%20Trade%20Thrives.htm.

[81] For a recent assessment, see Alyssa Ayres, "Musharraf's Pakistan: A Nation on the Edge," *Current History* 103 (Apr. 2004), 151–57.

Conclusion

This chapter started with a basic premise – that the international costs of aggressive foreign policies are not necessarily sufficient to stop a country from engaging in irredentism if domestic pressures are strong enough. Irredentism and self-destructive behavior go hand in hand in South Asia and around the world. While Kashmir is only one issue that divides the two countries, it is a very important one. Further, the dynamics that have exacerbated this specific dispute – ethnic politics in each country making moderation hard and rewarding extremism – also impact other contentious issues, challenging any effort to build bridges and reduce the rivalry. To develop lasting solutions to these conflicts, moderation must pay off domestically. Increased international economic ties may help to create constituencies that favor continued peace, offsetting the more extreme elements in each society. Recent events have raised hopes, but we should be clear about the chances for a long peace. Ultimately, progress will depend on the ability of leaders to not only survive (politically and physically) but to thrive. That is, if domestic incentives reward politicians' moderate stances, then there may be a chance for a more peaceful relationship. The problem is that there are still plenty of incentives for politicians to engage in self-destructive behavior – irredentism.

10   Institutional causes of the India–Pakistan rivalry

Reeta Chowdhari Tremblay and Julian Schofield

Introduction

The India–Pakistan rivalry has varied significantly in intensity across both time and issue area. This poses various puzzles that cannot adequately be answered by reference to geopolitics alone. Why, for example, has India been relatively restrained in Kashmir? Why does the rivalry activate some issues into disputes and ignore others? Why has the vulnerable Indus Waters Treaty not become a pawn of the competition? We argue that an examination of regime factors can explain some of the variation in the intensity of the India–Pakistan rivalry. This security competition has never been zero-sum. It depends to some extent on the opportunities and con-straints imposed on domestic political actors by the respective institutions.

The India–Pakistan rivalry has been dominated by contrasting regime types – Indian democracy and Pakistani military authoritarianism – for most of its duration. We propose that regime types aggravate or alleviate rivalries by the extent to which they are dispute- and war-prone, and their role in maintaining domestic stability. Whereas Indian democracy has been the least rivalry perpetuating, Pakistan's authoritarian military and hybrid (whether the military using democratic means to legitimize itself or popularly elected governments functioning under the threat of military intervention) governments have usually been more escalatory. We suggest that the story of the domestic sources of the India–Pakistan rivalry is complex and we need to disaggregate the regime type to provide a fuller explanation. This is necessary because we need not only answer questions of why Pakistan is more likely to initiate and escalate disputes than India and why Pakistan is eager to "take to task a much larger neighbor," we also must provide an explanation for the substantial river water cooperation between the two regimes. Why, for example, has India not sought to punish its smaller neighbor for its support of the cross-border insurgency in Kashmir by terminating the Indus Waters Treaty?

Our argument explaining the response of Pakistan's authoritarian regime to the India–Pakistan rivalry consists of the following parts:

(a) Pakistan's military regimes create structural and normative distortions in decisionmaking. The effects are twofold: first, normative biases influence military regimes to become involved in strategic disputes more often than regimes driven by domestic popularity, and second, while military regimes do not engage in disputes more often than non-military regimes, the former escalate disputes rapidly; (b) while the military regimes pursue confrontational policies, hybrid regimes have an even greater such tendency. Hybrid regimes are at least as dispute- and war-prone because they have the escalatory tendencies of purely military-led states without the latter's insulation from volatile popular issues. Hybrid regimes tend to seek popular legitimacy through disputes with the result that rivalry issues become symbolic rallying points for the regime; (c) while authoritarian regimes may generate nationalist radicalization as part of their regime-legitimizing propaganda, hybrid regimes rely upon it for their survival.

Our explanation of the Indian democracy's response to the India–Pakistan dispute goes beyond simple regime differentiation. Although we find that India's democracy is unlikely to initiate disputes, in order to fully comprehend India's policy stance on the three issues of Kashmir, nuclear weapons, and the water treaty, we need to disaggregate the state and use the framework of policy communities and networks to explain its restraint.

We approach the problem of explaining Indian democracy's impact on foreign policy issues through the policy community and policy network framework, which explains the different responses to these issues and posits that: (a) the policy process will be different across all policy sectors within a democratic state; (b) the policy communities consist of two sets of actors: the sub-government (i.e., state and societal) actors who determine policy within a given sector and are therefore close to the core; and the attentive public, who exist at the periphery, are less cohesive and organized but nevertheless try and influence the policy process. These policy communities differ across policy sectors and sub-sectors; (c) there is also an inherent mutual belief system (a set of core ideational and beliefs system), which exists within each policy domain, and a set of rules that governs the codes of conduct and communication between actors; there is therefore an underlying stability within each policy domain;[1] (d) policy change is generally a product of compromises which occur at the secondary level of belief system.[2]

---

[1] William Coleman and Grace Skogstad. "Policy Communities and Policy Networks: A Structural Approach," in William Coleman and Grace Skogstad (eds.), *Organized Interests and Public Policy* (Toronto: Copp-Clark, 1990), 14–33.

[2] Paul Sabatier, "An Advocacy Coalition Framework of Policy Change and the Role of Policy-Oriented Learning Therein," *Policy Sciences* 21 (Fall 1988), 129–68.

Regimes, disputes, and war

The broad empirical evidence has generally concluded that democracies are marginally more pacific in their external relations than military authoritarian states. Stam and Reiter found that the lower the proportion of the population that votes, the greater the likelihood that the state will initiate disputes. They also found that military and single party regimes are more likely to challenge democracies in disputes than the reverse.[3] In their survey, Geller and Singer conclude that regime attributes associated with non-democracies, such as government centralization, co-vary with a state's higher hostility level and its involvement in foreign conflict. They also cite studies whose surveys in turn suggest that democratic foreign policies are less conflict-prone than those of non-democracies.[4] Monadically, democracies are more likely to use diplomacy than war to resolve their disputes.[5] There is robust evidence that disputes between states that are both democracies (joint-democracy) are less likely and less escalatory.[6] Based on these research findings, we therefore expect to find that Pakistan has generally been more aggressive than India in their rivalry.

Pakistan – military and hybrid regimes

Pakistan's military and hybrid regimes propagate rivalry because of their dispute- and war-proneness, and their disruptive impact on domestic stability. There is a paucity of large-n evidence on the behavior of military regimes because the literature is dominated by comparisons between democratic and the less-discriminatory category of non-democratic regimes. We must therefore infer variations in foreign policy behavior from studies that examine characteristics typical of military regimes. The

---

[3] Dan Reiter and Allan Stam, "Identifying the Culprit: Democracy, Dictatorship, and Dispute Initiation," *American Political Science Review* 97 (May 2003), 333–37; see also R. J. Rummel, "Democracies Are Less Warlike than Other Regimes," *European Journal of International Relations* 1 (1995), 457–78; "Libertarianism and International Violence," *Journal of Conflict Resolution* 27 (Mar. 1983), 27–71.

[4] Daniel Geller and J. David Singer, *Nations at War* (Cambridge: Cambridge University Press, 1998), 52–53, 56; James Lee Ray, *Democracy and International Conflict: An Evaluation of the Democratic Peace Proposition* (Columbia: University of South Carolina Press, 1995).

[5] T. Clifton Morgan and Sally Howard Campbell, "Domestic Structure, Decisional Constraints, and War," *Journal of Conflict Resolution* 35 (June 1991), 187–211, 193.

[6] Melvin Small and J. David Singer, "The War-Proneness of Democratic Regimes, 1816–1965," *Jerusalem Journal of International Relations* 1 (Summer 1976), 50–69; Michael Doyle, "Kant, Liberal Legacies and Foreign Affairs," parts 1 and 2 *Philosophy & Public Affairs* 12 (Summer 1983), 205–35, and 12 (Fall 1983), 323–53.

behavioral evidence is that military regimes are more escalatory both within crises and from crises to war. Military regimes typically use a decisionmaking forum of four or less persons, significantly fewer than non-military governments. This may aggravate pessimistic misperceptions and insecurity that contribute to defensively aggressive policies.[7] Military states, characterized by authoritarian regimes, may also be better insulated from the costs of defeat and therefore less restrained from adopting risky foreign policies.[8] Vagts elaborates that military leaders are more likely to endorse aggressive policies because they are more familiar with that policy instrument. He also finds that in militarized regimes there is a heightened tendency to exaggerate military threats from outside the state, including the roles of preventive war, sensitivity to changes in the military balance, and opening and closing windows of opportunity.[9]

Military regimes create normative and structural distortions in decision-making as compared with democracies with balanced civil–military relations. Normative biases inherent in militarization have their origins in the doctrinal education of the military professionals, particularly in the middle and higher ranks of the officer corps that occupy positions of political power.[10] Normative biases heighten the tendency to exaggerate military threats from outside the state, sharpen sensitivity to changes in the military balance and opening and closing windows of opportunity, and promote a reliance on pre-emptive and preventive war solutions to these perceived threats.[11] While military leaders are no more hawkish than their civilian counterparts in recommending the use of coercion, they are far more likely to opt for a rapid escalation once hostilities are under way, particularly when they believe that war is inevitable. The military predisposition to escalate to the maximum use of force is based on the logic that less than the full commitment of resources lowers the chances or speed of victory.[12]

[7] Jonathan Wilkenfeld, Michael Brecher, and Sheila Moser, *Crises in the Twentieth Century* (Oxford: Pergamon Press, 1988), 197; Randolph Siverson, "Democracies and War Participation: In Defense of the Institutional Constraints Argument," *European Journal of International Relations* 1 (Dec. 1995), 481–89, 486.

[8] Reiter and Stam, "Identifying the Culprit," 333–37.

[9] Alfred Vagts, *Defense and Diplomacy* (New York: King Crown's Press, 1958), 3, 263.

[10] Samuel Huntington, *The Soldier and the State* (Cambridge, MA: Harvard University Press, 1967), 64–66, 70; Morris Janowitz and Roger Little, *Sociology and the Military Establishment* (New York: Russell Sage Foundation, 1965), 31, 103.

[11] Vagts, *Defense and Diplomacy*, 3, 263.

[12] Richard Betts, *Soldier, Statesmen, and Cold War Crises* (Cambridge, MA: Harvard University Press, 1977), 5.

The structural biases result from the imposition of the military's command system on a government. The military type of organizational decisionmaking is a narrow, hierarchical, and streamlined system that ensures quick responses under the stress of chronic uncertainty, but within parameters familiar to the military.[13] This has the effect of displacing and reducing the influence of the foreign office and institutions that mediate domestic politics, thus potentially undermining the quality of decisionmaking. This also insulates the regime from domestic calls for action. Military regimes proceed into disputes and war without careful attention to the behavior of allies or third parties. There also follows an increased tendency to make use of coercion as an instrument of diplomacy and for the maintenance of civil order. However, public disenfranchisement makes military rule unsustainable, and it gradually degenerates into hybrid forms with civilian coalitions necessary to maintain its legitimacy.

Hybrid governments are at least as dispute- and war-prone as military regimes because they possess the escalatory tendencies of pure military-led states without the insulation from volatile popular issues. Hybrid regimes emerge as militaries seek to stave off the erosion of their legitimacy, caused by their domestic mismanagement and their unrepresentativeness.[14] Hybrid regimes consist of policy coalitions of civilian and military interest groups who logroll their interests in order to aggregate their influence for a package of goals.[15] Hybrids manifest themselves under two circumstances. First, the extended stay of the military in government erodes public confidence, and short of widespread (and unsustainable) suppression, it does not have the instruments to generate public legitimacy. These military regimes incorporate civilian groups to enhance their legitimacy while simultaneously resisting their influence, but gradually accede to their demands as a condition for the maintenance of the coalition. The second instance involves civilian regimes that govern under the everpresent threat of military intervention in the background.[16]

Though insulated from public demands by coercive force and narrow bureaucratically dependent forms of governance, military regimes nevertheless disseminate legitimizing propaganda to cement their hold on power and advance their developmental agenda. From at least 1954, when the military became a key actor in Pakistan, it has made use of the power of the

---

[13] Janowitz and Little, *Sociology and the Military Establishment*, 31, 100.

[14] Larry Diamond, "Thinking About Hybrid Regimes," *Journal of Democracy* 13 (Apr. 2002), 21–35, 22.

[15] On the impact of military influences on governing coalitions, see Jack Snyder, *Myths of Empire* (Ithaca: Cornell University Press, 1991), 31–60.

[16] Diamond, "Thinking About Hybrid Regimes," 22; Aqil Shah, "Democracy on Hold in Pakistan," *Journal of Democracy* 13 (Jan. 2002), 67–75, 69.

state to propagate its versions of nationalism. The military-bureaucratic regime has not only defined the India–Pakistan conflict as a national issue, or what Waseem has called a "civilization issue," but it has also successfully generated a national consensus of Pakistan presenting itself as "a strong nation *vis-à-vis* the Indian threat."[17] Moreover, a (since established) national consensus that "a strong army equates with a strong nation" explains the continuity between both civilian and the martial law agencies.[18] In the 1980s, the military used the state to expound a domestic policy of Islamicization, whose legacy has survived the military regime.

While, on the one hand, the propagation of a radical form of the nationalist consensus by Pakistan's military regimes has served the purposes of maintaining domestic legitimacy and unifying the larger population with regard to foreign policy goals, on the other hand, it has provided the military regimes with the autonomy to set aside their hawkish attitudes and actions against India for brief periods of time and pursue other goals. The military regimes possess the institutional discipline not to suffer blowback from their own propaganda and, instead, to seek other goals. For example, the Pakistani military vetoed any action against attempts by India to incorporate Kashmir in the 1950s. Had the military succumbed to its own extreme nationalism, Pakistan would have intervened and disputes if not war would have resulted.[19] However, within official circles, President Ayub had remarked that "there were a dozen better reasons for going to war than Kashmir."[20] None of these developments seemed to provoke any serious military or political reaction in Pakistan – instead the matter was routinely brought to the UN for resolution. In fact, the Pakistan military was accommodating during this period, as indicated by its agreement over the Indus Waters Treaty in 1960, elaborated below. The military was even able to offer territorial concessions from Muslim-occupied sections of Kashmir to China in March 1963, something a nationalist civilian regime could not have achieved.[21]

---

[17] Mohammad Waseem, "The Dialectic between Domestic Politics and Foreign Policy," in Christopher Jaffrelot (ed.), *Pakistan – Nationalism Without a Nation?* (New Delhi: Manohar, 2002), 263–82.

[18] Ian Talbot, "Does the Army Shape Pakistan's Foreign Policy?" in Jaffrelot (ed.), *Pakistan – Nationalism Without A Nation?* 311–36.

[19] General Gul Hassan did not believe Kashmir had strategic value worth risking a war. Interview, Apr. 23, 1999, Rawalpindi; Kashmir's strategic value, its headwaters for irrigation and access to China, had already been secured in the First Kashmir War in 1947–48. Interview, *de facto* Pakistan army chief 1984–87, General K. M. Arif, Apr. 26, 1999, Rawalpindi; Interview, Pakistan army chief 1988–91, General Mirza Aslam Beg, Apr. 24, 1999, Rawalpindi.

[20] Agha Shahi, interview, Apr. 21, 1999, Islamabad.

[21] Khurshid Hyder, "Pakistan's Foreign Policy," *Survival* 9 (1967), 19–24, 21.

Unlike military regimes, hybrid governments are less insulated from public sentiment and are therefore much more vulnerable to blowback – they come to believe in and act on the propaganda disseminated by the state. Lacking coercive means, they become dependent on these national myths as legitimizing tools. Hybrids, which are structurally composed of a diverse constellation of factions, penetrate and fragment the military's hierarchical structure. In order to realize the dual requirements of such regimes, maintenance of domestic legitimacy and familiarity with the exercise of force, hybrid coalitions are prone to the use of military force to resolve security issues of domestic, symbolic importance and, because of military influence, rapidly escalate these. Hybrid regimes are therefore most dangerous because they desensitize military decisionmakers to the dangers of escalation by their close association with popular symbolic issues. We therefore expect states to be most dispute-prone as military rule degenerates into hybrid regimes.

Civilian rule exempt from military pressure existed only briefly in 1947–54 and 1971–77. The latter civilian period under Zulfikar Ali Bhutto was peaceful due to the after-effects of Indian military victory in East Pakistan. Pakistan's periods of non-hybrid military rule are limited to 1958–60, 1966–71, 1977–85, 1999–2004 (since 2002 under the Legal Framework Order). Periods of hybrid rule were present in 1960–65, and 1986–99. Hybrid rule is associated with fighting in Kashmir in 1965, the 1980s and 1990s, Dras-Kargil, and nuclear testing.

The 1958 coup and the 1965 war

Pakistan's early politics were civilian-dominated, but this did not preclude a war over Kashmir with India through to the end of 1948, nor two subsequent war scares in 1950 and 1951. Early democratization is usually associated with war-proneness (and this is not unusual).[22] Political crisis put a military cum bureaucratic coalition at the helm in 1954, and from 1958 Pakistan was firmly under the military rule of General Ayub Khan. Under his early reign, Kashmir and disputes over the use of the Indus River were relegated to the United Nations while Ayub concentrated on the integration of US military and economic aid. Though there were occasional frontier clashes, particularly over population movements in East Pakistan, the military period was notable for its relatively peaceful relations with India.

---

[22] Edward Mansfield and Jack Snyder, "Democratization and the Danger of War," *International Security* 20 (Summer 1995), 5–38.

Institutional military rule in its undiluted form was unpopular and led rather directly to a hybridized form of governance. General Ayub Khan had transformed himself into a civilian president in 1960 and consequently expanded the base of the military so that it could compete in legislative politics. Influential political figures were incorporated into Pakistan's government to provide it with expertise and widen its base of popular support. These typically included civilians able to mobilize support for Ayub's policies, such as the Nawab Kalabagh of Punjab. Another such individual, Zulfiqar Ali Bhutto, brought with him a plan to liberate Kashmir.

India's unexpected defeat by the Chinese army in the Aksai Chin portion of Kashmir in November of 1962, and its subsequent large-scale military build-up sensitized Pakistan to a closing window of opportunity that gradually became irresistible to an institution focused on fighting India. A territorial dispute over the Rann of Kutch, a remote desert frontier without population, natural resources, or domestic interest, began with Indian and Pakistani patrols confronting each other in early 1965. This operation typified the consequences of hybrid rule because it engaged an issue that had mainly domestic nationalist value – the confrontation with India – and implemented it in a highly escalatory fashion favored by the military. Pakistani forces ultimately defeated but did not pursue Indian forces. The foreign office was not solicited and therefore could not inform Ayub Khan that, as a consequence of Pakistani actions in the Rann, the US would impose an embargo, which it did shortly thereafter.[23] It is highly unlikely that a democratic regime, or a purely military one, would have escalated a dispute over such a remote and domestically marginal issue.

The subsequent *Operation Gibraltar*, the Pakistani attempt to seize Kashmir in August of 1965, was developed without consultation with the army's General Headquarters (GHQ). Rather, it was planned in isolation by the Kashmir Publicity Committee, established by Ayub Khan between January and March of 1964, under the influence of Bhutto.[24] The entry into the military bureaucracy of influential civilians like Bhutto precipitated politicization of the military that circumvented and fragmented the military's chain of command. The army's corps commanders were not informed, and would likely have rejected the planned attack into Kashmir.[25] *Op Gibraltar*, which ultimately included the infiltration of 7,000 volunteers into Kashmir in August 1965, failed

---

[23] Norman Palmer, "The Defense of South Asia," *Orbis* 9 (Winter 1966), 898–929, 908.
[24] Altaf Gauhar, *Ayub Khan* (Lahore: Sang-e-Meel Publications, 1993), 316.
[25] Gul Hassan Khan, *Memoirs* (Karachi: Oxford University Press, 1993), 225.

and triggered the escalation of move and counter-move that led ultimately to the 1965 India–Pakistan War.

The 1977 coup and the 1999 war

A recurrent military-hybrid shift occurred again in the 1980s through to the 1990s. After establishing a military regime through a coup in 1977, General Zia ul-Huq came to rely significantly upon Islamist groups for domestic political legitimacy. Despite providing preferential support to Islamist fighters battling the Soviets in Afghanistan, he resisted involvement in Kashmir. The democratization subsequent to his 1988 assassination nevertheless produced blowback in the form of Islamist state ideology that persisted in influencing Pakistan's interventionist foreign policy in Kashmir under both the Benazir Bhutto and Nawaz Sharif governments. The persistent threat of a coup, ultimately realized by President Pervez Musharraf in 1999, provided the military sufficient latitude to plan and execute military operations without reference to civil authorities.

The Dras-Kargil war of 1999, an Indo-Pakistani confrontation over Kashmir, was largely the result of the hybrid regime composed of Nawaz Sharif, Islamists, and Siachen/Kashmir-focused military interests. The conflict itself was over an issue of significant symbolic value, carried out with widespread public support in Pakistan. Conducted by Pakistan's Military Intelligence Branch, Kargil was essentially a military operation that was beyond the reach of civilian control. The civilian Islamist penetration of the military led to its fragmentation and high likelihood that the Kargil plans were not even approved of by the army's General Headquarters (though for similar reasons as 1965 – operational security and the threat that the corps commanders would have vetoed it). The apparent lack of consultation with the Foreign Ministry put Pakistan under sufficient pressure to compel it to abandon the field of battle to India.

The 1971 India–Pakistan War

The 1971 India–Pakistan War illustrates those aspects of military regimes that undermine domestic stability, and miscalculate international reaction to events. Pakistan's military regime set the conditions for the earlier 1965 war that sensitized India and perpetuated the rivalry and war. While it did not initiate the 1971 War, it set many of the conditions. The 1971 War erupted on 3 December and culminated in the break-up of East and West Pakistan into Pakistan and Bangladesh. The origins of the conflict can be traced to the economic and linguistic tensions between East and West Pakistan under Ayub Khan's military government, and to the disruption of the delicate constitutional arrangement between the two. When an election in December 1970 gave the Awami League, a predominantly East Pakistani party, an absolute majority in the assembly, the military government of General Yahya Khan reacted with a military crackdown on March 25, 1971 that led to widespread disruption; and millions of refugees fled to India. India's prime minister, Indira Gandhi, seized this rare opportunity to intervene in Pakistani affairs.[26]

General Yahya Khan, president of Pakistan since 1969, was dependent upon and therefore vulnerable to pressure from within the army, which also rendered him far less accessible to civilian institutions and advisors. This lack of balanced decisionmaking was one of the major causes of the international isolation that led ultimately to Pakistan's defeat.[27] For example, Pakistan's military decisionmakers became unrealistically reliant on China and the US for help in the event of a war with India.[28] However, Pakistani diplomatic efforts failed to determine that neither China nor the United States would come to its aid in the event of an Indian attack into East Pakistan – a repeat of the 1965 mistake – and it was subsequently unable to activate international concern over the threat of a third India–Pakistan war.[29] The military worsened the situation by conducting a preemptive strike whose effect was to further legitimate the Indian invasion.[30]

From the survey of hybrid regimes, we can conclude that Pakistan is least war-prone immediately after a military seizure of power (and when it has made the fewest concessions to civilian and domestic concerns in order to shore up its eroding public legitimacy). Pakistan would probably be most secure and least dispute-prone under a non-military, non-hybrid government, a condition that has only held true twice, in the early 1950s and mid-1970s. However, civilian regimes are not simply the result of political will on the part of Pakistan; the regional security environment has a role to play.

---

[26] J. F. R. Jacob, *Surrender at Dacca: Birth of a Nation* (New Delhi: Manohar, 1997), 35–36.

[27] Information Secretary Roedad Khan, interview, Apr. 22, 1999, Islamabad; Richard Sisson and Leo Rose, *War and Secession* (Berkeley: University of California Press, 1990), 108–09.

[28] Roedad Khan, who was present at a number of GHQ meetings, did not recall even a single discussion regarding the likelihood of China's promised intervention. Interview, Apr. 22, 1999, Islamabad.

[29] Agha Shahi. Interview, Apr. 21, 1999; Niaz Naik, interview, Apr. 23, 1999, Islamabad.

[30] Kamal Matinuddin, *Tragedy of Errors* (Lahore: Wajidalis, 1994), 479.

Rivalries as causes – regimes as effects

An important proviso of any theory of regime effects on policy is that rivalries may exist in the absence of the aggravating effects of institutions. More importantly, regime types may solely or in part be the effects of rivalries, requiring an appreciation of their reciprocal causation. Insecurity may lead to a ratchet-up effect on the preparation for war, which in turn selects for a regime able to manage the new security responsibilities. This must be controlled for if we are to conclude any effects on rivalry. This is captured by Harold Lasswell's garrison state concept, in which the preparation for defense and war puts such demands on society and the economy, that the state is gradually militarized.[31] Consequently, Pakistan's regime is predictably more militarized because of the asymmetrically stronger effects the rivalry has had on its decision-making institutions when compared with India. Even in the absence of institutional distortions, we can reasonably expect some level of insecurity in India–Pakistan relations. For example, Pakistan's civilian founder and Governor General Mohammad Ali Jinnah ordered provocative military interventions into Kashmir three times between September 1947 and April 1948, including the seizure of the Indian city of Jammu in October, at a time when the military had very little influence in government.[32] A military regime in Pakistan is not a prerequisite for aggressive confrontation with India. Conversely, India is less exposed to the effects of rivalry than Pakistan, posing less of a transformational threat to its democracy.

An important issue in the case of Pakistan is to what extent the military coups of 1958, 1969, 1977, and 1999 are the result of the security competition with India, and to what extent they are the result of interventions motivated by other (socio-economic developmental) goals that were not being met by the civilian authorities. The stated motives for the 1958 coup were civilian mismanagement. However, Pakistan's fear of India stimulated a search for aid culminating in US financial and military assistance in 1954, which elevated the military's role in decisionmaking, and facilitated the coup.[33] The 1969 intra-military coup displacing

---

[31] Raymond Aron, "Remarks on Lasswell's 'The Garrison State,'" *Armed Forces & Society* 5 (Spring 1979), 347–59, 356.

[32] Interview, aide-de-camp to Mohammad Ali Jinnah, 1948, Brig. Noor A. Husain, Apr. 21, 1999, July, 2003, Rawalpindi; interview with Armored Divisional Commander at the battle of Sialkot and later Pakistan foreign minister, General Yaqub Khan, Apr. 28, 1999, July 2003, Islamabad; Fazal Muqueem Khan (Major General), *The Story of the Pakistan Army* (Karachi: Oxford University Press, 1963), 92, 98–99; Shaukat Riza (Major General), *Izzat-O-Iqbal* (Nowshera: School of Artillery, 1980), 50.

[33] Ayesha Jalal, *The State of Martial Rule: The Origins of Pakistan's Political Economy of Defence* (Cambridge, MA: Vanguard, 1991), 49, 301.

President Ayub Khan, and the 1977 coup that deposed Zulfikar Ali Bhutto, were both in response to the deteriorating domestic popularity of the respective leaders linked to economic stagnation. The 1999 coup that removed Nawaz Sharif was motivated as much by the unprecedented displacement of military spending by debt servicing, as it was by civilian interference in military appointments. The military has a direct interest in the budgeting process that provides its operating funds, and its economic motives are inextricably linked with its security goals.[34] Therefore Pakistan's military regimes are in large part an indirect effect of its security competition with India. This does not mean that military governments are an optimal solution to Pakistan's decisionmaking challenges, but that Pakistan would unlikely have been any more frequently ruled by a military government than, for example, Bangladesh after 1971. Probably the coups of 1958, 1969, and 1999 would not have occurred had India not appeared such a threat to the Pakistani military. The 1977 coup does show that once the military was strong relative to civilian institutions, socio-economic issues were a sufficient cause for intervention. We can conclude that to some extent the endogenous effects of military regimes deepened the India–Pakistan rivalry.

Because the military has significant control over nuclear assets and policy in Pakistan, this is likely to remain a major avenue of military influence in any future regime type. It is difficult to be sure whether the anticipated cost of nuclear weapons use, both physical and damage to the nuclear taboo, would change the military's tendency to escalate disputes. It may in fact be more likely that the military, with its preference for escalation, would be conscious of its consequences and therefore less likely than non-military leaders to threaten nuclear use in given disputes. According to Brian Cloughley, "[Chief of the Army Staff (COAS), Gen. Pervez] Musharraf has never been a nuclear hawk. As a soldier he realizes more than most the terrible consequences of a nuclear exchange."[35]

In the context of the broader link between regime types and rivalry, institutions in Pakistan have affected rivalry in all of three ways. First, Pakistan's military regimes have expounded aggressive propaganda but are initially sufficiently institutionally strong to suppress domestic influences on its foreign policy preferences. Hybrid regimes are highly dispute-prone, as indicated in their repeated attempts at raising costs to India in Kashmir at such focal points as Kargil. Pakistan's civilian regimes are the

---

[34] Hasan-Askari Rizvi, *The Military and Politics in Pakistan, 1947–86* (New Delhi: Konark Publishers Limited, 1988), 125, 205.

[35] Brian Cloughley, former Australian defense attaché in Islamabad, Henry Stimson Center, *SAIF Cross-border Dialogue XII*, Oct. 18, 1999.

least dispute-prone. Second, military and hybrid military regimes suffer from poor diplomatic skills. They either ignore or misinterpret international signals that worsen the consequences of the disputes they involve themselves in. Third, military regimes, in particular, poison domestic arrangements that create instability and create opportunities for exploitation by rivals.

Disaggregating Indian democracy

India's democracy is less dispute or war-prone than its Pakistan rival because of domestic crosscutting cleavages that make aggressive unilateral policy difficult to implement. However, India's subordination of its military to civilian institutions means that defense policy has historically received a low priority. Viewing the India–Pakistan rivalry from the Indian side, there are three salient issues: two of confrontation (Kashmir dispute and nuclear rivalry) and one of cooperation (water sharing agreement). We present a two-level analysis in order to understand India's differing responses. The overarching focus of the first level of analysis points to the role played by the system-level norms and institutional structures (democratic institutions and norms) in determining India's responses to the rivalry. We share the view of the democratic peace theorists that constitutional, procedural, and normative features affect foreign policy decisionmaking in a democracy. Within these institutional constraints, particularly in a democracy which is in the initial stages of fulfilling the challenging tasks of nation-building and of economic development, the state and its elites acquire autonomy in making policy choices. It will not be an exaggeration to maintain that the maximum potential for state autonomy for the Indian state during the first two decades after independence was the product of a successful national movement, the dominant position of the Congress Party, its propagated and pronounced socialist agenda, a well-established operational bureaucratic structure, the task of nation-building, and the overall enthusiasm and haste to implement an indigenous political and economic agenda. The Indian case clearly suggests that the stronger executive has been able to pursue diplomacy and to show its resolve *vis-à-vis* its non-democratic neighbor, Pakistan. However, this state autonomy is constrained by the political leadership's need to acquire legitimacy and win the numerical electoral game. The democratic leadership must respond to the increasing levels of political mobilization, unfulfilled agendas, and the resultant problems of ungovernability.

Our second level of analysis employs the framework of policy communities. We assert at the outset that to treat all democracies in a

homogeneous fashion is a mistake. Domestic and international constraints cause democracies to behave differently and push them to make
different policy choices. Moreover, states may opt for different responses
to different issues depending upon domestic institutional and political
constraints. A sectoral analysis presents us with a better understanding of
a democratic state not responding in the same fashion to all issues underlying its enduring rivalry with a neighbor. We suggest that it is important
to study each issue separately and understand the limits to state autonomy or lack of it by exploring the nature of the actors involved in the
issue. Depending upon the issue, these political actors (the state and the
non-state actors, including the attentive public) form different policy
communities and policy networks. These policy communities range
from the very limited (for example, limited small autonomous bureaucratic structures) to the very broad and encompassing, depending upon
the issue. The ability to make policy changes, in the domestic and in
foreign affairs arenas alike, depends upon the policy communities' adher-
ence to their core belief systems. The stronger the commitment is to the
core value system, the less the scope for policy change. Both the state actors
and the attentive public are unwilling to make compromises. However, it is
within the context of the secondary belief system that compromises and
policy changes are to be witnessed. We can sum up the relationship
between these two levels of analysis as the institutional framework and
the systemic norms which specify the outline of policy output and implementation, the content of which is determined at the strata of different
policy areas and, within them, sectors and sub-sectors.[36] This two-level
analysis helps us to explain why there is cooperation with regard to the
water sharing issue and a severe conflict with regard to the Kashmir issue.
Moreover, it points to the fact that the nuclear policy arena, engaging a
limited policy community of scientists and the top political leadership, has
remained non-conflictual.

The institutional and policy communities operate within a broader
normative context, of which there are four major aspects that govern
the policy process in India. First, although partition was as traumatic an
experience for India as it was for Pakistan, India has, nevertheless,
accepted the reality of partition. It therefore has no ambition to absorb
its non-Himalayan neighbors, such as Bangladesh or Pakistan. Indeed,
since partition, while the Hindu nationalist parties and cultural organizations, such as the Bhartiya Jan Sangh and its later reincarnation the
Bhartiya Janta Party, the RSS and the Vishwa Hindu Parishad have not

---

[36] Coleman and Skogstad, *Organized Interests.*

adhered to this national norm and have frequently flirted with the idea of a unified Hindu India, this position has remained relatively marginal among the Indian population. Indian public opinion does fluctuate and may push for punishing Pakistan, for example, when it perceives India to be threatened by Pakistan's aggressive behavior such as the attack on India's Parliament in December 2002. Second, Pakistan does not pose a major threat to India, and India may in fact benefit from its position as a buffer. Third, for India, territorial integrity is essential and it insists on the territorial status quo in Kashmir. Fourth, India is principally interested in asserting its status as an influential global actor with economic and political clout, and this affects its security, nuclear, and even domestic (Kashmir) policy to the exclusion of the aggressive use of coercive force.

The institutional framework

India's democratic constitution and, in particular, the parliamentary and federal governance structures, constitute the normative framework which constrains India's response to India–Pakistan rivalry. The Kashmir conflict should be viewed within the context of the constitutional principles describing the relationship between India and the state of Jammu and Kashmir. This initial constitutional entente, which determines the state's distinct status within the Indian federal structure, has emerged as the normative guideline pushing India to seek a balance between its security and national identity requirements, and the pursuance of constitutional and democratic principles within the Kashmir Valley. On the one hand, India is committed to its territorial integrity and unwilling to abandon Kashmir (India has consistently maintained that Kashmir is an integral part of India). This is largely for two reasons: (a) India needs Kashmir for security purposes, and (b) India's secular identity is tied to its holding onto the Muslim-majority state of Jammu and Kashmir. On the other hand, the Indian state must respect the constitutional arrangement by which it has defined its asymmetrical federal relationship with Kashmir.

Kashmir's distinctness, unlike the other federal units in the Indian state, is enshrined in Article 370 of the Constitution. This Article, while restricting the national government's legislative powers to the areas of foreign affairs, defense, and communications, allowed the state government to legislate on residuary powers. Article 370 is also distinct in terms of allowing the state of Jammu and Kashmir to set up its own constitution, and place restrictions on non-state residents who wish to acquire and hold property or to obtain employment in Kashmir. Although over the years Article 370 has been diluted through the application and extension of several central legal and constitutional provisions with the approval of the state legislature, this legal constitutional principle has remained the symbol of Kashmir's distinctness within the Indian state. Through this legal category, the Indian state situates itself *vis-à-vis* Kashmir in a different manner than its neighbor. Unlike Pakistan, which lays claims to Kashmir on the basis of religious affinity, India points to a special relationship whereby the Indian state has simultaneously embraced and denied its differences from Kashmiri society: it recognizes the cultural and political identity of Kashmir; yet it asserts that the similarities between Kashmir and the Indian state are based on socialist and democratic principles.

In short, to implement the constitutional entente between India and the state of Jammu and Kashmir, the Indian constitution has set up institutional arrangements such as federalism (through Article 370), regular elections, and the requirements of public debate and accountability. These democratic institutional arrangements make it difficult (probably impossible) for the Indian leaders to commit themselves to large-scale violence and compel them instead to work out conflict within the democratic framework. This explains, to a large extent, India's reasons for maintaining democratic practices including regular elections in the state of Jammu and Kashmir and nevertheless using violence against the Pakistan-supported insurgency there. In other words, the institutional and normative framework provides the Indian state no choice but to remain committed to the democratic process in the state of Jammu and Kashmir. The existing state violence, justified by Indian leaders as a war on terror, is explained as a necessary reaction to outside interference.

Despite these democratic constraints and the Indian leadership's commitment to the pursuance of procedural democracy in the state of Jammu and Kashmir, the Indian state has used the authoritarian features of the Indian constitution to bring in line the dissident population of the Valley who have sought either independence for Kashmir or its association with Pakistan. Contrary to the initial constitutional bargain, there was a slow and a steady abrogation of Article 370 which over the years would become a symbol, particular amongst the chauvinist Hindus, of what was wrong with Kashmir. The years 1956 to 1974 witnessed the extension and application of various central laws and constitutional provisions with the approval of the state legislature. This includes the most repressive provisions of the Indian constitution such as Article 356 allowing the central government to impose the president's rule and Article 248, 249, and 250 empowering the Indian parliament to legislate in matters of state jurisdiction. All the elected governments have existed with the approval of the central government. Most of the elections to the state government have been rigged. Jammu and Kashmir politics has revolved around a one-party regime under a leadership which has not allowed political dissent. Whenever there has been an attempt to set up an opposition party, the group has been either absorbed into the ruling party or simply outlawed. All this has been done with the blessing and encouragement of the central government. Moreover, whenever the central government has feared the shifting of public opinion against India, it has used extra-constitutional measures such as the Terrorism and Disruptive Activities Acts (TADA) to suppress popular demands for autonomy. During the recent secessionist movement, which was initially accompanied by political insurgency in 1989, the Indian security forces committed serious human rights violations including arbitrary arrests, cordoned-off searches, shooting, killing, rape, and the arson of both commercial and civil properties.

India's integrationist measures to dilute the distinctness provisions for the state of Jammu and Kashmir, its wide-scale interference in the politics and the electoral process of the state, all this to the accompaniment of wide-scale human rights abuses by its security forces did give the upper hand to Pakistan. Pakistani and Kashmiri Muslim lobbies in the United States and the United Kingdom were able to place the agenda of human rights violations by the Indian state in Kashmir on the agenda of the US administration and several United Nations conferences. Pakistan was able to call into question the legitimacy of the accession of Kashmir to India. With increased pressure from international human rights groups and Pakistan's continued support for the Kashmiri cause in global forums, the Indian government took steps to discipline its security forces and set up its own agencies to monitor human rights violations. While Pakistan's Inter-Services Intelligence made a conscious decision militarily to support only the irredentist groups, thus marginalizing the more popular Jammu and Kashmir Liberation Front, India took advantage of this window of opportunity and undertook to revive the electoral process. In addition, September 11 has strengthened its hand *vis-à-vis* Pakistan demanding an end to cross-border terrorism and Pakistan's active support for militancy in the Kashmir Valley.

Nuclear policy

Related to this is India's nuclear policy, which has consistently remained firmly committed to the basic tenet that "the country's national security in a world of nuclear proliferation lies either in global disarmament or in exercise of the principle of equal and legitimate security for all."[37] This

---

[37] Jaswant Singh, "Against Nuclear Apartheid," *Foreign Affairs* 77 (Sep.–Oct. 1998), 41–52.

doctrine has evolved within the context of the democratic principle of civilian control over the military. India has nevertheless promulgated a minimal and reactive defensive policy that emphasizes its policy conservatism.[38] This doctrine implicitly rejects a doctrine of massive retaliation or flexible response to conventional attack. Nor has the deployment of its nuclear arsenal been tied-in to any geographic commitments. For one Indian government spokesman, "India shall not engage in an arms race, nor, of course, shall it subscribe to or reinvent the sterile doctrines of the Cold War."[39] An Indian nuclear democracy is therefore likely to try to be as unprovocative and undefined as its pre-nuclear deterrents (though Pakistan may not see it as unprovocative).

Prime Minister Nehru played an active role in the development of India's nuclear program, though he established the Indian nation's long-standing ambivalence about nuclear weapons. Following Gandhian principles, both the Indian public and the leadership have expressed moral doubts about possessing nuclear weapons, though these were justified on the grounds of self-sufficiency, technological prestige, security, and international leverage. Nehru believed nuclear technology, including arms, was essential for India's modernization. Nevertheless, there has always been a limited debate about the nuclear program amongst Indian parliamentarians and the political leadership. Certain events such as China's attack in 1962 ignited such a debate between the pro-bomb lobby and the critics of nuclear weapons. However, the decision with regard to the nuclear program has remained narrowly confined to the scientific community and the prime minister of India. Consequently, nuclear policy has remained an elite affair, insulated from popular inputs and the military.

Domestic politics plays an important role in India's nuclear decisions. The timings of both the 1974 and the 1998 test detonations were related to bolstering government support. Prime Minister Indira Gandhi's initial popularity after the successful liberation of Bangladesh in 1971 was eroded by domestic political and economic problems. A major nation-wide railway strike paralyzed the country while opposition parties demanded her resignation for violating election laws. Her 1974 nuclear test decision was heavily influenced by its diversionary benefits. The 1998 nuclear test decision by the BJP seemed indirectly motivated by their inability to secure legislative allies for a coalition government. Raju Thomas notes, "the nuclear tests of May 1998 may have been a method

---

[38] George Perkovich, *India's Ambiguous Bomb: Indian Practice, International Relations Theory, and Nonproliferation Policy* (Charlottesville: W. Alton Jones Foundation, 1997), 497.
[39] Singh, "Against Nuclear Apartheid," 50.

of consolidating the coalition government by inducing a feeling of pride and patriotism."[40] The tests secured both a coalition government and widespread national support for the party.

Water sharing

Since 1960 there has been an exceptionally cooperative relationship between Delhi and Islamabad in the area of river water disputes, potentially the most consequential security issue facing South Asia. Without this cooperation, fighting over the waters of the Indus and stoppages could desiccate Pakistani Punjab and create tens of millions of refugees. The headwaters of the Indus are for the most part in Indian territory, and its water principally benefits Pakistani users from the Punjab through to the Sindh. The river is also the politico-military boundary in the Punjab, and an important means of navigation.

From Pakistan's standpoint, conquest of the entire Indus water basin, which stretches northeastward into China, is infeasible. In April of 1948, the Pakistani army had secured those strategic headwaters in Kashmir that were attainable. A lack of resolution following the expiration of a standstill agreement in March of 1948 led to numerous water stoppages. In 1956, the Indian government informed Pakistan that it would divert five rivers for Indian use by 1962. This culminated in a major confrontation in March of 1956 at the Hussainiwala Headworks near Ferozipur that could have escalated to war.[41] The impossibility of a military solution on the part of the Pakistanis, and Indian disinterest in fighting led to the success of international mediation and World Bank financing in establishing the September 1960 Indus Waters Treaty. The Treaty delineated the sharing of river water from the Indus and its tributaries that has lasted without interruption.

India–Pakistan cooperation over the Indus waters is largely the result of three factors. First, the durability of the 1960 Indus Waters Treaty can be attributed in no large part to its operative depoliticization. Prime Minister Nehru and General Ayub Khan set aside their disputes and committed to a successful sharing formula. The origins of the problem as a pre-partition interprovincial dispute had temporarily at least kept it beyond the reach of central politicians until the signing of the Treaty. Second, World Bank backing and international involvement made it easier to turn a potentially

---

[40] D. R. SarDesai and Raju G. C. Thomas (eds.), *Nuclear India in the Twenty-First Century* (New York: Palgrave, 2002), 7.

[41] Sumit Ganguly, "Discord and Collaboration in Indo-Pakistani Relations," in Kanti Bajpai and Harish C. Shukul (eds.), *Interpreting World Politics* (New Delhi: Sage, 1995), 408–09.

political issue into a functional one. Third, once agreed upon by the political leadership that water would be shared according to the provisions outlined in the Treaty, the implementation of the agreement has been concentrated in the hands of a small bureaucratic community. The core belief system is guided by administrative values of efficiency rather than electoral politics. The criterion of efficiency has protected the water sharing from being used as political leverage against Pakistan. The Treaty is administered by technical specialists enjoying diplomatic privileges in both India and Pakistan, and excludes local, state, and national political involvement, shielding the Treaty from easy manipulation by national political leaders.[42] For example, even in the midst of the 1965 war in August and September, Indian payments to Pakistan as part of the Treaty continued uninterrupted, as did the work of engineers of both countries to control the opening and closing of sluices.[43] Key Indian politicians threatened abrogation of the Treaty in 2002 during the confrontation with Pakistan, and this may signal a move toward a genuine zero-sum competition between India and Pakistan.

Policy communities

While the institutional and the normative frameworks help explain why India is not usually the initiator of conflict in the India–Pakistan rivalry, the policy community approach allows us to describe, with regard to the three issue areas of Kashmir, nuclear and water sharing, the differing nature of participants, differences in the core and secondary belief systems to which participants adhere and the policy stability or instability in each of these issue areas.[44] We propose to show that, while the policy communities in the nuclear and water sharing areas are differently constituted and while they adhere to different belief systems, there has been policy stability in these sectors. The Kashmir issue is more complex and here the policy community is both constrained by and in conflict with the attentive public. The core and the secondary belief systems have an impact in terms of where the Indian state maintains policy stability and where it is willing to make policy changes. While the core beliefs are fundamental normative and ontological axioms and there is very little susceptibility to change, it is within the realm of secondary belief systems

---

[42] Salman Salman and Kishor Uprety, *Conflict and Cooperation on South Asia's International Rivers: A Legal Perspective* (Washington, DC: The World Bank, 2002), 38, 48, 52–53; Aloys Michel, *The Indus Rivers* (New Haven: Yale University Press, 1967), 521.
[43] Ganguly, "Discord and Collaboration in Indo-Pakistani Relations," 408–09.
[44] India was largely the conflict initiator in its invasion of East Pakistan in 1971, and in its seizure of Siachen in 1984.

that policy communities make compromises and initiate policy changes.[45] India thus approaches Kashmir as a multidimensional issue and, while it blames Pakistan, its democratic institutions afford it a complex perspective that does not resort solely to violent suppression and escalation with Pakistan of the Kashmir dispute.

With regard to Kashmir, the policy community is both diverse and complex. It consists of state, sub-state, and various sections of societal actors. However, the policy community is constrained and sometimes in conflict regarding the policy goals with the attentive public (which Coleman and Skogstad define as operating at the periphery, "less tightly knit," "more loosely defined," and "attempts to influence policy, but does not participate in policy-making on a regular basis"). In the Kashmir issue, one clearly sees a split between the policy community's commitment to the core belief system and its willingness to compromise within the secondary belief domain. The core belief system, which dictates that Kashmir is an integral part of India, is not to be compromised by the policy community both within Kashmir and *vis-à-vis* Pakistan. However, it is at the level of secondary belief systems that the policy community in India shifts its focus and accommodates the attentive public. The attentive public in this case is fractionalized, with its views on Kashmir ranging from the simple wish for better governance to the hope for autonomy and even the desire for independent statehood. The reactivation of civil society in the Kashmir Valley after the political insurgency, an attempt on the part of the Indian state to negotiate with the nationalist and the secessionist groups, the talk of autonomy for the state of Jammu and Kashmir within the Indian federal framework, are all compromises made by the policy community within the secondary belief framework. These are instrumental decisions necessary to implement core policy, which, in this case, is to maintain Kashmir as an integral part of India. The policy shift is necessary to maintain the support of the Kashmiri Muslim population. The accommodation of the Kashmiri demands within the secondary belief system allows India not to incur the cost of alienating the population and pushing them to support the secessionist demands, and thus allowing Pakistan the upper hand in the India–Pakistan rivalry over the Kashmir issue. It is the over-arching democratic institutional framework which fosters the Indian state's accommodation of the diversity of the policy community and of a conflictual attentive public. The policy stability with regard to the core belief system as well as the policy compromises and change within the secondary belief domain are the reason

---

[45] Sabatier, "An Advocacy Coalition Framework of Policy Change," 129–68.

why India remains restrained and does not initiate conflict with Pakistan; why it is not the aggressor but reacts to aggression.

The policy community in the nuclear sector is narrowly based and closely linked with the energy and scientific communities that helped develop it. It is a state-directed activity where state agencies control the formulation of policy, and addresses developmental and self-sufficiency issues that sometimes are at odds with the military's nuclear interests. The state agency has considerable capacity in its own right, is autonomous of all associational networks and is able to concentrate power for coordinated decisionmaking. It could also be described as an "epistemic community" consisting of "a network of professionals with recognized experts and competence in a particular domain or issue area."

The nuclear policy community shares a core belief system: that nuclear development in India is directly linked to India's modernization project; that it would allow India to become a strong regional power; and that the policy of nuclear haves and have-nots is wrong, and India has every right to join the have group. This core belief system is shared by Indian popular opinion at large. The closed policy community and the shared consensus on the core belief system have allowed the policy to remain stable over the last four decades. The narrow and the closed nature of the policy community has kept the policy outside the political framework except for short interludes (the BJP and the Kashmir government tried to link the nuclear tests of 1998 to the resolution of the Kashmir issue). This policy is neither perceived by the public nor presented by the policy community as directed against Pakistan. Within India's policy framework, the nuclear issue is a non-issue as far as the India–Pakistan rivalry is concerned.

The preoccupation of Indian democracy with domestic politics, and bureaucratized or elite control over key issues, may have permitted the rivalry with Pakistan by contributing to an incoherent defense policy. From independence, Prime Minister Nehru's concerns over the threat of military intervention and his emphasis on military subordination to civil authority established institutional constraints in the domain of national security.[46] While this minimized the threat of military takeover, the provocation of neighbors, involvement in the Cold War, and large military budgets, it also made policy inputs from the military nearly impossible.[47] This low priority given to defense under Nehru, and

---

[46] Raju G. C. Thomas, "Defense Planning in India," in Stephanie Neuman (ed.), *Defense Planning in Less-Industrialized States – The Middle East and South Asia* (Lexington: Lexington Books, 1984), 239–64, 249.

[47] Stephen Philip Cohen, *The Indian Army – Its Contribution to the Development of a Nation* (Berkeley: University of California Press, 1971), 173.

continued since with only occasional deviations, may have had a permissive effect on the Chinese attack in 1962, and Pakistani provocations in 1965 and in Kashmir in the 1990s.[48] The military has been consistently unable to warn the political leadership of its weaknesses, particularly in the run-up to the 1962 and 1965 wars, and during the 1999 Kargil episode in Kashmir.[49] The military is also often the agent of policies that suffer from an absence of military relevance, such as the occupation of Siachen Glacier in 1984.

Conclusion

The foregoing analysis suggests the following conclusions. First, rivalries are perpetuated by unresolved disputes. Military and democratic regimes and their respective hybrids differ substantially. Military regimes tend to suffer from information deficits in the area of domestic politics and international relations, and have a tendency to become transfixed on power balances and the rapid escalation of disputes. On balance, the greater dispute- and war-proneness depend on the availability of relevant disputes. Military regimes are more likely to seek disputes that affect the strategic balance between states, or whose initiation can affect that balance. Hybrid regimes are at least as dispute- and war-prone as military regimes because they have a tendency to become involved in disputes which carry domestic symbolic importance, and escalate them beyond what a democratic regime would have permitted. Second, we have suggested in this chapter that in democratic regimes the system-level norms and institutional structures (democratic institutions and norms) act as the major constraints in the India–Pakistan rivalry. It is reasonable to assume that joint democracy would lead to regional peace, but this may underrate the existential threat Pakistan sees in India simply given its size. In terms of negotiations, the short life-span of Pakistani regimes and emerging traces of extremism in India may make long-term commitments difficult. Third, within India's democratic framework, a sectoral policy analysis involving the concepts of policy communities and policy networks helps us explain India's different responses to the issues underlying India–Pakistan rivalry. Fourth, democratic regimes may abet disputes and war through deterrence policies that project weakness rather than reassurance. Fifth, any democracy established within Pakistan would

[48] Surjit Singh, *India's Search for Power – Indira Gandhi's Foreign Policy 1966–1982* (New Delhi: Sage Publications, 1984), 43.
[49] Sumit Ganguly, "Deterrence Failure Revisited: The Indo-Pakistani War of 1965," *Journal of Strategic Studies* 13 (Dec. 1990), 77–93, 78.

potentially remain insecure. Our findings indicate that for democracy to establish itself in Pakistan, security assurances would have to be forthcoming from India, effectively reducing the military's incentive to reintervene in politics. Awareness of the role of the security dilemma makes joint-democracy more attainable. Sixth, a prerequisite to bringing about an end to the India–Pakistan rivalry is the erosion of the legacy within Pakistan of a strong anti-India consensus. We would expect that democracy with genuinely crosscutting policy communities would foster a less confrontational national consensus than is likely to be attained under either military or hybrid regimes.

Part IV

Conclusion

11 South Asia's embedded conflict: understanding the India–Pakistan rivalry

T. V. Paul and William Hogg

The contributors to this volume have endeavored to provide both theoretical and policy-oriented analyses and prescriptions on the India–Pakistan conflict, one of the longest lasting rivalries in the contemporary world. In attempting to offer a novel approach, this volume brought together specialists from both international relations and comparative politics. As such, the analyses they have offered examined a variety of factors – global and regional balance of power and power distribution, nuclear weapons, political systems, national identity, religion, and levels of economic interactions – variables drawn from both international and domestic politics levels, in order to understand both the persistence and possible pathways for termination of the rivalry. One of the main concerns of the volume's editor was whether area specialists could communicate fruitfully with international relations theorists, and vice versa. International relations theory, as highlighted in some of the chapters in this volume, does not yet offer a strong framework for explaining the rivalry between India and Pakistan. International relations paradigms, such as realism, and theories such as balance of power and power transition that draw on systemic level explanations offer only partial clues to the understanding of the ongoing conflict.[1] A comprehensive yet convincing theoretical framework is wanting. Area specialists, on the other hand, have been apt to offer explanations based on idiosyncratic variables pertaining to decisionmaker, nation-state, or regional level factors.[2] If the two subfields can exchange views with each other, perhaps a comprehensive explanation for the persistence of this multifaceted conflict could be developed.

---

[1] For these theories, see T. V. Paul, James J. Wirtz, and Michel Fortmann (eds.), *Balance of Power: Theory and Practice in the 21st Century* (Stanford: Stanford University Press, 2004), chs. 1, 2, and 5.

[2] For examples outside of this volume, see Sumit Ganguly, *Conflict Unending: India–Pakistan Tensions Since 1947* (New York: Columbia University Press, 2001); Sumantra Bose, "Kashmir: Sources of Conflict, Dimensions of Peace," *Survival* 41 (Autumn 1999), 149–71.

Table 11.1 *Factors determining persistence and possible termination of the rivalry*

	Persistence	Termination
International Level	● Great power involvement	→Major change in great power policies (US/China)
	● Systemic/structural factors (e.g., bipolar competition)	→post-Cold War, post- 9/11 constraints/opportunities
Regional Level	● Territorial divisions	→Territorial settlement
	● Nuclear weapons (stability/instability paradox)	→Nuclear stability
	● Truncated power asymmetry	→Preponderance of status quo power
	● Lack of effective regional institutions	→Strengthening of regional institutions
	● Dearth of economic interaction	→Deepening economic interdependence
Domestic Level	● Problems of national identity	→Secure identities
	● Institutional incompatibility	→Full democratization (Pakistan)
	● Secession/irredentism	→Change in strategies and goals, e.g., abandonment of irredentism/low-intensity war (Pakistan)/limited war options (India)
		→Autonomy for Kashmir
Decisionmaker Level	● Dysfunctional learning	→Functional learning
	● Leadership priorities/strategies	→Change in leadership priorities/strategies

In order to accomplish this objective, the contributors were asked three core sets of questions. First, to what extent is the India–Pakistan conflict an enduring rivalry? Second, what specific factors explain the persistence of this conflict? Can its stasis be attributed to structural elements, such as great power politics and regional power distribution and, in recent years, the possession of nuclear weapons by the two principal states? Or, are domestic variables – national identities, state strategies such as irredentism, or internal power structures, especially the role of the armed forces within them – at the source of the rivalry? Finally, when and how can this enduring rivalry end? The contributors were encouraged to offer ideas on possible external and internal changes, the arrival of which would be required to bring an end to the longstanding conflict. Table 11.1 outlines the contributors' core arguments for persistence, and conditions for termination of the rivalry. They are listed under international, regional, domestic, and decisionmaker levels of analysis.

The India–Pakistan conflict as an enduring rivalry

In their theoretical overview, Paul Diehl, Gary Goertz, and Daniel Saeedi define an enduring rivalry as a strategic competition between the same pair of states over an extended period of time. These rivalries commonly find their roots in sets of internal or external political shocks.[3] While most conflicts between states occur due to some type of internal or external shock, the vast majority terminate quickly – almost 95 percent. Only approximately 5 percent of all conflicts will become embedded or enduring. These conflicts are characterized by an "outstanding set of unresolved issues," "strategic interdependence," "psychological manifestations of enmity," and "repeated militarized conflict", between the parties.[4] What factors cause conflicts to evolve into enduring rivalries? A set of core issues, be they security-based, identity-based, or some other type, becomes central to the goals of participants on both sides of the conflict that leads to actor inflexibility. Domestic actors with narrow political goals capture the policymaking process. Some of these actors tend to have specific preferences for seeing that the conflict persists until their goals are met, or they would lose power altogether. Well-entrenched domestic forces make it hard for imaginative leaders to make the concessions necessary to satisfy the demands of the opposing side. And the conflict continues. An enduring rivalry has to be ripe for reconciliation as a result of either external or internal changes, and visionary leaders on both sides have to emerge to initiate the conflict resolution process.

The India–Pakistan conflict fits the above criteria neatly. A massive political shock took place in 1947 with the partition of the subcontinent. The rivalry has deeper roots in pre-1947 history, especially in the visions of statehood espoused by the Congress Party and the Muslim League.[5] But the key source of the rivalry emerged over control of the territory of Jammu and Kashmir. The 1947–48 War between the two states did not

---

[3] For further research into the role of shocks in enduring rivalries, see William R. Thompson, "Explaining Rivalry Termination in Contemporary Eastern Eurasia with Evolutionary Expectancy Theory." Paper presented at the REGIS Security Workshop, McGill University, Montreal, Nov. 2004.

[4] Zeev Maoz and Ben D. Mor, *Bound by Struggle: The Strategic Evolution of Enduring International Rivalries* (Ann Arbor: University of Michigan Press, 2002), 5.

[5] For an overview of these different visions, see Stanley Wolpert, *A New History of India* (Oxford: Oxford University Press, 1999), 301–49; Ayesha Jalal, *Democracy and Authoritarianism in South Asia: A Comparative and Historical Perspective* (Cambridge: Cambridge University Press, 1995), 1–28.

settle the territorial issue. Since then, the rivalry has involved multiple strategic decisions on war and peace by the principal actors, all contributing to the prolongation of the conflict.[6]

Causes of the rivalry's persistence and conditions for its termination

In order to understand what led to prolongation of the rivalry, a multivariate examination of its stasis is necessary. Taken as a whole, this multivariate examination does not ease the task of developing a comprehensive explanation for rivalry persistence, or for rivalry termination. First, the variables presented by the contributors have varying degrees of explanatory power. Second, given that the variables discussed below can explain different historical events in the India–Pakistan rivalry, the analytical power of each variable is not static – it changes over time and with events.

The list given above is comprehensive, outlining the key variables that can help to explain the rivalry's persistence. The authors have also indicated that there are many links between the different variables, both within and between the different levels of analysis. A parsimonious explanation is not forthcoming, as it was inter-disciplinary richness and comprehensiveness that motivated this enterprise. The contributors have, however, helped us better understand the different dimensions of the conflict in the light of different theories on enduring rivalries drawn from both international and domestic levels of analyses.

Explaining the persistence of the conflict is only part of the endeavor as understanding the most likely conditions under which the conflict could end is crucial as well. The need to find a solution to the conflict is reinforced by the increasing costs in terms of lives sacrificed and opportunities lost.[7] The urgency for resolution has been highlighted by the crucial post-1998 crises – Kargil (1999) and the attack on the Indian Parliament (2001), followed by the Indian military mobilization (2002–03). When

---

[6] On the Kashmir conflict, see Sumantra Bose, *Kashmir: Roots of Conflict, Paths to Peace* (Cambridge, MA: Harvard University Press, 2003); Victoria Schofield, *Kashmir in Conflict: India, Pakistan and the Unfinished War* (New York: I. B. Tauris, 2000); Raju Thomas (ed.), *Perspectives on Kashmir: The Roots of Conflict in South Asia* (Boulder, CO: Westview Press, 1992); Robert G. Wirsing, *Kashmir in the Shadow of War* (Armonk, NY: M. E. Sharpe, 2003).

[7] Since 1989, it is estimated that there have been between 38,000 and 100,000 deaths attributable to the enduring rivalry. In addition, the political and economic rights of millions of people on both sides of the conflict have been ignored. South Asia remains one of the least developed regions of the world, and the India–Pakistan conflict has robbed the states of the chance to develop economically and to build fruitful regional economic and political cooperation. See http://ploughshares.ca/content/ACR/ACRBriefs/ACR-IndiaKashmirBrief.html

finite territorial considerations (especially when defined as vital to national identity and sovereignty) are central to the preferences of the major stakeholders in the conflict, how do we get parties to sit down at the bargaining table in good faith, willing to conclude, ratify, and implement an agreement that terminates the conflict forever?

Conflict resolution requires both favorable general conditions and individual leadership efforts. The general conditions may be external (e.g., changing position of the chief ally) or internal (e.g., rapidly declining economic conditions, "mutually hurting stalemates"[8]). Imaginative leaders are needed to translate windows of opportunity offered by changes in general conditions into diplomatic openings and the eventual ending of the conflict. The rapprochement between East and West Germany in 1972, the normalization of US–China relations during 1972–79, and the Egypt–Israel peace agreement in 1979 were all made possible because leaders used favorable conditions to negotiate an end to their rivalries.[9] The most significant example remains the end of the East–West rivalry and the Cold War, due largely to initiatives by Mikhail Gorbachev, who made use of a deep economic slump in the former Soviet Union to initiate revolutionary changes.[10]

The contributors to this volume have briefly outlined possible sets of solutions. The following discussion sheds light on the reasons for the persistence of the conflict and the changes in conditions that might bring an end to this rivalry.

International level factors

The international level factors for the rivalry's persistence are centered on the changing systemic conditions in general and the politics among great powers that are deeply involved in the conflict. Systemic changes such as the end of the Cold War or the post-September 11, 2001 power configurations could offer political shocks as well as opportunities for change in the regions. In South Asia, these systemic changes do seem to have affected the dynamics of the regional conflict pattern. In chapter 2, Goertz, Diehl, and Saeedi

---

[8] Tony Armstrong, *Breaking the Ice* (Washington, DC: United States Institute of Peace, 1993), 32. See also Saadia Touval and I. William Zartman (eds.), *The Man in the Middle: International Mediation in Theory and Practice* (Boulder, CO: Westview Press, 1985); Daniel Druckman, "Negotiating in the International Context," in I. William Zartman and J. Lewis Rasmussen (eds.), *Peacemaking in International Conflict: Methods and Techniques* (Washington, DC: United Institute of Peace Press, 1999), 81–123.

[9] On these, see Armstrong, *Breaking the Ice*; Thompson, "Explaining Rivalry Termination."

[10] On this, see Richard K. Herrmann and Richard Ned Lebow, *Ending the Cold War* (New York: Palgrave-Macmillan, 2004).

argue that a massive external shock caused by systemic conditions could give rise to new variables that could impact on an enduring rivalry. However, no such shock has been sufficient to dramatically alter the positions of the rival states in the India–Pakistan dyad. The impact of the systemic factors has been in terms of long-term stasis as opposed to dramatic policy alterations. In Chapter 6, Ashok Kapur argues that the shifting patterns of alliance formation and changing configurations in international politics involving great power actors – especially the US, China, and Russia – have, contrary to the best intentions of outside powers, only helped to embed the conflict. Cold War politics, the major powers and their interest in maintaining "manageable instability" in the region and containing India as a potential major power actor, led to building up Pakistan as a credible challenger, which has helped to embed the rivalry. The peculiar conflict dynamics of the South Asian regional security complex have provided the great powers the opportunity to penetrate the region in pursuit of furthering their own global and regional interests.[11]

From a great-power-centered perspective, the US alliance with Pakistan and American arms transfers to Islamabad in the 1950s, 1960s, and 1980s encouraged the Pakistani military to resort to war, as in 1965 and 1999. The 1965 War led to the 1971 War, as the Bengali population was increasingly alienated from the foreign policy goals of Punjabi-dominated West Pakistan. The role of the US, USSR, and China in 1971, as opponents or alliance partners of the parties, did not help to end the conflict.[12] The bifurcation of Pakistan in 1971 increased the bitterness in Pakistan toward India, while the conflict in Kashmir, although subsiding for a brief period, resurfaced in the 1980s. The Afghan War, and Pakistan's central place in it, assured a massive flow of US military and economic aid to Pakistan during this period. Pakistan became the host country for millions of Afghan refugees and mujahidin forces fighting to eject the Soviet forces from Afghanistan. At the end of the war, the US exited the region, leaving the guerrilla network in place. This led to the rise of the Taliban and al-Queda, and the shift in Pakistan's military strategy toward an insurgency war with India.[13]

---

[11] A regional security complex is defined as "durable patterns of amity and enmity taking the form of subglobal, geographically coherent patterns of security interdependence." Barry Buzan and Ole Waever, *Regions and Powers: The Structure of International Security* (Cambridge: Cambridge University Press, 2003), 46.

[12] On the role of the US in the 1971 War, see Leo Rose and Richard Sisson, *War and Secession* (Berkeley: University of California Press, 1991).

[13] Mary Anne Weaver, *Pakistan: In the Shadow of Jihad and Afghanistan* (New York: Farrar, Straus, and Giroux, 2002), 62–085; Dennis Kux, *The United States and Pakistan 1947–2000* (Washington, DC: Woodrow Wilson Center Press, 2001), 256–320.

How can possible changes to great power politics or international level conditions pave the way to rivalry termination? Kapur argues that external powers must refrain from intervening in the conflict, especially in support of the revisionist goals of the weaker challenger, Pakistan. Great powers must also help the Pakistani leadership to learn that they cannot win a military conflict with India, with or without external support. A weakness of this approach, however, is exposed by those who examine the role of learning in the rivalry – Pakistan will not allow the great powers to remove themselves from the conflict nor will the great powers abandon Islamabad due to its geostrategic prominence in both the Cold War and the post-9/11 strategic environments. Additionally, great powers have at times acted as mediators or facilitators of peace (e.g., Russia in 1965 and the US in 2004), although they need not have persisted in their efforts. And their lack of persistence has ramifications for peace in the region.

Among the systemic variables, the somewhat changed position of the United States *vis-à-vis* the rival states since the end of the Cold War and in particular since the September 11, 2001 terrorist attacks, is the most crucial one for understanding the deescalation in 2004. The American-led war on terrorism has offered both India and Pakistan a limited policy window to work toward rivalry deescalation. The region has become the fulcrum of global efforts led by the US to root out terrorism. International pressure brought about by this ongoing war against terrorism means that outside states may be able to help induce both India and Pakistan to sit at the negotiating table to resolve their longstanding issues, especially the conflict over Kashmir, as it is a source of terrorism and insecurity for India. As a key ally of America in the war on terrorism, Pakistan has been under pressure to wage war on al-Queda and curtail its insurgent operations to a limited extent in Indian Kashmir to focus on that war. Reducing and eventually ending support for the insurgents in Kashmir by Pakistan could demoralize these non-state actors, and, as such, a reduction in conflict levels could be achieved. The question still very much in the open though is whether it is sustainable and whether it will lead to an eventual full termination of the rivalry.

China is the other major power playing a significant role in the rivalry's dynamics. From a realpolitik perspective, the Chinese policy of letting the India–Pakistan conflict persist has helped partially to prevent India from emerging as a peer competitor in Asia. During the 1970s, this policy pushed India toward forming a limited counter-coalition with the USSR. The policy has also hampered economic ties between China and India. Since 2000, Sino-Indian relations, especially in the economic area, have improved and this seems to have exerted some impact on Pakistani calculations. The termination of Sino-Indian rivalry may also help to deescalate the India–Pakistan rivalry, especially if China emerges as an honest broker for peace in the region. Thus, as of early 2005, the great-power-related variables were still evolving; some changes seem to have occurred since the September 11, 2001 attacks, raising hopes for a more positive engagement of both the US and China with the two South Asian states and the deescalation of the rivalry itself.

Regional level factors

At the regional level, contested territorial divisions, truncated power asymmetry, and nuclear weapons are seen as key variables explaining the rivalry's persistence. The contributors, Diehl, Goertz and Saeedi, Vasquez, and Geller, all give significant weight to territorial considerations in the ongoing rivalry. Kashmir has acted as a catalyst for political and strategic stasis between India and Pakistan. These contributors point out that 81 percent of all enduring rivalries have been partly or predominantly caused by territorial issues and, therefore, until these territorial issues are solved, rivalries tend to continue. The territorial dispute in the dyad is thus a fundamental factor in its persistence.

Beyond territory, the arms race between the two states has engendered considerable instability over the years. In particular, nuclear arms, while introduced late into the rivalry, have had a varied effect on the level of conflict. Continued stasis was assured when both powers developed their nuclear arsenals during the early 1990s, achieving nuclear weapons state status almost simultaneously. But theorists and practitioners are unsure what lessons have been drawn by both sides about the utility of nuclear weapons in the conflict. To John Vasquez, nuclear weapons in South Asia, unlike the US–Soviet context, have not served as a deterrent but as a factor that fostered increased conflict. This is because the conditions of the India–Pakistan rivalry are markedly different from the conditions of the US–USSR rivalry. On issues such as the role of territory in the rivalry, tolerance of the status quo, war experience, the observance of the "rules of the game," crisis management learning, and arms control agreements, the India–Pakistan rivalry is disturbingly different. As such, nuclear weapons have become more of a factor for instability than for stability. For Daniel Geller, the risk of conflict has increased with nuclear acquisition by the two states. To Saira Khan, nuclear weapons have made the rivalry even more deeply embedded, as both sides understand that the chance for a major war is slim, and are much less interested in making the compromises necessary to terminate the rivalry. There has also been a marked increase in the number of crises in the nuclear era, showing the presence of a stability–instability paradox, i.e., absence of major wars but an increasing number of minor skirmishes and crises.

At the regional level, what can be done to bring about rivalry termination? It is highly unlikely that either state will give up its nuclear weapons, and, as such, these weapons are now a permanent facet of the rivalry. What effect will this have on chances of rivalry termination? Will nuclear weapons over time cause a new balance that will stabilize relations, or will it lead to further tensions (learning and perceptions are key here)? Time may prove that both states would achieve a stable relationship on the basis of nuclear deterrence and nuclear confidence building measures. The current instability may be because new nuclear weapons states take a period of time to learn and apply crisis and conflict management techniques properly. From an optimistic point of view, the nuclear predicament that these states are in may eventually help the two actors to find an answer to the territorial question of Kashmir. Nuclear crises could act as catalysts for rapprochement. Similarly, over time, the elites from both sides could believe that their country's existential security is guaranteed and therefore they could make meaningful territorial concessions.[14]

In the regional context, beyond nuclear stability, economic variables could play a major role in conflict termination. The development of economic interdependence between the two states may exert the most effect on the prospects for rivalry termination. Barring a few skeptics, most scholars on economic interdependence highlight the conflict-reducing role of this variable in relations between trading states.[15] Within the region, the creation of the proposed South Asia Free Trade Area (SAFTA) and the strengthening of the South Asian Association of Regional Cooperation (SAARC) could evolve in a manner similar to ASEAN (Association of Southeast Asian Nations) and its free trade arrangements and this could lead to regional peace and prosperity.

[14] On the different nuclear scenarios in South Asia, see Ashley J. Tellis, *India's Emerging Nuclear Future* (Santa Monica, CA: RAND, 2001), ch. 6; see also various chapters in Lowell Dimmer (ed.), *South Asia's Nuclear Security Dilemma* (Armonk, NY: M. E. Sharpe, 2005), especially ch. 6, Timothy D. Hoyt, "Strategic Myopia: Pakistan's Nuclear Doctrine and Crisis Stability in South Asia."

[15] The logic behind this liberal theory is that high levels of economic exchanges between open market economies would inhibit parties from engaging in inter-state military conflict as they become sensitive to its impact on their economic prospects. Further, economic interdependence increases interactions between governmental and non-governmental actors. The business communities will emerge as major stakeholders in pressing governments not to escalate a conflict if it arises. For an overview of the arguments linking interdependence and conflict reduction, see Edward D. Mansfield and Brian M. Pollins (eds.), *Economic Interdependence and International Conflict: New Perspectives on an Enduring Debate* (Ann Arbor: University of Michigan Press, 2003).

In this respect, the proposed gas pipeline from Iran to India via Pakistan and the mutual granting of most-favored-nation (MFN) trade status could form the basis for sustained cooperation leading to greater economic interdependence. Other options for rivalry termination may be found in following Track II diplomatic efforts.[16]

At the regional level, the role of India is crucial. India's increasing global and regional power ambitions and deeper insertion into economic globalization may propel New Delhi to make meaningful efforts to settle territorial disputes with its neighbors. With its rapidly growing economy, India may over time become preponderant *vis-à-vis* Pakistan, economically and militarily, but is unlikely to achieve the kind of overwhelming superiority the US accomplished with Mexico. In the near term, its truncated asymmetry with Pakistan is likely to continue due to the involvement of the great powers, the presence of nuclear weapons, the strategic terrain in Kashmir, and the use of asymmetric strategies by Islamabad. In this context, India may find a way to limit Pakistani antagonism through accommodation in different core areas of the dispute.

Domestic level factors

Territorial issues affect the domestic politics of both the rival states as, until they are solved, the rivalry is likely to continue. Territory acts as a symbolic, economic, and political rallying point for important actors on both sides of the conflict. These actors hold significant domestic political power and, in this case, they are not ready to terminate the rivalry. Vasquez posits that the practice of realpolitik *vis-à-vis* Kashmir by the parties is one of the causal factors for stasis in the rivalry. This tendency is partially a result of domestic politics in the two states. In his chapter, Vali Nasr argues that the roots of the conflict lie in Pakistani domestic politics. A lack of a clear Pakistani national identity has given the country's military and militant Islamists significant power over policymaking. These actors subsequently captured the policymaking process, thus establishing the symbolic links between the India–Pakistan–Kashmir conflict and national identity formation. In the absence of other unifying themes, the territorial conflict with India over Kashmir acts as a beacon for national unity, prolonging and embedding the conflict.

---

[16] On the role of Track II diplomacy, see Hussein Agha, Shai Feldman, Ahmad Khalidi, and Zeev Schiff, *Track II Diplomacy: Lessons from the Middle East* (Cambridge, MA: MIT Press, 2004). In the South Asian context, see http://www.atimes.com/atimes/South_Asia/FB16Df03.html

In this context, domestic politics has other pertinent dimensions. Stephen Saideman extends the argument developed by Nasr by contending that it is the domestic politics of all three key actors (India, Pakistan, and Kashmir) that ensures the continuation of the conflict. Within each of the actors there are sets of dominant stakeholders with irredentist interests in the continuation of the enduring rivalry. As these actors have significant policymaking power, they have captured the dynamics of the conflict, and stasis is a result. The irredentist claims of Pakistan, the mixed motives of the Kashmiris, and the counter-irredentist policies of India have led to the prolongation and the deadly nature of the conflict. The important question is why conflict-oriented actors have been able to capture the policymaking process for such a long period of time. The answer may be found in Reeta Tremblay and Julian Schofield's examination of domestic political and institutional structures that helped to perpetuate the rivalry. They argue that it is the inability of Pakistan to develop a stable democratic political system that ensures the continuation of the conflict. In Pakistan, radical Islamists and the military control the domestic and international agenda of the country due to the absence of proper democratic political structures.

What changes in these variables could produce an end to the conflict? Nasr requires the development of a strong and vibrant Pakistani national identity, one free of radical Islam and the excessive control of the military establishment. The over-reliance on religion and the military in Pakistan makes Kashmir a pivotal and sensitive issue, and ensures its continuing vital role in the India–Pakistan enduring rivalry. The changing identity formations in India, alternating between secular and mild *Hindutva* (Hinduness) also do not bode well for the conflict. A caveat here is to be noted; proper national identity formation is difficult to control, as the effects of globalization, religious antagonisms based on radicalized worldviews, irredentism, and a host of other factors that influence the conflict also impact identity, making it difficult to manipulate the variable to congruent patterns. However, as Saideman argues, by identifying the key supporters of the irredentist conflict, and then modifying their preferences through manipulating incentives and disincentives, a solution may be possible. One key incentive is the development of economic ties, both within the region and beyond, in order to develop stakeholder constituencies in India, Pakistan, and Kashmir that would favor continued peace, rather than conflict escalation.

Institutional compatibility by way of stable democratic domestic political structures is what Tremblay and Schofield argue should be the focus for those searching for a solution. Goertz, Diehl, and Saeedi also echo this argument. Authoritarian and hybrid democracies are much more dispute- and war-prone, and push conflicts farther than strong democratic regimes would. The incompatibility of the political systems thus has been a major constraint on ending the India–Pakistan rivalry.

Can democratization of Pakistan lead to rivalry termination?[17] It depends on what type of democracy Pakistan develops into. As some contributors point out, during the short periods of democratic rule in Pakistan, little headway was made on resolving the points of contention, and in fact tensions became more acute during the hybrid-democratic phases. Further, it seems, being the main unifying force and the key power holder, the Pakistani military may be the institution that can strike meaningful deals with India. But a change in the military's larger strategic goals will be essential to achieve this objective. In order for Pakistan to change its position, political actors may need to understand that a peaceful resolution to the rivalry will benefit their country, both economically and politically. Conflict with a major regional power has robbed Pakistan of democracy, the development of a robust civil society, and much-needed economic development, as it expends a significant portion of its GNP on defense. A realization of this nature may require the curtailment of power of the Pakistani armed forces and the development of a robust democratic civil society while eradicating the fundamentalist and intolerant elements in the educational system, especially as evident in the curriculum of the *madrassas* or religious schools.[18]

Beyond Pakistani domestic politics, the India–Pakistan rivalry is also heavily influenced by the domestic politics of Kashmir. The struggle of different Kashmiri groups for autonomy, outright independence, or accession to Pakistan has generated much of the space for outbidding by the two rival states. The goal of an independent Kashmir is unlikely to materialize, however, as not all regional parties – India, Pakistan, and to a certain extent China – support the creation of such a state. The attempt to achieve this is also constrained by a "profound conservatism" prevalent in the international system which supports stability and order over change and reform. The world community fears that international and regional order and stability would be threatened, as one entity's secession would lead to similar demands elsewhere. For instance, the Kurds argue that

[17] For an overview of the democratic peace literature, see Michael Brown, *et al.* (eds.), *Debating the Democratic Peace* (Cambridge, MA: MIT Press, 1996); and Bruce Russett, *Grasping the Democratic Peace* (Princeton: Princeton University Press, 1993). The basic argument of those who support the democratic peace thesis is that democratic institutions and civil society constrain decisionmakers' choices to go to war, especially with another democracy. The argument is also normative, as it is assumed that democracies tend to share specific ideas and values that inhibit the use of violence *vis-à-vis* one another.

[18] On the prospects of this outcome, see Stephen Philip Cohen, *The Idea of Pakistan* (Washington, DC: Brookings Institution Press, 2004), ch. 8.

they deserve a nation-state, but are unlikely to receive one any time soon due to regional systemic realities. Further, there exists an international norm against forced territorial divisions.[19]

Part of the constraint in this regard is the high likelihood that an independent Kashmir will not be democratic, secular, or liberal. If the examples of Pakistan, Afghanistan, and Bangladesh are any indication, minorities, in this case the substantial Hindu and Buddhist populations, are unlikely to be integrated into the Kashmiri mainstream. The ethnic cleansing of the Kashmiri Hindu *Pandit* groups since the 1980s reinforces this argument. The new state could be subject to the machinations of Pakistan, India, and China and of the fundamentalists from the region and elsewhere. An independent state would thereby serve as a great source of insecurity for the regional powers. A land-locked Kashmir would also require security guarantees and substantial economic aid from the three principal powers, and it is unlikely to get this aid without falling under the influence of one actor or the other.[20] An independent Kashmir is unlikely to be economically or militarily viable, as it will not be able to survive on tourism alone.[21] Moreover, the end to the India–Pakistan enduring rivalry is a necessary pre-condition for Kashmir to realize its economic and political potential. Independence for Kashmir may not bring an end to the India–Pakistan rivalry.[22]

However, for Kashmiri independence demands to end, both India and Pakistan have to redouble their efforts to integrate the existing Kashmiri populations into their respective national mainstreams in a legitimate

[19] On this, see Viva Bartkus, *The Dynamics of Secession* (Cambridge: Cambridge University Press, 1999), 221–22; Mark Zacher, "The Territorial Integrity Norm," *International Organization* 55 (Spring 2001), 15–50; Robert Jackson, *Quasi-States: Sovereignty, International Relations and the Third World* (Cambridge: Cambridge University Press, 1993).

[20] See http://news.bbc.co.uk/1/shared/spl/hi/south_asia/03/kashmir_future/html/default.stm for an assessment of the costs and benefits associated with different political solutions to the Kashmir question.

[21] We owe this point to Reeta Tremblay.

[22] Some elements of the Irish Agreement of April 1998 may be applicable here. That agreement created a North–South ministerial body to deal with issues of common concern, and a British–Irish Council, and Equality Commission and a Human Rights Commission and normalization of security arrangements. On these, see Mari Fitzduff, *Beyond Violence: Conflict Resolution Process in Northern Ireland* (Tokyo: United Nations University Press, 2002), 15. In recent years, offering both portions of Kashmir loose sovereignty within India and Pakistan but without an international personality has been proposed as a solution by the Kashmiri Study Group comprising scholars and former officials. On this, see Teresita C. Schaffer, "Toward a Peaceful Kashmir," Upadhaya Lectures (Washington, DC: Center for Strategic and International Studies, Sept. 26, 2003). However, this may be unworkable without substantial improvement in India–Pakistan relations.

way, whereby[7] Kashmiri culture and traditions and regional autonomy are properly maintained. This they may achieve only by convincing an over-whelming majority of Kashmiris of the benefits of membership in India and Pakistan and the costs of separation.

Beyond domestic level factors, the contributors have identified some decisionmaker-level variables in the continuation and possible termination of the rivalry.

Decisionmaker-level factors

What role has leadership learning played in the enduring rivalry? Vasquez posits that the practice of realpolitik by the Indian and Pakistani leaders is one of the causal factors explaining rivalry persistence. The psychological and sociological aspects of the conflict are critical here. Russell Leng argues that the divergent learning patterns of both the Indian and Pakistani leaderships led to the embedded character of the conflict. The Indian elites have learned, rightly or wrongly, that power politics works, and that Islamabad is untrustworthy. Pakistani decisionmakers, on the other hand, have learned that they cannot take Kashmir by direct application of force, and as such they need proxy wars and intervention by external actors on their behalf. Failure in one crisis bred more determination on the part of the challenger to try again, as a peculiar sort of learning took place in the coercive bargaining of the actors. Leng argues that the wrong realpolitik-oriented lessons have led to misperceptions about each other's intentions and capabilities. These misperceptions have led to a series of never-ending crises and stasis in the rivalry.

What then is necessary from this perspective for rivalry termination to occur? From Leng's point of view, actors need to focus on getting the leaderships in both states to learn the right lessons. Indian and Pakistani leaders need to go beyond the lessons of realpolitik and coercive diplomacy, as these lessons only feed into the conflict cycle. For the rivalry to be terminated, both countries' elites need to change their understanding of means and ends. Hostility in relations must be eliminated, and empathy toward the other side's goals and constraints needs to be present. Goertz, Diehl, and Saeedi also see the need for imaginative leaders as a necessary requirement for rivalry termination, as such leaders can bring about some of the psychological conditions Leng proposes.

The problem with focusing excessively on leadership learning is that while it may help us understand the role that perceptions play in prolonging the conflict, it does not offer much by way of concrete policy prescriptions. Of course, sometimes right leadership learning could occur,

because of the realization of impending decline of a country's economic
and military position *vis-à-vis* a conflict rival (as in the case of
Gorbachev), but it is often difficult to predict the timing of such learning.
In addition, it is difficult to teach national leaders the right lessons as crisis
learning could go either way – functional or dysfunctional.

Directions for future research

The chapters in this volume suggest that a multivariate analysis is useful
and may well hold the key to understanding the conflict in its wider
manifestations. The singular focus on international or domestic level
factors will not help us to grasp this multifaceted conflict or its possible
termination trajectories. Even when external conditions change, especially in terms of the positions of the great powers, a true accommodation
will only happen when changes occur internally in the two countries, i.e.,
if they move toward becoming compatible democracies with a willingness
to focus more on economic cooperation than on political and strategic
divisions. Clearly, imaginative leaderships in both countries need to rise
above the narrow interests of societal groups in order to find a solution to
one of the world's remaining enduring rivalries that began with decolonization and has acted as a major impediment to the economic and political
development and modernization of South Asia. In this context, the dis-
ciplines of international relations and comparative politics have much
more to accomplish.

The India–Pakistan rivalry has not been given its deserved prominence
in the international relations literature on enduring rivalries and protracted conflicts. The conflict resolution literature has also been notably
silent on this conflict. The complexity of the conflict is one explanation
for this feature as the multivariate nature of the sources of the conflict
makes its study difficult. During the Cold War, the conflict was deemed
peripheral, except during a major crisis or war in the subcontinent. This
has changed with the end of the Cold War and the nuclear acquisition
by the two states. The post-September 11 international focus on transnational terrorism has made South Asia, and the India–Pakistan relationship, central to international security. There now exists a fertile ground
for studying different dimensions of this rivalry in more meaningful ways.
In addition, the India–Pakistan conflict is the only remaining active
dyadic rivalry between two nuclear weapons states.

Several research trajectories are possible for future work on this conflict. The potential research questions include: are the lessons learned
during the Cold War relevant to South Asia? Are the lessons of rivalry
termination between the US and the USSR relevant to this conflict?

How does nuclear deterrence operate in this context of two geographically close neighbors fighting over issues of territory and national identity? How would the continued proliferation of nuclear weapons in the region affect the rivalry? Can the unstable nuclear relationships be transformed into stable ones? How dependent is the rivalry's de-escalation on the continued emphasis of the US on the region in the "war on terror"? These and other questions need further research. What this volume has offered is a sketch of different dimensions of the conflict, each one of which can be studied further on its own singularly or in combinations for greater understanding of the India–Pakistan conflict and the greater phenomenon of enduring rivalry itself.

Index